What's on the CD?

The CD-ROM included with the *MCSE: Exchange 5 Study Guide* contains several valuable tools to help you prepare for your MCSE exams. The contents of the folders you'll find on the CD and the steps for installing the various programs are described below. Please read the README file located in the root directory of the CD for further information.

The Edge Tests: Exchange 5 Exam Prepara

This Edge Test similar to those you'll encounte exam. Two versions of the test 3.11 systems, and one for Window systems. To install the Edge Test for Windows 3.1, Windows NT 4, or Windows 95 run the SETUP.EXE file located in the EdgeTest folder. Once installation is complete, run the DELIVERY.EXE file to start the program.

Microsoft's TechNet Technical Information Network

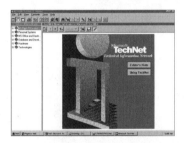

An evaluation copy of a vast database of information related to Microsoft products and technologies. It includes more than 100,000 pages of articles, technical notes, service packs, and Knowledge Bases. To install the TechNet Technical Information network program to your computer, run the SETUP.EXE file located in the TECHNET folder. For further installation instructions, please read the MANSETUP text file located in the TECHNET folder. This text file also contains the user license agreement for this product.

Microsoft *Train_Cert Offline* Web Site and *Internet Explorer 3.0*

Look to Microsoft's *Train_Cert Offline* Website, a quarterly snapshot of Microsoft's Education and Certification Website, for all the information you need to plot your course for MCSE certification. You'll need to run *Internet Explorer 3.0* to access all of the features of the *Train_Cert Offline* Website, so we've included a free copy on the CD. To install *Internet Explorer 3.0*, run the SETUP.EXE file located in the MICROSOFT\IE3\CD folder. To install the *Train_Cert Offline* Website to your system, copy the TCWEB.EXE file located in the MICROSOFT\OFFLINE folder to your hard drive and then open the file.

Transcender Corporation's Certification Sampler

Copyright © 1994-1997 Transcender Corporation.

Provides sample exam questions to give you a clear idea of the types of questions you'll encounter when you take your MCSE exams. To install the program, simply run the SETUP.EXE file located in the TRANSCEN folder. Please read the accompanying README file in the TRANSCEN folder for more information about the programs and the Transcender Corporation.

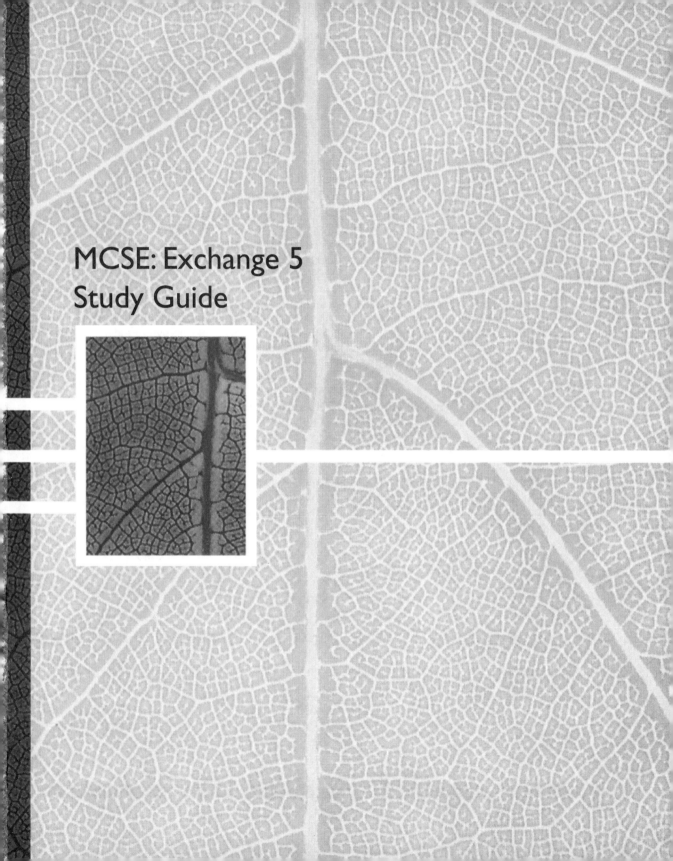

MCSE: Exchange 5
Study Guide

October 9, 1996

Dear SYBEX Inc. Customer:

Microsoft is pleased to inform you SYBEX Inc. is a participant in the Microsoft® Independent Courseware Vendor (ICV) program. Microsoft ICVs design, develop, and market self-paced courseware, books, and other products that support Microsoft software and the Microsoft Certified Professional (MCP) program.

To be accepted into the Microsoft ICV program, an ICV must meet set criteria. In addition, Microsoft reviews and approves each ICV training product before permission is granted to use the Microsoft Certified Professional Approved Study Guide logo on that product. This logo assures the consumer that the product has passed the following Microsoft standards:

- The course contains accurate product information.
- The course includes labs and activities during which the student can apply knowledge and skills learned from the course.
- The course teaches skills that help prepare the student to take corresponding MCP exams.

Microsoft ICVs continually develop and release new MCP Approved Study Guides. To prepare for a particular Microsoft certification exam, a student may choose one or more single, self-paced training courses or a series of training courses.

You will be pleased with the quality and effectiveness of the MCP Approved Study Guides available from SYBEX Inc.

Sincerely,

Holly Heath
ICV/OCV Account Manager
Microsoft Channel Programs, Education & Certification

MICROSOFT INDEPENDENT COURSEWARE VENDOR PROGRAM

MCSE: Exchange 5
Study Guide

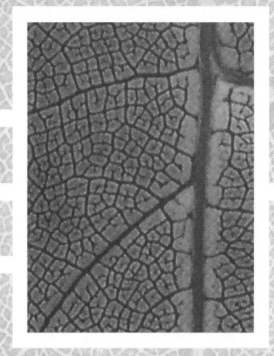

Richard Easlick
with
James Chellis

San Francisco • Paris • Düsseldorf • Soest

Associate Publisher: Guy Hart-Davis
Acquisitions Manager: Kristine Plachy
Acquisitions & Developmental Editor: Neil Edde
Editor: Kathy Grider-Carlyle
Project Editors: Jeff Chorney and Davina Baum
Technical Editor: Rob Sanfilippo
Book Designer: Patrick Dintino
Graphic Illustrators: Steve Brooks and Andrew Benzie
Electronic Publishing Specialist: Bill Gibson
Production Coordinators: Michael Tom and Amy Eoff
Production Assistants: Katherine Cooley, Eryn Osterhaus, and Duncan Watson
Indexer: Matthew Spence
Companion CD: Molly Sharp and John D. Wright
Cover Designer: Archer Design
Cover Illustrator/Photographer: John Gadja

Screen reproductions produced with Collage Complete.

Collage Complete is a trademark of Inner Media Inc.

SYBEX, Network Press, and the Network Press logo are registered trademarks of SYBEX Inc.

TRADEMARKS: SYBEX has attempted throughout this book to distinguish proprietary trademarks from descriptive terms by following the capitalization style used by the manufacturer.

The author and publisher have made their best efforts to prepare this book, and the content is based upon final release software whenever possible. Portions of the manuscript may be based upon pre-release versions supplied by software manufacturer(s). The author and the publisher make no representation or warranties of any kind with regard to the completeness or accuracy of the contents herein and accept no liability of any kind including but not limited to performance, merchantability, fitness for any particular purpose, or any losses or damages of any kind caused or alleged to be caused directly or indirectly from this book.

Microsoft Internet Explorer ©1996 Microsoft Corporation. All rights reserved. Microsoft, the Microsoft Internet Explorer logo, Windows, Windows NT, and the Windows logo are either registered trademarks or trademarks of Microsoft Corporation in the United States and/or other countries.

SYBEX is an independent entity from Microsoft Corporation, and not affiliated with Microsoft Corporation in any manner. This publication may be used in assisting students to prepare for a Microsoft Certified Professional Exam. Neither Microsoft Corporation, its designated review company, nor SYBEX warrants that use of this publication will ensure passing the relevant Exam. Microsoft is either a registered trademark or trademark of Microsoft Corporation in the United States and/or other countries.

Library of Congress Card Number: 97-68479
ISBN: 0-7821-1967-0

Manufactured in the United States of America

10 9 8 7 6 5 4

Software License Agreement: Terms and Conditions

The media and/or any online materials accompanying this book that are available now or in the future contain programs and/or text files (the "Software") to be used in connection with the book. SYBEX hereby grants to you a license to use the Software, subject to the terms that follow. Your purchase, acceptance, or use of the Software will constitute your acceptance of such terms.

The Software compilation is the property of SYBEX unless otherwise indicated and is protected by copyright to SYBEX or other copyright owner(s) as indicated in the media files (the "Owner(s)"). You are hereby granted a single-user license to use the Software for your personal, noncommercial use only. You may not reproduce, sell, distribute, publish, circulate, or commercially exploit the Software, or any portion thereof, without the written consent of SYBEX and the specific copyright owner(s) of any component software included on this media.

In the event that the Software or components include specific license requirements or end-user agreements, statements of condition, disclaimers, limitations or warranties ("End-User License"), those End-User Licenses supersede the terms and conditions herein as to that particular Software component. Your purchase, acceptance, or use of the Software will constitute your acceptance of such End-User Licenses.

By purchase, use or acceptance of the Software you further agree to comply with all export laws and regulations of the United States as such laws and regulations may exist from time to time.

Software Support

Components of the supplemental Software and any offers associated with them may be supported by the specific Owner(s) of that material but they are not supported by SYBEX. Information regarding any available support may be obtained from the Owner(s) using the information provided in the appropriate read.me files or listed elsewhere on the media.

Should the manufacturer(s) or other Owner(s) cease to offer support or decline to honor any offer, SYBEX bears no responsibility. This notice concerning support for the Software is provided for your information only. SYBEX is not the agent or principal of the Owner(s), and SYBEX is in no way responsible for providing any support for the Software, nor is it liable or responsible for any support provided, or not provided, by the Owner(s).

Warranty

SYBEX warrants the enclosed media to be free of physical defects for a period of ninety (90) days after purchase. The Software is not available from SYBEX in any other form or media than that enclosed herein or posted to *www.sybex.com*. If you discover a defect in the media during this warranty period, you may obtain a replacement of identical format at no charge by sending the defective media, postage prepaid, with proof of purchase to:

SYBEX Inc.
Customer Service Department
1151 Marina Village Parkway
Alameda, CA 94501
(510) 523-8233
Fax: (510) 523-2373
e-mail: info@sybex.com
WEB: HTTP://WWW.SYBEX.COM

After the 90-day period, you can obtain replacement media of identical format by sending us the defective disk, proof of purchase, and a check or money order for $10, payable to SYBEX.

Disclaimer

SYBEX makes no warranty or representation, either expressed or implied, with respect to the Software or its contents, quality, performance, merchantability, or fitness for a particular purpose. In no event will SYBEX, its distributors, or dealers be liable to you or any other party for direct, indirect, special, incidental, consequential, or other damages arising out of the use of or inability to use the Software or its contents even if advised of the possibility of such damage. In the event that the Software includes an online update feature, SYBEX further disclaims any obligation to provide this feature for any specific duration other than the initial posting.

The exclusion of implied warranties is not permitted by some states. Therefore, the above exclusion may not apply to you. This warranty provides you with specific legal rights; there may be other rights that you may have that vary from state to state. The pricing of the book with the Software by SYBEX reflects the allocation of risk and limitations on liability contained in this agreement of Terms and Conditions.

Shareware Distribution

This Software may contain various programs that are distributed as shareware. Copyright laws apply to both shareware and ordinary commercial software, and the copyright Owner(s) retains all rights. If you try a shareware program and continue using it, you are expected to register it. Individual programs differ on details of trial periods, registration, and payment. Please observe the requirements stated in appropriate files.

Copy Protection

The Software in whole or in part may or may not be copy-protected or encrypted. However, in all cases, reselling or redistributing these files without authorization is expressly forbidden except as specifically provided for by the Owner(s) therein.

Acknowledgements

My thanks to Kathy Grider-Carlyle, the copy editor, and Rob Sanfilippo, the technical editor, for all their hard work and contributions. I also appreciate the great work from all the people at Sybex: Neil Edde, Jeff Chorney, Davina Baum, Michael Tom, and Bill Gibson. And finally, thanks to Louise for letting me use her green room as my office and lab. Thanks to all of you!

Contents at a Glance

Table of Contents

Introduction

The Microsoft Certified Systems Engineer (MCSE) certification is *the* hottest ticket to career advancement in the computer industry today. Hundreds of thousands of corporations and organizations worldwide are choosing Windows NT for their networks. This means that there is a tremendous need for qualified personnel and consultants to help implement NT and related products, such as Exchange Server 5.0. The MCSE certification is your way to show these corporations and organizations that you have the professional abilities they need.

This book has been developed in alliance with Microsoft Corporation to give you the knowledge and skills you need to prepare for one of the key elective exams of the MCSE certification program: Implementing and Supporting Microsoft Exchange Server 5.0. Certified by Microsoft, this book presents the information you need to acquire a solid foundation in Exchange Server 5.0, to prepare for the Implementing and Supporting Microsoft Exchange Server 5.0 exam, and to take a big step toward MCSE certification.

Is This Book for You?

If you want to learn how Microsoft Exchange 5.0 works, this book is for you. You'll find clear explanations of the fundamental concepts you need to grasp.

If you want to become certified as a Microsoft Certified Systems Engineer (MCSE), this book is also for you. Microsoft Certified Professional Magazine recently completed a survey that revealed that the average MCSE is earning well over $70,000 (US) per year, while the average MCSE consultant is earning over $95,000 per year. If you want to acquire the solid background you need to pass Microsoft's most popular elective exam, take a step closer to your MCSE, and boost your career efforts, this book is for you.

You can read the entire MCP Magazine annual salary survey at http://www.mcpmag.com/members/97janfeb/fealmain.htm.

What Does This Book Cover?

Think of this book as your guide to Microsoft Exchange Server 5.0. It begins by covering key technologies that make up Exchange, such as:

- Client/server messaging

- MAPI and RPC

- X.400 and X.500

Next, it covers the architecture of Exchange, including:

- Core components

- Optional components

- Component communication

Then, it continues with the following important topics:

- Installing Exchange Server

- Creating recipients

- The architecture, installation, and configuration of Microsoft Exchange clients

- Forms, public folders, and advanced security

- Internet clients for Exchange Server

Finally, a number of advanced topics are included:

- Managing an Exchange environment

- Connecting sites

- Internet mail and Exchange

- Microsoft Mail and Exchange

- Migrating other mail systems to Exchange

- Planning an Exchange environment

How Do You Become an MCSE?

Attaining Microsoft Certified Systems Engineer (MCSE) status is a challenge. The exams cover a wide range of topics and require dedicated study and expertise. This is, however, why the MCSE certificate is so valuable. If achieving the MCSE was too easy, the market would be quickly flooded by MCSEs and the certification would become meaningless. Microsoft, keenly aware of this fact, has taken steps to ensure that the certification means its holder is truly knowledgeable and skilled.

To become an MCSE, you must pass four core requirements and two electives. Most people select the following exam combination for the MCSE core requirements for the most current track:

Client Requirement

70-073: Implementing and Supporting Windows NT Workstation 4.0

Networking Requirement

70-058: Networking Essentials

Windows NT Server 4.0 Requirement

70-067: Implementing and Supporting Windows NT Server 4.0

Windows NT Server 4.0 in the Enterprise Requirement

70-068: Implementing and Supporting Windows NT Server 4.0 in the Enterprise

For the electives, you have about ten choices. The two most popular electives are:

70-076: Implementing and Supporting Microsoft Exchange Server 5.0

70-059: Internetworking Microsoft TCP/IP on Microsoft Windows NT 4.0

This book is a part of a series of MCSE study guides, published by Network Press (Sybex), that covers four core requirements and a choice of several electives—the entire MCSE track.

Where Do You Take the Exams?

You may take the exams at any of more than 800 Sylvan Prometric Authorized Testing Centers around the world. For the location of a testing center near you, call (800) 755-EXAM (755-3926). Outside the United States and Canada, contact your local Sylvan Prometric Registration Center.

To register for a Microsoft Certified Professional exam:

1. Determine the number of the exam you want to take.

2. Register with the Sylvan Prometric Registration Center that is nearest to you. At this point you will be asked for advance payment for the exam. At this writing, the exams are $100 each. Exams must be taken within one year of payment. You can schedule exams up to six weeks in advance or as late as one working day prior to the date of the exam. You can cancel or reschedule your exam if you contact Sylvan Prometric at least two working days prior to the exam. Same-day registration is available in some locations, although this is subject to space availability. Where same-day registration is available, you must register a minimum of two hours before test time.

3. After you receive a registration and payment confirmation letter from Sylvan Prometric, call a nearby Sylvan Prometric Testing Center to schedule your exam.

When you schedule the exam, you'll be provided with instructions regarding appointment and cancellation procedures, ID requirements, and information about the testing center location.

What the Implementing and Supporting Microsoft Exchange Server 5.0 Exam Covers

The Implementing and Supporting Microsoft Exchange Server 5.0 exam covers concepts and skills required for the support of Microsoft Exchange Server 5.0. It emphasizes the following areas of Exchange Server support:

- Internet protocols

- Managing Exchange Servers and clients

- Backing up and restoring Exchange Servers

- Configuring and managing site-to-site communication

- Microsoft Exchange coexistence with foreign systems

- Migrations to Exchange

- Troubleshooting Exchange

The exam focuses on fundamental concepts relating to Microsoft Exchange Server operation. But it can also be quite specific about operational settings and troubleshooting situations. Careful study of this book, along with hands-on experience with Exchange Server, will be especially helpful in preparing you for the exam. The Microsoft Exchange Server Resource Guide is another good reference for preparing for the exam.

How Microsoft Develops the Exam Questions

Microsoft follows an exam-development process consisting of eight mandatory phases. The process takes an average of seven months and contains more than 150 specific steps. The phases of Microsoft Certified Professional exam development are:

1. Job analysis

2. Objective domain definition

3. Blueprint survey

4. Item development

5. Alpha review and item revision

6. Beta exam

7. Item selection and cut-score setting

8. Exam live

Microsoft describes each phase as follows:

Phase 1: Job analysis   Phase 1 is an analysis of all the tasks that make up the specific job function, based on tasks identified by people who are currently performing the job function. This phase also identifies the knowledge, skills, and abilities that relate specifically to the performance area to be certified.

Phase 2: Objective domain definition The results of the job analysis provide the framework used to develop objectives. The development of objectives involves translating the job function tasks into a comprehensive set of more specific and measurable knowledge, skills, and abilities. The resulting list of objectives, or the objective domain, is the basis for the development of both the certification exams and the training materials.

Phase 3: Blueprint survey The final objective domain is transformed into a blueprint survey in which contributors—technology professionals who are performing the applicable job function—are asked to rate each objective. Contributors may be selected from lists of past Certified Professional candidates, from appropriately skilled exam development volunteers, and from within Microsoft. Based on the contributors' input, the objectives are prioritized and weighted. The actual exam items are written according to the prioritized objectives. Contributors are queried about how they spend their time on the job, and if a contributor doesn't spend an adequate amount of time actually performing the specified job function, his or her data is eliminated from the analysis.

The blueprint survey phase helps determine which objectives to measure, as well as the appropriate number and types of items to include on the exam.

Phase 4: Item development A pool of items is developed to measure the blueprinted objective domain. The number and types of items to be written are based on the results of the blueprint survey. During this phase, items are reviewed and revised to ensure that they are:

- Technically accurate

- Clear, unambiguous, and plausible

- Not biased for any population subgroup or culture

- Not misleading or tricky

- Testing at the correct level of Bloom's Taxonomy

- Testing for useful knowledge, not obscure or trivial facts

Items that meet these criteria are included in the initial item pool.

Phase 5: Alpha review and item revision During this phase, a panel of technical and job function experts reviews each item for technical accuracy, then answers each item, reaching consensus on all technical issues. Once the items have been verified as technically accurate, they are edited to ensure that they are expressed in the clearest language possible.

Phase 6: Beta exam   The reviewed and edited items are collected into a beta exam pool. During the beta exam, each participant has the opportunity to respond to all the items in this beta exam pool. Based on the responses of all beta participants, Microsoft performs a statistical analysis to verify the validity of the exam items and to determine which items will be used in the certification exam. Once the analysis has been completed, the items are distributed into multiple parallel forms, or versions, of the final certification exam.

Phase 7: Item selection and cut-score setting   The results of the beta exam are analyzed to determine which items should be included in the certification exam based on many factors, including item difficulty and relevance. Generally, the desired items are those that were answered correctly by anywhere from 25 percent to 90 percent of the beta exam candidates. This helps ensure that the exam consists of a variety of difficulty levels, from somewhat easy to extremely difficult.

Also during this phase, a panel of job function experts determines the cut score (minimum passing score) for the exam. The cut score differs from exam to exam because it is based on an item-by-item determination of the percentage of candidates who answered the item correctly and who would be expected to answer the item correctly. The cut score is determined in a group session to increase the reliability among the experts.

Phase 8: Exam live   Microsoft Certified Professional exams are administered by Sylvan Prometric.

Tips for Taking the Exam

Here are some general tips for taking your exam successfully:

- Arrive early at the exam center so you can relax and review your study materials, particularly tables and lists of exam-related information.

- Read the questions carefully. Don't be tempted to jump to an early conclusion. Make sure you know *exactly* what the question is asking.

- Don't leave any unanswered questions. They count against you.

- When answering multiple-choice questions you're not sure about, use a process of elimination to get rid of the obviously incorrect questions first. This will improve your odds if you need to make an educated guess.

- Because the hard questions will eat up the most time, save them for last. You can go back to them when you have completed the easier questions.

- This test has many exhibits (pictures). It can be difficult, if not impossible, to view both the questions and the exhibit simulation on the 14- and 15-inch screens usually found at the testing centers. Call around to each center and see if they have 17" monitors available. If they don't, perhaps you can arrange to bring in your own. Failing this, some have found it useful to quickly draw the diagram on the scratch paper provided by the testing center and use the monitor to view just the question.

- The Implementing and Supporting Microsoft Exchange Server 5.0 exam is often perceived as the most difficult of the Microsoft Certified Professional tests. Many participants run out of time before they are able to complete the test. If you are unsure of the answer to a question, you may want to choose one of the answers, mark the question, and go on—an unanswered question does not help you. Once your time is up, you cannot go on to another question. However, you can remain on one question indefinitely when the time runs out. Therefore, when you are almost out of time, go to a question you feel you can figure out—given enough time—and work until you feel you have got it (or the night security guard boots you out!).

This is not simply a test of your knowledge of Exchange, but on how it is implemented in Windows NT. You will need to know about Windows NT domain models, local and global group concepts, and administration functions. Once you have completed the exam, you will be given immediate, online notification of your pass or fail status. You will also receive a printed Examination Score Report indicating your pass or fail status and your exam results by section. (The test administrator will give you the printed score report.) Test scores are automatically forwarded to Microsoft within five working days after you take the test. You do not need to send your score to Microsoft. If you pass the exam, you will receive confirmation from Microsoft, typically within two to four weeks.

How to Use This Book

This book can provide a solid foundation for the serious effort of preparing for the Implementing and Supporting Microsoft Exchange Server 5.0 exam.

To best benefit from this book, you might want to use the following study method:

1. Study a chapter carefully, making sure you fully understand the information.

2. Complete all hands-on exercises in the chapter, referring to the content of the chapter so that you understand each step you take.

3. Answer the exercise questions related to that chapter. (You will find the answers to these questions in Appendix A.)

4. Note which questions you did not understand, and study those sections of the book again.

5. Study each chapter in the same manner.

6. Before taking the exam, try The Edge Tests' practice exams included on the CD that comes with this book. They will give you a brief overview of what you can expect to see on the real thing. The Edge Tests include simulations of the actual Microsoft exams with references to the SYBEX MCSE Study Guides. It is an excellent way to make the best use of your SYBEX study guides and your limited study time. For more information call 1-800-800-1638 or visit http://www.edgetest.com.

If you prefer to use this book in conjunction with classroom or online training, you have many options. Both Microsoft-authorized training and independent training are widely available. Cyberstate University offers excellent online MCSE courses across the Internet, using Sybex materials. Their program includes an online NT lab where you can practice some of the exercises in this book, as well as videos, software, and lectures, all centered around the Sybex MCSE Study Guide series. You can reach Cyberstate at 1-888-GET-EDUC (888-438-3382) or at http://www.cyberstateu.com.

In order to complete the exercises in this book, there are certain minimum hardware requirements, detailed in Tables a.1, a.2, and a.3.

T A B L E a.1 Server requirements	Resource	Minimum	Recommended
	CPU	Pentium 60	Pentium 133 or higher
	RAM	24 MB	32 MB or higher
	Free disk space	250 MB	(depends on user storage)
	Network adapter/ cable/etc.	(almost anything) e.g. Ethernet, Token Ring, etc.	n.a.
	Operating system	Windows NT Server v3.51 Service Pack 5 or above	Windows NT Server 4.0 (Service Pack 2 is necessary if you are installing the Active Server Components)

T A B L E a.2 Windows 95/NT client requirements (using Microsoft Outlook)	Resource	Minimum	Recommended
	CPU	n.a.	n.a.
	RAM	8 MB for Windows 95 16 MB for Windows NT	16 MB or higher
	Free disk space	26 MB	46 MB
	Network adapter/ cable/etc.	(almost anything) e.g. Ethernet, Token Ring, etc.	n.a.
	Operating system	Windows 95 Windows NT Workstation 3.51 or 4.0	n.a.

T A B L E a.3 Windows 3.x client requirements (using Microsoft Exchange Client)	Resource	Minimum	Recommended
	CPU	n.a.	n.a.
	RAM	8 MB	12 or 16 MB
	Free disk space	12 MB	22 MB

	Resource	Minimum	Recommended
T A B L E a.3 *(cont.)* Windows 3.*x* client requirements (using Microsoft Exchange Client)	Network adapter/ cable/etc.	(almost anything) e.g. Ethernet, Token Ring, etc.	n.a.
	Operating system	Windows 3.*x*	n.a.

To learn all the material covered in this book, you will need to study regularly and with discipline. Try to set aside the same time every day to study, and select a comfortable and quiet place in which to do it. If you work hard, you will be surprised at how quickly you learn this material. Good luck.

What's on the CD?

The CD contains several valuable tools to help you study for your MCSE exams:

- Microsoft's Train_Cert Offline is a good place to start, if you want to gain an overview of Microsoft education and the process of becoming an MCSE.

- Microsoft's TechNet Technical Information Network demonstration copy is a vast database of technical information relating to Microsoft products. It can also be a helpful study aid.

- Internet Explorer 3.02 will allow you to view Train_Cert Offline, and will also function as a Web browser.

- The Edge Tests for Exchange Server 5.0 demo provides excellent simulations of the real exam questions.

Contact Information

To find out more about Microsoft Education and Certification materials and programs, to register with Sylvan Prometric, or to get other useful information, check the following resources. Outside the United States or Canada, contact your local Microsoft office or Sylvan Prometric testing center.

Microsoft Certified Professional Program—(800) 636-7544 For information about the Microsoft Certified Professional program and exams, and to order the latest Microsoft Roadmap to Education and Certification.

Sylvan Prometric testing centers—(800) 755-EXAM To register to take a Microsoft Certified Professional exam at any of more than 800 Sylvan Prometric testing centers around the world, or to order this Exam Study Guide.

Microsoft Certification Development Team—on the Web at http://www.microsoft.com/Train_Cert/mcp/examinfo/certsd.htm To volunteer for participation in one or more exam development phases or to report a problem with an exam. Address written correspondence to: Certification Development Team, Microsoft Education and Certification, One Microsoft Way, Redmond, WA 98052.

Microsoft TechNet Technical Information Network—(800) 344-2121 For support professionals and system administrators. Outside the United States and Canada, call your local Microsoft subsidiary for information.

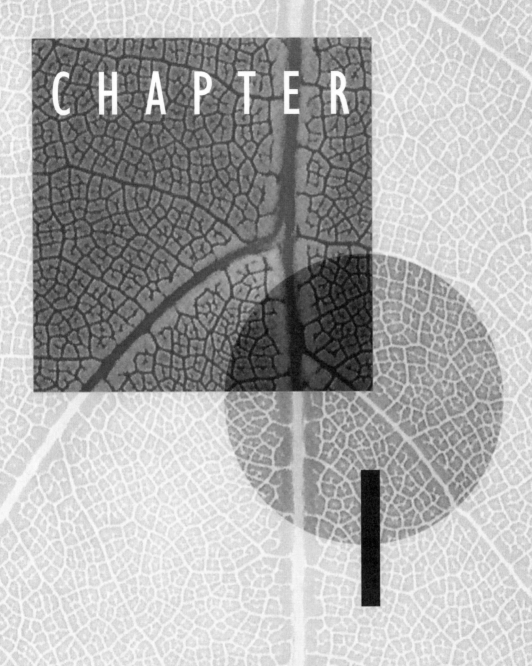

CHAPTER

1

Introduction to Microsoft Exchange

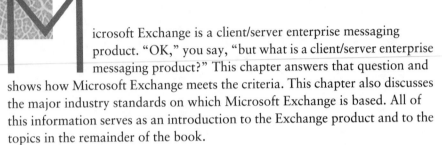

icrosoft Exchange is a client/server enterprise messaging product. "OK," you say, "but what is a client/server enterprise messaging product?" This chapter answers that question and shows how Microsoft Exchange meets the criteria. This chapter also discusses the major industry standards on which Microsoft Exchange is based. All of this information serves as an introduction to the Exchange product and to the topics in the remainder of the book.

In this chapter, we will address the following subjects:

- Messaging systems

- The client/server model

- Enterprise-wide computing

- Industry standards used by Exchange

The first three items relate to our previous question, "What is a client/ server enterprise messaging product?" Messaging systems relate to *what* Exchange does, client/server models relate to *how* it does it, and enterprise-wide computing relates to the *context* in which it does it.

Messaging Systems

An enterprise needs information in order to get work done. Information is its oxygen. Frequently information *is* the work *and* the product (for example, a consulting company). In this context electronic messaging has become a mission-critical function in most organizations. While electronic mail (e-mail) is still the core ingredient, other applications are now included in this category. The category of messaging can be divided into the following subcategories:

- E-mail
- Electronic forms
- Groupware
- Other messaging applications

Each of these categories, and how Exchange addresses them, are briefly discussed in the following text.

> Due to the multiple functionality of some of the client programs, a single program could fit into more than one of the previous categories. For example, Microsoft Outlook includes e-mail functions and groupware functions like group scheduling.

E-Mail

An e-mail program allows a user to create, send, read, store, and manipulate electronic messages and attachments. E-mail is an example of *push-style* communication, meaning that the sender initiates the communication. Because of the importance of e-mail in the overall communication of organizations, these programs have evolved from merely creating and sending text messages, into multifeatured programs.

Microsoft ships two powerful e-mail client applications with the Exchange product. Exchange Client runs on 16-bit and 32-bit systems. Outlook runs on 32-bit systems only.

Microsoft also has server components that enable Internet clients to be Exchange e-mail clients. Those Internet clients include:

- Web browsers
- Internet e-mail programs with the Post Office Protocol version 3 (POP3)

Figure 1.1 illustrates these e-mail client applications.

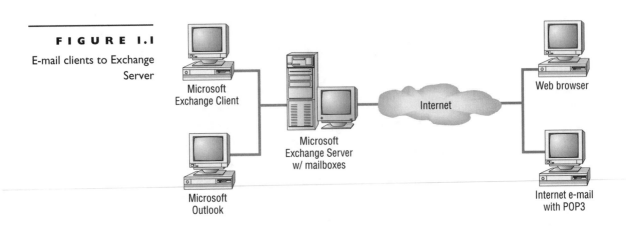

FIGURE 1.1

E-mail clients to Exchange Server

Microsoft Exchange Client

The Exchange Client is a feature-rich e-mail program. Some of its features include the following:

- **Universal inbox (mailbox)**   This central storage area can hold not only e-mail messages, but other data such as word processing documents, spreadsheet files, faxes, electronic forms, even voice mail files.

Two terms refer to a user's mailbox, *mailbox* and *inbox*. The most common usage in this book will be mailbox. This is our primary term for two reasons. One, Microsoft divides a mailbox into folders, one of which is labeled the inbox. Using the term inbox for only the folder helps prevent confusion. The other reason is that the Exchange object name for a mailbox is *mailbox*.

- **Hierarchical data storage**   The Exchange Client organizes the client's mailbox into four default folders: Inbox, Outbox, Deleted Items, and Sent Items. Users can also create their own folders, thereby creating a personalized organization of their data.

- **Customized views**   Users have the ability to determine what and how data is presented to them on their screens. Messages can be ordered by sender, date, priority, subject, and other properties.

- **Search tool**   Users can search and retrieve messages in their mailboxes using a variety of search criteria, such as sender, date, and subject.

- **AutoAssistants** Exchange includes software routines that can automatically carry out actions based upon rules the user defines. This functionality is referred to as AutoAssistants. Some of the actions AutoAssistants can perform are alerting, deleting, moving, copying, forwarding, and replying.

- **Rich-text message content** Historically, most e-mail content was simple text. The Exchange Client message editor enables the creation of rich-text message content which can include multiple fonts, sizes, colors, alignments, and other formatting controls.

- **Microsoft Word as message editor** Even though the Exchange Client includes a rich message editor, it can be configured to use Microsoft Word as its message editor.

- **Compound messages and drag-and-drop editing** The Exchange Client program is OLE 2.0 (Object Linking and Embedding) compliant, and therefore allows the creation of compound documents. For example, a user could drag-and-drop a group of cells from a spreadsheet into an e-mail message.

- **Secure messages** Digital signatures and message encryption are advanced security features built into the Exchange Client.

- **Remote mail** Because more and more workers spend some of their work time outside of the office, special features relating to remote mail have been incorporated. One example is the ability to remotely access a mailbox and selectively download new mail to the remote computer, and to send out all outgoing mail that was created on the remote computer.

- **Delegate access** Some users need to allow other users to access their mailbox. For example, a manager might want a secretary to read meeting request messages in order to handle the manager's schedule. In many mail systems, this would be accomplished by having the secretary log on as the manager. This creates an obvious security hole. Microsoft solves this problem by allowing the manager to grant the secretary permission to access the manager's mailbox. This permission can be restricted to certain folders. The secretary can also be granted permission to send messages "on behalf of" the manager, or even send messages as the manager, called "send as."

- **Send/Receive electronic forms**   Users can send and receive electronic forms through the Exchange Client application.

These are just some of the many features of the Exchange Client program. Chapters 6 and 7 discuss these features in greater detail.

Microsoft includes versions of this e-mail program for the following operating system platforms:

- MS-DOS

- Microsoft Windows 3.*x*

- Microsoft Windows for Workgroups

- Microsoft Windows 95

- Microsoft Windows NT

- Apple Macintosh

Microsoft Outlook

Outlook is a new e-mail client that ships with Exchange Server and Microsoft Office 97 as a stand-alone product. It is a 32-bit application that was built for the 32-bit Windows operating systems—Microsoft Windows 95 and Windows NT. Outlook is referred to as a desktop information manager because it is more than just an e-mail client. It also performs such tasks as calendaring, scheduling, and task and contact management. Outlook is intended to be a central program for client management of data.

Microsoft Outlook includes the feature set listed previously for the Exchange Client, but also adds some additional advanced features. Some of them that specifically relate to e-mail are listed here:

- **MessageFlags**   These tags can be associated with e-mail messages to help the user prioritize follow-up action. MessageFlags include reply, read, and "for your information." Users can sort their messages by these MessageFlags which helps with task management.

- **Voting**   Outlook has the ability to add voting buttons in the header of a mail message and to collect the responses. This allows surveys to be conducted through e-mail.

- **MessageRecall** Permits a sent message to be recalled, provided the recipient has not opened the message. Users can also replace a sent message with a new message.

- **AutoPreview** Outlook can automatically display the first three lines of a mail message so users can quickly decide which messages to read or delete.

- **AutoCreate** Outlook can automatically convert one Outlook item into another. For example, a mail message may contain an action item which the user can simply drag-and-drop into the Task folder. Outlook would automatically convert the mail message into a task. This saves the user from retyping.

These are just some of the e-mail features of Microsoft Outlook. This client program will be discussed further in Chapters 6 and 7.

Web Browsers

Exchange ships with a server component, consisting of Active Server Pages, that enables Internet Web browsers to access Exchange mailboxes. Through a Web browser, users can access their Exchange mailboxes and read or send mail, read their schedules, browse the Exchange Directory, and access public folders. Any standard Web browser can be used, such as Microsoft Internet Explorer or Netscape Navigator. This Exchange functionality permits users of other operating system platforms, such as UNIX or IBM's OS/2, to also be Exchange clients. Chapter 11 covers the Exchange components required for web browser clients.

Internet E-Mail Programs with POP3

Exchange ships with a server component, called the Microsoft Exchange POP3 Mail Service, that allows Internet e-mail programs that are POP3-enabled to access an Exchange mailbox and download their mail messages to their remote machine. POP3 (which stands for Post Office Protocol, version 3) is a mail retrieval protocol. An example of an application that fits this category is Qualcomm's Eudora. Chapter 11 will discuss the Exchange components that relate to POP3.

Electronic Forms

Electronic forms are electronic messages with built-in fields. They can be used instead of paper-based forms to automate and streamline organizational processes. Items such as expense reports, order entry, and purchase requests can all be implemented with electronic forms.

The two Exchange e-mail clients—Exchange Client and Outlook—can send and receive electronic forms. Exchange also ships with two programs that can be used to create customized electronic forms:

- Microsoft Exchange Forms Designer

- Microsoft Outlook Forms Designer

Microsoft Exchange Forms Designer

The Exchange Forms Designer is a visual, nonprogrammatic design and creation tool for electronic forms. Users simply draw a form's appearance and choose its behavior. The Forms Designer program is actually a special version of Microsoft's Visual Basic development tool. Because of this, forms created in the Forms Designer environment can be further modified in Visual Basic.

Electronic forms can be used with two types of applications:

- Stand-alone form applications

- Folder-based applications

Stand-alone form applications are electronic forms that are going to be sent from one person to another person or persons. An example is an expense report form that would be filled out and sent to the user's manager.

Folder-based applications utilize *public folders* and can have electronic forms associated with them. Both public folders and the way in which electronic forms relate to them will be discussed in the Groupware section that follows. Chapter 8 will cover the topic of forms in detail.

Microsoft Outlook Forms Designer

The Outlook Forms Designer is a program that can create 32-bit forms. It contains the basic functionality of the Exchange Forms Designer, and adds some powerful new functions. One of those new functions is the ability to use Microsoft Office 97 applications to create templates for Outlook forms. Chapter 8 will cover the topic of the Microsoft Outlook Forms Designer.

Groupware

A simple definition of *groupware* is any application (the *ware* in groupware) that allows *groups* to store and share information. That is a very broad definition, and one that includes applications like e-mail and electronic forms. And indeed, as you will see, they are important ingredients in groupware. But the emphasis in groupware is collaboration, not merely sending something—but enabling many people to collaborate.

Microsoft Schedule+, which comes with the Exchange Server, is a straightforward groupware application. One of its functions is to enable many people to share calendar and scheduling information. A user, with the necessary permissions, can view the schedule of another user. This allows people to collaborate on their schedules. Microsoft Outlook also incorporates many groupware functions such as the ability to share a calendar, schedule, task list, and contact list.

Another example of groupware is *folder-based* applications. These applications utilize public folders. A public folder is a special storage area for group access. Various types of information can be contained in a public folder, such as documents, spreadsheets, graphics, e-mail messages, forms, and many other types of information. Along with storing information, a public folder can be assigned security, so that only selected users or groups can access the public folder. Other features like views and rules can be assigned to a public folder. A simple folder-based application would be where a sales department places all their sales letters in a specified sales public folder. Only the employees in the sales department would be given permission to access this public folder.

Folder-based applications can also utilize electronic forms. A specific electronic form or forms can be associated with a public folder. Users can then fill out and "post" the form to the public folder. Other users can access the public folder and view the posted information. An example of this type of application is a discussion-and-response application. A product manager could create a public folder for discussion about a product under development. That manager could also create customized electronic forms that people could use to enter their comments and then send, through e-mail, to the public folder. The product manager and product developers could then access the public folder to read the comments. It is even possible to set up customized views of the content in the public folder in order to view only data on a specific topic. A marketing person might want to see only comments relating to the possible market for the product. Folder-based applications are examples of *pull-style* communication, because users go to the information and decide what is relevant to them. See Chapter 9 for more on the topic of public folders. Figure 1.2 illustrates folder-based applications.

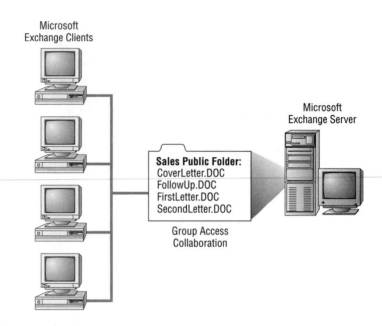

FIGURE 1.2

Folder-based applications

Other Messaging Applications

Along with e-mail, electronic forms, and groupware, there are many other types of messaging applications. Exchange provides an open platform that encourages the integration of other types of applications, some of which include:

- **Workflow** Workflow software builds on e-mail and electronic forms by adding automatic routing to electronic messaging.

- **Fax** Fax software can be integrated with the Exchange clients so that e-mail and faxes can be sent and received from the same location, as well as share the same address book.

- **Paging** Some paging products can enable an Exchange client to send an electronic page through an Exchange server, to a wireless paging service, and to another person's pager.

- **Video conferencing** Products like Microsoft's NetMeeting can be integrated with the Exchange clients to provide video conferencing, as well as other features like *whiteboard conferencing* (i.e., collaborative drawing) and text-based chatting.

- **Voice mail**   There are various voice mail products that integrate with Exchange and store their messages in an Exchange mailbox.

Client/Server Model

Microsoft Exchange uses a client/server computing model to implement its messaging system. To better understand the client/server model, two other models will be briefly discussed to provide a contrast to the client/server model. The three models discussed in this section are:

- Host-based computing

- LAN-based shared-file computing

- Client/server computing

Host-Based Computing

Host-based computing consists of a powerful host computer, such as a mainframe computer or minicomputer, and numerous input-output devices attached to the host, such as terminals, printers, and personal computers running terminal emulation software. The advantages of this architecture are the powerful, centralized computing processing, administration, and backup. These features permit a large number of users on these systems. The disadvantages are that these features incur high costs, that personal computing power and applications are not leveraged, and that most of these systems have a proprietary architecture. Examples of messaging systems that use this type of model are IBM PROFS (Professional Office System) and SNADS (SNA Distribution Services).

Figure 1.3 illustrates the host-based computing model.

LAN-Based Shared-File Computing

This network computing model works in a local area network (LAN) context. At least one powerful personal computer is used as a server computer to store files. Users, working on their own networked personal computers, access and share the files on the server computer. Microsoft Mail is a messaging system that uses this type of architecture.

FIGURE 1.3

Host-based computing
model

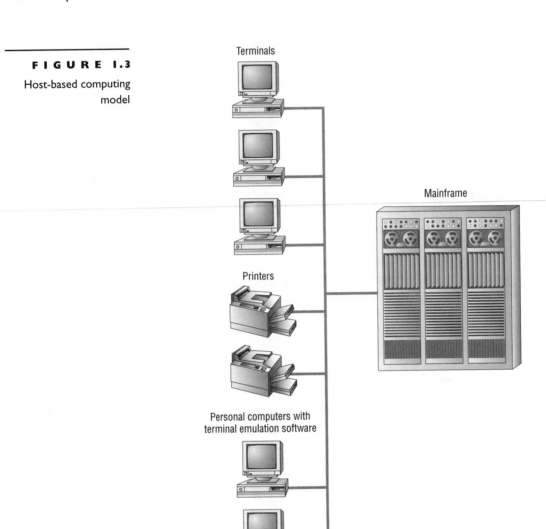

Using this model, a shared-file mail system has *active clients* and *passive servers*. Each mail user is assigned a mailbox. A mailbox is actually a directory on the server where mail messages will be placed. The server software is passive in that its main task is to store mail messages.

The client software is said to be active because it performs almost all mail activities. Along with the normal mail activities of creating and reading mail, the client software is also responsible for sending mail to mailboxes and checking for new mail (this is referred to as *polling*).

This could be compared to a postal system where people must take their outgoing mail to the post office and place it in the respective recipients' mail slots. They must also visit the post office to check their mail slots for any new mail. The primary duty of the post office is to store the mail. This is analogous to the shared-file mail system in that the clients are active and the server is passive.

The advantages of shared-file mail systems include the following:

- **Minimal server requirements**   Because the server has a passive role, it does not need to run on a high-end hardware platform.

- **Minimal server configuration in a single-server environment**   Because the server is mainly a storage location, it does not need a lot of configuration.

The disadvantages of shared-file mail systems include the following:

- **Limited security**   Because the client software is responsible for sending mail to a recipient's mailbox, each client must have *write permissions* on each mail directory. Each client must also have *read permissions* on the entire mail directory structure in order to read forwarded or copied messages. From a security standpoint, this is considered an excessive level of permissions.

- **Increased network traffic**   The periodic client polling of mailboxes for new mail increases network traffic.

- **Increased client load**   The active clients do almost all of the processing work.

- **Limited scalability**   These systems cannot accommodate large numbers of users due to the shared-file model. Users must access common files that can be opened by only one process at a time.

Figure 1.4 illustrates a shared-file mail system.

FIGURE 1.4

Shared-file mail system

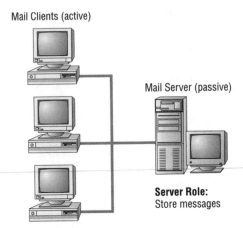

Mail Clients (active)

Mail Server (passive)

Server Role:
Store messages

Client Role:
– Poll mail directory for new mail
– Read mail (necessitates read
  permission over entire mail
  directory structure)
– Create mail
– Send mail (necessitates write
  permission over entire mail
  directory structure)

Client/Server Computing

Client/server computing is where a computer task is divided between the client processes and server processes. Each side, while performing specific parts of the task, works to accomplish the task. The two processes are usually running on separate computers and are communicating over a network. The communication is in the form of requests and replies passed back and forth through messages.

The client side includes a user's personal computer or workstation and client software. The client software provides the interface to the user for manipulating data and making requests to and receiving replies from the server. The processing power to carry out those tasks is provided by the client's computer.

The server side includes the server computer and server software. The server software receives and processes client requests, provides storage capabilities, implements security, provides for administrative functions, and performs many more duties. The server's processor, or processors, power these functions.

When this model is applied to a mail system, both the client side and the server side are active participants. Mail activities are divided between the two sides in a way that takes advantage of both parties. The client software enables users to initiate mail activities like creating, sending, reading, storing, and forwarding mail and attachments.

The server software also has an active role. Some of its tasks are implementing security, placing messages in mailboxes (as opposed to the client software doing it), notifying clients of new mail (which eliminates clients polling their mailboxes), and performing specified actions on mail, such as applying rules, rerouting messages, along with many other tasks. Many of the mail activities that are initiated by the client software are actually implemented on the server. For example, when a client initiates the reading of a message, the client software sends a read request to the server where the message physically resides. The server software receives this request, processes it (for example, checks security to see if this user is permitted to read this message), and then sends the message to the client. The user can then use the client software and processor to manipulate the message (edit the message, for example). This illustrates how both sides are active.

In this model, the software running on the client machine is frequently referred to as the *front-end* program, while the software running on the server is referred to as the *back-end* program.

The advantages of the client/server model include the following:

- **Distributed computer processing**   The computer processing power of both the client and server machines are utilized. The client processor handles the end-user mail activities, such as creating, reading, and manipulating mail, while the server processor (or processors) handles the security, routing, and special handling of mail. This spreads the processing load over a multitude of client processors, while still utilizing the powerful processing of the server machine.

- **Tight security**   The server software is responsible for the security of the mail system. The server software is the entity that actually places messages in mailboxes. The clients therefore do not need permissions to all mailboxes. This creates a much more secure mail system.

- **Reduced network traffic**   Because the server software informs clients of new mail, the client software does not have to poll the server, thus reducing network traffic.

The Big Ox Fallacy

Grace Hopper, one of the developers of the COBOL programming language, once told a story about a farmer who came upon a huge tree that had fallen across his road. The farmer brought out his ox and some rope and tried in vain to move the tree. The farmer's next act was to take the ox and breed it with another big ox hoping to produce an even bigger ox. He figured he would do this until he had bred an ox big enough to move that huge tree. Grace Hopper's commentary was that obviously the farmer's logic was flawed. What the farmer should have done was simply go get all his neighbors' oxen and hook them up to the tree and pull the tree off the road. This story illustrates the need to utilize the distributed processing power of all the machines on a network.

- **Scalable**   The term *scalable* relates to the ability to grow easily. A client/server mail system can scale to any size organization.

The primary disadvantage of the client/server model is the following:

- **Increased server hardware requirements**   Because the server has an active role in the messaging environment, there are greater requirements for the server hardware platform. This should not be seen as much of a disadvantage in light of the advantages of scalability, central administration, backup, and other advantages.

Figure 1.5 illustrates the client/server mail system.

Exchange is a client/server messaging system. The Exchange Server software runs as an application on a Windows NT Server. It provides server-side messaging functions for the client applications. Exchange also ships with the client applications noted earlier in this chapter. These programs, along with third-party applications like Web browsers, provide the client-side functions such as making requests to the server and creating and manipulating data.

So far we have learned *what* features make up Exchange 5, and *how* the system is implemented, namely the client/server model. Now we need to turn our attention to the context or scale in which Exchange can be implemented.

FIGURE 1.5

Client/server mail system

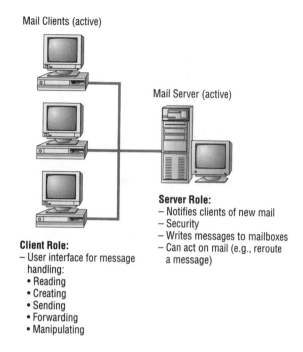

Mail Clients (active)

Mail Server (active)

Server Role:
- Notifies clients of new mail
- Security
- Writes messages to mailboxes
- Can act on mail (e.g., reroute a message)

Client Role:
- User interface for message handling:
  • Reading
  • Creating
  • Sending
  • Forwarding
  • Manipulating

Enterprise-Wide Computing

Microsoft Exchange was designed to be an *enterprise* messaging system, meaning one that spans an entire organization. While an enterprise can be of small or medium size with straightforward requirements, it can also be very large and have very complex requirements. For Exchange to be an enterprise messaging system, a large number of technologies had to be included or leveraged from other products (such as Microsoft Windows NT Server). This section briefly discusses the technologies that make Exchange a true enterprise messaging system. Those technologies fall into six categories:

- Enterprise-quality application platform

- Scalability

- Interoperability

- Performance

- Administration

- Reliability

Enterprise-Quality Application Platform

Before a determination can be made as to whether or not a product can scale to the size an organization needs, it must be determined that the product can do the things it needs to do. Exchange provides the necessary application platform to meet the requirements of almost any organization. The following are some of the elements of the Exchange application platform:

- **Supports large number of messaging services**   E-mail, electronic forms, groupware, and add-on products for fax, paging, video conferencing, voice mail, and many services are supported.

- **Supports large number of client platforms**   There is client software that runs on MS-DOS, Windows 3.*x*, Windows 95, Windows NT Workstation, Apple Macintosh, UNIX, and IBM OS/2.

- **Integrates with other client applications**   The Exchange client programs that ship with Exchange have very tight integration with the most popular application suite on the market, Microsoft Office.

- **Provides open architecture/extensibility**   Exchange uses an application programming interface (API) for messaging services, called Messaging API (MAPI), that is a published specification and can be used to create additional applications for the Exchange environment.

- **Based on industry standards**   MAPI is not only an open architecture, but it is considered an industry standard. Exchange also uses other open standards for the vast majority of its messaging functions. Some examples are:

    Internet mail   Simple Mail Transfer Protocol (SMTP), Post Office Protocol 3 (POP3). See Chapter 11.

    Internet directory access   Lightweight Directory Access Protocol (LDAP). See Chapter 11.

> **Internet news services**   Network News Transfer Protocol (NNTP). See Chapter 11.
>
> **Internet Web protocols**   HyperText Transfer Protocol (HTTP) and HyperText Markup Language (HTML). See Chapter 11.
>
> **CCITT message transfer**   (International Telegraph and Telephone Consultative Committee): X.400. See the section "Industry Standards" later in this chapter.
>
> **CCITT directory**   X.500. See the section "Industry Standards" later in this chapter.

- **Security features**   Messages can be sent with a digital signature to confirm the identity of the sender, and message content can be encrypted. (Chapter 10 discusses these two features.) Further security features, and ones that are leveraged from Microsoft Windows NT Server, include:

  > **Mandatory logon**   A user must have a domain account and password to log on to a Windows NT Server domain.
  >
  > **Discretionary access control**   An Exchange administrator can use NT security to control access to Exchange resources. For example, one administrator could have security to manage one particular Exchange server, but not other servers.
  >
  > **Auditing**   Windows NT can be configured to monitor and record certain events. This can help diagnose security events. The audit information is written to the Windows NT Event Log.

Scalability

Once a product has been determined to accomplish the types of things you need to get done, then you must find out if it can do it on the scale you need. Exchange is extremely scalable due to the following features:

- **Software scalable**   Exchange can be implemented with a single Exchange server, or dozens of servers, depending on the message requirements. Even with multiple Exchange servers, a single enterprise messaging system exists. This is due to the Exchange features that enable communication between servers. Some of those features include message routing, directory replication, and data replication. This functionality permits Exchange to scale from a single server to multiple server implementations. Microsoft itself uses Exchange for its worldwide messaging system.

- **Hardware scalable** Scalability is also evidenced by the maximum hardware specifications that Exchange can utilize.

  - **CPUs** Scalable from 1–8 processors.

  - **RAM** Maximum is 4 gigabytes.

  - **Disk Storage** Maximum for mail messages is 16 gigabytes of physical storage per server. Logical storage can be greater because of single-instance storage.

Interoperability

For a product to fit into an enterprise, it might need to work with an existing messaging system. This is called *interoperability* or coexistence. An organization might need to move all its existing messaging data to a new messaging product. This is called a *migration*. Exchange addresses both of these issues.

To interoperate with various non-Exchange systems, referred to as *foreign systems*, Microsoft had to write special software programs called *connectors*. Connectors are similar to translators who understand both Exchange and the foreign system and translate between them. Third-party companies also have written similar programs. Microsoft refers to these programs as *gateways*. Some of the messaging systems that Exchange can interoperate with include:

- Internet mail

- X.400 mail systems

- Microsoft Mail

- Lotus cc:Mail

- Lotus Notes

- IBM PROFS and SNADS

- Digital Equipment Corporation (DEC) All-IN-1

- Verimation MEMO

 For Exchange to interoperate with some of the previous systems, third-party software is required. Chapters 14 and 15 discuss interoperability in more detail.

Some of the messaging systems that Exchange can perform a migration with include:

- Microsoft Mail

- Lotus cc:Mail

- Novell GroupWise

- Netscape Collabra

- IBM PROFS and OfficeVision/VM

- DEC All-IN-1

- Verimation MEMO

For Exchange to perform a migration with some of the previous systems, third-party software is required. Migration is discussed in Chapter 16.

Performance

A messaging system requires adequate performance to be used on an enterprise scale. Exchange meets that requirement by being a 32-bit, multithreaded program running on a high-performance operating system, Microsoft Windows NT Server. Exchange also ships with a program to help optimize performance, called the Exchange Optimizer. Another Exchange program that relates to performance is Load Simulator. This program can simulate load on the system and predict the system's performance.

Administration

An important element of any enterprise application is the ability to effectively and efficiently administer it. Exchange meets this need by including powerful administration programs, one of which is the Exchange Administrator program. This program provides a single point of administration for an entire Exchange organization. Exchange servers anywhere in the enterprise can be managed from this program, and such activities as creating mailboxes, configuring a server, and managing connections to foreign systems, can all be managed from this program. The Exchange Administrator program also enables the creation of mailboxes in a batch process, and provides for the tracking of messages. The Exchange Administrator program includes these administrative utilities:

- **Link Monitor** Examines the link between two servers.

- **Server Monitor** Examines the status of a particular server.

Along with its own administrative utilities, Exchange can also leverage the administrative capabilities of the Windows NT Server operating system. Exchange integrates with Windows NT Server utilities like Performance Monitor and Event Viewer.

Reliability

Because of the importance of a messaging system to an enterprise, it must be reliable. Exchange provides reliability through the following:

- **Transaction logs** These logs provide fault tolerance and recoverability.

- **Windows NT Backup program** When Exchange is installed, it adds extensions to the Windows NT Backup program, allowing Windows NT to back up Exchange information.

- **Replicas** Exchange can be configured to have multiple copies, called *replicas*, of a single public folder on different servers. This prevents a single point of failure in terms of data access.

- **Intelligent message routing** This feature allows multiple routes to a destination, thereby preventing a single point of failure for message delivery.

- **Windows NT Server fault tolerance** Exchange takes advantage of the many fault tolerant features of the Windows NT Server operating system, such as disk mirroring and disk striping with parity.

Industry Standards

Microsoft Exchange is based on industry standard technologies. Someone once joked that the best thing about standards was that there were so many of them from which to choose. But being a standards-based product ensures an open architecture and therefore extensibility (i.e., the ability to easily add on to the product). An adequate understanding of the standards used in Exchange will help in utilizing it. This section presents a brief coverage of the following standards:

- Messaging Application Programming Interface (MAPI)

- The Remote Procedure Call (RPC) protocol

- CCITT X.400

- CCITT X.500

The Internet standards are also very important in Exchange, and they will be discussed in Chapters 11 and 14.

Messaging Application Programming Interface (MAPI)

To understand MAPI, you must first understand what an application programming interface is. At the code level, a program's functions are invoked through specific instructions. The collection of those instructions are referred to as an application programming interface (API). That phrase is appropriate because the API allows a programmer to interface with the functions of a program. For example, if a program has the ability to read a message, there is a specific API instruction, also called a *function call*, that can invoke that ability. If two programs need to interact, they must do so with an API they both understand. For example, if program A sends the instruction Read_Message 4 to program B, but program B only understands the instruction Message_4_Read then the instruction will not be understood. Humans can use slightly different grammar and still understand one another, but computers are not that forgiving.

In the past, many client/server messaging products had their own APIs for the client/server interaction. If someone wrote a client program, it would only work with the messaging system whose API it used. If a user needed to connect to multiple messaging systems, multiple client programs were needed (see Figure 1.6).

FIGURE 1.6

Multiple messaging APIs require multiple programs

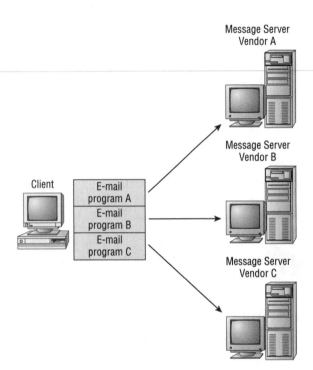

Microsoft decided to remedy that situation by creating a standard messaging architecture, referred to as the Messaging API (MAPI). MAPI accomplishes two broad goals. One, it provides a standard API for client/server messaging interaction. This role makes MAPI a type of *middleware*, meaning that it stands in the middle between clients and servers. Some authors refer to middleware as the slash (/) between the words client and server. MAPI makes it possible for a single client application to access different messaging servers (see Figure 1.7 for an illustration).

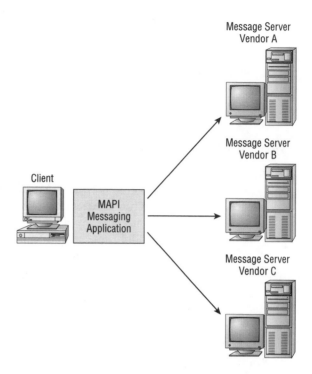

FIGURE 1.7

Accessing different
messaging servers
through MAPI

The second broad goal of MAPI is to provide a standard set of services to client messaging applications. These services include address books, message storage, and transport mechanisms. Even when using different types of MAPI applications, like e-mail, fax, and voice mail, a user can access a single address book (universal address book) and store different data types in the same folder (universal inbox). The transport mechanisms relate to a single client application connecting to different messaging systems. A single MAPI e-mail application can access a Exchange server, a Microsoft Mail post office, an Internet mail server, and others. Chapter 6 examines the MAPI services in more detail.

Although MAPI includes individual API instructions, it most often communicates those instructions in an object-oriented manner. An object is a container: in this context, it functions as a container of API instructions. The Microsoft specification for object-oriented programming is called the Component Object Model (COM). MAPI, OLE, ActiveX, and other technologies are part of the COM standard.

The original version of MAPI (called Simple MAPI) was developed by Microsoft. But in the subsequent version (MAPI 1.0), Microsoft worked with over 100 different vendors to develop an industry standard. Microsoft has also turned over the vast majority of the MAPI specification to standards organizations, while still taking a leadership role by including the core MAPI component with the Microsoft Windows 95 and Windows NT operating systems.

While MAPI deals with instructions, the next section discusses the protocols that enable those instructions to be passed between clients and servers.

Procedure Calls

We now know the instruction standard used by the Exchange client/server messaging applications, namely MAPI. But client/server applications are divided across physical machines. When a client issues a read instruction for a message, that message could be on the server. The server could understand that instruction and could send the message, but the instruction has to get to the server and the message has to get back to the client. MAPI does not handle those procedures. From MAPI's perspective, the physical distinction of the client and the server does not exist, it is transparent. Microsoft uses the Remote Procedure Call protocol (RPC) to pass instructions and data between machines. Before discussing the RPC protocol, we will first define what a procedure call is, and discuss the two types of procedure calls, local and remote.

Procedure calls handle the transfer of instructions and data between a program and processor, or processors. When a program issues an instruction, that instruction is passed to the processor for execution, and the results of the execution are passed back to the program. There are two main types of procedure calls:

- Local procedure calls

- Remote procedure calls

Local Procedure Calls

When a program issues an instruction that is executed on the same computer as the program executing the instruction, the procedure is referred to as a *local procedure call*. When Exchange Server components perform activities on that server, they issue instructions that are executed by that server's CPU or CPUs. That is an example of a local procedure call. Exchange uses a Microsoft protocol called the Local Procedure Call (LPC) to implement this mechanism. Examples of how Exchange uses LPCs will be forthcoming in Chapter 2.

Remote Procedure Calls

A *remote procedure call* is similar to a local procedure call in that it relates to the transfer of instructions and data between a program and processor. But unlike a local procedure call, a remote procedure call enables an instruction issued on one computer to be sent over the network to another computer for execution, with the results being sent back to the first computer. The computer making the instruction and the computer performing the execution are remote from each other. The transfer of instructions and data between the computers is totally transparent to the original program and to the user. To the program issuing the instruction, all its instructions appear to be locally executed. Remote procedure calls are a key ingredient in distributed processing and client/server computing.

The RPC mechanism permits the optimizing of different computers for specific tasks. For example, some programs require lots of processor power, memory, storage, or all three. It would be impractical to give every computer running these applications those level of resources. But one specialized computer could be given, for example, 4 processors, 512MB of RAM, and 16GB of storage. Clients could use those resources through the RPC mechanism.

Because the request/reply aspect of RPC is intended to be transparent to the client program and user, the speed of network communication is a factor. The computers involved in a RPC session need to have a high-speed permanent link between them, such as a local area network (LAN) or a high-speed wide area network (WAN).

Exchange uses remote procedure calls in many of its communications. The protocol that Exchange uses to implement remote procedure calls is also called Remote Procedure Call (RPC). This protocol is discussed in the following section.

Remote Procedure Call (RPC) Protocol

As previously stated, the protocol that Exchange uses to implement remote procedure calls is also called Remote Procedure Call (RPC). It is based on a protocol created by the standards group Open Software Foundation (OSF) and is part of the OSF's Distributed Computing Environment (DCE) protocol suite. Microsoft includes the RPC protocol with their Windows NT operating system, and this is what Exchange uses for much of its communication.

When a user chooses to read a message, the Exchange client program issues a MAPI instruction (MAPIReadMail). The RPC protocol on the client transfers this instruction to the Exchange server where the message physically resides. This is called a *request*. The RPC protocol on the server receives this request, has it executed, and sends the message back to the client's screen. The is called a *reply*. RPC clients make requests, and RPC servers make replies. RPC is sometimes referred to as a request/reply protocol. RPCs are also used in some Exchange server-to-server communications. Figure 1.8 illustrates the RPC mechanism.

FIGURE 1.8

The Remote Procedure Call protocol

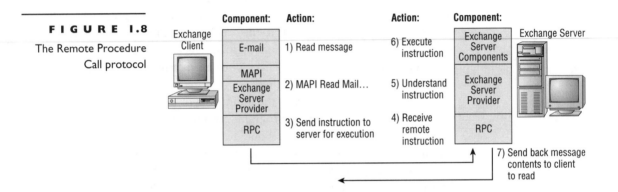

CCITT X.400

For most of the history of electronic messaging in the private sector, there were no widely accepted messaging standards. Different messaging products used vastly different messaging protocols. This prevented, or made difficult and costly, interoperability between different systems. To address this situation, different standards organizations began to develop what they hoped would become internationally recognized messaging standards. One of those standards organizations was the Comité Consultatif International Telegraphique et Telephonique (CCITT). This is translated in English as the International Telegraph and Telephone Consultative Committee. One of the standards they developed was the X.400 Message Handling System (MHS) standard. Exchange uses some of the technologies of the X.400 standard.

The CCITT is now a subdelegation of the International Telegraph Union (ITU), which is an agency of the United Nations. The State Department is the voting member from the United States.

The different versions of the X.400 standard are referred to by the year they were officially published and by a specified color. Versions to date are:

- 1984 "Red Book"

- 1988 "Blue Book"

- 1992 "White Book"

The Message Handling System (MHS) discussed in this section is not the same standard as the Novell-related Message Handling System (MHS).

X.400 is a set of standards relating to the exchange of electronic messages (messages can be e-mail, fax, voice mail, telex, etc.). The goal of X.400 is to enable the creation of a global electronic messaging network. Just as you can make a telephone call from almost anywhere in the world to almost anywhere in the world, X.400 hopes to make that a reality for electronic messaging. X.400 only defines application-level protocols and relies on other standards for the physical transportation of data (e.g., X.25, and others).

X.400 Addressing: Originator/Recipient Address

Try to imagine the American telephone system if different parts of the country used different numbering schemes: different number lengths, different placement of the area code, etc. Obviously that would lead to a lot of complexity and problems: hence a standard numbering scheme exists. A global addressing system is needed to in order to avoid the same sort of chaos.

One might think that you could simply list people's names in alphabetical order. But there are many problems with that scheme. The addressing scheme needs to potentially scale to the entire world's population. An alphabetical list would be quite long. There is also the problem of what constitutes a last name, different countries have different methods (e.g., Anwar el-Sadat, Willem de Kooning). A truly global address scheme needs to be totally unambiguous.

The address scheme that X.400 uses is called the Originator/Recipient Address (O/R Address). It is similar to a postal address in that it uses a hierarchical format. While a postal address hierarchy is country, zip code, state, city, street, and recipient's name, the O/R address hierarchy consists of countries, communication providers (like AT&T), companies or organizations, and other categories. Figure 1.9 and Table 1.1 present some of these categories, called *fields*.

FIGURE 1.9

X.400 Originator/
Recipient address example

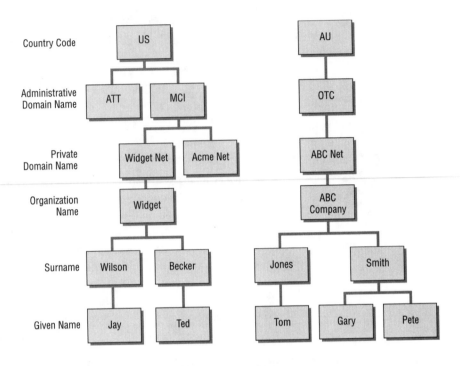

Country Code			
Administrative Domain Name			
Private Domain Name			
Organization Name			
Surname			
Given Name			

TABLE 1.1

Some X.400 Originator/
Recipient address fields

Field	Abbreviation/ Example	Description
Country code	c=us	Country
Administrative Management Domain (ADMD)	a=mci	The third-party networking system used (e.g., ATT, MCI, Sprint, etc.)
Private Management Domain (PRMD)	p=WidgetNet	Subscriber to the ADMD (company name)
Organization	o=Widget	Name of company or organization
Surname	s=Wilson	Last name
Given name	g=Jay	First name

The O/R Address specifies an unambiguous path to where the recipient is located in the X.400 network (it does not specify a path the message might take, only the path to where the recipient is located).

In actual practice, this addressing scheme is not as standardized as Table 1.1 seems to indicate, nor is it used in the standardized way. Although the address fields have always been specified, the order in which to write them was not specified until 1993. Consequently, you will see them written in different ways. Some X.400 implementations have modified the standard.

X.400 Message Format: Interpersonal Messaging (IPM)

X.400 also specifies the protocols for formatting messages. The most common one is called Interpersonal Messaging (IPM), and is used for e-mail messages. There are other protocols for other types of messaging, such as electronic data interchange (EDI).

X.400 Message Routing: Message Transfer Agent (MTA)

Another very important X.400 protocol is Message Transfer Agent (MTA). MTA is the protocol that runs in the message routing machines (i.e., routers). MTA is like a local post office, in that it receives and routes messages to their ultimate destinations. And just like a postal system (a snail mail system), electronic messages can go through several MTAs before they arrive at their ultimate destinations. This type of delivery method is called *store and forward*. An MTA machine receives a message, stores it so it can calculate its next route, and then forwards it either to another MTA machine or its ultimate destination. This method eliminates the need for the sender's application and the recipient's application to perform any simultaneous actions in order to exchange data. A sender's message is simply packaged with all the necessary addressing information, and is sent to the next store-and-forward MTA machine (i.e., router). That MTA can route it to the next MTA, and so on, until it reaches it final destination.

Other X.400 Information

While the X.400 standard does not define the protocols for the physical transporting of messages, it does specify what other standards it can use. They include the following OSI (Open Systems Interconnection) protocols:

- TP0/X.25

- TP4 (CLNP)

- TP0/RPC 1006 to TCPIP

TP stands for Transport Protocol.

Third-party X.400 networks that can be subscribed to include: AT&T Mail, AT&T EasyLink, MCI Mail, Sprintmail, Atlas 400 (France), Envoy 100 (Canada), Telebox 400 (Germany), and Telecom Australia. Microsoft Exchange is an X.400 messaging product.

CCITT X.500

The CCITT X.500 standard defines the protocols for a global directory service. A directory service is a database of information about resources. Resources can be user accounts, user groups, mailboxes, printers, fax machines, and many other items. These resources are officially referred to as objects. The information about an object, such as a mailbox, can include the owner of the mailbox, the owner's title, phone number, fax number, and many other types of information. The information about an object is referred to as its *properties* or *attributes*. A directory enables objects and their properties to be made available to users and administrators.

The directory's importance cannot be overstated. To use a telephone analogy, imagine the current global telephone system without telephone directories. The technology to make a call would be in place, but you would have a hard time locating a person's number to call. Compare a directory to a phone book, or the yellow pages. Both provide assistance in locating resources. This analogy is also good for the relationship of X.400 to X.500. X.400 relates to how applications exchange messages. X.500 relates to how users locate resources, such as another user's e-mail address. The creation of a global, electronic yellow pages could go a long way toward solving the "I know it's out there, I just can't find it" problem.

To create a directory service, X.500 addresses two main areas:

- **Directory structure**   How resources should be organized.

- **Directory access**   How one is able to read, query, and modify a directory.

X.500 Directory Structure

The X.500 directory structure is hierarchical, which facilitates a logical organization of information, which leads to finding information easier. Figure 1.10 illustrates the X.500 directory structure, and Table 1.2 explains it.

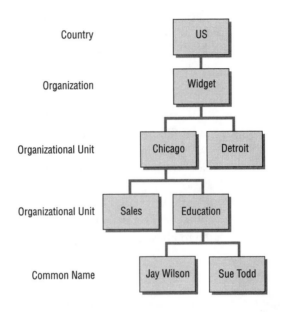

TABLE 1.2	**X.500 Object**	**Abbreviation/Example**	**Description**
Descriptions of X.500 objects	Country	c=us	Country of the organization
	Organization	o=Widget	Name of the organization
	Organization Unit	ou=Chicago ou=Detroit	Subcategory of the organization
	Organization Unit	ou=Sales ou=Education	Subcategories under the ou=Chicago
	Common Name	cn=JayWilson	Name of a specific resource (username, fax name, printer name, etc.)

The X.500 terminology for the structure of a directory is the Directory Information Tree (DIT). The term for the information in the directory is Directory Information Base (DIB).

To communicate the location of an object in the directory hierarchy, list the path to that object, starting at the top and moving down. This is called a Distinguished Name (DN). The DN of the example in Figure 1.10 is:

c=us; o=widget; ou=Chicago; ou=Education; cn=jaywilson

The differences between an X.500 address, the distinguished name (DN), and an X.400 address are due to their different purposes. A DN is the location of an object in the directory, whereas the X.400 address is the location of an object in a message system. Getting back to the telephone analogy, a DN is the location of a person in the phone book, and an X.400 address is where they are in the physical telephone system. This is illustrated by the fact that an X.400 address can include information about third-party messaging networks used to physically deliver a message, some examples being AT&T, MCI, and Sprint.

The 1988 release of X.400 incorporated the use of a DN address instead of, or along with, an O/R address. Some implementations of X.400 also incorporated some of the X.500 fields, like ou= and cn=.

A directory also puts a more natural interface to network resources. Many communication objects have long numeric identifiers that are hard to remember. A directory allows objects to be presented to users by a natural descriptive term. The directory then maps the descriptive term to the numeric.

X.500 has a 1988 version and a 1993 version.

Directory Access

Having a directory is only half the equation. Users and administrators must also be able to access it to read, query, and write to it. A user might query the directory for a printer in the sales department, fourth floor, and the directory could respond with the needed information about the printer. Other issues that must be addressed are security (e.g., who can access an object and modify its properties) and directory replication (a true global directory would need to be on more than one machine). These issues are addressed by directory access protocols.

The standard access protocol in the X.500 recommendations is the Directory Access Protocol (DAP). DAP is considered more of a model than a real-world protocol. This is because DAP is very computer-resource intense (i.e., heavy) on client machines, and the few implementations of it were proprietary. But a newer access protocol that is getting a lot of attention today is the Lightweight Directory Access Protocol (LDAP). LDAP is an Internet protocol derived from the X.500 DAP. One of the reasons LDAP is called lightweight is because it requires fewer computer resources on the client. While LDAP is an Internet protocol, it is designed to enable access to an X.500-type directory. Almost every major software vendor has pledged support for LDAP.

Summary

The Exchange product is a powerful client/server enterprise messaging product.

The types of applications in an Exchange environment are:

- Electronic mail (e-mail)

- Electronic forms

- Groupware

- Other applications, such as workflow, fax, paging, video conferencing, and voice mail

The client applications that are shipped with Exchange are:

- Exchange Client

- Exchange Forms Designer

- Schedule+ 7.5

- Outlook

- Outlook Forms Designer

The network computing model that Exchange uses to implement its messaging system is the client/server model. This model utilizes the computing power of both client computers and server computers.

Exchange was designed for enterprise-wide implementations and consequently meets the following requirements:

- Enterprise-quality application services

- Scalability

- Interoperability

- Performance

- Administration

- Reliability

The following industry standards are used by Exchange:

- Messaging Application Programming Interface (MAPI)

- Remote Procedure Call (RPC)

- X.400

- X.500

Review Questions

1. The type of utility that would allow you to transfer data from a foreign message system to Exchange is:

   A. Administrative tool

   B. Security utility

   C. X.500

   D. Migration tool

2. This type of mail system has a passive server:

   A. Shared-file mail system

   B. Client/server mail system

   C. Host-based mail system

   D. Exchange server

3. Which of the following is NOT a feature of a client/server messaging system?

   A. Distributed processing

   B. Tight security

   C. Passive client application

   D. Reduced network traffic

4. Microsoft Outlook is a desktop information manager application that runs on the following operating system:

   A. Windows 3.*x*

   B. Windows for Workgroups

   C. Windows NT

   D. 32-bit UNIX

5. The following types of components can be used to connect Exchange to a foreign messaging system:

   A. Gateway

   B. Connector

   C. Groupware

   D. Key Management

6. The universal inbox is part of this software:

   A. Exchange Client

   B. SMTP clients

   C. POP3 clients

   D. LDAP clients

7. The following is an e-mail protocol:

   A. LDAP

   B. PNP

   C. PPP

   D. POP3

8. Which of the following could NOT be used as an Exchange e-mail client?

   A. Word processing program

   B. Web browser

   C. Internet e-mail program

   D. Microsoft Outlook

9. Which Exchange Client feature enables e-mail content to include multiple format types, such as fonts, sizes, and colors?

   A. WordPerfect

   B. This software cannot do this

   C. Richman message content

   D. Rich-text message content

10. This Microsoft technology enables the Exchange Client to create compound documents using drag-and-drop:

  A. OLE

  B. OOP

  C. DLL

  D. SNADS

11. Recalling a sent, but unopened, message is a feature of what program or programs?

  A. Outlook

  B. Exchange Client

  C. Public folders

  D. Forms

12. Which of the following relate to the performance of Exchange?

  A. Load Simulator

  B. 32-bit program

  C. Multithreaded

  D. Auditing

13. Since Exchange is scalable, it cannot be used in small to medium environments.

  A. True

  B. False

14. Exchange could use the Internet as part of its WAN design.

   A. True

   B. False

15. The following feature enables a Exchange client to create rules for processing incoming mail:

   A. Search tool

   B. Customized views

   C. Universal inbox

   D. AutoAssistants

16. What is the name of the mechanism when two Exchange components on the same machine pass instructions and data?

   A. Remote procedure call

   B. Remote instruction call

   C. Local instruction call

   D. Local procedure call

17. What is the name of the mechanism when a client-read instruction is sent to an Exchange server for execution?

   A. Local procedure call

   B. Local instruction call

   C. Remote instruction call

   D. Remote procedure call

CHAPTER

2

Microsoft Exchange Architecture

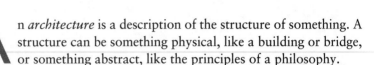

An *architecture* is a description of the structure of something. A structure can be something physical, like a building or bridge, or something abstract, like the principles of a philosophy. When applied to a software product, an architecture is a description of the software components of the product, what they are, what they do, and how they relate to each other. Part of what software components do is create and manage *objects* (i.e., resources) like servers, mailboxes, public folders, address books, etc. How those objects are structured or organized is also part of a software architecture.

There are many practical benefits to understanding the architecture of Microsoft Exchange. It will aid a person in designing, installing, administering, and troubleshooting an Exchange system. For example, understanding component functionality will assist in deciding what optional components, if any, to choose during an installation. Troubleshooting can frequently benefit from a good understanding of an architecture; just understanding some error messages requires this knowledge. This chapter also serves as a good conceptual background for the topics in the remainder of the book.

In this chapter, we will address the following issues:

- The organization of Microsoft Exchange objects

- Core components of Microsoft Exchange

- Optional components of Microsoft Exchange

Microsoft Exchange Object Organization

Many of the Microsoft Exchange components create and manage objects. Objects, as stated earlier, are resources such as servers, mailboxes, public folders, and address books. The organization of these objects is part of the architecture of Microsoft Exchange. Finding an object in the Exchange directory requires understanding object organization and object management. As you will learn, if a number of objects need the same configuration, and those objects are all grouped under a single object, the configuration can be given to the single object and then inherited by the objects underneath it.

Exchange is organized hierarchically. A *hierarchy* is the grouping and arrangement of items by rank, order, class, etc. A family tree is a good example of a hierarchy. At the top of the tree is the family patriarch and matriarch. Below them are their children, and their children below them, and so on. The family tree shows the relationships between people. One of these relationships is the parent-child relationship. Inherent to that relationship is the passing of traits from parent to children. A person can be both a parent and a child. A person will always be a child in reference to their parents, and that person can have children, making them also a parent. All of these concepts will relate to Microsoft Exchange.

Three objects constitute the main structures in the Exchange hierarchy:

- Organization

- Sites

- Servers

These objects contain other objects, but these three form the major structure of the hierarchy. Later in this chapter, under "Core Components" and "Directory Service," additional information will be given on them, as well as the other objects contained in them. Figure 2.1 illustrates the three main structures.

Organization

The largest unit, and the one at the top of the Exchange hierarchy, is the organization. All other Exchange structures are contained under this unit. The organization is the parent to the sites. This relationship permits an administrator to configure something at the organization level and have it apply or be available at all the sites (its children).

Because an organization encompasses an entire Exchange system, each company or business should create only one organization.

FIGURE 2.1

Three main structures of the Microsoft Exchange hierarchy

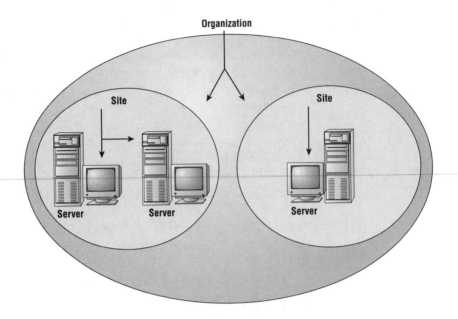

Sites

Sites are logical groupings of one or more Exchange servers. Even though resources reside on different servers in the site, the site groups all those resources without reference to their locations. This grouping makes using resources in the site very easy. For example, let us say that a certain mailbox physically resides on site server A. That site server is called the mailbox's *home server*. Senders do not need to know the physical location of the mailbox in order to send messages to it. They simply see the mailbox in the site listing, and send it a message. The same principle applies to public folders in a site. The particular server a public folder is stored on is of no concern to the users wanting to access it. They simply see the public folder listed in their site and access it. This is called *location transparency*. From the user's perspective, a site creates a transparent messaging environment.

A site also creates a smaller, more manageable Exchange network within the larger network of the organization. Administrators can assign a setting to the site (the parent), and it will be inherited by its site servers (the children).

There are two primary prerequisites for a site to be created:

- **Permanent, high-speed connections between the site servers**   All communication that takes place within a site is done with RPCs. As you learned earlier, the RPC protocol transfers instructions issued at one machine to another machine for execution, and waits for the data to be sent back (a request/reply mechanism). For this to work efficiently, there must be a relatively high-speed connection between all the machines in the site. The connection also needs to be permanent. It is strongly recommended that all site servers be within a local area network (LAN) or high-speed wide area network (WAN) with permanent links.

- **All the site servers must be in the same Windows NT security context (*context* relates to location)**   When an Exchange component on one site server initiates communication with a component on another site server, the initiating component logs on to the other site server. The Windows NT account that is used to log on with is called the Site Services Account (the actual name of the account could be anything, Jane, Steve, etc., but it is referred to as the Site Services Account). This means all the site servers must be in the same Windows NT domain or domains with trust relationships.

Servers

Exchange servers comprise the final main structure in the Exchange hierarchy. These computers run the Windows NT Server operating system (version 3.51 or above) and the Exchange Server software. The Exchange servers are the physical location for mailboxes, folders, and other data and information for the site. Individual servers, while inheriting certain configuration parameters from the site (the parent), can also be individually configured. For example, even though recipients can be managed at the site level, they can also be managed at the server they were created on, their home server. All Exchange objects, as well as all related processes, are created and managed by the software components that make up the Exchange product. These components are divided into two main groups, core components and optional components, which are covered in the following discussion.

Core Components

The Exchange components are executable programs that perform the Exchange functions. Some are in the form of EXE files, others are in the form of Dynamic Link Libraries (DLLs). They are referred to as core components because they are necessary for Exchange to be operational. They are also referred to as services, because they run as services on the Microsoft Windows NT Server operating system. The core components include:

- Directory Service (DS)

- Information Store (IS)

- Message Transfer Agent (MTA)

- System Attendant (SA)

Table 2.1 uses a post office analogy to illustrate the functions of the core components.

T A B L E 2.1 Post office analogy for core components	**Exchange Core Component**	**Post Office Service**
	Directory Service	Creation of a comprehensive address book
	Information Store	Storage and delivery of mail
	Message Transfer Agent	Routing decisions for mail to be sent between post offices
	System Attendant	Post office management

Directory Service (DS)

The Directory Service (DS) component creates and manages the storage of all information about Exchange objects in an organization. Objects are resources, such as mailboxes, distribution lists, public folders, and servers. The database that stores the objects is called the Directory. Objects in the Directory are organized in a hierarchical structure. The main purpose of the Directory is to allow users and administrators to easily locate resources to use or configure. The other Exchange components also reference the Directory for information. The Exchange Directory is patterned after the X.500 standard.

Structure and Objects of the Directory

As with the X.500 directory structure, the DS Directory is also organized in a hierarchical manner. The three main structures (organization, sites, and servers) have already been mentioned in the first section of this chapter. This section provides additional details about these three and information on the other objects in the Directory. Figure 2.2 and Table 2.2 illustrate an X.500 directory structure along with the corresponding Exchange structures.

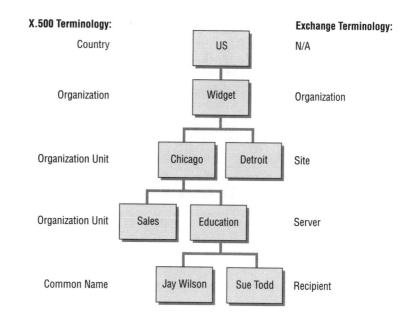

F I G U R E 2.2

The Exchange Directory
and X.500

X.500 Object	Example	Description	Mapping to Exchange
Country	c=us	Country of the organization	N/A
Organization	o=Widget	Name of the organization	Organization name
Organization Unit	ou=Chicago ou=Detroit	Subcategory of the organization	Site name
Organization Unit	ou=Sales ou=Education	Subcategories under the ou=Chicago	Server names
Common Name	cn=Jay Wilson cn=Sue Todd	Name of a specific resource (e.g., username, fax name, printer name, etc.)	Recipient (e.g., mailbox, public folder)

T A B L E 2.2

The Exchange Directory
and X.500

As can be seen in Figure 2.2 and Table 2.2, the Exchange Directory uses the same basic hierarchical structure as X.500. A minor difference is the naming conventions. For example, the Exchange Directory refers to site names and X.500 refers to organization units, but they are easily mapped to each other.

The Exchange Directory, like X.500, contains objects. Objects are the representation, or abstraction, of a resource. That resource can be a person (e.g., Jay Wilson), or even an entire Exchange organization (e.g., Widget). Objects have properties, which are the characteristics of the object. The Jay Wilson object can have *properties* such as first name, last name, job title, telephone number, e-mail address, and many others. Properties are also called *attributes*. Figure 2.3 illustrates the properties of an object.

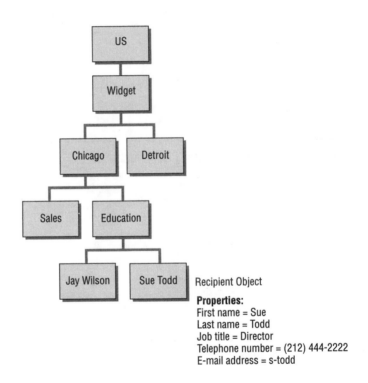

FIGURE 2.3

Properties of an object

While the Exchange Directory objects map to the main structures in the X.500 hierarchy, Exchange also adds some additional objects. The three main structures (organization, site, server) are discussed next, along with the other objects within them.

Organization Object As stated earlier, the organization encompasses all the Exchange objects of a company or other enterprise. The organization structure is an object and, as an object, it has properties. The primary property is *permissions,* which determine what functions the specified people can perform at the organization level. For example, one Exchange administrator can be given permission to create child objects under the organization, such as additional sites.

Because other objects are contained under the organization object, it is considered a container object. Along with site objects, two other objects are under the organization object:

- **Global Address List (GAL)** The GAL object contains a comprehensive list of all the published mail addresses in the organization. Client software can access this list in order to send information to anybody in the organization. The global address list is considered a *container object* because it contains other objects, in this case, message recipients. These objects include mailboxes, distribution lists (multiple addresses grouped as one), and public folders. Each of these objects are considered *leaf objects*, because they do not have any other objects contained in them.

- **Folders** The folders object contains public and system folders. An example of a public folder could be a folder named Technical Help containing a listing of all the people who provide technical help on the network. Examples of system folders are the organization forms and offline address book. An example of a folder property is replicas, which are the Exchange servers that contain a copy of that folder.

See Figure 2.4 for a depiction of the organization container.

Site Object A site is a logical grouping of Exchange servers. The purpose of the grouping is to create a transparent messaging environment (users do not need to know on which server a resource is located). The properties of a site are the same type as with the organization object, the main one being permissions. Permissions can be assigned to a particular administrator allowing that administrator to create or modify child objects (like mailboxes) in the site. The difference between permissions granted at the organization object versus the site object is the *context* (i.e., the location in the hierarchy). Permissions granted at a site only apply to objects in that site, not other sites and not the organization.

FIGURE 2.4

The organization
container object

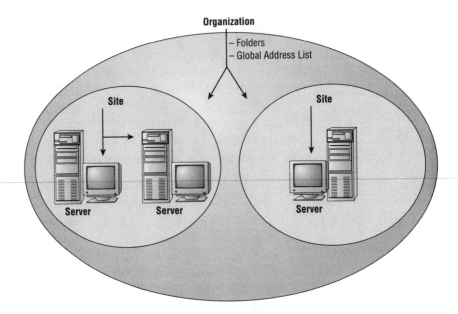

Sites are also container objects with the following objects under them:

- **Configuration**   This container object holds seven additional container objects that pertain to numerous aspects of a site configuration. There are also four non-container objects under Configuration. These eleven objects are listed here (each item will be discussed in Chapter 12):

  - **Add-Ins** (container object)

  - **Addressing** (container object)

  - **Connections** (container object)

  - **Directory Replication** (container object)

  - **Monitors** (container object)

  - **Protocols** (container object)

  - **Servers** (container object)

  - **DS Site Configuration**

  - **Information Store Site Configuration**

  - **MTA Site Configuration**

  - **Site Addressing**

- **Recipients** These are objects to which Exchange users can send messages. Recipient objects include:

  - **Mailboxes** A location from which messages can be received, sent, stored, etc. Also stores other types of data.

  - **Distribution lists** A grouping of individual recipients.

  - **Public folders** A storage container for group access.

  - **Custom recipients** E-mail addresses that represent a foreign mail system address.

See Figure 2.5 for an illustration of the site container.

FIGURE 2.5

The site container object

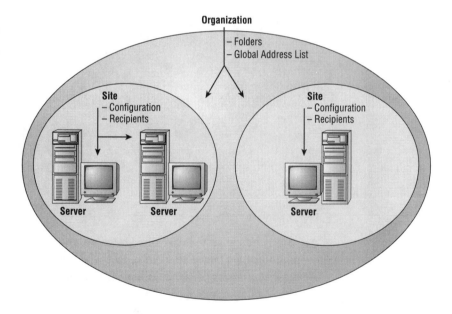

Servers Object Configuration The Servers container object is under the Configuration container. This object contains a listing of all the servers in the selected site. Each particular server object can be managed individually and contains the following two container objects:

- **Protocols** This object contains the protocols, such as LDAP, NNTP, and POP3, that can be configured on the selected server. (These protocols will be discussed in Chapter 11.)

■ **Server Recipients**   This object contains all the recipient objects (mailboxes, distribution lists, public folders, and custom recipients) stored on the selected server.

Figure 2.6 illustrates the server container and its objects.

F I G U R E   2.6

Exchange server container
and objects

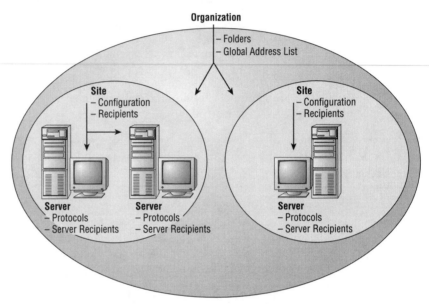

Directory Replication

All Exchange servers in a site contain a complete copy of the directory information of that site. This is accomplished by automatic directory replication between servers of a site. When an Exchange object, for example a mailbox, is created on a particular Exchange server, that mailbox information is automatically copied to all the other servers in that site. This is an important factor in creating a transparent messaging environment. Users see all site recipients in their site address book. And while users do not need to know the physical location of a recipient, each Exchange server can route a message to the correct server because it has a copy of the site directory which contains this information.

There can also be directory replication between sites. This is not an automatic process, and must be configured by an administrator. This ability allows administrators to decide what resources to share with other sites. But directory replication between sites can be used to create an enterprise messaging environment. More on the topic of directory replication appears in Chapter 13.

Directory Access to the DS Directory

The DS component supports directory access through the MAPI interface and through the LDAP interface. This enables both Microsoft Exchange Client software and Internet LDAP-enabled applications to access the Exchange directory. Administrators access the directory through the Microsoft Exchange Administrator program, which is a MAPI program.

The DS directory content is located in a file called DIR.EDB.

Benefits of the DS

There are many benefits to having an object-oriented hierarchical directory like the one the DS creates and manages. Because all Exchange configuration information is stored in the directory, the other Exchange components know where to go to reference information. Exchange administrators benefit from a graphical view of the Exchange environment, which helps in creating and managing Exchange resources. Administrators manage the Exchange environment by configuring the properties of objects in the directory. Users also benefit from a graphical view of resources, such as public folders and mailboxes, which makes it much easier to find resources. See Figure 2.7 for a review of the main points of the Directory Service.

Information Store (IS)

The Information Store (IS) creates and manages the message database on an Exchange server. All types of data can be stored in this database, including e-mail messages, electronic forms, word processing documents, spreadsheets, and graphics. Users access the IS content through their mailbox and folders in their client applications. Chapter 1 discussed the Exchange client programs and many of their features. The Information Store is the back-end component that makes many of those features possible.

FIGURE 2.7

Directory Service (DS)

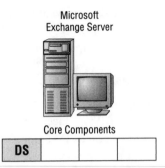

Microsoft
Exchange Server

Core Components

DS			

DS Main Functions, Characteristics, Benefits:

Creates and manages directory

Characteristics of directory:
- Directory contains objects
- Objects have properties
- Directory structure is hierarchical
- Main hierarchy structures are:
  - Organization
  - Sites
  - Servers

Benefits of the directory:
- Central location of all Exchange information
- Easy to find information because of the hierarchical structure

Two separate databases comprise the IS:

- Public Information Store

- Private Information Store

Public Information Store

The Public Information Store contains all the public folders of a particular server. Public folders are containers for shared information. In a sense, they are like a public mailbox. Different types of data can be stored in a public folder, such as e-mail messages, word processing documents, graphic files, and many other types. Public folders are used to create groupware applications. The Public Information Store is contained in the file PUB.EDB and stored on an Exchange server. The storage limit of this database is 16 gigabytes per server.

Private Information Store

The Private Information Store contains all user mailboxes. Security makes mailboxes accessible only to their owners and to others who have been given access permission. This database is contained in the file PRIV.EDB and stored on an Exchange Server. Its storage limit is 16 gigabytes per server.

By default, a user's messages are stored in their mailbox in this database. Although mailboxes are always located in the Private Information Store on an Exchange server, messages do not have to be stored there. A user can specify a personal location for message storage. This type of folder is called a personal folder and has a PST file extension. A personal folder can be located on a user's local computer or on a server share point. Even when a user is using a personal folder for message storage, their mailbox is still on their Exchange server and in the Private Information Store. When they are sent a message, the message still first goes to their mailbox in the Private Information Store, and then is rerouted to a personal folder. The advantage of storing messages in a personal folder, especially if it is on a local computer, is that the user can access it without logging on to the server. The advantages of keeping message storage in the Private Information Store, which is the default, are centralized backup and fault tolerance.

Dedicated Servers

By default, an Exchange server contains both the Public and Private databases. But Exchange servers can also be configured to store only one of the two. If only the Private Information Store were configured, that server would act as a dedicated mailbox server. A dedicated folder server would only have the Public Information Store configured. Dedicated servers are created to improve the performance of information access.

Microsoft Mail Connector

An Exchange system can interoperate with a Microsoft Mail system through the Microsoft Mail Connector. Microsoft Mail is a mail product for PC or AppleTalk networks. The Microsoft Mail Connector can translate Exchange messages to and from the Microsoft Mail format. This permits Exchange users and Mail users to exchange mail. You will find more on the Microsoft Mail Connector in Chapter 15.

If an Exchange system and a Microsoft Mail system want to interoperate, they must share their directory information (e.g., listings of mailboxes, distribution lists, and folders). This involves Exchange exporting its directory information to Microsoft Mail, and importing directory information from Microsoft Mail. The Exchange component that performs this is the Directory Synchronization Agent (DXA). Chapter 15 will provide more information on the DXA.

Lotus cc:Mail Connector

This connector permits Exchange to interoperate with a Lotus cc:Mail system. Users of each system can exchange mail with the other system. As with the other connectors, this connector permits organizations to implement Exchange with another messaging system and still have interoperability. Chapter 15 provides further discussion on the Connector for Lotus cc:Mail.

Information Store Management Properties

Before we can begin an in-depth discussion of IS management, we need to introduce some IS properties that relate to management issues:

- **Replication**   Public folders can be configured to be replicated (copied) to other Exchange servers. This can be done for different reasons, including locating folders for easier network access and fault tolerance.

- **Storage limits**   The IS can be configured to set a storage limit for each mailbox.

- **Aging**   Folders can be configured to mark and delete information that has been in them for a specified length of time.

- **Views of resource usage**   An administrator can view the resources used by a user in the IS. An administrator can view resources by either mailbox or public folder. Resources viewed include disk space, number of stored items, log on time, and last log off time.

Chapter 9 discusses the management of public folders. Chapter 12 discusses the overall management of an Exchange server, which includes managing the IS.

As an analogy, the IS as a service can be compared to a postal worker who stores letters and packages. If a letter's destination is that post office, this person will place the letter in the correct mailbox. The IS as a database is like the mailboxes and other storage at the post office. Figure 2.8 depicts the Information Store and some of its features.

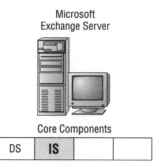

FIGURE 2.8

Information Store (IS)

Microsoft
Exchange Server

Core Components

DS	**IS**		

IS Main Functions:

Creates and manages information storage
• Public Information Store (e.g., public folders)
• Private Information Store (e.g., mailboxes)

Notifies clients of new messages

Delivers message when sender and recipient are
on the same server

Message Transfer Agent (MTA)

The Message Transfer Agent (MTA) manages the *routing* of messages within a site, between sites, and to foreign message systems. The MTA uses other components, called *connectors,* to manage the transfer of data, while the MTA handles the routing functions. The MTA could be compared to a post office that receives mail and routes it to another post office. The MTA component is based on the CCITT 1984 and 1988 X.400 standard.

The main routing functions of the MTA component include:

- Addressing messages: O/R Addresses

- Translating message formats

- Making routing decisions

Addressing Messages: O/R Addresses

Because the MTA component is based on X.400, it also uses an Originator/Recipient Address (O/R Address). Chapter 1 discussed the X.400 addressing scheme. Figure 2.9 and Table 2.3 provide a review of the O/R Address and how Exchange information is applied to this addressing scheme.

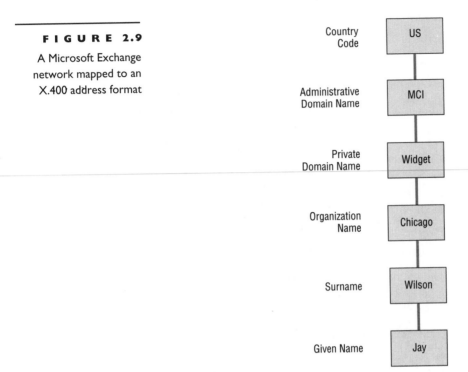

FIGURE 2.9

A Microsoft Exchange
network mapped to an
X.400 address format

Country Code — US

Administrative Domain Name — MCI

Private Domain Name — Widget

Organization Name — Chicago

Surname — Wilson

Given Name — Jay

TABLE 2.3

An X.400 addressing
scheme and Microsoft
Exchange

Field	Abbreviation	Description	Mapping to Exchange
Country code	c=us	Country	Country
Administrative Management Domain (ADMD)	a=mci	The third-party networking system used (e.g., ATT, MCI, Sprint, etc.)	Abbreviation of third-party network, or if not using one, leave field with a space
Private Management Domain (PRMD)	p=Widget	Subscriber to the ADMD (i.e., company name)	Exchange organization name
Organization	o=Chicago	Name of company or organization	Exchange site name

Field	Abbreviation	Description	Mapping to Exchange
Surname	s=Wilson	Last name	Last name attribute field for a mailbox
Given name	g=Jay	First name	First name attribute field for a mailbox

TABLE 2.3 *(cont.)* An X.400 addressing scheme and Microsoft Exchange

The example in Figure 2.9 and Table 2.3 could be written the following way:

c=us; a=mci; p=widget; o=Chicago; s=wilson; g=jay

If you compare the way Exchange uses the X.400 address format (Figure 2.9 and Table 2.2) and the X.500 name format (Figure 2.2 and Table 2.2), you will notice a difference in how Exchange uses the organization field. In the X.400 organization field, Exchange places the site name rather than the Exchange organization name. This is probably due to the fact that the 1984 X.400 standard, which predated the X.500 standard, did not include the organization unit field. But when X.500 was published in 1988, the X.400 standard was revised to include X.500 names, such as organization unit and common name. Microsoft Exchange adheres to both the 1984 and 1988 X.400 standard. Exchange by default places the Exchange site name in the organization field. This value can be left in place, or the administrator can easily change it to the Exchange organization name. The administrator can also include an organization unit (ou=) field, placing the site name as its value. Using this format, the X.400 address would look like the following:

c=us; a=mci; p=widget; o=widget; ou=chicago; s=wilson; g=jay

The directory location to modify these addresses is Site/Configuration/Site Addressing.

Translating Message Content Format

If a message is being routed from Exchange to an X.400 message system, the MTA translates the message from the Exchange format, called the Microsoft Database Exchange Format (MDBEF) to the X.400 message format, called the Interpersonal Message (IPM) format.

This translation ability allows Microsoft Exchange clients to exchange mail with X.400 mail users, or use an X.400 network as a backbone to another Exchange environment and the user on that system. Figure 2.10 illustrates this latter scenario.

FIGURE 2.10

An X.400 network as a backbone for Exchange networks

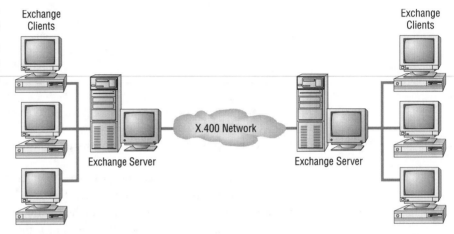

Making Routing Decisions

When an MTA component receives a message to be forwarded, it first stores it, in order to determine a route. Then, it looks at the message recipient's Distinguished Name (DN). If that address cannot resolve the next route, the MTA looks at the O/R address. In either case, the MTA compares the address with the various locations and paths in the routing table (called the Gateway Address Routing Table, GWART, more on this in Chapter 13). If the MTA finds a path to send the message on, it sends it on its way. Because there could be more than one path, the X.400 standard allows an administrator to assign *costs* to different paths. Costs allow priorities to be given to different routes. When faced with multiple paths, the MTA chooses the lowest cost path. If the MTA cannot forward a message, a Non-Delivery Report (NDR) is sent to the message originator. Chapter 13 discusses message routing in greater detail. Figure 2.11 depicts the role of the MTA.

The Microsoft Exchange MTA is based on the 1984 and 1988 versions of X.400 standards.

FIGURE 2.11

Message Transfer Agent
(MTA)

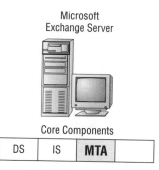

Microsoft
Exchange Server

Core Components

DS	IS	**MTA**	

MTA Main Functions:

Addressing messages

Translating message content format
(only if a message is moving from Exchange
to an X.400 mail system)

Making routing decisions

System Attendant (SA)

This service monitors and logs information about the other Exchange services. It also builds and maintains the routing tables for the site. The primary functions of the System Attendant are as follows:

- **Monitoring**   Two Exchange features, Link Monitor and Server Monitor, use the SA component to monitor. The Link Monitor sends test messages between servers to see if there is a connection between them. The Server Monitor checks the status of Exchange or other NT services on a server by sending test messages to that server. Both of these features use the SA component to send and receive the test messages.

- **Verifying information**   The SA verifies the accuracy of a server's directory replication information. If it is incorrect, the SA will repair the inconsistencies.

- **Logging**   The SA writes message tracking information to the message tracking log. Information tracked includes the route a message took, and if the message arrived at its destination.

- **Building routing tables**   The SA builds the routing tables of a site. The MTA references these tables when making routing decisions.

- **Generating e-mail addresses**   When new recipients are created by the DS, the SA ensures that their e-mail addresses are generated.

- **Assisting with advanced security**   The SA accepts client requests for advanced security initialization and passes those requests on to the Exchange Server advanced security components. Advanced security relates to digital signatures and data encryption. Advanced security will be introduced later in this chapter under the "Optional Exchange Components" section. It is also covered in more detail in Chapter 10.

Figure 2.12 illustrates the main functions of the SA component.

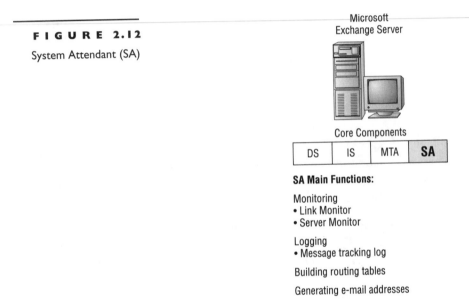

FIGURE 2.12

System Attendant (SA)

manage the transferring of messages. Using the postal analogy, if the MTA component is compared to the postal manager who makes routing decisions, then a connector component is like the postal manager who supervises the transfer of mail between post offices.

Many of the optional components are connector components. Some do not use the word *connector* in their title, like the Internet Mail Service, but they are connector components nevertheless. Microsoft refers to a connector component written by a third-party vendor as a *gateway*.

Internet Mail Service (IMS)

The Internet Mail Service (IMS) connector enables an Exchange system to interoperate with an SMTP mail system. SMTP, Simple Mail Transfer Protocol, is the standard mail exchange protocol for the TCP/IP protocol suite. It is used in many intranet mail systems (inside a company or organization), as well as on the Internet. The IMS permits Exchange users and SMTP mail users to send and receive mail to each other. Organizations that already have an SMTP mail system can add Microsoft Exchange, gaining its rich feature set, and yet still have enterprise messaging because of the interoperability through the IMS. The IMS connector also permits an organization with geographically disperse locations to use the Internet as a messaging backbone. Messages can be sent from one Exchange user, through the Internet, to the Exchange recipient. Figure 2.13 illustrates the IMS component. Chapter 14 provides further information on the IMS.

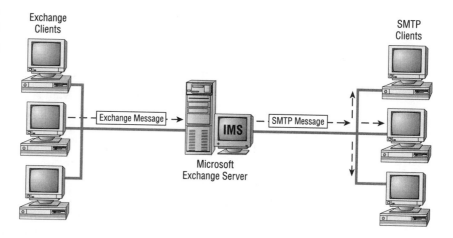

FIGURE 2.13

Internet Mail Service (IMS)

Internet News Service (INS)

The Internet News Service (INS) connector permits an Exchange system to interoperate with USENET newsgroups. USENET is a network of host machines containing posted discussions on various topics. A discussion area is referred to as a newsgroup. Users can access a newsgroup and read the text of a discussion or post their own comments. The USENET uses the Internet, as well as other networks. USENET uses Network News Transport Protocol (NNTP) to replicate newsgroup information between hosts.

The Microsoft Internet News Service includes the NNTP protocol and can download newsgroup information from the USENET into an Exchange public folder, and vice versa. The Internet New Service is discussed in more detail in Chapter 11.

Active Server Components

The Active Server Components are ActiveX programs that ship with Microsoft Exchange, but that run on a Microsoft Internet Information Server 3.0 (IIS). These components make Exchange resources, such as mailboxes, public folders, schedules, and calendars, available to users on the World Wide Web (WWW). A Web user, through a Web browser, establishes an HTTP connection to the IIS server. The Active Server Components on the IIS server then transfer the connection, using the RPC protocol, to the Exchange server. The Exchange resources are translated from MAPI services to HyperText Markup Language (HTML) for the Web users. Because of the scope of the WWW, remote access to Exchange is greatly expanded. Figure 2.14 illustrates the Active Server Components. Chapter 11 provides additional information on the Active Server Components.

Microsoft Mail Connector

An Exchange system can interoperate with a Microsoft Mail system through the Microsoft Mail Connector. Microsoft Mail is a mail product for PC or AppleTalk networks. The Microsoft Mail Connector can translate Exchange messages to and from the Microsoft Mail format. This permits Exchange users and Mail users to exchange mail. You will find more on the Microsoft Mail Connector in Chapter 15.

If an Exchange system and a Microsoft Mail system want to interoperate, they must share their directory information (e.g., listings of mailboxes, distribution lists, and folders). This involves Exchange exporting its directory information to Microsoft Mail, and importing directory information from Microsoft Mail. The Exchange component that performs this is the Directory Synchronization Agent (DXA). Chapter 15 will provide more information on the DXA.

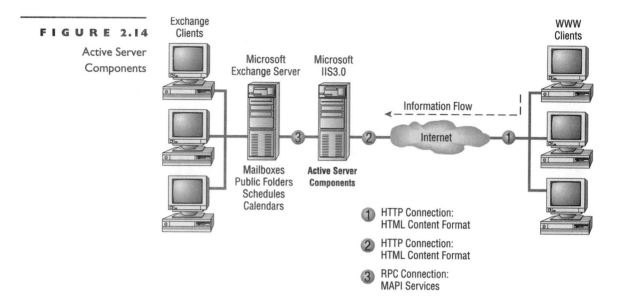

FIGURE 2.14

Active Server Components

Connector for cc:Mail

This connector permits Exchange to interoperate with a Lotus cc:Mail system. Users of each system can exchange mail with the other system. As with the other connectors, this connector permits organizations to implement Exchange with another messaging system and still have interoperability. Chapter 15 provides further discussion on the Connector for Lotus cc:Mail.

Schedule+ Free/Busy Connector

Microsoft Schedule+ performs personal and group calendaring, scheduling, and task management. The group scheduling feature allows a user who wants to schedule a meeting to view the schedules of other users. The user scheduling the meeting can see if a particular time period is unscheduled for the other users, called *free*, or if it is already scheduled, called *busy*.

Microsoft Exchange ships with Schedule+ 7.5, while Microsoft Mail ships with the earlier version 1.0. These two versions are incompatible in terms of viewing each others free/busy status. To solve this incompatibility, Microsoft Exchange ships with the Schedule+ Free/Busy Connector which allows the two versions to share their free/busy information. This connector requires the Microsoft Mail Connector. Further information on the Schedule+ Free/Busy Connector is found in Chapter 15.

Key Management

The key management components provide additional security features such as encryption and digital signatures. Encryption prevents unauthorized people from reading messages as they are being sent over the network. Digital signatures ensure that the person whose name appears in the From field is the actual sender of the message. Chapter 10 covers the topic of key management.

Third-Party Gateways

Gateways, like connectors, are software components that provide interoperability between Exchange and other foreign message systems ("foreign" from the perspective of Exchange). The difference between gateways and connectors is that connectors are written by Microsoft, and gateways are written by third-party vendors. An example of a foreign message system that has a gateway written for it is the IBM mainframe-based messaging product PROFS (Professional Office System). For further information on gateway components, refer to the specific vendor product literature.

Summary

The three main objects (structures) of the Exchange hierarchy are the organization, sites, and servers. Each company or enterprise defines one Exchange organization object. The organization object encompasses all the other objects of an Exchange implementation. Two of the objects contained within the organization object are the Global Address List (GAL) and Folders. The GAL is a comprehensive listing of all e-mail addresses of the organization. The folders object contains public folders and systems folders.

Sites are logical groupings of Exchange servers. They create a transparent messaging environment. Site users can use Exchange resources in the site without regard to the physical location of those resources. Two of the objects contained within the site object are the Configuration object and the Recipients object. The Recipients object holds all the recipients created in that site. Examples of recipients are mailboxes, distribution lists, public folders, and custom recipients.

Servers are the computers running the Exchange Server components. They are the physical location of the Exchange mailboxes, public folders, and other information.

Exchange Server is made up of various software components. The components that are required for Exchange to be operational are called core components. The following are the four core components:

- Directory service

- Information store

- Message transfer agent

- System attendant

Other components, called optional components, provide additional functionality that could be needed depending on the particular implementation.

Review Questions

1. The following is NOT a core component of Exchange:

   A. Internet Mail Service

   B. System Attendant

   C. Message Transfer Agent

   D. Information Store

2. The Information Store is made up of these two databases:

   A. SQL and ODBC

   B. Message tracking log

   C. Private and public information store

   D. MTA and SA databases

3. This component generates new e-mail addresses:

   A. Directory Service

   B. System Attendant

   C. Global Address List

   D. Client components

4. This component is involved in advanced security:

   A. Directory Service

   B. Information Store

   C. Key Management

   D. Message Transfer Agent

5. This component builds routing tables:

   A. System Attendant

   B. Key Management

   C. Information Store

   D. Internet Mail Service

6. This component notifies clients of new mail:

   A. Directory Service

   B. Microsoft Mail Connector

   C. Information Store

   D. System Attendant

7. The Internet Mail Service relates to which protocol?

   A. X.400

   B. RPC

C. OSF

D. SMTP

8. Which of the following is NOT an example of a foreign system?

   A. An Exchange server in a different site

   B. IBM SNADS

   C. SMTP system

   D. Microsoft Mail system

9. This component calculates the route a message could take to its destination:

   A. System Attendant

   B. Message Transfer Agent

   C. Information Store

   D. Internet Mail Service

10. This standard is used as the pattern of the Exchange Directory:

   A. X.400

   B. SMTP

   C. LDAP

   D. X.500

11. The following object creates a transparent messaging environment for Exchange users:

   A. Site

   B. System Attendant

   C. Protocols

   D. INS

12. The Global Address List is contained in this object:

    A. Site

    B. Server

    C. Enterprise

    D. Organization

13. Users must know the name of the server on which a public folder is homed in order to access the public folder.

    A. True

    B. False

14. This component enables World Wide Web users to access Exchange resources:

    A. Active Server Components

    B. SNMP

    C. X.400

    D. X.500

15. The Message Transfer Agent is based on this standard:

    A. SNMP

    B. SMTP

    C. X.500

    D. X.400

CHAPTER

3

Component Communication

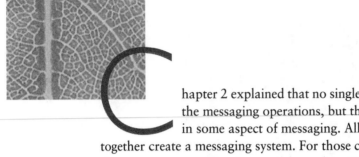

hapter 2 explained that no single Exchange component does all the messaging operations, but that each component specializes in some aspect of messaging. All of the components working together create a messaging system. For those components to work together, they must communicate between themselves. Within a single Exchange site, component communication falls into two basic categories:

- Component communication within a single Exchange server

- Component communication between Exchange servers in a site

In this chapter, you will learn about both categories (see Figure 3.1). Understanding component communication is as beneficial as understanding the architecture. It will aid you in designing, installing, administering, and troubleshooting an Exchange system.

Component communication between sites will be covered in Chapter 13.

Component Communication within a Single Exchange Server

Components within an Exchange server communicate with each other. This communication is necessary for the server to carry out messaging operations, including receiving, sending, and storing messages. This section will show what components communicate with what other components. First, we will discuss the core components, then the optional components. The final part of this section will outline some common messaging operations (e.g., sending a message) and will explain how component communication accomplishes those operations.

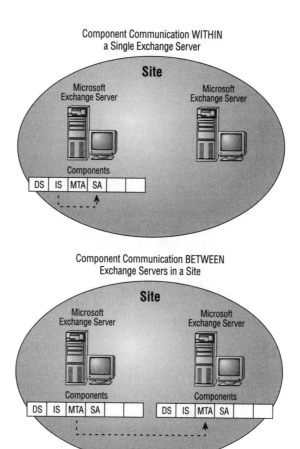

Component Communication WITHIN
a Single Exchange Server

Component Communication BETWEEN
Exchange Servers in a Site

Core Component Communication

The core components and their communication is obviously very important because an Exchange server cannot be operational without them. Almost all component communication is *event driven*. That means when a specific event occurs, such as when the IS receives a message from a client, the relevant components communicate in order to accomplish the message operation, such as delivering a message. The following text explains the events that involve the specific core components and the associated component communication.

Directory Service (DS)

For the most part, other components initiate communication with the DS; the DS does not initiate communication with them. This makes sense in light of the DS role (keeper of directory information). The only time the DS initiates communication with another component is during directory replication. As Chapter 2 mentioned, directory replication is the copying of an Exchange directory to other Exchange servers. If the servers are in the same site, the DS on one server communicates with the DS on the other server. This will be discussed later in this chapter (see "Component Communication between Exchange Servers in a Site"). If the servers are in different sites, the DS uses the MTA for the replication. This scenario will be covered in Chapter 13.

Information Store (IS)

As Chapter 2 explained, the IS manages the storage of data on an Exchange server. This data includes mail messages and public folder content. Three primary operations that require the IS to initiate communication with other components are:

- Local delivery of a message

- Remote delivery of a message

- Creation of a new folder

Local Message Delivery   When the IS receives a message for delivery, the IS references the DS to determine the physical location of the recipient's mailbox. This process is referred to as *resolving* an address. If the recipient's mailbox is located on the same server the IS is on, the IS will potentially deliver the message to that mailbox. This is called a *local delivery*. The phrase "potentially deliver" was used because after resolving the address, the IS then references the properties of that mailbox. The mailbox could have properties that determine whether or not the message should be delivered, such properties as message rejection and rules that would refuse the message. The mailbox could also have properties that determine how the message should be delivered, such as an alternate recipient who is supposed to get any messages for this mailbox instead of, or along with, the mailbox owner.

A message recipient can be a distribution list (DL). A DL is a grouping of recipients. DLs make it easy for users to communicate with a group of recipients. Instead of creating and sending a message to every individual recipient, a user can send a single message to the DL. Exchange then processes and sends the message to each member of the DL. When the IS receives a message addressed to a DL, it passes the DL to the Message Transfer Agent (MTA) which determines the individual members of the DL. This is called expanding a distribution list (there is more on this in the "MTA" section). Once the DL has been expanded, the IS delivers the message to those recipients.

When a mailbox receives a new message, the IS notifies the mailbox owner, through the client application, of the new message. The user can configure the client application for the type of notification, be it a sound, a changing cursor, or a pop-up message to the user's screen.

If IS message tracking is enabled, the last component that the IS communicates with is the SA. Whenever the IS is involved in a messaging operation, such as a message delivery, the IS notifies the SA of this event in order for the SA to write the event to the log files.

Remote Message Delivery   If after referencing the DS when resolving an address, the IS learns from the DS that the message recipient's mailbox is located on another server, the IS passes the message to the MTA for routing. The IS also notifies the SA of the event for logging purposes.

New Folder Creation   Whenever a user creates a new folder in the IS, the IS communicates this information to the DS. The DS then creates a new directory entry for that folder. Table 3.1 and Figure 3.2 summarize and illustrate this information.

TABLE 3.1 Information Store initiated communication with other components	Component	Purpose of Communication
	Directory Service	■ Resolve addresses ■ Read mailbox properties ■ Create new directory entries for folders
	Message Transfer Agent	■ Deliver remote messages ■ Expand distribution lists
	Local Gateways	■ Deliver remote messages to a foreign system
	System Attendant	■ Write events to tracking log files
	Client Applications	■ Notify of new messages

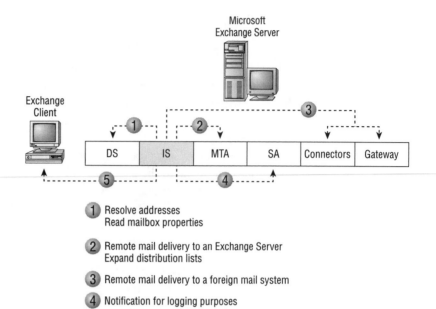

1 Resolve addresses
Read mailbox properties

2 Remote mail delivery to an Exchange Server
Expand distribution lists

3 Remote mail delivery to a foreign mail system

4 Notification for logging purposes

5 Notification of new messages

Message Transfer Agent (MTA)

The MTA manages the routing of messages. The first step in making a routing decision is for the MTA to reference the DS to resolve the address of the message. If the message recipient is a distribution list, the MTA will reference the DS in order to expand the distribution list, and then resolve the addresses. If the message is destined for a remote Exchange server, the MTA will deliver the message to the remote server's MTA. If the message is destined for a foreign system, the MTA routes the message to the home server of the connector. If the message is received from a remote MTA, it is delivered to the IS. The MTA will then inform the SA of this event for its inclusion in the tracking log files.

If while referencing the DS, the MTA learns that the message is destined for that server, the MTA passes the message to the IS for delivery. As with a remote delivery, the MTA then communicates its actions to the SA for tracking logging purposes. Figure 3.3 and Table 3.2 summarize and illustrate this information.

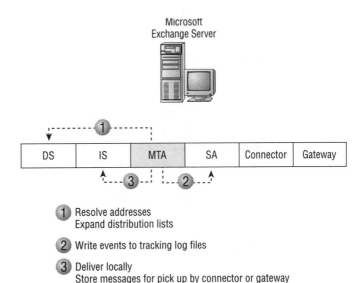

FIGURE 3.3

Message Transfer Agent
initiated communication
with other components

Component	Purpose of Communication
Directory Service	■ Resolve addresses ■ Expand distribution list
Information Store	■ Local delivery of messages ■ Store message for pick up by connector or gateway
Connectors or Gateways	■ Delivery to remote Exchange Server ■ Delivery to connector or remote Exchange Server
System Attendant	■ Write events to tracking log files

TABLE 3.2

Message Transfer Agent
initiated communication
with other components

The MTA handles some additional processes itself, such as route calculation, but the preceding scenarios describe the other components with which the MTA communicates. For a more complete description of message routing, see Chapter 13.

System Attendant (SA)

The SA has many functions, but primarily initiates communication with three other components, the DS, IS, and Key Management components. Whenever a recipient object is created in the DS, the SA manages the generation of its e-mail addresses. By default, the addresses created are for Microsoft Mail, X.400, Lotus cc:Mail, and SMTP. The e-mail addresses allow an Exchange recipient to receive messages from a foreign mail system (there would have to be a connector or gateway set up also). The SA generates these addresses and communicates the information to the DS for inclusion in the directory. More information on this topic appears in Chapter 5, which covers Exchange recipients.

One of the functions of the SA is to build a site's routing tables that will be used by the MTA. To do this, the SA references server information contained in the DS.

The SA is involved in Link Monitors and Server Monitors. The Link Monitors test the link between Exchange servers by sending a test message. Link Monitors use the SA to send the test message. To have the message delivered, the SA places it in the IS. The IS then passes it to the MTA for routing. The Server Monitor program tests the Exchange services of a server. It also uses the SA to send messages to the server to be tested. Again, the SA places the test message in the IS for delivery. In the course of addressing either of these types of test messages, the SA might need to access the DS to resolve an address.

Another process that requires the SA to communicate with another component is directory replication. The SA monitors the status of various processes. One of the most important processes it monitors is directory replication. The SA accesses the DS to verify that directory information is correct, and if it is not, it corrects inconsistencies.

Although the Key Management components are the primary programs for advanced security, the SA is also involved. The SA retrieves user requests for the initialization of advanced security features. The SA also assists in managing *security keys*. A key is a number used in encrypting data. Figure 3.4 and Table 3.3 summarize and illustrate this information.

Chapter 10 covers advanced security.

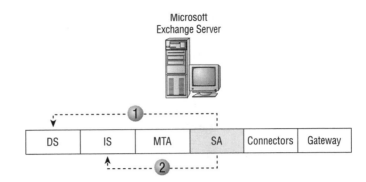

FIGURE 3.4

System Attendant initiated communication with other components

1 Create e-mail addresses
Check on directory replication status
Resolve addresses for sending test messages
Reference information for building routing tables

2 Send Link Monitor test messages
Send Server Monitor test messages

TABLE 3.3

System Attendant initiated communication with other components

Component	Purpose of Communication
Directory Service	■ Writes e-mail addresses ■ Resolve addresses for sending test messages ■ Monitor directory replication status ■ Reference information to build routing tables
Information Store	■ Send Link Monitor test messages ■ Send Server Monitor test messages
Key Management	■ Assist in collecting and managing security keys

Optional Components Communication

The Exchange optional components provide additional messaging functionality. Most of these components are connectors or gateways and therefore provide interoperability with foreign messaging systems. Because connectors, gateways, and other related components are involved in the same type of events and communicate with the same components, we will group them together. The other optional components are discussed under their own headings.

Components that Communicate with Foreign Systems

All of the components discussed in this section help to enable Exchange to interoperate with a foreign messaging system. The following components use the same component communication:

- Internet Mail Service (IMS)

- Microsoft Mail Connector

- Connector for Lotus cc:Mail

Third-party gateways are also included in this discussion. Three primary events initiate component communication for a connector/gateway:

- Receiving a foreign message for local delivery

- Receiving and routing a foreign message (remote delivery)

Receiving a Foreign Message for Local Delivery   When a connector/gateway receives a foreign message, it passes the message to the IS for local delivery.

Receiving and Routing a Foreign Message (Remote Delivery)   Connectors pick up outbound messages from the IS. Figure 3.5 and Table 3.4 summarize and illustrate this information.

FIGURE 3.5

Connectors/Gateways initiated communication with other components

Microsoft
Exchange Server

DS	IS	MTA	SA	Connectors/Gateways

1 Deliver inbound messages
Pick up outbound messages

	Component	Purpose of Communication
TABLE 3.4 Connector/Gateway initiated communication with other components	Information Store	■ Submit inbound messages ■ Pick up outbound messages

You will learn about two other components and how they relate to interoperability with a foreign system under the following two headings:

- Directory Synchronization Agent (DXA)

- Schedule+ Free/Busy Connector

Directory Synchronization Agent (DXA)   The Directory Synchronization Service (DSS) handles the *exporting* and *importing* of directory information between Exchange and an MS Mail or compatible foreign directory. When a change is made to the Exchange directory, such as the creation of a recipient, the DXA communicates the new information sent to the foreign system. This is called exporting directory information.

If a foreign system sends directory information to the DXA, which is referred to as importing directory information, the DXA communicates this information to the DS. Figure 3.6 and Table 3.5 summarize and illustrate this information.

FIGURE 3.6

Directory Synchronization Agent initiated communication with other components

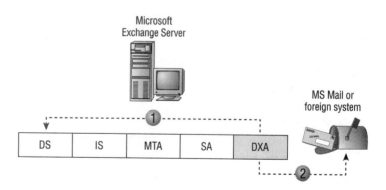

① Communicating imported foreign directory information

② Routing Exchange directory information to be exported to a foreign system

TABLE 3.5 Directory Synchronization Agent initiated communication with other components	Component	Purpose of Communication
	Directory Services	■ Communicate imported foreign directory information
	Foreign System	■ Export new changes to foreign system

For the DXA component to communicate with a foreign message system directory, the foreign system must use the Microsoft Mail directory synchronization protocol.

Schedule+ Free/Busy Connector   Microsoft Schedule+ performs personal and group calendaring, scheduling, and task management. Microsoft Exchange ships with version 7.5 of Schedule+, while Microsoft Mail ships with version 1.0. In order to interoperate with the two versions, Microsoft created the Schedule+ Free/Busy Connector.

This connector communicates with the Microsoft Mail Connector in order to send and receive free/busy information. It also stores free/busy information that it receives from the Microsoft Mail users in the IS. The Schedule+ Free/Busy Connector also interfaces with the DS. It references the DS to resolve addresses. Figure 3.7 and Table 3.6 summarize and illustrate this information.

FIGURE 3.7

Schedule+ Free/Busy Connector initiated communication with other components

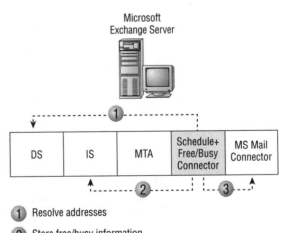

T A B L E 3.6 Schedule+ Free/Busy Connector initiated communication with other components	**Component**	**Purpose of Communication**
	Directory Service	■ Resolve addresses
	Information Store	■ Store free/busy information
	MS Mail Connector	■ Send Exchange users' free/busy information to Mail users

Key Management

Key Management provides an Exchange system with additional security, such as message encryption and digital signatures. The DS and SA are the other primary Exchange components with which Key Management communicates. Key Management uses the SA to assist in collecting and managing security key information. It uses the DS to store various security information. Chapter 10 covers Key Management in more detail. Figure 3.8 and Table 3.7 summarize and illustrate this information.

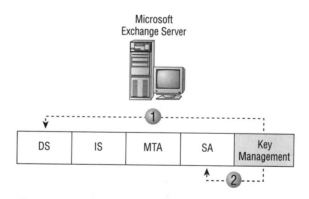

Microsoft
Exchange Server

DS	IS	MTA	SA	Key Management

1 Stores various security information

2 Collects and manages security keys

	Component	Purpose of Communication
T A B L E 3.7 Key Management initiated communication with other components	Directory Service	■ Store various security information
	System Attendant	■ Collect and manage security keys

Internet News Service (INS)

The Internet News Service enables the publishing of USENET newsgroup content to Exchange public folders. Exchange public folders can also be published to USENET newsgroups. The primary component that the INS communicates with is the IS. Communication is straightforward because public folders are part of the IS. Figure 3.9 and Table 3.8 summarize this information.

F I G U R E   3.9

Internet News Service initiated communication with other components

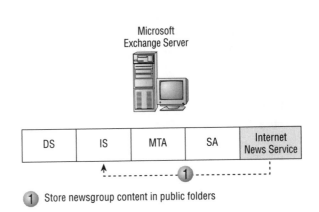

1 Store newsgroup content in public folders

	Component	Purpose of Communication
T A B L E 3.8 Internet News Service initiated communication with other components	Information Service	■ Store newsgroup content in public folders

Active Server Components

The Active Server Components are shipped with Microsoft Exchange but run on a Microsoft Internet Information Server 3.0 (IIS). These components make

Exchange resources available to World Wide Web (WWW) clients. They accomplish this by translating MAPI services to a HyperText Markup Language (HTML) format.

Web users, through the Active Server Components, communicate with the IS to send and receive messages and to access public folders. They also access the DS to look up directory information, such as the Global Address List. Figure 3.10 and Table 3.9 summarize and illustrate this information.

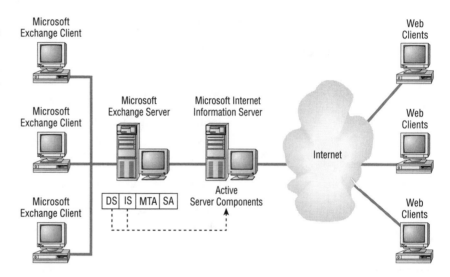

FIGURE 3.10

Active Server Components initiated communication with other components

TABLE 3.9

Active Server Components initiated communication with other components

Component	Purpose of Communication
Directory Service	■ Look up directory information
Information Store	■ Send messages ■ Receive messages ■ Access public folders

Common Messaging Operations

We will now discuss several common messaging operations and how the various Exchange components enable those operations. By starting with a real-world operation and then explaining how the various components enable that operation, we will tie our earlier discussions together. The operations that will be discussed are two of the most common in a site. They are:

- Local message delivery

- Reading mail

Local Message Delivery

The following steps trace the sending of a message to another Exchange user on the same Exchange server. Steps 1, 2, and 3 correspond to Figure 3.11.

1. Client A looks up client B's address by accessing the Global Address List in the Directory. The RPC protocol is used for the client/server interaction.

2. Client A creates a message to be sent to client B.

3. Client A sends this message. The message is received on the Exchange server by the IS.

FIGURE 3.11

Sending mail:
Steps 1, 2, and 3

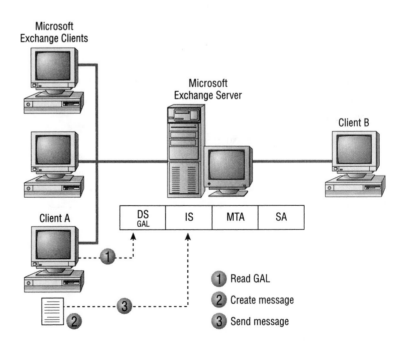

Steps 4 and 5 correspond to Figure 3.12.

4. In order to deliver the message, the IS accesses the Directory to determine the physical location of the recipient's mailbox (using a local procedure call, LPC). In this scenario, the recipient's mailbox is on the same server. The IS also references the properties of the destination mailbox, some of which are stored in the Directory. For example, the mailbox could have forwarding rules, reject messages from, and other properties.

5. The IS places the message in the recipient's mailbox.

FIGURE 3.12

Sending mail:
Steps 4 and 5

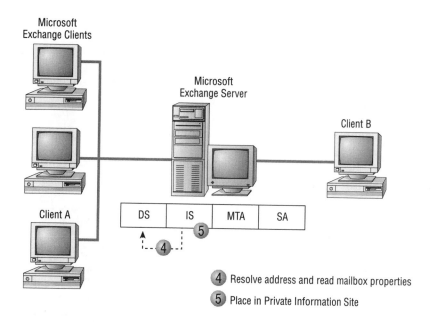

Reading Mail

Reading Mail

The following steps trace the way a message is read on an Exchange server. Steps 1 and 2 correspond to Figure 3.13.

1. The IS notifies client B of the new message.

2. Client B, using an RPC, sends a read request to the IS.

FIGURE 3.13

Reading mail:
Steps 1 and 2

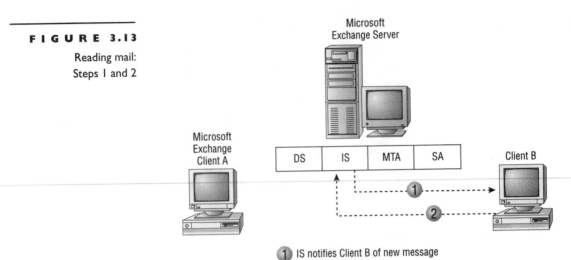

FIGURE 3.13

Reading mail:
Steps 1 and 2

1 IS notifies Client B of new message

2 Client issues a read request that is executed as an RPC request sent to the server

Step 3 corresponds to Figure 3.14.

3. The IS sends the message to client B (in response to client B's RPC in Step 2).

FIGURE 3.14

Reading mail:
Steps 3 and 4

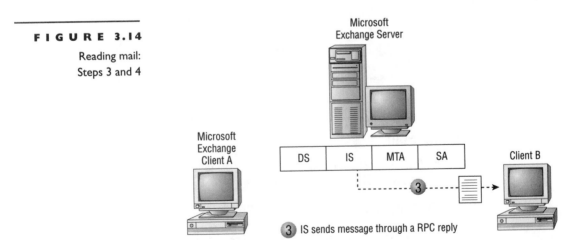

3 IS sends message through a RPC reply

Component Communication between Exchange Servers in a Site

An Exchange site, by grouping messaging functions, presents a single messaging environment to users and administrators. For example, although mailboxes can be created and reside on different home servers, they all appear in the address book without reference to their physical location. Users do not need to know the physical location of a recipient. They simply create and send messages. If a message recipient is on another server, the various Exchange components transparently deliver the message to that server.

The underlying mechanism that creates this single messaging environment is component communication between Exchange servers in a site. This server-to-server communication within a site is called *intrasite* communication.

Communication between sites, called intersite communication, will be covered in Chapter 13.

Two main components implement the transfer of all information between Exchange servers within a site, they are:

- Directory Service (DS)

- Message Transfer Agent (MTA)

The DS and MTA run under the security context of the site service account. Each Exchange site must have a single, designated user account that serves this purpose. This allows Windows NT security to ensure no unauthorized access is made to Exchange services. The use of a single designated account means that all the Exchange components are under the same security context.

As with client/server interactions, the server-to-server interactions also use the RPC protocol. A server sending a request to another server is in the client role, and the server sending the reply is in the server role.

Three main communication processes take place within a site; they are:

- Directory replication

- Mail message transfer

- Link Monitor message transfer

The following sections cover each process by discussing the Exchange components and steps involved in each process.

Directory Replication

Directory replication is the mechanism by which Exchange servers in an organization share directory information. For instance, when a directory object, such as a mailbox, is created, modified, or deleted on a server, that information will be communicated with all the other Exchange servers in its site. Each Exchange server is responsible for updating the other Exchange servers in its site. The result is that each server contains a comprehensive copy of all the resources in the site. This scheme is sometimes called the *multimaster* model because each server contains the entire site directory, rather than one central server maintaining the directory and the other servers having to collect information from the central server.

Directory replication within a site takes place automatically and does not need the intervention of an administrator (there are some parameters that can be set, but they are optional). Directory replication between sites (intersite) does require configuration by the administrator (this topic will be covered in Chapter 13).

The Directory Service component implements the directory replication mechanism. A DS component on one server transfers directory information to the DS component on another server. For intrasite replication, this process does not use the MTA component.

Directory replication includes a tracking method that ensures all new changes to a directory are replicated throughout the site. This tracking method is called the *update sequence number* (USN). Each Exchange server is automatically assigned a unique number for its USN value. Each server also contains a list of the last known USN values for all the other servers in the site.

USNs allow the directory service to copy only modified information during directory replication. If USNs were not used, directory replication would have to copy entire directories between servers, rather than only the modifications. USNs also contribute to the fault tolerance features of Exchange by ensuring a current and accurate directory throughout a site.

Directory Replication Procedure

The following steps occur during the directory replication process. Steps 1 and 2 are illustrated in Figure 3.15, and Steps 3, 4, and 5 are illustrated in Figure 3.16.

FIGURE 3.15

Directory replication:
Steps 1 and 2

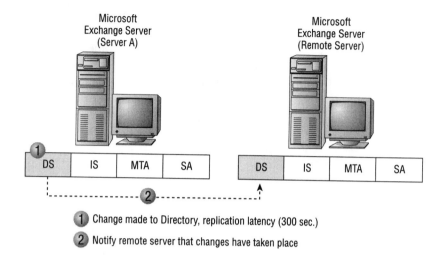

1. Change made to Directory, replication latency (300 sec.)
2. Notify remote server that changes have taken place

I. On Server A, which contains a modified directory, the DS will delay starting the replication process for a period of 300 seconds (5 minutes). This allows the DS to replicate changes in a batch manner (i.e., all at once) rather than one at a time. This delay is referred to as the *replication latency* and can be configured in the Registry at the following location:

```
HKEY_LOCAL_MACHINE

     System

          CurrentControlSet

               Services

                    MSExchangeDS

                         Parameters

                              Replicator notify pause after
                              modify(secs)
```

2. At the end of the replication latency, the DS on Server A starts to send notifications to the other servers in the site. It knows what servers to notify because it has a list of the other Exchange servers in the site. This replication list is discussed later in this chapter. From Server A's perspective, the other servers are referred to as *remote servers*.

The notification that is sent does not contain the actual changes, but only a notice that changes have been made. The DS sends this notification to one remote server at time, pausing after each notification before continuing with the next remote server. This pause allows the notified server to perform some actions (Step 3). The default pause period is 30 seconds and can be modified in the Registry at the following location:

HKEY_LOCAL_MACHINE

    System

        CurrentControlSet

        Services

            MSExchangeDS

            Parameters

                Replicator notify pause between DSAs (secs)

FIGURE 3.16

Directory replication: Steps 3, 4, and 5

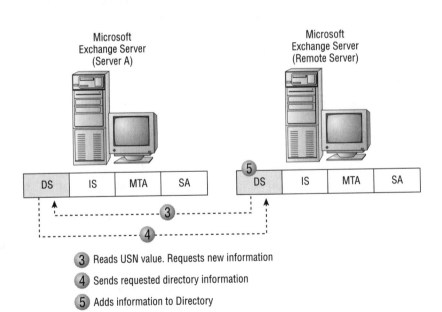

3 Reads USN value. Requests new information

4 Sends requested directory information

5 Adds information to Directory

3. When a remote server receives the notification, it compares the USN value in the notification with the value it has recorded for Server A. If Server A's (i.e., the server sending the notice) USN is greater than what the remote server has recorded for it, the remote server knows there are changes to Server A's directory. The remote server then requests that Server A send it all of its directory objects with a USN higher than the remote server's last known USN for Server A.

4. The DS on Server A then uses the RPC mechanism to transfer the requested information to the DS on the remote server.

5. The DS on the remote server adds the new information to its directory.

Directory Replication Fault Tolerance Features

Because directory information is so important, Microsoft has included various fault tolerance features for directory replication. The three main fault tolerance features are:

- Update Sequence Numbers (USNs)

- Replication lists

- Knowledge Consistency Checker (KCC)

Update Sequence Numbers (USNs) As stated earlier, directory replication includes a tracking method that ensures that all new changes to a directory are replicated throughout a site. This tracking method is called update sequence numbers (USNs).

Replication Lists Each Exchange server directory contains lists of other Exchange servers in its site. REPS-TO is a list of the servers that are to receive directory updates. REPS-FROM is a list of the servers from which directory updates can be accepted. These lists are *cached* (i.e., stored) in a server's memory.

Replication lists provide fault tolerance by ensuring that each server knows the other servers that should be involved in directory replication.

Knowledge Consistency Checker (KCC) The knowledge consistency checker (KCC) runs on every Exchange server. The KCC on each server compares its replication lists to the replication lists on other servers. It makes sure there are no Exchange servers in the site that are not on its replication lists.

That situation is called a *mismatch*. If there is a mismatch, the KCC updates its lists by requesting replication lists from another server. This ensures that an Exchange server's replication lists are accurate.

The KCC process runs by default every 3 hours. It can also be manually started through the Directory Service.

The KCC process is also involved in intersite directory replication, which will be discussed in Chapter 13.

Events That Trigger Fault Tolerance Features

The fault tolerance features of directory replication are operational during normal operation of Microsoft Exchange. However, there are certain circumstances under which these features are especially relevant:

- When a server has been offline and is now back online

- When there is failed communication because a server is down, removed, or reconfigured

- When installing an Exchange server to an existing site

In the first two circumstances, the fault tolerant features of directory replication work in a straightforward manner. The third circumstance, when a new server is added to a site, warrants a short discussion.

Directory Replication for a New Server in a Site   When a new Exchange server has been added to a site, it must collect the directory information for that site. During setup, the installer is prompted for the name of an existing Exchange server. This existing server will be the one that the SETUP program connects to and copies its directory information. The steps are outlined here:

1. The SETUP program adds the name of the new server to the existing server's directory. This event also notifies the existing server that it needs to send its Directory to the new server.

2. The existing server sends a modified directory, without the site recipients, to the new server. This directory without recipients is referred to as the STUB directory. Using the STUB allows the SETUP program to efficiently finish its installation process because it does not need to spend time copying all the recipients to the new server. Instead, SETUP can efficiently copy the essential parts of the site directory and then finish its installation functions. Recipients are copied to the new server during Step 4.

3. Using the STUB directory, the new server builds its replication lists.

4. The new server can now connect to the other site servers and instruct them to begin directory replication. This is how the new server receives a copy of the recipients list.

Directory replication ensures that accurate information needed for messaging is distributed throughout a site. It serves as a foundation for the next communication process to be discussed, the transferring of mail messages.

Message Transfer

All communication within a site, with the exception of directory replication, uses the MTA component. That includes the two most common types of communication, transferring of mail messages and the updating of public folder data. Both forms of communication use mail messages to send their content, and both use the MTA to deliver messages to other servers. In this section, you will learn about:

- Formatting mail messages: X.400 interpersonal messages (IPMs)

- Addressing mail messages: X.400 and X.500

- Transferring messages within a site

- Expanding a distribution list

Formatting Mail Messages: X.400 (IPMs)

When a user of the Microsoft Exchange Client application creates a mail message, that message is created in the X.400 interpersonal message (IPM) format. An IPM message is comprised of two main parts, the message content and the message envelope (see Figure 3.17).

Message Content   This is the information that the user is sending. It is similar in concept to an office memo in that it is subdivided into two parts:

- **Heading**   The heading, also called the header, contains information such as the originator of the message (the sender), the recipient (or recipients) of the message, and information about how the message is to be handled (such as an expiration time).

- **Body**   The body contains the actual data of the IPM. Common types of data are text and graphics. Other types of data include facsimile (fax), telex, and voice.

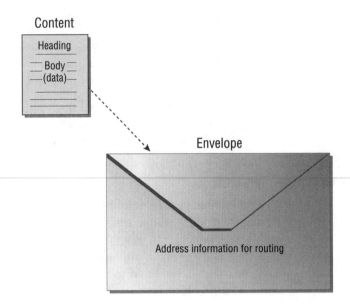

Message Envelope   Message content, like memos or a letter, must be placed
in an envelope in order to be mailed. The protocol used by Microsoft
Exchange to accomplish this is the X.400 P1 protocol. The X.400 envelope,
just like a postal envelope, is used to route a message to its destination. Some
of the information on the X.400 envelope is the same as on the mail message
header, such as the originator and recipient of the message. The delivery priority of the message can also be on the envelope.

X.400 and X.500 Addressing

Exchange uses both X.400 and X.500 addresses to address and route messages. The X.500 address, called a Distinguished Name (DN), is the path to
the location of an object in the directory hierarchy. An example DN is:

o=Widget; ou=Chicago; cn=Recipients; cn=JayWilson

Whenever a user creates and addresses a message, Exchange uses a DN as
the address format. The Exchange MTA component uses DNs for all routing
within an Exchange organization.

But Exchange also generates an X.400 address, called an Originator/Recip-
ient Address (O/R Address), for each message. This is in case the message will
be sent outside the organization to, or through, an X.400 network. The

Exchange MTA will always first try to resolve a route with the DN, and failing, will then use the O/R Address. An example of an O/R Address is:

c=us; a=mci; p=WidgeNet; o=Widget; s=Wilson; g=Jay

Transferring Mail Messages within a Site

A mail message can be used to send an e-mail message to another server and to update public folder data on another server. The following process transfers a message within a site from one Exchange server to another Exchange server. Even though we are focusing on the role of the MTA component, other steps are included to provide a better context to the mail message transfer process.

1. A user, through an Exchange client application, creates and sends an e-mail message, or edits data inside a public folder (an e-mail message will be used for the rest of this example). To do this, the user must:

   ■ Choose recipients for the message.

   ■ Create the content of the mail message.

   Then Exchange must:

   ■ Format the message in the IPM format.

   ■ Assign addresses to the message in the form of a distinguished name (DN) and an Originator/Recipient (O/R).

2. When a message is created, it is initially stored in the IS. The IS performs the following actions:

   ■ Resolves the recipient's address by referencing the DS.

   ■ If the recipient's mailbox is on this Exchange server, the IS delivers the message to the recipient's mailbox and notifies the recipient that they have new mail. This is a local delivery.

   ■ If the recipient's mailbox is on another Exchange server in the site, the IS passes the message to the MTA. (This option is used in the example.) This is a remote delivery.

3. The MTA accesses the DS to learn the recipient's home server.

4. The MTA uses the RPC protocol under the context of the site service account to open a session with the MTA on the recipient's home server.

5. The MTA transfers the message to the MTA on the recipient's home server.

6. The MTA on the recipient's server temporarily stores the message and notifies the IS that a message has arrived.

7. The IS retrieves the message from the MTA and notifies the client application of the recipient that there is new mail.

If the MTA cannot deliver the message, the message is sent back to the sender in a nondelivery report (NDR).

If the MTA on the sender's server (Steps 3, 4, and 5) receives a message that has multiple recipients, and those recipients reside on different servers, the MTA will create an individual message for each of the destination servers. You will learn more about this in the next section.

Expanding a Distribution List

A distribution list is a grouping of recipients. One of the functions of the MTA is to expand a distribution list recipient into its individual members. The following are the steps involved in this process:

1. The IS receives a message addressed to a distribution list recipient.

2. The IS passes this message to the MTA.

3. The MTA determines the individual members of the distribution list. These members can be any Exchange recipient, such as mailboxes, custom recipients, public folders, and other distribution lists. The process of determining the members is also referred to as *expanding* or *resolving* the distribution list.

4. The MTA creates an individual message for each destination server MTA containing members of the distribution list.

Link Monitor Messages

One of the administrative features of Exchange is the testing of connections between Exchange servers within a site. This is done through the Link Monitor utility, which sends test messages between Exchange Servers.

The Link Monitor utility uses the System Attendant to create and receive test messages (test messages are actually mail messages used for these purposes).

The SA uses the MTA to send the test messages. The following steps explain this process:

1. An administrator configures the Link Monitor to send test messages from one Exchange server, the local server, to other Exchange servers, referred to as the monitored servers.

2. At the specified intervals, the SA creates test messages addressed to the monitored servers.

3. The MTA delivers the test messages to the MTAs on the monitored servers.

4. The MTAs on the monitored servers pass the test messages to their respective SAs.

5. The SA on a monitored server responds to the test message by sending back a reply message.

The use of Link Monitor messages can help administrators continually test connections and therefore assist in providing a high level of network service. More information on this topic, including exercises, appears in Chapter 12.

Summary

Because no single Exchange component performs all messaging services, components must communicate amongst themselves to create a messaging system. Component communication takes place within a single Exchange server and between Exchange servers in a site. The latter is called intrasite communication.

Component communication is involved in such activities as accessing the Global Address List, sending and reading a message, and delivering local messages. Component communication between servers involves activities like directory replication, message transfer, and Link Monitor messages.

Review Questions

1. The IS communicates with this component to perform a remote delivery:

    A. SA

    B. IS on other server

    C. Key Manager

    D. MTA

2. This component is referenced by other components when resolving an address:

    A. DS

    B. IS

    C. MTA

    D. SA

3. Intrasite Directory replication uses the MTA to route directory information.

    A. True

    B. False

4. The IS notifies clients of new messages.

    A. True

    B. False

5. This component assists in the implementation of advanced security:

    A. IS

    B. SA

C. MTA

D. DXA

6. The Active Server Components run on this system:

A. Microsoft Exchange server

B. Web client

C. Internet router

D. Microsoft IIS server

7. The INS communicates with this component for the storing of USENET content:

A. Microsoft IIS server

B. DS

C. SA

D. IS

8. Connectors, such as the Connector for Lotus cc:Mail, CANNOT place foreign messages in the IS.

A. True

B. False

9. When routing a message, the MTA may communicate with this component for the physical transfer of the message:

A. Connector or gateway

B. MTA on another server

C. Key Manager

D. SA

10. The DS uses this information when performing a directory replication:

    A. Site number

    B. Update Sequence Number (USN)

    C. Server DS number

    D. Combination site and server number

11. The Link Monitor utility uses this component to send test messages:

    A. LDAP

    B. INS

    C. Key Security

    D. SA

12. To expand a distribution list, the MTA references this component:

    A. IS

    B. DS

    C. Key security

    D. SA

13. When addressing messages for delivery within an Exchange organization, this address format is used:

    A. Distinguished Name

    B. MS Mail name

    C. Exchange lengthwise address

    D. cc:Mail name

CHAPTER

4

Installing Microsoft Exchange Server

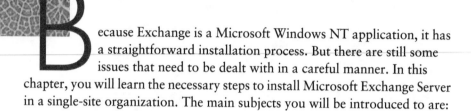

ecause Exchange is a Microsoft Windows NT application, it has a straightforward installation process. But there are still some issues that need to be dealt with in a careful manner. In this chapter, you will learn the necessary steps to install Microsoft Exchange Server in a single-site organization. The main subjects you will be introduced to are:

- Preinstallation considerations

- Installing Microsoft Exchange Server

- Postinstallation considerations

- Troubleshooting a Microsoft Exchange installation

- Upgrading Microsoft Exchange Server

Planning would be a normal step to perform before executing an installation. But the topic of planning cannot be covered at this time because the necessary prerequisite knowledge has not been covered. However, by the end of this book you will have that knowledge. Consequently, the last chapter in this book, Chapter 17, is on planning.

Preinstallation Considerations

Several important issues must be dealt with before you install Exchange Server. Having the correct information and making the right decisions about these issues will go a long way to ensuring a successful installation. The preinstallation issues that will be covered in this section are:

- Minimum system requirements

- The NT user accounts related to the Exchange installation
- Licensing issues
- The relationship between Exchange sites and NT domains
- Installation scenarios

Minimum System Requirements

This section lists the minimum requirements for the computer system upon which Exchange is to be installed. These minimums are valid when you install only the core components. Using additional Exchange components, depending on the particular performance demands, could require more resources than the following minimum requirements.

Hardware Requirements

The minimum hardware requirements for installing Exchange are listed below:

Microprocessor	Intel Pentium 60 MHz or higher (recommended: Pentium 133MHz or higher), or RISC microprocessor such as Digital Alpha AXP
Random Access Memory (RAM)	24MB RAM for Intel platform; 32MB RAM for RISC platform (recommended: 32MB for Intel and 48MB for RISC)
Hard Disk Space	250MB free disk space; 300MB for RISC (recommended: 500MB for all platforms)

The Microsoft Exchange Server software comes on a compact disc. If the machine intended to be the Exchange Server has no compact disc drive, the administrator may copy the necessary files from the compact disc to a shared hard disk or share a compact disc drive on another machine. The Exchange files take approximately 110MB of space for Intel and approximately 90MB for Alpha.

Software Requirements

The software requirements for an Exchange installation are listed below:

Operating System	■ Microsoft Windows NT Server version 3.51 with Service Pack 5, or later ■ Microsoft Windows NT Server version 4.0 (Service Pack 2 is required if you are installing Active Server Components) ■ The operating system needs to be configured for a page file size equal to 50MB of disk space plus the amount of RAM in the machine. (For example, if the machine has 48MB of RAM, the page file size should be 50 plus 48, equaling 98MB. The recommended size is 100 MB of disk space plus amount of physical RAM)
Apple Macintosh clients (optional)	Windows NT Services for Macintosh is needed if Macintosh Exchange clients will access the Exchange server or if the Microsoft Mail Connector will be installed for interoperability with clients using MS Mail for AppleTalk.
Novell NetWare clients (optional)	The Microsoft Gateway Services for NetWare (GSNW) is required on the Exchange server. If the NetWare clients are using IPX/SPX, then the Exchange server will also require Microsoft NWLink.
Internet SMTP clients (optional)	Windows NT Transmission Control Protocol/ Internet Protocol (TCP/IP) is required if the Internet Mail Service will be installed for Internet client connectivity.
World Wide Web clients	A Microsoft Internet Information Server 3.0 running the Active Server Components is required for Web browser access to an Exchange server.

Remember that the minimum requirements probably will not provide the optimal operational performance, or take into account the requirements for any future growth of system demand. The actual system requirements of any installation will depend on the particulars of that specific environment. To determine your real-world requirements, refer to the *Microsoft Exchange Server Concepts and Planning Guide*.

NT User Accounts Related to the Exchange Installation

Both during and after installation, Microsoft Exchange utilizes the following Windows NT user accounts:

- Windows NT administrator account

- Site services account

Windows NT Administrator Account

To install Exchange Server on a Windows NT Server, a user must log on to that computer with a *user account* that has administrator privileges (i.e., an account that is in the local administrator's group). This level of privileges is needed because during installation services will be started, files will be copied to the \<winnt_root>\SYSTEM32 directory, and rights will be granted to the site services account.

Site Services Account

The Exchange Server components, also called services, need an NT user account to operate. This account is referred to as the *site services account*. The Exchange services use this account to log on to the NT system and carry out their functions. The following facts and parameters relate to the site services account:

- It must be created before performing the Exchange Server installation. The Exchange Server installation will prompt you for the account name and password to use for this account.

- The Exchange Server installation program will automatically grant the following rights to the account you specify as the site services account:

  - Act as part of the operating system

  - Log on as a Service

  - Restore files and directories

Licensing Issues

Licensing issues relate to matters of legality (specifically, the number of servers Exchange can be loaded on and the number of clients that can access a server).

Four main licenses pertain to the various Microsoft Exchange product packages:

- Server License

- Connector License

- Client Access License (CAL)

- Client Pack License

Server License

The basic server license provides the legal right to install and operate Microsoft Exchange Server on a single-server machine. A couple of specific components can be installed on additional machines without additional licenses. These components are the Microsoft Exchange Administrator Program and the Source Extractor software contained in the Microsoft Exchange Migration Utilities. The license for the Source Extractor software permits the migration of data only to a Microsoft Exchange system.

Connector License

X.400 software is licensed for installation and use on a single Microsoft Exchange Server. In addition other Exchange servers that do not have the X.400 connector installed, but are utilizing the X.400 connector on another Exchange server, will also need a license. This scenario is illustrated in Figure 4.1.

FIGURE 4.1

Connector licenses

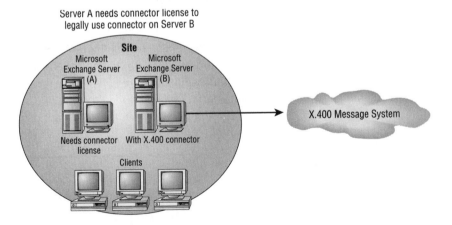

Since many licensing policies can change over time, always check for the latest policy to ensure your compliance.

Client Access License (CAL)

A Client Access License (CAL) gives a user the legal right to access an Exchange server. An organization designates the number of (CALs) it needs when a Microsoft Exchange server is purchased. Each CAL provides a user the legal right to access the Exchange Server. Any client software that has the ability to be a client to Microsoft Exchange Server is legally required to have a CAL purchased for it. Microsoft Exchange Client software and third-party client software need CALs.

Client Access Licenses are NOT included in any version of Microsoft Windows or in Microsoft Office. For example, the Microsoft Exchange Inbox in the Windows 95 operating system legally requires a CAL.

There are two options for applying CALs during the installation of an Exchange Server:

- Per Server mode
- Per Seat mode

The Per Server mode allows the installer to specify the legal number of concurrent client connections to that particular Exchange Server. The CAL in this mode logically resides on the Exchange Server.

The Per Seat mode allows Exchange clients to hold the legal right to access any Exchange Server. The CAL in this mode logically resides on the client machine.

After an installation, an administrator can perform a one-time conversion from the Per Server to the Per Seat mode. Administrators may also use the License Manager program, included in the NT Administrative Tools group, to set license quantities and track license usage for an entire organization.

Client Pack License

The Client Pack License includes both Exchange client software and 20 CALs. The Client Pack is offered primarily for using the Exchange client software to connect to non-Exchange back-ends, such as Microsoft Mail.

Exchange Sites and Windows NT Domain

A Windows NT *domain* is a logical grouping of NT Servers and clients which use the same security accounts manager (SAM). The SAM is a database containing information on the resources and configurations of a domain, such as users, groups, permissions, and rights. The domain creates a logical network. Users log on to a particular domain by using an account from that domain's SAM. This is called being *authenticated*. Once logged on from the domain, a user has access to the resources of that domain, depending on the permissions granted.

An organization can have more than one domain. The domains can be totally separate, or they can work with each other. This is done by creating a *trust relationship* between the domains. While there are multiple implementations of trust relationships between domains, the following describes one straightforward implementation for the purpose of review. If Domain B wanted to allow the users of Domain A to use its resources, Domain B could "trust" Domain A. To trust another domain means to allow its SAM (e.g., its users and groups) to have access to your domain. Even though there are two domains, each with its own SAM, from the perspective of Domain B there is one virtual SAM which includes Domain B and Domain A. See Figure 4.2 for an illustration of this concept.

FIGURE 4.2

A trust relationship between domains

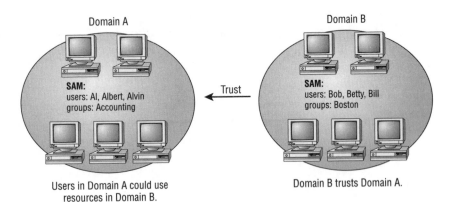

Domain A

Domain B

SAM:
users: Al, Albert, Alvin
groups: Accounting

Trust

SAM:
users: Bob, Betty, Bill
groups: Boston

Users in Domain A could use resources in Domain B.

Domain B trusts Domain A.

A *Microsoft Exchange site* is a logical grouping of Exchange Servers and clients (it must include at least one Exchange Server). Exchange sites and NT domains relate to two different environments. They are not the same thing. But while different, there is an operational connection between the two.

Microsoft Exchange sites utilize NT domain SAMs. For example, for Exchange services to operate they must use a site service account, which is contained in a domain SAM. If an Exchange site has multiple Exchange Servers, they must all use the same site services account in order to communicate with each other. There are two ways to accomplish this. The easiest is to have the Exchange site map directly to the NT domain (see Figure 4.3). All the Exchange Servers would have direct access to the same SAM, and therefore to the same site service account.

FIGURE 4.3

An Exchange site mapping directly to an NT domain

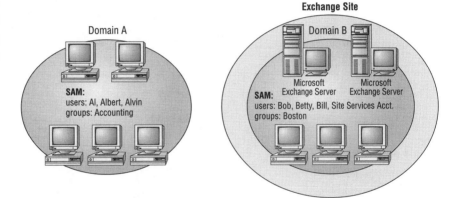

But imagine an Exchange site planned to encompass multiple domains with the Exchange Servers located in the different domains (see Figure 4.4).

The Exchange site servers need to use the same site service account, but there are multiple domains and therefore multiple SAMs. The solution is to establish trust relationships between the domains. This would allow domains to access each other's SAMs and, in effect, create one single, virtual SAM. The Exchange site servers could then use the same site service account. See Figure 4.5 for an illustration of one way to implement this concept.

FIGURE 4.4

A single Exchange site and
multiple domains

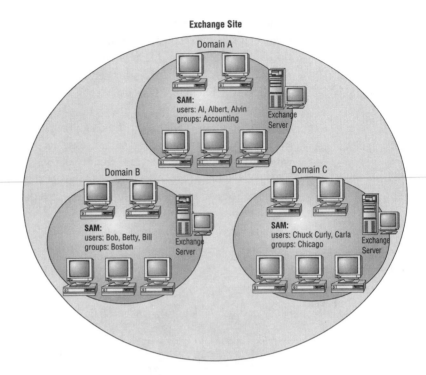

FIGURE 4.4

A single Exchange site and
multiple domains

FIGURE 4.5

An Exchange site and
multiple trusted NT
domains

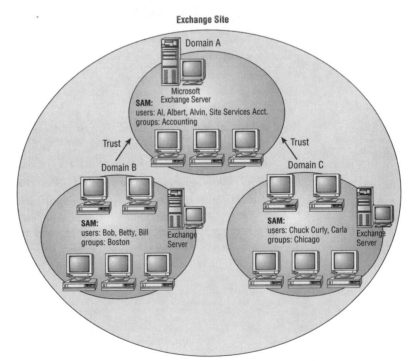

For communication between sites, not within a site but between sites, the Exchange Servers do not have to use the same site service account. See Figure 4.6 for an illustration of this concept. The logical boundaries between sites are called *site boundaries*.

FIGURE 4.6

Communication between sites

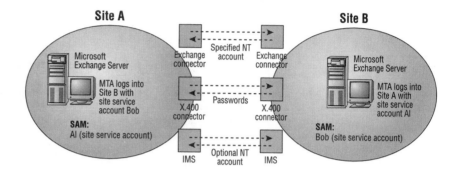

If an organization plans to have multiple Exchange sites (which they do not have to have, they could have only one site), there are many factors relating to the Exchange organization design. Some are logical factors, like the previous situation with domains and the site service account. Some are physical, like the speed of the connections between the Exchange Servers. Because Exchange Servers within a site communicate through RPCs, there needs to be a permanent, high-speed connection between all the Exchange Servers. There is more information on multiple site networks in Chapter 13.

Designing the number of sites and the location of the site boundaries is important for numerous reasons, some of which are performance, security, and access to NT accounts. Another reason is that if you later want to redesign your Exchange organization, you will have to reinstall and reconfigure the Exchange Servers.

Installation Scenarios

During the Exchange Server installation, you will have the option of having this new server create a new site, or having it join an existing site. Both scenarios are discussed in the following text.

Creating a New Site

While executing the SETUP program, one of the dialog boxes (shown in Figure 4.7) will present the installer with the option to create a new site. This would be the choice for the first installation of Exchange in an organization, or when an existing Exchange implementation requires a new site to be added to the organization.

FIGURE 4.7

Setup dialog box for creating or joining a site

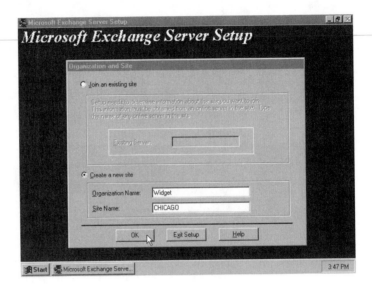

If you choose the Create a New Site option, you will be prompted to enter information on the following topics:

- **Exchange organization name**   The organization is at the top of the Exchange hierarchy. This case-sensitive field can be up to 64 characters in length. The organization name is associated with every object in the Exchange directory, such as mailboxes, public folders, and distribution lists. The organization name cannot be modified after the installation.

- **Exchange site name**   Site names distinguish between multiple sites, and are also associated with directory objects within the site. They must be unique names within the organization and can be up to 64 characters in length and are also case-sensitive.

- **Name of the directory for installation**   The default directory location and name is C:\EXCHSRVR, but this can be modified by the installer.

- **Site Service account and password**   When creating a new site, the default site service account will be the account currently logged in during the installation. This can be changed by the installer.

- **CD Key**   The setup program will present you with a dialog box requesting the CD Key or product ID number (PID). The CD Key is a unique 11-digit number found on the Exchange Server compact disc case.

Joining an Existing Site

There are many reasons to add an Exchange server to an existing site. The primary reasons are for performance, capacity and scaling, and fault tolerance. Each is briefly discussed below.

- **Performance**   An organization could place certain Exchange services on additional Exchange Servers, making those servers dedicated to those functions. Examples are:

  - **Public and/or private information stores**   These databases could be located on an additional Exchange Server dedicated to those functions.

  - **Connector software**   The same principle relates to running connector software on a dedicated Exchange Server.

- **Capacity and scaling**   If the physical limits of a particular system are being approached, Exchange services and their related physical resources (e.g., disk space) can be spread out among multiple Exchange servers. This issue also relates to performance issues.

- **Fault tolerance through redundancy**   Many Exchange services and resources are replicated throughout an Exchange organization. This redundancy implements a built-in level of fault tolerance. For example, all the Exchange servers within a site share the same directory information through replication. If one particular Exchange server were taken offline, when it came back online its directory information would be automatically updated by another Exchange server through the replication mechanism.

To join an existing site, the installer must know the name of an existing Exchange server in the site, as well as the password of the site service account. After the installer supplies the existing server name, SETUP will search the Exchange directory of that server and then automatically supply the name of the Exchange organization and site to this new installation. It will also automatically supply the site service account.

Adding a server to an existing site will create a new object under the Configuration container in the Exchange hierarchy. This requires the installer's user account to have certain Exchange permissions at the site object and configuration object. Those permissions are granted by assigning the user with one of the following security roles:

- Admin.

- Permissions Admin.

- Service Account Admin.

These roles give the installer the ability to create a new server object under the Configuration container in the Exchange hierarchy. These roles are assigned through the Microsoft Exchange Administrator program and the Permissions tab of the site object and Configuration object.

As with creating a new server, the installer must also have NT administrator privileges.

Installing Exchange Server

This section explains the installation options and then walks you through an actual installation. So boot up your Windows NT Server, grab your Exchange CD, and get ready to rumble... that is, do an installation.

Installation Options

As with most, if not all Microsoft products, the installation program for Exchange Server is named SETUP.EXE. This program is found on the Exchange Server CD under the SETUP directory and the I386 subdirectory for the Intel platform, and the ALPHA subdirectory for the Digital RISC platform.

When SETUP runs, it checks for a current installation of Exchange on this machine. If it finds one, it goes into maintenance mode and lets you modify some of the configuration. If it does not find one, it prompts you for the type of installation to undertake. There are three installation options:

- Typical

- Complete/Custom

- Minimum

After a brief explanation of these three options, you can take an exercise through an actual installation.

Typical Installation

The Typical Installation option installs the Microsoft Exchange Server software and the Exchange Administrator program. No connectors, client software, or online documentation are installed. Those items can be installed from CD at a later time.

Complete/Custom Installation

This option provides the ability to install all the Exchange software, including the following:

- Microsoft Exchange Server software

- Microsoft Exchange Administrator program

- Connectors

    - Microsoft Mail Connector

    - Connector for Lotus cc:Mail

    - X.400 Connector

- Online documentation

- Active Server Components

This is also the option used when installing the Microsoft Exchange Administrator program on an administrator's Microsoft Windows NT workstation. The installer deselects all the options, except the Microsoft Exchange Administrator program, and then continues with the installation.

Minimum Installation

The Minimum installation option installs only the Microsoft Exchange Server software. This option does not install the Administrator program or connectors. You would use this option to install an additional Exchange Server in a site when the server does not need the Administrator program. Not every Exchange Server needs the Administrator program because all servers can be centrally managed from one machine running the Administrator program.

Performing the Installation

The following exercises provide the actual steps to install Microsoft Exchange Server. Exercise 4.1 outlines the steps for creating and configuring the site services account that will be used in the installation and operation of Microsoft Exchange. Exercise 4.2 provides the installation steps, using the Complete/ Custom option and the Create a New Site option, and discusses the Join an Existing Site option.

EXERCISE 4.1

Creating the Site Service Account for Microsoft Exchange Server

1. In the Administrative Tools program group, start User Manager for Domains.

2. Select the New User option from the User menu.

3. In the Username field type **SiteAcct**. We will use this user account for the Exchange site service account. This could be any legal NT name you choose.

4. In the Full Name field, enter **Site Service Account**. This is an optional field and is for your information only.

5. In the Description field, enter **Site Service Account for Exchange Server**. This is also an optional field and is for your information.

6. Enter the password **12*12** in the Password and Confirm Password fields.

EXERCISE 4.1 (CONTINUED FROM PREVIOUS PAGE)

7. Clear the check box for the option User Must Change Password At Next Logon.

8. Select the Password Never Expires check box.

9. Click Add to finish creating the site service account.

10. Click Close to exit from User Manager for Domains.

Now that the site services account is created and configured, you may begin the installation steps for Microsoft Exchange Server. Those steps are outlined in Exercise 4.2.

EXERCISE 4.2

Installing Microsoft Exchange Server

1. Insert the Microsoft Exchange Server CD into the server's compact disc drive. (Other options are to share the CD on another machine on the network and then connect to that share, or to copy the CD to the server's hard drive.)

2. Start Microsoft Explorer or My Computer, and double-click on the drive letter pointing to the CD drive.

3. Navigate the CD directory structure until you are at \SETUP\ <processor type>. If you are installing on an Intel machine, the path would be \SETUP\I386.

4. Locate the file SETUP.EXE in this directory and double-click on it to execute it.

5. The Microsoft Exchange Server Setup message box appears. Click OK.

6. The Microsoft Exchange Server Setup dialog box lists the installation options. Using the Change Directory button on the screen, you can select the directory into which Exchange Server will be installed. For this book, we will assume the location is C:\EXCHSRVR. Next click Continue to continue the setup. If this is the first Exchange Server in the site, click Complete/Custom.

EXERCISE 4.2 (CONTINUED FROM PREVIOUS PAGE)

7. The Microsoft Exchange Server Setup - Complete/Custom dialog box appears (see below). For this exercise, we will not install the Active Server Components. Clear the check box. This will prevent the components from installing during this setup. This dialog box also allows you to select the components that will be installed with the Microsoft Exchange Server option. For this exercise, leave the default selections by clicking Cancel.

8. The Choose Licensing Mode dialog box appears. You may choose the Per Server option or the Per Seat option. For this installation, choose the Per Server option. Next, enter the number of client access licenses that you have purchased into the Concurrent Connections box. You must enter a number greater than zero in this field or clients will not be able to connect to this Exchange server. After you have entered a number, click Continue.

9. A Per Server Licensing dialog box appears, showing the Client Licensing agreement. Read this and if you agree, click on the I Agree check box. Then click OK.

10. The Organization and Site dialog box appears next. This is where you either join an existing site, or create a new site. If joining a site, you will select the Join an Existing Site option, and then enter the name of an existing Exchange server in that site in the Existing server field. SETUP will communicate with that server and automatically insert the name of the Exchange organization and site. If you are creating a new site, you will need to choose the option Create a New Site. You then must supply the name of the organization and site. For this exercise, click on Create a New Site, and then enter a name in the Organization Name field, like **Widget**, and a name in the Site Name field, like **Chicago**. (The names Widget and Chicago will be used throughout the remainder of this book, so you should use them for consistency). After entering this information, click OK.

11. A message will now appear prompting you to confirm the creation of a new site. Click Yes.

12. The Site Services Account dialog box appears. Click Browse and pick the SiteAcct account you created in Exercise 4.1 from the list provided. Then enter the password 12*12 and click the OK button.

13. A message screen will appear stating that the user account you just entered has been granted the rights to "Log on as a service," "Restore files and directories," and "Act as part of the operating system." Click OK. The SETUP program will now create Exchange directories and download files from the Exchange CD to those directories.

14. The next dialog box to appear will inform you that "Microsoft Exchange Server Setup has completed successfully." This dialog box will also present the option to run the Exchange Server Optimizer program, which is discussed later in this chapter. Do not run it at this time, instead click Exit Setup.

Postinstallation Considerations

This section discusses some of the results of the Exchange installation, and two postinstallation actions that the installer could take. During the installation of Exchange, some of the activities of SETUP.EXE include: creating an Exchange directory structure, copying files to that directory structure, creating share points to the directory structure, and adding keys and values to the NT Registry. Knowing the results of these activities is helpful for the Exchange administrator, especially when troubleshooting situations (which will be discussed later in this chapter). Here we will cover the preceding topics under the following headings:

- Default Directory and File Structure for Exchange

- Share Points and Permissions for Exchange Directories

- Exchange Entries in the NT Registry

As mentioned, we will also discuss two postinstallation actions that the installer could perform:

- Execute the Microsoft Exchange Performance Optimizer program

- Install the Microsoft Exchange Administrator program

Default Directory and File Structure for Exchange

The default root directory for Exchange is EXCHSRVR. The SETUP program creates subdirectories under that root directory and copies Exchange files to those subdirectories. Knowing this information could be useful in some troubleshooting situations. Table 4.1 is a listing of the default Exchange subdirectories under the root and the type of files in those subdirectories.

	Folder	Contents
T A B L E 4.1 Default Exchange Directories and their contents	ADD-INS	The ADD-INS directory contains subdirectories with program files that can be used to give additional functionality to Microsoft Exchange. These types of files are sometimes referred to as *extensions,* meaning they extend the basic functionality of Exchange. These files are implemented as DLL files. The complete installation copies files here that pertain to the use of the Microsoft Mail Connector, the Microsoft Schedule+ Free/Busy Connector and the Internet Mail Service.

	Folder	Contents
T A B L E 4.1 *(cont.)* Default Exchange Directories and their contents	ADDRESS	The ADDRESS directory contains subdirectories with program files (DLLs) that can be used to generate foreign addresses for Exchange recipients. When an Exchange Server uses a connector or gateway to create interoperability with a foreign system, the System Attendant component automatically generates a foreign address for each Exchange recipient. This foreign address, also referred to as a proxy address or simply an e-mail address, is what the users of the foreign mail system see and where they send mail. The program files in these subdirectories have the functionality to generate these proxy addresses. The complete installation downloads files for the following foreign mail systems: Microsoft Mail, SMTP systems, X.400 systems, and Lotus cc:Mail.
	BIN	The BIN directory contains many of the files that are the components and services of Microsoft Exchange Server and the Microsoft Exchange Server Administrator program.
	CCMCDATA	Files for cc: Mail Connector
	CONNECT	The CONNECT directory contains subdirectories that hold the files that are the Microsoft connectors. The complete installation downloads files for the following connectors: the Microsoft Mail Connector, the Internet Mail Service, the Microsoft Schedule+ Free/Busy Connector, and the Microsoft Exchange Connector for Lotus cc:Mail. An additional subdirectory contains files for translating messages into other languages.
	DSADATA	The DSADATA directory contains the file (DIR.EDB) that is the Directory Service database. This directory also holds the transaction log files (*.LOG) for the directory database.
	DXADATA	The DXADATA directory contains the file (XDIR.EDB) that is the Directory Synchronization database.
	IMCDATA	The IMCDATA directory contains subdirectories that are used by the Internet Mail Service (IMS) for working files. When the IMS is receiving mail, sending mail, or creating log files, it uses these subdirectories.
	INSDATA	This directory and its subdirectories are used by the Internet News Service to store data related to USENET feeds.

	Folder	Contents
T A B L E 4.1 *(cont.)* Default Exchange Directories and their contents	MDBDATA	The MDBDATA directory contains the files that are the Private Information Store (PRIV.EDB), the Public Information Store (PUB.EDB), and the database transaction log files (*.LOG) for both Information Stores.
	MTADATA	The MTADATA directory holds the files that make up and relate to the Message Transfer Agent (MTA).
	RES	Holds files that contain message strings used when Exchange logs events to the NT Event Log.
	SAMPAPPS	The SAMPAPPS directory contains subdirectories holding sample Exchange applications and forms. One of the subdirectories, CLIENTS, contains the file SAMPAPPS.PST which provides documentation on creating custom Exchange applications and forms. This information can be copied to a public folder.
	TRACKING.LOG	The TRACKING.LOG directory contains the log files for the messaging tracking feature of the Microsoft Exchange Administrator program.
	WEBDATA	Files for Web Connector.

Share Points and Permissions for Exchange Directories

Table 4.2 lists the Exchange directories that are shared on the network with the specified share names and permissions. (The software requirements mentioned in the *Preinstallation Considerations* section assumes that Exchange was installed on the C: drive.)

	Folder	Shared As	Permissions
T A B L E 4.2 Microsoft Exchange share points and permissions	C:\EXCHSRVR\ADD-INS	Add-ins	Administrators and Site Service Account: Full Control; Everyone group: Read
	C:\EXCHSRVR\ADDRESS	Address	Administrators and Site Service Account: Full Control; Everyone group: Read

	Folder	Shared As	Permissions
TABLE 4.2 *(cont.)* Microsoft Exchange share points and permissions	C:\EXCHSRVR\CONNECT	connect$	Administrators and Site Service Account: Full Control; Everyone group: Read
	C:\EXCHSRVR\CONNECT\ MSMCON\MAILDATA	maildat$	Administrators and Site Service Account: Full Control; Everyone group: Full Control
	C:\EXCHSRVR\SAMPAPPS\CLIENTS	Samples	Administrators and Site Service Account: Full Control; Everyone group: Full Control
	C:\EXCHSRVR\RES	Resources	Administrators and Site Service Account: Full Control; Everyone group: Read
	C:\EXCHSRVR\TRACKING.LOG	tracking.log	Administrators and Site Service Account: Full Control; Everyone group: Read

Exchange Entries in the NT Registry

During installation, SETUP creates entries in the NT Registry. Some of these entries are mentioned here.

Registry information about the presence of the Exchange application on this machine, as well as the directory location of the installation, is found in the following Registry location:

```
HKEY_LOCAL_MACHINE

        \SOFTWARE

                \Microsoft

                        \Exchange

                                \Setup
```

The following Registry location records the settings for the various Event Logs created by the different Exchange components.

```
HKEY_LOCAL_MACHINE
            \SYSTEM
                    \CurrentControlSet
                        \Services
                            \EventLog
                                \Application
                                    \<Exchange components>
```

The Exchange component settings are stored in the Registry at the following location:

```
\HKEY_LOCAL_MACHINE
                \SYSTEM
                    \CurrentControlSet
                        \Services
                            \<Exchange component>
```

License settings for Exchange are stored in:

```
\HKEY_LOCAL_MACHINE
        \SYSTEM
                \CurrentControlSet
                    \Services
                        \LicenseInfo
                            \MSExchangeIS
```

The Microsoft Exchange Performance Optimizer Program

One of the programs included in the Microsoft Exchange program group is the Performance Optimizer. This is a Windows NT-based application that analyzes the hard disk and memory of the server machine to determine the best place to locate Exchange files and databases. The Exchange components and files for which a change in directory location may be recommended are:

- Information Store

- Directory Service database

- Message Transfer Agent

- Transaction log files

Performance Optimizer will also recommend the amount of memory for caching data from the Information Store and Directory Service. At the end of an Exchange installation, SETUP offers the installer the option to run Performance Optimizer. The program can also be run at a later time.

Microsoft Exchange Administrator Program

A powerful feature of Microsoft Exchange is the ability to centrally administer an entire Exchange organization. This is accomplished through the Microsoft Exchange Administrator program. This Windows NT program can run on any NT machine, server or workstation, on the Exchange network. From this single point, an administrator can administer all the Exchange Servers in the organization. This is sometimes referred to as single-seat administration.

The executable program for Microsoft Exchange Administrator is ADMIN.EXE, which is stored in the \EXCHSRVR\BIN directory. While the Exchange setup program can install the Administrator program on their Exchange Server machine, the administrator will probably also want this program on the Windows NT workstation. Installing this program also installs a new version of Windows NT Backup and installs extensions to the User Manager for Domains and Performance Monitor programs. These changes enable those programs to work with Exchange Server.

The Administrator program uses RPCs to communicate with the various Exchange Servers. But some network links, due to slow speeds, do not support RPC connections. If that is the case between the machine running the Administrator program and a particular remote Exchange server, then a copy of the Administrator program must be running on the remote Exchange server's local area network.

Troubleshooting an Exchange Installation

If any problems arise during an Exchange installation, you may want to investigate the following areas:

- **The security context of the Site Service Account** This account must be accessible by all servers in the site.

- **The setup log** While SETUP is running, it creates a log of what it is attempting. This log file, called Exchange Server Setup.LOG, is stored in the root directory of the drive on which Exchange is installed.

- **Share point permissions** Make sure the necessary Exchange directories are shared.

- **Observe the Exchange Server boot process** If there are any problems with the Exchange boot process, alert messages can be sent to the console and/or written to the NT Event Log. The installer may also want to check that all the necessary Exchange services have been started. This can be done by going to Control Panel/Services, or by going to a command prompt and executing NET START. Some Exchange services are dependent on other NT services being started. If the dependent service is not started, the Exchange service will not start.

Upgrading a Server

Because of the changes in Exchange Server since version 4.0, two issues must be considered before performing an upgrade. One relates to the Service Pack being used with Exchange Server 4.0. The second issue relates to security.

Exchange Server 4.0 Service Pack 2

Service Pack 2 for Exchange Server 4.0 (also known as Exchange Server 4.0a) instituted some new changes to the Exchange directory *schema*. A schema is the set of rules defining a directory's hierarchy, objects, attributes, etc. If you have installed Service Pack 2 on all your Exchange Servers, you can upgrade those servers in any order. But if you have not installed that Service Pack on all the Exchange Servers, you must choose between two upgrade strategies. One strategy is to install Service Pack 2 on all Exchange Servers, and then upgrade the Exchange Servers to version 5.0 in any order you would like.

A different strategy can be used in a multiple-site environment. In a multiple-site network, one Exchange Server in each site is designated as the server to send directory replication information to another site, that server is called the *directory bridgehead server*, or *directory replication bridgehead*. (Chapter 13 discusses directory replication bridgeheads.)

In this scenario you could first upgrade the directory bridgehead servers by installing Service Pack 2 and then upgrading to Exchange Server 5.0. Then upgrade the other Exchange Servers in the site in any order.

In either scenario, single-site or multiple-site, you should, after installing Service Pack 2 on the Exchange servers, wait a period of time to allow the new information to replicate. The time period will depend on the size and traffic of your network. After the new information is replicated, you can continue upgrading the Exchange Servers to version 5.0.

Security

Post Office Protocol 3 (POP3) is one of the new protocols included with Exchange Server 5.0. POP3 is an Internet protocol that permits clients to download messages to their remote machines. POP3 requires that the Site Service account have the Windows NT right to act as part of the operating system. When a remote Internet client connects with POP3 to an Exchange Server, the POP3 component on that server impersonates the user by logging on to allow the retrieval of messages by the remote user. With Exchange Server 5.0, this right is granted automatically to the Site Service. But when upgrading from 4.0 to 5.0, the installer must manually grant this right to the Site Service account.

Summary

Although installing Microsoft Exchange Server is a straightforward process, you still must understand some important concepts.

One of the most important phases of an installation is preinstallation. Before starting the actual installation, you must make sure the minimum requirements for Exchange are met. You must also create the site service account which is used by the Exchange services for operation. License issues must be addressed to ensure compliance with legal issues. Because Exchange utilizes user accounts from Windows NT Server accounts databases, Exchange sites must interface with NT domains. Finally, you must know whether the planned new Exchange server is going to join an existing site or create a new site. When joining a site, you must know the name of an existing Exchange server in that site. When creating a site, you must know the name of or create a name for the organization, and enter a name for the new site.

There are three types of installation options:

- **Typical**   This option installs all the Exchange Server software, the Administrator program, but none of the connectors or online documentation.

- **Complete/Custom**   This option installs all the Exchange Server software, the Administrator program, connectors, and online documentation.

- **Minimum**   This option installs only the Exchange Server software.

After an Exchange Server installation, you should know the directory structure that SETUP has created. The default directory name for the installation is EXCHSRVR. Share points and modifications to the NT Registry are also made by SETUP.

At the end of the installation procedure, you have the option of running the Performance Optimizer program. This program will analyze the server's hard disk and memory configuration. It will then recommend any changes to the location of Exchange directories and the memory configuration.

Once the installation is complete, the installer should consider installing the Microsoft Exchange Server Administrator program. If the Typical or Complete/Custom options were used during installation, this program is already installed on the Exchange Server machine. But as the administrator of the Exchange system, you will probably want this program on your Windows NT workstation.

Review Questions

1. The minimum amount of RAM needed by Microsoft Exchange Server is:

   A. 24

   B. 48

   C. 64

   D. 128

2. When the installation option "Typical" is chosen, the Microsoft Exchange Server Administrator program is not installed.

   A. True

   B. False

3. One of the reasons to install an additional Exchange server in a site is to locate the public or private information stores on another machine.

   A. True

   B. False

4. The Site Services Account must be configured:

   A. As a regular user account

   B. As a member of the Mail group

   C. After the Exchange installation

   D. As a member of the Domain Administrators global group

5. A Client Access License (CAL) is not required for the Windows 95 Inbox.

   A. True

   B. False

6. Which file would be useful in a troubleshooting situation?

   A. Exchange Server Setup.LOG

   B. ERROR.LOG

   C. SETUP.EXE

   D. VIEWLOG

7. The default location of the Exchange directory is:

   A. \EXCHANGE

   B. \MICROSOFT\EXCHANGE

   C. \EXCHSRVR

   D. \\EXCHANGE

8. The Microsoft Exchange Server Administrator program can be run on a Windows NT workstation.

   A. True

   B. False

9. The Internet Mail Service requires this protocol to be running on the Exchange Server:

   A. NWLink

   B. Ethernet

   C. TCP/IP

   D. SNA

10. This Windows NT-based program analyzes your Exchange Server machine and makes recommendations for better performance:

   A. Administrator program

   B. SETUP.HLP

C. ANALYZER

D. Performance Optimizer

11. If there is a problem with the Exchange Server boot process, one action would be to view:

    A. The Event Log

    B. My Computer

    C. Microsoft Explorer

    D. Administrator Tools / User Manager for Domains

12. The following is one of the configuration requirements for the operating system that Microsoft Exchange Server uses:

    A. Page file size equal to 50 plus the amount of RAM

    B. NETBEUI

    C. NWLink

    D. Ethernet

13. Two sites, siteA and siteB, were both using version 4.0 of Exchange Server. The two sites also had directory replication configured between them. But after upgrading some of the servers in siteA to version 5.0, directory replication between the two sites stops working. Which of the following is a solution?

    A. Uninstall version 5.0, and reinstall version 4.0.

    B. Directory replication between sites cannot work until all servers have the same version.

    C. Internet Mail Service must be used for directory replication.

    D. Upgrade all directory bridgehead servers to version 5.0.

14. When adding a Microsoft Exchange Server to an existing site, which two pieces of information do you need to know?

A. The name of an existing Exchange Server in that site, and the password for the site service account in that site

B. Organization name, and site name

C. Site name, and administrator's user account

D. Organization name, and administrator's user account

CHAPTER

5

Recipients in a
Microsoft Exchange Environment

ne of an administrator's most important tasks is to create and configure Exchange *recipients*. A recipient is an object that can receive a message. In this chapter, we will discuss the types of recipients, their creation, and their properties. Exchange has four main types of recipients:

- **Mailboxes**   A mailbox is a storage location on a Microsoft Exchange server that, along with a client program, allows information to be sent, received, and organized. E-mail messages, forms, and file attachments are some of the typical types of information that can be sent to and stored in a mailbox.

- **Distribution lists (DL)**   A distribution list is a grouping of recipients. A single DL can represent a number of other recipients. Using DLs makes mass mailing easy. A message sent to a DL can be read by all the members of that DL.

- **Custom recipients**   A custom recipient is an e-mail address to a non-Exchange e-mail user. By using custom recipients, Exchange users can see a directory listing of non-Exchange mail users and send them messages. (The necessary connector components and other software must be in place.)

- **Public folders**   A public folder is like a public mailbox. It is a container for information to be shared among a group of people. Public folders can contain e-mail messages, forms, word processing documents, spreadsheet files, and files of many other formats. Public folders can also be configured to send information to other recipients.

The rest of this chapter discusses the creation and properties of these four recipient objects as well as some related management tasks.

> ### Don't Want to Be Distracted by Those Other People
>
> A pastor answered his telephone one Sunday afternoon. The caller wanted to know if the pastor's church would be open for worship on Sunday evenings. "Yes, it is open, but the regular worship service is on Sunday mornings," the pastor replied. He then asked if the caller would like to worship with the rest of the congregation on Sunday mornings. "Oh no!" answered the caller, "I do not want to be distracted by all those other people."
>
> Although distractions are part of any communal enterprise, those other people are essential to the enterprise. The recipients talked about in this chapter represent those other people.

Mailbox Objects

As mentioned, a mailbox is a specific storage area on an Exchange server where information can be sent, received, and organized. An Exchange mailbox, along with client software, enables users to perform a wide range of powerful messaging functions. A mailbox and the client software that uses it are analogous to a container box and the person who uses it. The box has certain characteristics, like shape, width, length, depth, etc., that determine what the person can do with the box. But the *person* is the active party who uses the box for some activity. As with all analogies, this one cannot be pushed too far. Exchange mailboxes also have active features, such as AutoAssistants. Now we will examine the creation and configuration of mailbox objects.

Creating a Mailbox

The vast majority, if not all, of your users are going to need a mailbox. Mailboxes must be created before any Exchange client software can be used. The following programs can be used to create and configure a mailbox:

- Microsoft Exchange Administrator program
- Microsoft Windows NT User Manager for Domains program
- Microsoft Exchange extract and import tools

Exchange Administrator Program

One of the functions of the Microsoft Exchange Administrator program (ADMIN.EXE) is creating and configuring mailboxes. To create a mailbox within this program, choose the File menu and then the New Mailbox option. You will then be presented with a number of property pages that can be used to configure the mailbox (these will be discussed shortly).

Part of the process of creating a mailbox is to assign it a primary Windows NT *user account*. The user account can be an existing account, or a new account created while in the Administrator program. The last function is possible because the Microsoft Exchange Administrator program has built-in functionality to create accounts in the NT domain SAM. This allows the Administrator program to create new Windows NT user accounts, at the same time it creates a mailbox. Later in this chapter, Exercise 5.2 will provide the steps to create a mailbox through this program.

Windows NT User Manager for Domains Program

Another program that can be used to create a mailbox is the Microsoft Windows NT User Manager for Domains. When Microsoft Exchange Server is installed, an Exchange module, MAILUMX.DLL, is added to the User Manager for the Domains program. This dynamic link library adds some of the functionality of the Exchange Administrator program to User Manager for Domains. Whenever a Windows NT user account is created in User Manager for Domains, an Exchange mailbox can also be created. This also applies to deleting a mailbox when the NT user account is deleted. Later in this chapter, Exercise 5.3 will provide the steps to create a mailbox through this program.

Exchange Extract and Import Tools

Microsoft Exchange can create Exchange recipients from existing user accounts. Two types of software tools, called *extract tools* and *import tools*, work together to accomplish this. Extract tools collect information about the user accounts. Import tools take that information and use it to create Exchange recipient objects.

Extract tools and import tools can also be used to create Exchange recipients from user accounts that are on an existing non-Exchange mail system. In this scenario, these tools can be used to not only create an Exchange mailbox, they can also create a Windows NT account, copy the contents of the foreign mailbox, and copy address book and folder information. This process is referred to as a *migration*. Migrations are covered in Chapter 16.

Extract Tools   The Microsoft Exchange Administrator program can be used to extract and import user information from Windows NT and NetWare systems. Each is discussed here:

- **Extract Windows NT Account List**   The Extract Windows NT Accounts List tool can take data from a trusted Windows NT or LAN Manager domain and prepare that data for the creation of recipient objects on a Microsoft Exchange Server. This extraction tool can be executed through the Exchange Administrator program, Tools menu, and the Extract Windows NT Account List option. It can also be executed using the command prompt. The user account executing this program must have administrative privileges and must select a domain controller in the relevant domain. Exercise 5.4, later in this chapter, will provide the steps to perform this type of extraction.

- **Extract NetWare Account List**   This program works like the previous tool, except that it prepares NetWare user accounts as the source data. The NetWare server can be any NetWare 2.x, 3.x, or 4.x running in bindery emulation mode. This tool can be executed through the Exchange Administrator program, Tools menu, and the Extract NetWare Account List option. The user executing this program will be prompted to log on to the NetWare server. They must log on as a user with supervisor rights to that NetWare server.

Additional extraction tools that can be used to migrate non-Exchange mail users will be discussed in Chapter 16.

Import Tools   After the data from the other system is prepared with the relevant extraction tool, the Microsoft Exchange Directory Import tool can be used to create Exchange recipient objects and import other specified data. This program is executed through the Microsoft Exchange Administrator program, using the Tools menu, Directory Import option.

Along with creating recipients, the Directory Import tool can also be used to modify existing recipients. For example, you could use the Import tool to add a large number of existing recipients to a distribution list. Exercise 5.5 shows the steps for performing an import.

Properties of a Mailbox

A mailbox object, like all objects, has properties. Those properties are configured and viewed through property pages and the individual attributes on those property pages. Many of the attributes are straightforward and do not warrant any explanation (e.g., phone number). This section describes each property page and the important individual attributes. Exercise 5.3 will walk you through the creation of a mailbox object.

The terms "properties" and "attributes" are used interchangeably.

Mailbox Property Pages

The property pages of a mailbox, or any recipient object, are accessed in one of two ways. With a mailbox highlighted, you can use the File menu and the Properties option to access the property pages. A quicker way is to simply double-click on the mailbox object; this will also bring up the property pages of that particular mailbox. The property pages of a mailbox object are listed in this section, with some of the individual attributes also discussed.

General Page This page records general information about the mailbox, such as name, title, company, department, and address (see Figure 5.1). The following information is on this page:

- **Display name** This is the name of the mailbox that will be seen in the Administrator window and the GAL. By default, the display name is automatically generated by combining the first and last name values. For example, if a first name is "Sue," and a last name is "Todd," then the display name would be "Sue Todd." The display name can also be manually edited.

- **Alias** This is a name that will be used to generate foreign e-mail addresses for this mailbox. By default, the alias name is automatically generated by using the primary NT account as the mailbox alias. For example, if the NT account name was "STodd," then the alias would be "STodd." The alias can also be manually edited.

- **Primary Windows NT Account** This is the NT user account that is associated with this mailbox.

- **Home server** This is the Microsoft Exchange Server on which this mailbox will physically reside. If a server is not specified by the administrator, the Administrator program assumes the home server is the one to which the Administrator program is currently attached.

FIGURE 5.1

The General page of a mailbox

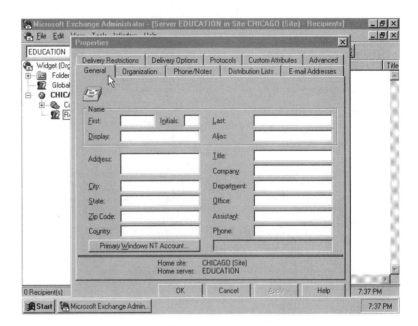

The Exchange administrator can determine the default naming convention that will be used to automatically generate the display name and alias. These default naming conventions are configured in the Exchange Administrator program under the Tools menu and Options submenu and the Auto Naming property page. Standard naming conventions that could be used include "first last" (e.g. Sue Todd), "last, first" (e.g. Todd, Sue), and "first initials last" (e.g. Sue L. Todd). A custom naming convention could also be entered by the administrator. For example, if new display names needed to be last name followed by the initial of the first name, the administrator could enter "%Last %1First" (the percent sign is the symbol for a variable). If a mailbox was created for Sue Todd with this naming convention, her display name would be "ToddS." The display name and alias name generation can have separate naming conventions.

Organization Page   This page contains optional information about listing the manager of the mailbox user, and any *direct reports* of the mailbox user (i.e., people the mailbox owner manages).

Phone/Notes Page   This page contains information on phone numbers, including business, home, fax, mobile, page, and others.

Permissions Page   This page allows you to view and configure the permissions that users and groups have for this mailbox. It should be noted that multiple users could be assigned as the owner of a mailbox. This is useful when you want to create a mailbox that will be used by a group of people, such as a help desk department. A single mailbox could be created and all users of that department could be made an owner of that mailbox.

Distribution Lists Property Page   This page specifies the distribution lists of which this mailbox is a member.

E-mail Addresses Page   Each time an Exchange mailbox is created, a number of non-Exchange mail addresses, also called foreign mail addresses or proxy addresses, are automatically generated for that Exchange mailbox. This allows Exchange mailboxes to be prepared to receive mail from foreign mail systems. Microsoft Exchange automatically generates foreign addresses for the following systems:

- Lotus cc:Mail

- Microsoft Mail

- SMTP

- X.400

If an administrator does not want a particular e-mail address generated for new mailboxes, they can disable that type of address through the Site Addressing properties. This will be covered in Chapter 12.

Delivery Restrictions Page   This page contains information regarding from whom this mailbox will accept or reject messages. The default is to accept messages from everyone (All), and reject messages from nobody (None).

Delivery Options Page This page can specify a list of users who can send mail "on behalf of" this mailbox user. It also allows mail sent to this mailbox to be rerouted to another mailbox, referred to as an *alternate recipient*. The alternate recipient feature can be configured to receive mail instead of the original mailbox, or along with the original mailbox.

Protocols Page This page can specify various message protocols and character sets that can be used with this mailbox. Two of the message protocols supported by an Exchange mailbox are POP3 and NNTP (these two protocols are discussed further in Chapter 11). Protocol options for encoding messages include:

- **MIME** (Multipurpose Internet Mail Extensions) This is a popular Internet protocol for including multimedia data like graphics, sound, animation, etc. in a mail message.

- **BINHEX** (Binary Hex) This protocol is popular with Apple computers.

- **UUENCODE** (UNIX-to-UNIX Encode) This is a popular Internet protocol for encoding binary data in a mail message.

- **Microsoft Exchange rich-text format**

Options for character sets include:

- **US-ASCII**

- **Various foreign language character sets**

Custom Attributes Page This page permits the viewing of any unique properties that have been defined in the DS Site Configuration object. An administrator can create up to ten custom-made properties. Examples could be employee identification numbers, birthdays, hobbies, bowling averages, or any other information a company might want to store. After the custom attributes have been created, these property fields can be displayed and filled in on every recipient in a site through the Custom Attributes property page.

Advanced Page Figure 5.2 depicts the Advanced property page.

FIGURE 5.2

The Advanced property
page of a mailbox

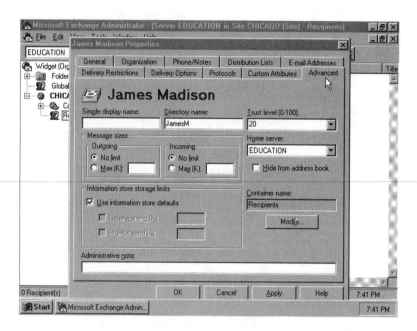

FIGURE 5.2

The Advanced property
page of a mailbox

The following attribute fields are found on the Advanced property page:

- **Simple Display Name** This mailbox name would be used by a non-Exchange mail system that cannot interpret all the characters that could be used in an Exchange mailbox name, such as spaces or characters like *Kanji* (which are icons used in the Japanese language).

- **Directory Name** This read-only field contains the name used for the mailbox within the Directory Service.

- **Trust level** (0-100) Directory synchronization is a process where directory information is exchanged between Exchange and a non-Exchange mail system, such as Microsoft Mail or Lotus cc:Mail. One factor that synchronization uses to determine what objects to synchronize is the trust level of the object. Directory synchronization will be further discussed in Chapter 15.

- **Message sizes** This property can set limits on the maximum outgoing and incoming message sizes (in kilobytes) for this object. The default is No limit.

- **Home server** The home server is the Exchange server on which this mailbox is physically stored.

- **Hide from address book** If this property is chosen, this mailbox name will not appear in the Global Address List, similar to an unlisted telephone number. Users can still send mail to this recipient, but they will need to know the mail address to manually enter it.

- **Information store limits** This property can be used to limit the storage used by this mailbox. The default is to use the server-wide settings.

- **Container name** This read-only field contains the name of the recipient's container where this object resides.

- **Administrative note** This field can contain any comments the administrator wants to enter.

Mailbox Roles

As mentioned earlier, the Permissions property page allows you to view and configure the permissions that users and groups have for this mailbox (see Figure 5.3). By default, the Permissions property tab is not seen, it is configured through Exchange Administrator to be hidden. To view this tab, you must open the Tools menu, the Options menu, and the Permissions tab. On the screen you will see an option stating "Show Permissions page for all objects." Check the option box if you want to see the Permissions tab for all Exchange objects. Exercise 5.1 outlines these steps in preparation for the following exercises on creating mailboxes.

EXERCISE 5.1

Configuring the Show Permissions Page

1. Start the Microsoft Exchange Administrator program by selecting Start ➢ Programs ➢ Microsoft Exchange ➢ Microsoft Exchange Administrator.

2. In order to view the Permissions page for any Exchange object, open Tools ➢ Options ➢ Permissions. Now check the box next to the option stating "Show Permissions page for all objects." Click OK.

FIGURE 5.3

The Permissions page of a
mailbox

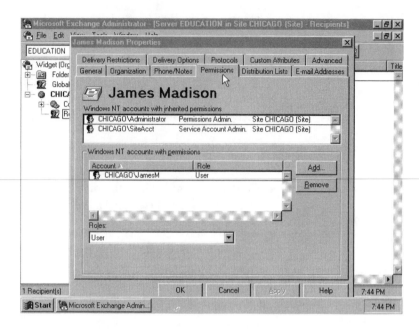

After you have completed Exercise 5.1, you will be able to see the Permissions tab for recipients. The first field on the Permissions page shows the Windows NT accounts with inherited permissions for this mailbox. This information is read-only. The second field on this page shows the Windows NT accounts with permissions, and allows the accounts and permissions to be edited. You assign permissions by giving a user or group a *role* for the mailbox. Roles are sets of permissions that define what activities a user or group can do with regards to this mailbox. Four roles are predefined, and you can create a custom role.

Admin. Role (Administrative)   The Admin. role includes two rights that allow all attributes of a mailbox to be modified. Those rights are:

- Modify User Attributes

- Modify Admin. Attributes

Permissions Admin.   The Permissions Admin. role includes three rights that allow all attributes and the permissions of a mailbox to be modified. Those rights are:

- Modify User Attributes

- Modify Admin. Attributes

- Modify Permissions

Send As   The Send As role includes one right that allows another user or group member to send mail addressed from this mailbox.

User   The User role, which is the default permission, includes the following three rights:

- Modify User Attributes

- Send As

- Mailbox Owner

The Mailbox Owner right permits a user or group to use this mailbox and receive mail. The user account that is automatically given this right is the primary NT account assigned to this mailbox on the General page.

Now that you know the property pages and attributes of a mailbox, we can proceed with the promised exercises on the different methods of creating a mailbox. Exercise 5.2 outlines the steps in creating and configuring a mailbox through the Microsoft Exchange Administrator program.

EXERCISE 5.2

Creating and Configuring a Mailbox through the Exchange Administrator Program

1. Highlight the Recipients container in the left pane.

2. Select File menu ➣ New Mailbox. A Properties window will appear with a number of property tabs relating to a mailbox.

3. On the property tab that is open, the General tab, locate the Name area of the page and enter the name **George** in the First field. In the Last field enter the name **Washington**. Notice that the Display field and the Alias field are automatically completed.

4. You may enter information into the Address fields (such as City: Mount Vernon and State: Virginia) and into the Title field (such as President).

5. Click the Primary Windows NT Account button. A window labeled "Primary Windows NT Account" will appear. Two radio buttons will be on this window. Select the second radio button, labeled "Create a New Windows NT Account." Then click OK. Another dialog box, labeled "Create Windows NT Account," will appear. Select the NT domain in which you want to create this new account. Then, if you like, you may edit the Account Name that has been generated automatically for you (which in this case is GeorgeW). When you are finished, click OK. A dialog box labeled "Microsoft Exchange Administrator" will appear stating "The password for the Windows NT Account you just created was given a blank password. The user will be required to change the password upon first logon." After reading the message, click OK.

6. You may click on the Organization tab and the Phone/Notes tab. Feel free to enter any information you like.

7. Click on the Permissions tab to view the accounts that have permissions to this mailbox. You will see that your site service account has inherited the role of Service Account Admin., and that GeorgeW has the permissions associated with the User role.

8. Click on the E-mail Addresses tab to view the non-Exchange addresses that the System Attendant automatically generates for each Exchange recipient.

9. You may click on the remaining property tabs. Feel free to add any information you want.

Exercise 5.3 will take you through the steps for creating a mailbox through the Windows NT User Manager for Domains program.

EXERCISE 5.3

Creating and Configuring a Mailbox through the Windows NT User Manager for Domains Program

1. Start the User Manager for Domains program by clicking on Start ➤ Programs ➤ Administrative Tools ➤ User Manager for Domains.

2. While in User Manager for Domains, click on User ≻ New User. The New User dialog box will appear, giving you the ability to input the information you want associated with this new user.

3. The only field that requires information is the Username field. Enter the name **JohnA**. In the Full Name field, enter the name **John Adams**. Enter any other information you would like in any of the other fields.

4. Click Add. The next dialog box you will see will be labeled "JohnA Properties." This is the Exchange properties page for a mailbox for the user JohnA.

5. Enter **John** in the First name field and **Adams** in the Last name field. Notice the Primary Windows NT Account that will be associated with this mailbox, JohnA. Enter any other information you would like in any of the other fields or property tabs.

6. Click OK. You will then be taken back to User Manager for Domains for the creation of any additional user accounts. In preparation for future exercises, create two additional users called Thomas Jefferson and James Madison. Using the same naming conventions (ThomasJ and JamesM), create mailboxes for both users. When you are finished, click Close.

7. Go to the Microsoft Exchange Administrator program and examine the JohnA mailbox.

Exercise 5.4 shows you the steps to extract all the Windows NT user accounts in the specified domain and prepare that information for the creation of mailboxes for those users. In preparation for this exercise, make sure you have created some users who do not have Exchange mailboxes. If you want to follow our Presidents theme and have the same screen information that this book will have, then create users called JamesM (James Monroe), JohnQA (John Quincy Adams), and AndrewJ (Andrew Jackson). Do not create mailboxes for these users now. You will do that in Exercise 5.5.

EXERCISE 5.4

Extracting User Information in Preparation for Creating a Mailbox

1. While in the Microsoft Exchange Administrator program, click on Tools ≻ Extract Windows NT Account List. The Windows NT User Extraction screen will appear.

2. Choose the domain and domain controller from which you want to extract user accounts.

3. Click Browse. In the File name field, you must enter a file name for the information that will be extracted. Choose the file name exercise.csv. Click Save.

4. Click OK. The extraction will now take place. If it is successful, you will see an information dialog box labeled "NT User Extractor Complete" and stating "Extraction of Windows NT user account information to file C:\exchsrvr\bin\exercise.csv is complete. No errors were encountered." Click OK. The next step is the import, which is found in Exercise 5.5.

Now that the Windows NT user account information has been prepared, it can be imported and used to create Exchange mailboxes for those user accounts. Exercise 5.5 shows those steps.

EXERCISE 5.5

Importing Extracted Windows NT User Accounts and Creating Exchange Mailboxes

1. While in the Microsoft Exchange Administrator program, click on Tools ≻ Directory Import. The Directory Import dialog box will appear.

2. Choose the domain that you chose in Exercise 5.4 and the Exchange server on which you want the mailboxes created.

3. Click Import File. This will enable you to choose the extraction file that has the information you want to import. Choose the exercise.csv file and then click Open.

4. Click Import to start the import process. If the import is successful, you will see an information dialog box labeled "Directory Import Complete" and stating "The directory import from file C:\exchsrvr\bin\ exercise.csv is complete. No errors were encountered." Click OK.

5. To confirm the import, go to the main screen of the Exchange Administrator program, and locate a user account that did not have a mailbox, for example, AndrewJ. You will see that mailboxes have indeed been created for those accounts. Double-click on one of the names to bring up its property pages. Notice that many of the mailbox attributes are blank. You can input information for those attributes. You also could have used a mailbox template during the import process.

Distribution Lists

A distribution list (DL) is a grouping of recipients. A single DL object can represent a number of other recipients. This allows easy mass mailing. You can send a message to a DL and all the members of that DL will receive a copy of your message. An electronic distribution list is light-years more efficient than the old paper-based distribution list stapled to a memo or report that moved from person to person.

Creating and Configuring a Distribution List

Creating and configuring a DL object is very simple. While in the Microsoft Exchange Administrator program, choose the File menu and then the New Distribution List option. You will then be presented with various property pages. Following an explanation of DL properties, Exercise 5.6 will list the steps in creating and configuring a DL.

Properties of a Distribution List

Two property pages connected to distribution lists need to be explained: the General property page and the Advanced property page. We have already discussed the other property pages.

General Property Page

The General property page (see Figure 5.4) contains some of the basic attributes of a distribution list.

FIGURE 5.4

The General properties
page of a distribution list

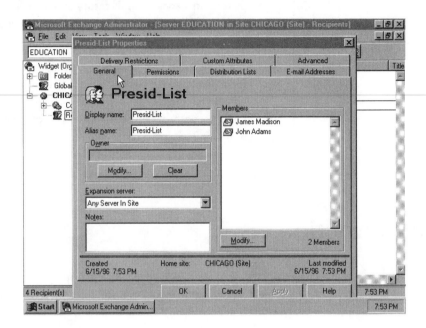

The basic attributes are:

- **Display name**   This is the name that will be seen in the Address Book.

- **Alias name**   This is a shorter name that can be used to refer to the DL and is used to generate some of the non-Exchange addresses for this distribution list.

- **Members**   This is the list of the recipients who are included in this distribution list.

- **Owner**   This is the recipient who owns and therefore manages this distribution list. The owner can modify the membership of the distribution list from an Exchange client, without having administrative rights.

- **Expansion server** When a message is sent to a distribution list, a server must *expand* the distribution list into its individual members in order for them to receive the message. Expanding the distribution list entails verifying that members do exist and determining a routing plan to distribute the message. This field lets you specify the server to carry out the functions of the expansion server. The default selection is "Any Server In Site," which means that any server in the site where the DL is homed can execute the expansion server functions. This process can be processor-intensive, so sometimes it is good practice to isolate one server in the site (perhaps with few or no user mailboxes) that will be responsible for all DL expansion in that site.

- **Notes** This field lets you enter additional information, up to 256 characters.

Advanced Property Page

Figure 5.5 illustrates the Advanced property page of a DL.

FIGURE 5.5

The Advanced page of a distribution list

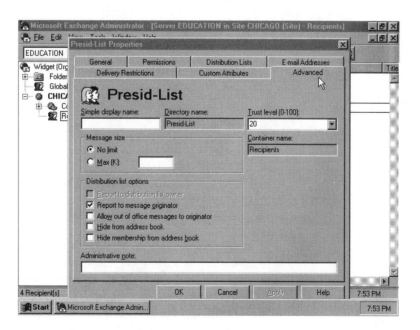

The following attribute fields are contained on the Advanced property page of a DL:

- **Simple display name**   This name will appear to non-Exchange clients that cannot read all the Exchange display name characters, such as spaces or Kanji characters.

- **Directory name**   This read-only field contains the name used for the DL within the Directory Service database.

- **Trust level** (0-100)   As we saw with mailboxes, the directory synchronization process exchanges directory information with non-Exchange mail systems. One of the factors this process uses to determine what objects to synchronize is the trust level of the object.

- **Message sizes**   This property can set limits on the maximum size (in kilobytes) of messages sent to this object. The default is No limit.

- **Container name**   This read-only field contains the name of the recipients container where this object resides.

- **Distribution list options**   This section of the Advanced page has options for the following:

  - **Report to distribution list owner**   If checked, this option notifies the distribution list owner when a message sent to the DL has requested a delivery notification or is undeliverable. By default, this is not checked.

  - **Report to message originator**   If checked, this option sends a separate delivery status notification for each DL member to a user who sends a message to the DL. When this option is not checked, a message originator receives reports from the list itself, not notification for each member. By default, this is checked.

  - **Allow out of office messages to originator**   "Out of Office" is an intelligent agent mechanism of a mailbox. This mechanism allows the owner of the mailbox to notify senders that they are unavailable to read messages (see Chapter 7). If checked, this option sends an Out of Office notification to the sender of a message to this DL on behalf of any members of this list who have enabled their Out of Office setting.

- **Hide from address book**   If this property is chosen, this distribution list will not appear in the Global Address List, in a fashion similar to an unlisted phone number. Users can still send mail to the DL, but they will have to know the DL name and manually enter it.

- **Hide membership from address book**   If this option is checked, the name of this distribution list will appear in the Global Address List, but the individual members of the list will not appear when its properties are viewed.

Exercise 5.6 outlines the steps for creating and configuring a distribution list.

EXERCISE 5.6

Creating and Configuring a Distribution List

1. While in Microsoft Exchange Administrator, select File ➢ New Distribution List. A Properties dialog box will appear with a number of property tabs relating to a distribution list. (If you do not have the Recipients object highlighted in the left pane when you create a new recipient, you will see the message: "Recipients cannot be created in the selected parent container. Do you want to switch to the 'Recipients' container of the site <site name>?" If you click OK, your view in the Exchange Administrator will change to the Recipients container and the Properties pages for the recipient you want to create will appear.)

2. On the General tab, locate the field labeled "Display name" and enter **SalesReps**. Enter the same information in the Alias field.

3. In the Members field, click Modify. In the left list box that contains a listing of Exchange recipients, choose a number of those recipients. One way to do this is to hold down the Control key and click on the recipients you want added as members of this distribution list. After you have selected the recipients, click Add to make them members of the distribution list. As soon as you are finished, click OK.

4. Find the field labeled "Expansion server," and click on the down-arrow to display a list of Exchange servers in the site. You may choose a specific Exchange server to be the expansion server, or leave the default, which is "Any Server In Site."

5. If you have any comments, enter them in the Notes field.

6. When you are finished, click OK.

Custom Recipients

A custom recipient is the address of a non-Exchange mail recipient. The custom recipients are part of the Exchange Global Address List, and therefore permit Exchange clients to send messages to non-Exchange mail users. This also assumes that the necessary connector or gateway is in place between the Exchange system and the foreign system.

Creating and Configuring a Custom Recipient

Custom recipients are created through the Exchange Administrator program, using the File menu and the New Custom Recipient option. You are prompted to select the type of e-mail address to create, and to enter the foreign e-mail address. The standard options for the types of foreign addresses are:

- cc:Mail address

- Microsoft Mail address

- MacMail address (this is Microsoft Mail for AppleTalk)

- Internet address

- X.400 address

- Other address

After an explanation of the properties of a custom recipient, Exercise 5.7 will walk you through the creation and configuration of this type of recipient.

Properties of a Custom Recipient

The properties of a custom recipient are very similar to those of a standard Exchange mailbox. The main difference is that you will be prompted to input the foreign mail address of the custom recipient. This address will be in the format of the foreign mail system (for example, joesmith@widget.com). In this example, joesmith is the username, and widget.com is the domain name.

After inputting the non-Exchange address of the custom recipient, you will be presented with the standard property pages seen with a mailbox recipient. Exercise 5.7 outlines the steps to create and configure a custom recipient.

EXERCISE 5.7

Creating and Configuring a Custom Recipient

1. While in the Exchange Administrator program, select File ➢ New Custom Recipient.

2. The New E-mail Address dialog box appears next. For this exercise, choose the Internet Address option. Then click OK.

3. The next screen to appear will be the Internet Address Properties screen. Type an Internet address, such as:

   joesmith@widget.com.

4. When you are finished, click on the OK button.

5. The Properties dialog box appears next. This dialog box presents the various property pages relating to a custom recipient. On the General page, the only mandatory fields are the Display field, and the Alias field. Feel free to fill in any fields on this page or any of the other property pages for this recipient.

6. When you finish inputting information for this recipient, click OK.

Public Folder Recipients

A public folder is a sharable container of information. It is a recipient object because, in addition to being able to view information in it, users can send information to it. Public folders have four main features:

- **Permissions** Public folders can have various levels of security attached to them. For example, a particular public folder could allow one group of users to read and add information, while another group is limited to only reading information.

- **Forms** Electronic forms can be associated with a public folder to provide a format for entering information to the public folder, or to provide a way to view information in the public folder.

- **Views**   In order to better organize and find information, a public folder can be configured by various views, such as by sender, recipient, subject, and time frame.

- **Rules**   A public folder can be configured with rules that pertain to the automatic processing of information sent to it. Actions that could be automatically performed on an incoming message include deleting it, moving it, forwarding it, and replying with a specified message.

Like mailbox objects, public folders are created and stored on a specific home server. But because users on different servers and in different sites could need access to that public folder, public folders can be configured to be copied automatically to other Exchange servers. This is called *replication,* and each copy of the same public folder is called a *replica* (more on this topic in Chapter 9).

While the other recipients are created from the Microsoft Exchange Administrator program, public folders are created through the various Microsoft Exchange client applications, such as the Microsoft Exchange Client and Microsoft Outlook. Many of the properties of a public folder can also be configured through the client software. Because the installation of the Exchange client applications has not yet been covered, the creation and configuration of public folders will be covered in Chapter 9.

Basic Management of Recipient Objects

Even after they have been created, recipient objects still require care from administrators. Some of those basic management activities are:

- Using templates for mailbox creation

- Finding a recipient

- Moving a recipient

- Cleaning a mailbox

- Modifying recipients in a batch process

Each of those activities will be covered briefly in the following discussions.

Using Templates for Mailbox Creation

A *template* is a pattern that can be used to more efficiently create something, in this case, a mailbox. A template mailbox, or multiple template mailboxes, can be created with the desired default values. These default values can then be used when creating mailboxes through the Duplicate command, Directory Import command, or Migration programs, which all can use a template.

Any mailbox can be used as a template. But no matter what mailbox is used, the first name, last name, display name, alias name, directory name, and e-mail address are not copied to the new mailbox or mailboxes.

A template mailbox is created in exactly the same manner as a user's mailbox, by using the Exchange Administrator program, File menu, New Mailbox option. The properties and values that will be the default are then entered. The template mailboxes should be named something that clearly expresses the nature of the mailbox. They could also be hidden from the GAL so mail is not accidentally sent to them.

Finding a Recipient

The Find Recipients function in the Exchange Administrator program has a function that can search for recipients anywhere in the organization. This function is found in the Tools menu, Find Recipients option. Search criteria can be inputted such as first name, last name, title, department, and others. See Figure 5.6 for an illustration of the Find Recipients window.

FIGURE 5.6

The Find Recipients window

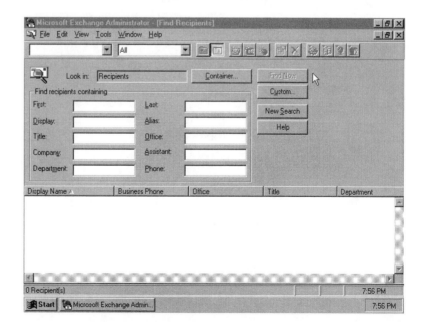

Moving a Mailbox

Mailboxes and their contents physically reside on their home server. Mailboxes can be moved to other servers within the same site. This is done through the Administrator program by highlighting the mailbox in the Contents window (the right window pane), selecting the Tools menu, the Move Mailbox option, and choosing the new server to hold the mailbox.

When moving mailboxes to a new home server, the size of the mailbox contents can increase. This is because when a message is sent to multiple recipients homed on the same server, Exchange stores only one copy of the message on the server, and gives all the recipients on that server a pointer to that single copy. This is called *single-instance storage*. But when a mailbox is moved to another server, the single-instance storage for that mailbox is lost on the new home server because each message must be copied into that mailbox.

For example, if you wanted to move 10 mailboxes, each one containing five messages of 1 MB each, and containing a pointer to five single-instance messages of 1 MB each, the size of the Private Information Store on the new home server would increase by 100 MB (10 mailboxes times 10 MB of mailbox storage).

Mailboxes can also be manually moved to a new home server in a different site. This is done by copying the mailbox contents to a personal folder and then copying that personal folder to the new mailbox in the new site. However, if other recipients try to use the Reply function to a message sent before a mailbox was manually moved, the message will not be delivered because the mailbox that is referenced no longer exists.

Mailboxes might be moved for several reasons:

- To balance the load between servers

- To move mailboxes to a server that is on the same local area network as the mailbox owners

- To take a server down for maintenance reasons and still allow users access to their mailboxes

Because distribution lists and custom recipients are purely logical entities, they do not need to be moved, and therefore cannot be moved.

Cleaning a Mailbox

Cleaning a mailbox refers to deleting certain messages stored in the mailbox. This function is found in the Administrator program, Tools menu, Clean Mailbox option. The administrator can select various criteria and input values to be used in the cleaning process (see Figure 5.7). Some of the criteria are:

- All messages older than (days)

- All messages greater than (K)

- Read items

- Unread items

FIGURE 5.7

The Clean Mailbox
dialog box

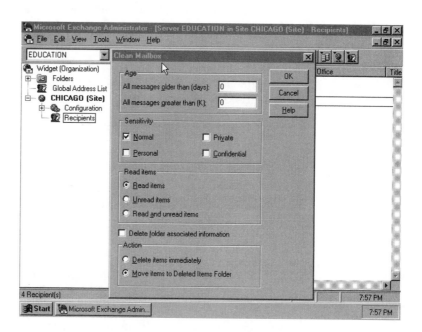

The administrator also has the option to delete the specified messages immediately, or to have them moved to the Deleted Items Folder.

Modifying Recipients in a Batch Process

There could be instances where a large number of Exchange recipients need to be modified. For example, you might need to change the area code of the business telephone attribute for all your recipients. This could obviously be done by modifying each individual recipient, but there is an easier way. You could use the Directory Export and Directory Import utilities to perform these modifications in a batch process.

The Directory Export utility, located on the Tools menu in Exchange Administrator, can be used to export the properties of all your recipients to an export file. An export file is a text file in comma-separated value format (the file extension of an export file is .CSV for comma-separated value). The format of the export file allows it to be read by many different applications, such as Microsoft Excel. An example of this file's format is seen below:

```
Obj-Class,Mode,Display Name,Alias Name,E-mail addresses,
    Telephone-Office1

Mailbox,modify,Mike Andrews,MAndrews,SMTP:MAndrews@widget.com,
    201-555-6161

Mailbox,modify,Amy Smith,ASmith,SMTP:ASmith@widget.com,201-555-6161
```

The header line lists the object class (e.g. mailbox, distribution list, etc.), the mode (e.g. create, modify), and the various attributes. The remaining lines list the objects and their properties that have been exported.

This export file could then be opened by an application, such as Microsoft Excel, in order to modify or add to the contents of the file. For example, you could modify the value for the attribute of "Telephone Office1" (the business telephone number) by using the Excel features of sorting and macros to replace the old area code with the new one for every recipient in this export file.

Once the export file has been modified, the Directory Import utility could take this file (now called the import file) and copy those recipients back into the Exchange Directory. If you have multiple users to modify, this could be a good way to accomplish it.

Summary

Recipients are objects that can receive information. The four main types of recipients are:

- Mailboxes

- Distribution lists

- Custom recipients

- Public folders

A mailbox is a storage location on an Exchange server that allows information to be sent, received, and organized. E-mail messages, forms, and file attachments are some of the typical types of information that can be sent to and stored in a mailbox.

A distribution list is a grouping of recipients. A single distribution list can represent a number of other recipients. This allows easy mass mailing. A message sent to a distribution list can be read by all the members of that distribution list.

A custom recipient is a non-Exchange e-mail address to which Exchange clients can send mail. An Internet user who has a connection to an Exchange server could have an e-mail address defined on the Exchange system. This is an example of a custom recipient and permits Exchange clients to send mail to that Internet user.

A public folder is like a public mailbox. It is an information container that can hold files and forms that multiple users can access.

Review Questions

1. The Microsoft Exchange Administrator program is the only method for creating Exchange mailboxes.

   A. True

   B. False

2. The following is an example of a mailbox attribute:

    A. Operating system

    B. Groups

    C. Server operating system

    D. Home server

3. Permissions to a mailbox are assigned through:

    A. Roles

    B. UNIX permissions

    C. Custom recipients

    D. DLs

4. The following permits easy mass mailing:

    A. A mailbox with multiple owners

    B. Distribution list

    C. A mailbox with multiple users

    D. A mailbox set to forward messages

5. Within the Exchange environment, a foreign mail user would be this type of Exchange recipient:

    A. Mailbox

    B. A member of the Custom distribution list

    C. Custom recipient

    D. A mailbox with a foreign owner

6. An expansion server is the server that sends e-mail messages to their destinations.

   A. True

   B. False

7. Public folders are created in the Microsoft Exchange Administrator program.

   A. True

   B. False

8. Which of the following does NOT relate to a feature of a public folder?

   A. Views

   B. Rules

   C. Permissions

   D. Expansion Server

9. Copies of the same public folder located on several Exchange servers are called:

   A. Clones

   B. Clone folders

   C. Folder images

   D. Replicas

10. A mailbox can be created that uses the settings of an existing mailbox.

   A. True

   B. False

11. This menu option relates to selectively deleting messages in a mailbox:

   A. Clean Mailbox

   B. Purge Mailbox

   C. Delete Mailbox

   D. Remove Mailbox

12. This feature of a mailbox allows it to store and send messages containing formatting, such as underlining, bolding, and fonts:

   A. Font format

   B. Word format

   C. Rich-text format

   D. Data compression

13. Microsoft NT User Manager for Domains can be used to create Exchange mailboxes.

   A. True

   B. False

14. This type of program assists in the creation of mailboxes for NetWare users:

   A. Extract tool

   B. NetWare synchtool

   C. Microsoft-NetWare synchronization tool

   D. Cannot be done

15. The default permission for the primary NT account of a mailbox is:

   A. Admin. role

   B. Send as

   C. Permissions Admin.

   D. User

C H A P T E R

6

The Architecture and Installation
of the Microsoft Exchange Clients

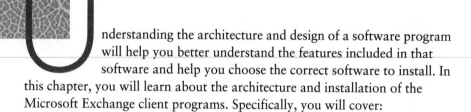

nderstanding the architecture and design of a software program will help you better understand the features included in that software and help you choose the correct software to install. In this chapter, you will learn about the architecture and installation of the Microsoft Exchange client programs. Specifically, you will cover:

- Client platforms for Microsoft Exchange

- Additional information on the MAPI architecture

- Microsoft Exchange Client

- Microsoft Schedule+

- Microsoft Outlook

- Installation of the Microsoft Exchange clients

Client Platforms for Microsoft Exchange

The very first order of business is to define what is meant by *clients* for Microsoft Exchange. The best way to do that is to compare and contrast an Exchange client to an Exchange correspondent (this term is the author's). An Exchange client application has the ability to access an Exchange mailbox as the owner of that mailbox, whereas an Exchange correspondent has only the ability to send and receive mail to and from an Exchange user. If an Exchange mailbox was a physical mailbox at the post office, a client would have the key for accessing their mailbox, while a correspondent would only be able to send mail to that mailbox or receive mail from it. An example of a client application is Microsoft

Outlook, and Lotus cc:Mail is an example of an application that could only correspond with an Exchange mailbox. This latter functionality is enabled through Microsoft Exchange connectors or gateways. Applications that can only correspond with Exchange are also referred to as foreign mail clients, and are the type of clients that are made a custom recipient within Exchange. This allows Exchange users to send mail to foreign mail users. (Exchange interoperability with foreign systems is covered in Chapters 14 and 15.)

There are two main Exchange client application architectures:

- **MAPI (Messaging Application Programming Interface)** MAPI is the Microsoft API used for messaging functions. Examples of MAPI client applications that ship with Microsoft Exchange Server are:

  - Microsoft Exchange Client (versions available for MS-DOS, Windows 3.x, Apple Macintosh, Windows 95, and Windows NT)

  - Microsoft Schedule+ 7.5

  - Microsoft Outlook (designed for Windows 95 and Windows NT)

- **Internet protocols** Some Internet applications can also be used as clients to Microsoft Exchange. Examples are:

  - Internet mail applications that support Post Office Protocol 3 (POP3)

  - Web browsers (e.g., Microsoft Internet Explorer, Netscape Navigator)

The forms design tools, Microsoft Exchange Forms Designer and Microsoft Outlook Forms Designer, are also MAPI clients that ship with Microsoft Exchange Server, but they will be discussed in Chapter 8.

The Internet clients are discussed in Chapter 11. This chapter covers the MAPI client applications. Figure 6.1 illustrates foreign mail users communicating with Exchange, and Figure 6.2 illustrates Exchange clients.

FIGURE 6.1

Foreign mail user
communication with
Exchange

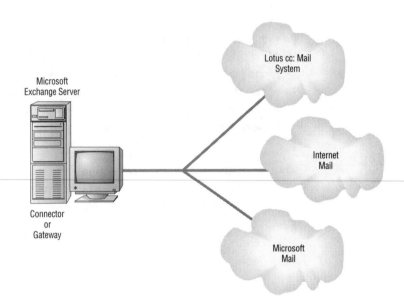

FIGURE 6.2

Exchange clients

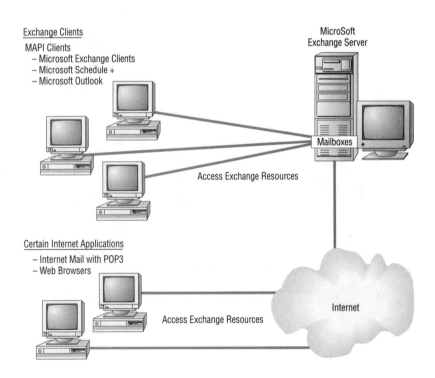

MAPI Architecture

Many messaging systems are divided into a *client-side* and a *server-side*. The client-side provides an interface to users and permits them to read, save, create, and send mail. The server-side programs carry out the client requests. For example, if a client issues a read request for a certain message, the server responds by transmitting the message to the client. The client software is sometimes referred to as the *front-end* to the server software, which can be referred to as the *back-end*. The front-end programs can be thought of as consumers, and the back-end programs as producers.

Historically, messaging systems have been implemented using "closed" application programming interfaces (APIs). An API is a collection of instructions, also called *function calls*. When a user wants to read a message stored on the server, the client program issues the relevant API function call and the server responds accordingly.

The problem with the closed API model is that it is proprietary and different vendors have their own APIs. When someone writes a client program to be used with one of these proprietary systems, it will only work with that system. With this architecture, multiple client programs are needed to connect to multiple messaging systems (see Figure 6.3).

Microsoft decided to remedy this situation by creating a standard messaging architecture, known as MAPI. MAPI provides a way for client messaging applications to communicate with multiple messaging systems (see Figure 6.4). Although MAPI is an abbreviation for Messaging Application Programming Interface, it is much more than an API. It is an architecture that specifies components, how they should act, and how they should interface with each other.

Figure 6.5 illustrates the basic architecture of MAPI. The top layer, the client application layer, includes client applications that enable users to perform messaging activities. These client applications are the front-end programs requesting services from the back-end server programs. Client applications can include different messaging services (such as e-mail, fax, voice mail, and paging), as long as they are written to the MAPI specification. The concept of having messages from multiple sources delivered to one place is referred to as the *universal inbox*.

FIGURE 6.3

FIGURE 6.3

Multiple client programs
for multiple message
systems

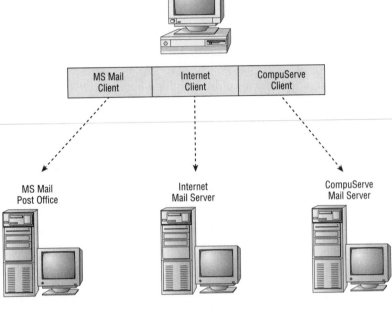

FIGURE 6.4

A single MAPI application
accessing multiple
message systems

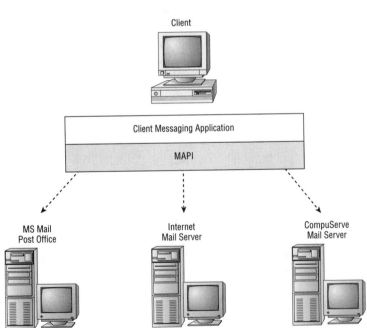

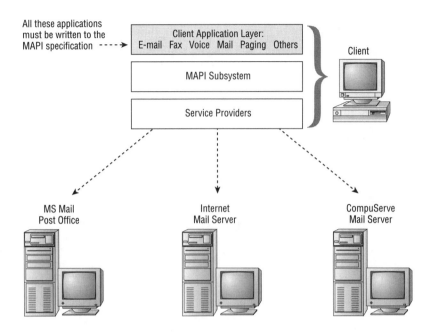

FIGURE 6.5

The Basic MAPI architecture

Previously, a single client program could not communicate with more than one server program, because the server programs all used different APIs. The MAPI architecture solves this limitation by providing a single layer through which the client programs and the server programs can communicate. This is the second layer and is called the MAPI subsystem (see Figure 6.6). The MAPI subsystem is referred to as *middleware,* because it acts as a broker between two other layers.

Server programs can still use their own APIs on the back-end. But the vendors of these programs must write a type of client component, called a *service provider,* that will interface their back-end system with the MAPI subsystem. Service providers comprise the third layer in the MAPI architecture (see Figure 6.7). Client software communicates with the MAPI subsystem, which communicates with a service provider, which communicates with the back-end message server. This is how a single client application, using multiple service providers, communicates with multiple back-end message servers.

Now we will turn our attention to the three basic layers of the MAPI architecture.

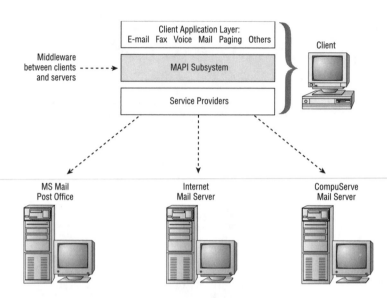

FIGURE 6.6

The MAPI subsystem

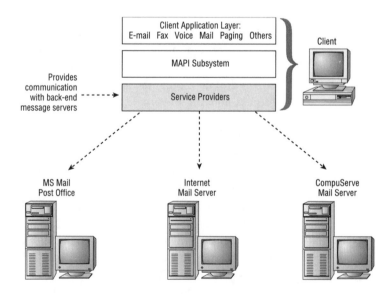

FIGURE 6.7

MAPI service providers

Client Application Layer

Client applications that need to perform messaging functions can be implemented through the usage of MAPI function calls. Examples of these calls are MAPIReadMail, MAPISaveMail, and MAPISendMail. When these instructions are executed in a client application, they initiate an action in the MAPI subsystem, which then interfaces with service providers, which interface with a server messaging system, such as Microsoft Exchange Server or CompuServe Mail.

MAPI encompasses three major API sets:

- **Simple MAPI**   This is a set of 12 straightforward messaging functions, like reading (MAPIReadMail) and sending (MAPISendMail) messages. It is included in *messaging-aware* applications like Microsoft Word.

- **Common Mail Call (CMC)**   This is a set of 10 messaging functions similar to Simple MAPI. CMC is geared for cross-platform, operating system independent development. CMC was developed by the X.400 Applications Programming Interface Association (XAPIA).

- **MAPI 1.x** (also called Extended MAPI)   This is the newer, more powerful MAPI standard. It includes the abilities of Simple MAPI, but adds many other instructions for complex messaging functions, such as custom forms.

See Figure 6.8 for a depiction of these three APIs in the MAPI architecture.

These three API sets allow developers to create client messaging applications that fall into two broad categories:

- **Messaging-aware applications**   These are applications like Microsoft Word that have some messaging functions included, like a send option on the File Menu. Messaging is not essential to these applications. Simple MAPI or CMC is most conveniently used as the messaging API.

- **Messaging-based or messaging-enabled applications**   These are applications like Microsoft Outlook that require messaging functionality. The comprehensive function call set of Extended MAPI is normally required to implement these applications.

F I G U R E 6.8

The three MAPI API sets

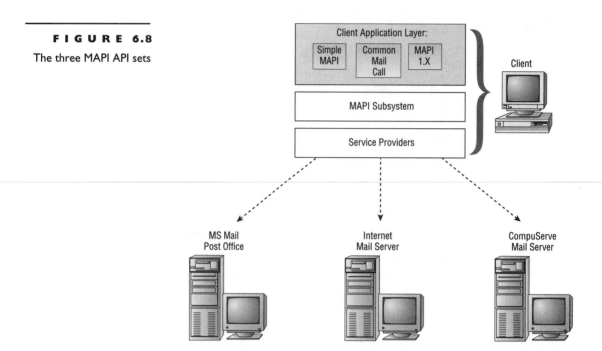

MAPI Subsystem

The second layer of the MAPI architecture is the MAPI subsystem (see Figure 6.9). This component is shared by all applications that require its services and is therefore considered a *subsystem* of the operating system. Microsoft includes the MAPI subsystem with the 32-bit Windows 95 and Windows NT operating systems, and the file MAPI32.DLL is the primary function library for these operating systems. The MAPI subsystem for 16-bit Windows 3.*x* is loaded with the installation of the Exchange client and the file MAPI.DLL is the primary function library.

The MAPI subsystem is also referred to as the *MAPI runtime.*

FIGURE 6.9

MAPI subsystem

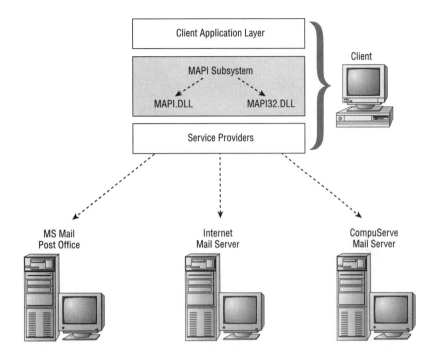

The MAPI subsystem provides a single interface for client applications. Communication with all MAPI compliant server messaging systems is facilitated by interfacing with the MAPI subsystem. It is the middleware or broker in the messaging environment. The subsystem manages memory, administers profiles, routes client requests to the relevant service provider, and returns results from servers via service providers.

The MAPI subsystem also presents a single, virtual address book and a single, virtual storage area to the user. As you will learn in the next section, multiple service providers can create multiple address books and multiple message stores. The MAPI subsystem presents all of these through a unified interface. Consequently, even though an e-mail program and a fax program are being used, the user can view all addresses in one virtual address book. Because all data can be kept in the same virtual storage area, users can organize information based upon logical categories (e.g., all communication from Jane) rather than by application (e.g., e-mail directory, fax directory, etc.).

MAPI Service Providers

The third layer contains components called service providers. These replaceable components (manifested as DLL files) communicate with the messaging system back-end. There are three main types of service providers:

- Address book providers

- Message store providers

- Message transport providers

The following three sections discuss these service providers.

A *provider* is sometimes called a *driver*.

Address Book Providers

An address book provider is a component that interacts with a database of message recipients. Some of these providers create their own address databases, called personal address books (PAB), others can access address books on a server. Address book providers can be written for many kinds of back-end systems; and because they all interface with the MAPI subsystem, a user can still have a single, virtual address book.

The following are three examples of address book providers:

- **Global Address List (GAL)**   This provider enables a client application to view an Exchange server's Global Address List (GAL). The GAL is a database of all the recipients in an Exchange organization, such as mailboxes, distribution lists, custom recipients, and public folders.

- **Personal Address Book (PAB)**   This provider, also called the Local Address Book, enables the creation of a customized address book. Users can include frequently used e-mail addresses, as well as custom recipients and distribution lists the user creates. Message recipients are not the only type of information that can be stored. Phone and fax numbers, postal addresses, and other information can be stored here. This address book can be stored on the user's machine or on a server. The file extension of this address book is PAB, for Personal Address Book.

- **Offline Address Book (OAB)**   This address book provider permits an Exchange server's GAL to be downloaded to a user's machine. This can be useful when working offline. The file extension of this local database is OAB, for Offline Address Book.

See Figure 6.10 for a depiction of the address book providers in the MAPI architecture.

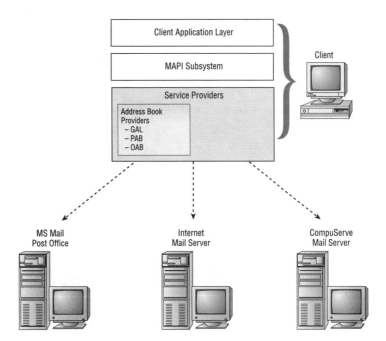

FIGURE 6.10

Address book providers

Message Store Providers

Message store providers are components that manage a database of messages. This entails client message storage, organization, submission for sending, and retrieval of messages and attachments. Storage is organized in a hierarchical tree of folders. Views can be created to allow the user to see messages based on certain criteria, like subject or date. Searches can also be conducted to retrieve specific information.

Message store providers can use server-based storage or client-based storage. The following are three examples of message store providers (see Figure 6.11):

FIGURE 6.11

Message store providers

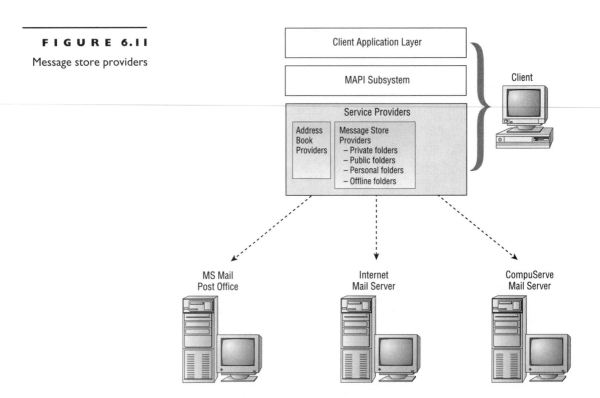

- **Private folders**   This provider enables client access to an assigned mailbox on an Exchange server (i.e., the home server of the mailbox). *Private folders* is another name for what is more commonly referred to as *mailboxes*. They are called "private" because they are, more often than not, associated with a single user (even though several users can be given permission to use a single mailbox). All private folders are stored on an Exchange server in the Private Information Store which is managed by the Information Store service. The advantages of this type of storage are compression, security, and centralized backup.

- **Public Folders**   Public folders are the groupware component of Exchange Server. This provider allows a client to access the hierarchical tree of public folder storage to which everyone in the Exchange organization has access. Public folders are stored on Exchange servers in the Public Information Store which is managed by the Information Store service.

- **Personal folders (PST, Personal STore)**   A personal folder store is a file-based storage container independent of the Exchange Server back-end. The file that comprises a set of personal folders has the PST extension. A PST file can be stored on the user's local machine or on a shared directory on a network server. As with private folders, a user can create a hierarchical tree of folders within a personal folder store. Up to 16,000 entries and 2GB of data can be placed in a personal folder store. Personal folder stores can be assigned a password for protection. Personal folders can also be designated as the location to where incoming mail messages are moved. Although all mail is always sent to private folders on an Exchange server first, users can configure their private folders to route messages to their personal folders. Because of storage technologies used in the Private Information Store, information moved from that location to a personal folder will take up more space in the personal folder.

Passwords assigned to a personal folder cannot be viewed by the Exchange administrator. Therefore, if a user forgets this password, the information in that folder is inaccessible.

- **Offline folders (OST, Offline STore)**   If mailbox storage is left in the default location (the Private Information Store) and offline access to that data is also needed, the user can utilize an offline folder. An offline folder is a local copy of the user's private folders from the Private Information Store. The mailbox on the server remains the master copy. Offline folders have the OST file extension.

Message Transport Providers

Message transport providers manage the physical transportation of messages between a MAPI client and a back-end system (see Figure 6.12). They are like gateway components. They take a MAPI message and translate it to the format of the back-end system and send it. They do the reverse for incoming messages.

Message transport providers work with any of the Microsoft supported network protocols, such as TCP/IP, IPX/SPX, and NetBEUI.

Examples of back-end systems that have message transport providers are:

- Microsoft Exchange Server

- Microsoft Network online service (MSN)

- Microsoft Fax

- Microsoft Mail

- Internet Mail

- CompuServe Mail

FIGURE 6.12

Message transport
providers

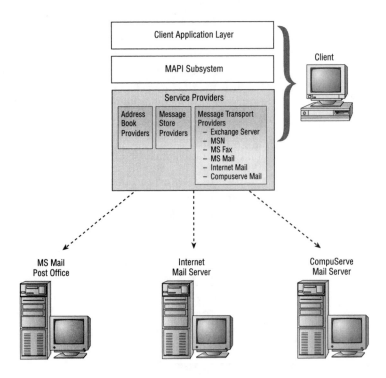

Message Spooler

The message spooler is an independent process that manages the flow of messages between the message store and the transport providers. It is like a queue where incoming and outgoing messages are sent, and from there are routed to the necessary provider. When a message is marked for sending, a message store provider will send it to the message spooler. The message spooler then selects, based on the destination address, a message transport provider that can send the message to the relevant messaging system.

Messaging Profiles

A messaging profile is a collection of configuration parameters for MAPI operations. The first time a user starts a MAPI-based application, the Profile Wizard runs and prompts for various operational parameters relating to messaging. For example, the user is prompted to choose the *information services* to be used, such as Microsoft Exchange Server, Microsoft Fax, Internet Mail, and others. Information services are collections of the various providers described earlier. The user is also prompted to configure his personal address book information service. Other information in the profile relates to message handling, such as saving sent mail or generating a delivery receipt. When the MAPI subsystem starts, it reads this profile to see what services to load and how to operate (see Figure 6.13).

A user can have several profiles for one particular machine. For example, a user's computer might be a laptop that is used both at the office and on the road. When at the office, the user profile connects the user to an Exchange server at the office. When traveling, a different profile connects the laptop to the Internet. (As you will learn in Chapter 10, you can also connect to an Exchange server through the Internet.) Multiple profiles for a particular machine are also useful when several people use the same machine.

Common Features of MAPI-Based Applications

Many common features are found in MAPI-based applications, including the following:

- **Universal inbox**   Information from multiple sources (e.g., Exchange Server, Internet, etc.) and of varying types (e.g., e-mail, faxes, documents, and voice mail) is delivered to a single Inbox folder.

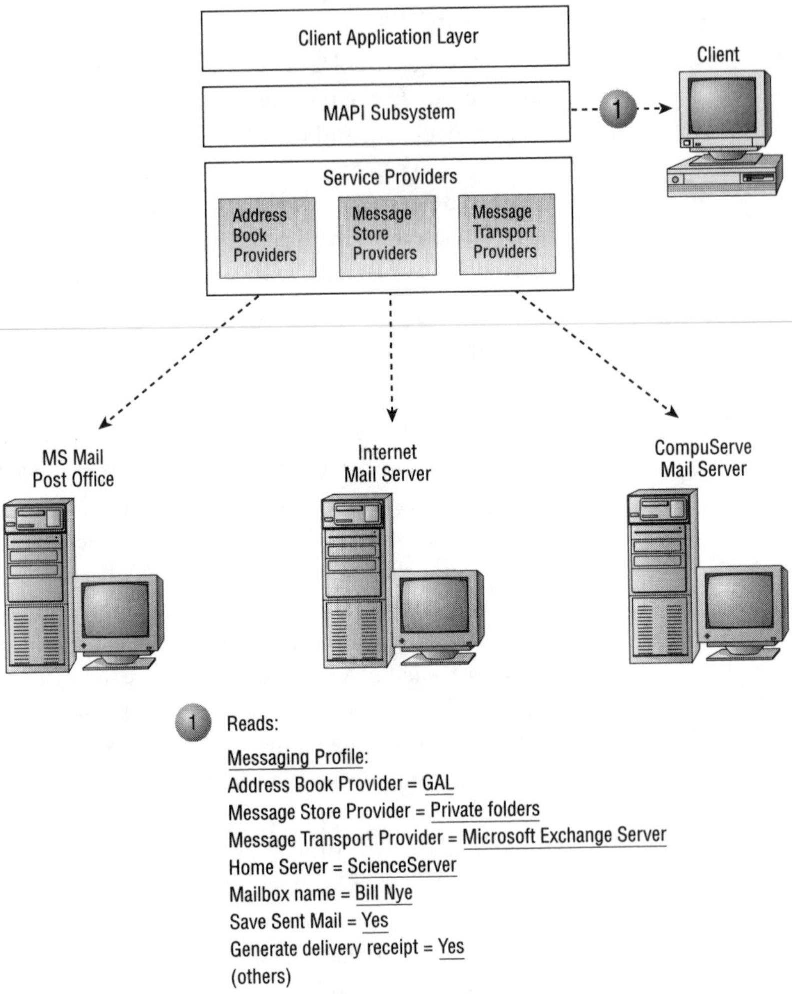
Client Application Layer
MAPI Subsystem
Client
Service Providers
Address Book Providers
Message Store Providers
Message Transport Providers
MS Mail Post Office
Internet Mail Server
CompuServe Mail Server
Reads:
Messaging Profile:
Address Book Provider = GAL
Message Store Provider = Private folders
Message Transport Provider = Microsoft Exchange Server
Home Server = ScienceServer
Mailbox name = Bill Nye
Save Sent Mail = Yes
Generate delivery receipt = Yes
(others)

FIGURE 6.13
Messaging profile

- **Single address book** A standard user interface to the address book is provided. Information from all the address books configured in the current profile is consolidated into one place.
- **Hierarchical storage** Messages and other items can be organized into a user-customizable hierarchical tree of folders. Four special folders are always present in the default store. They are the Inbox, Deleted Items, Sent Items, and Outbox folders.

- **Custom views**   Information stored in folders can be sorted and viewed using many types of criteria, such as author, date, keyword, or type of content.

- **Rich-text formatting**   Users can create message content that uses the rich-text format, which includes underlining, italic, bolding, bullet points, colors, fonts, different character sizes, and letter strikethrough.

Microsoft Exchange Client

The Microsoft Exchange Client is a feature-rich e-mail program designed to run in 16-bit environments like MS-DOS and Microsoft Windows 3.*x,* as well as the 32-bit Windows 95 and NT environments. There is also a version for the Apple Macintosh operating system. Each of these versions is shipped with Microsoft Exchange Server. As with all client applications that access Microsoft BackOffice server products, a Client Access License (CAL) must be purchased for each client to legally access a server.

Table 6.1 lists some features that Microsoft Exchange Client has in addition to the common MAPI-based features listed earlier.

TABLE 6.1 Additional features of Microsoft Exchange Client	Feature	Description
	Public folders	Public folders are the groupware component of Exchange Server. They allow all users in the Exchange organization to share information.
	Inbox Assistant	When running against an Exchange server back-end, software agents, also called *rules,* can be applied to a mailbox to automatically process messages. Actions that can be taken include automatically placing incoming messages in certain folders, automatically forwarding certain messages to specified users, or automatically generating a reply to a message.
	Search tool	Users can search and retrieve messages in their mailboxes using a variety of search criteria, such as sender, date, and subject.

	Feature	Description
TABLE 6.1 (cont.) Additional features of Microsoft Exchange Client	Microsoft Word as message editor	Even though the Exchange Client includes a rich-message editor, it can be configured to use Microsoft Word as the message editor instead.
	Compound messages and drag-and-drop editing	The Exchange Client is OLE 2.0 (Object Linking and Embedding) compliant, and therefore allows the creation of compound documents. For example, a user can drag-and-drop a group of cells from a spreadsheet into an e-mail message.
	Secure messages	Exchange Server allows the usage of digital signatures and encryption for advanced security during message transfer. These features can be invoked using the Exchange client (more on this in Chapter 10).
	Remote mail	Because more and more workers spend some of their work time outside of the office, special features relating to remote access have been incorporated. These features allow the remote mail user to more efficiently use online time. For example, a remote user can access a mailbox and selectively download incoming mail to a remote computer. Outgoing mail created at a remote computer can be held and then sent out at one time.
	Delegate access	Some users need to allow other users to access their mailboxes. For example, a manager might want a secretary to read meeting request messages in order to handle the manager's schedule. In many mail systems, this would be accomplished by having the secretary log on as the manager, creating an obvious security hole. The Exchange Client solves this problem by allowing the manager to grant the secretary permission to access the manager's mailbox. This permission can even be applied on a folder-by-folder basis. The secretary can also be granted permission to send messages on behalf of the manager, or even send messages addressed from the manager with no indication that the secretary was involved.
	Send/Receive electronic forms	Users can send and receive electronic forms through the Microsoft Exchange Client application.

A program referred to as "Microsoft Exchange," "Inbox," or "Windows Messaging" is included with Windows 95. Although their names are the same, the program included with Windows 95 and the one included with Microsoft Exchange Server are not the same. The one that comes with Windows 95 cannot be used as a client to Exchange Server, but can be upgraded to the program included with Exchange Server as long as a CAL is purchased.

Microsoft Exchange Client for MS-DOS

Due to operating system constraints, the Microsoft Exchange Client for MS-DOS has fewer features and a different interface than the Windows-based versions. The following are the major differences:

- Forms are not supported

- Microsoft Mail messages (MMF files) and personal address books (PAB files) cannot be imported

- Remote features, such as downloading headers only, are not available

- Only one AutoSignature entry is permitted

Microsoft Exchange Client for Macintosh

The Microsoft Exchange Client for Macintosh was designed to be as similar to the Windows versions as possible. Still, due to operating system differences, there are some setup and operational differences.

The following features are not supported in the Macintosh version (setup differences will be covered when installation is discussed later in this chapter):

- MAPI programmability

- Additional MAPI service providers

- Interoperability with Microsoft Exchange forms

- Integrated remote functionality through Remote Access Service (RAS)

- Person-to-person key security (this is covered in Chapter 10)

Also, note that Macintosh PST files (personal store files) are not compatible with Windows-based PST files.

Microsoft Schedule+

Microsoft Schedule+ version 7.5 is a MAPI program that includes scheduling, contact, and task management functions. All of these functions apply to both individual and group use. Schedule+ 7.5 is included with Exchange Server and can be used as a client to Exchange Server. It is designed to work with the Exchange Client, and is available for 16-bit and 32-bit environments.

Architectural Design

Four of the major design elements of Microsoft Schedule+ 7.5 are:

- **Integration with Microsoft Exchange Server** Many of the features of Schedule+ (such as meeting requests and notifications) utilize the messaging functions of Microsoft Exchange Server.

- **Contact list** Schedule+ includes a type of electronic Rolodex of contacts, including names, addresses, phone and fax numbers, and other types of information.

- **Time management functions** Users can manage their schedules, events, tasks, and projects. This applies to groups as well as individuals.

- **User permissions** Because it can function as a groupware application, Schedule+ enables permissions to be assigned to information to control who can access it, and what they can do to the information.

These major design elements are implemented through the Schedule+ user interface which includes four main tools (see Figure 6.14 for an illustration of the Schedule+ main screen). You will learn more about these tools in the following discussion.

Tabs

The Schedule+ Tabs are found on the left side of the main screen. They are the main navigation feature of Schedule+ because they enable switching between different views of information. Table 6.2 describes the six default tabs.

FIGURE 6.14

The Schedule+ main
screen

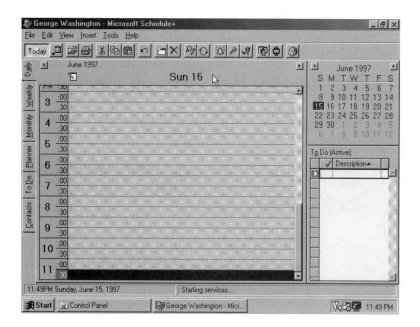

FIGURE 6.14

The Schedule+ main
screen

TABLE 6.2

The six default tabs of
Schedule+

Tab	Description
Daily	Displays the Daily Calendar in a format similar to most paper-based day schedulers.
Weekly	Displays a Weekly Calendar with any scheduled events.
Monthly	Displays a Monthly Calendar with any scheduled events.
Planner	Displays a calendar (number of days depends on screen size) for the purpose of scheduling meetings. Current meetings are shown with lists of attendees.
To Do	Displays the To Do List functions that allow a user to enter, organize, and display tasks.
Contacts	Displays the Contacts List, which is like a paper-based cardfile, but allows much more information.

Daily Calendar

The current day's calendar is displayed in this view, although any day of the year can be displayed. The calendar shows any appointments, meetings, or events scheduled for the day. Users can navigate backward or forward a day by clicking on the Previous or Next buttons at the top of the daily calendar.

Date Navigator

The Date Navigator appears in the top-right of the main screen, and enables users to select any day of the month to view its daily schedule. A different month can be selected by clicking the Previous and Next buttons on the top of the calendar.

To Do List

The To Do List enables the creation, organization, and display of tasks or projects. The display will show what is scheduled for the day chosen in the Daily Calendar and all incomplete tasks that aren't scheduled for any particular day.

Microsoft Schedule+ Features

Table 6.3 summarizes information on the main features of Schedule+.

TABLE 6.3 Features of Microsoft Schedule+	**Features**	**Description**
	Creating appointments	Users can schedule an activity for a specific time. This can be done while in any of the calendar views by choosing the Insert menu, Appointment option. Appointments can be designated private, tentative, or recurring: ■ Private means details of the appointment are hidden to all users except those with special access permission. Other users can still see that the time is blocked. ■ Tentative means the appointment does not show up as a busy time slot. ■ Recurring appointments occur at regular time intervals, such as 9 AM every Tuesday. Alarms can be set to remind the user of an appointment.

T A B L E 6.3 (cont.) Features of Microsoft Schedule+	**Features**	**Description**
	Inviting attendees	When scheduling a meeting, you can invite other attendees. Schedule+ sends an Exchange message to the people specified and they can either accept, accept tentatively, or reject the meeting.
	Viewing other people's free/ busy times and schedule details	By default, users can view free and busy times of all other users, but they are prevented from viewing the details of other people's schedules. Permissions can be set to allow different degrees of access to details of user schedules.
	Task management	A task is a specific activity that needs to be tracked but does not have to be assigned to a specific time slot. Tasks are displayed in the To Do List. Tasks can be created with a priority setting, the date to be completed, the number of days to completion, and even the percentage of the task completed. Tasks can be made private or public.
	Project management	Tasks are grouped together into projects. This allows for easier viewing and management. Projects can be made private or public.
	Alarms	Alarms are reminders that can be set for appointments, events, or tasks. The alarm is in the form of a pop-up message and optionally plays a sound.

There is no Schedule+ for MS-DOS.

Microsoft Outlook

Microsoft Outlook fits into several application categories. It is a personal information manager (PIM) because it functions as a personal calendar, scheduler, contact management, and task management. It is also a messaging application because it includes a powerful e-mail program and forms program. And finally, it is a groupware application because it can access Exchange Server public folders and enables calendars, schedules, contact information, and task information all to be used in a group context. All of this functionality exists through a single, integrated, desktop environment. Microsoft Outlook is the combination of the functions of Microsoft Exchange Client and Schedule+, along with many new and powerful features.

Microsoft Outlook is included with Microsoft Exchange Server as one of its client applications. It is also part of the Microsoft Office 97 suite of applications, and as such is tightly integrated with the other Office 97 applications. Outlook can also be purchased as a stand-alone product. Outlook is fully MAPI compliant. Because it is a 32-bit Windows program, it must run on the Microsoft 32-bit operating systems, either Windows 95 or Windows NT.

Even though Microsoft Outlook is shipped with Microsoft Exchange Server, it requires a Microsoft Exchange Client Access License (CAL) to legally access an Exchange server. This is the same requirement for all client applications that access Exchange Server.

Architectural Design

Microsoft Outlook is designed to be a desktop information manager. This means it integrates personal and groupware tools, as well as their information, in a unified manner. This goal was achieved by including the following design features:

- **Single application, multiple functionality**   From a single interface, users can execute numerous programs like e-mail, calendar, contact list, and task list.

- **Integrated user interface**   All the tools in Outlook are seamlessly integrated. For example, Outlook includes a feature called the *Outlook Bar*. This is a navigation tool that creates shortcuts to a user's e-mail inbox, calendar, contacts, tasks, and folders. Outlook, as a MAPI program, provides a single address book that can be used for e-mail, phone dialing, faxing, and other functions. The Outlook interface permits users to access both local file folders and Exchange public folders.

- **Custom forms using Office 97**   Outlook is tightly integrated with Microsoft Office 97. One example of this is Outlook's ability to create and send forms that include objects created in any of the Office 97 applications. For instance, an expense report form that includes an Excel spreadsheet can be created. Because of Microsoft object technology (see note), the spreadsheet contained in the form will not be merely rows and columns, but will include the Excel code to execute the functions of the spreadsheet. The form's users can input their numbers, have the spreadsheet calculate them, and then have the form automatically sent to a designated person. Outlook, along with Microsoft Office 97, enables the creation of instant groupware applications.

ActiveX is an object technology developed by Microsoft. It is an extension of the earlier OLE technology. ActiveX allows programs to exchange objects that include both presentation data (i.e., what you see on the screen) and native data (i.e., the executable code to manipulate the presentation data).

Features of Microsoft Outlook

Microsoft Outlook includes some very powerful messaging, groupware, and personal productivity features. Tables 6.4, 6.5, and 6.6 describe many of the those features.

T A B L E 6.4 Messaging features of Microsoft Outlook	**Main Function**	**Features**
	E-mail	**AutoNameCheck** Outlook will check the name typed in message headers against the address book as soon as the user tabs out of the entry fields.
		Message recall A user may recall a sent message, assuming the recipient has not already opened it.
		Voting Users can create messages that include voting buttons in the message when received. Recipients can click one of the button choices and submit their choice back to the sender. The sender can automatically track responses to a question or issue.
		Message tracking All the information about delivery, receipt, recall, and voting notifications is tabulated on the original message in the sender's mailbox.

T A B L E 6.4 (cont.) Messaging features of Microsoft Outlook	**Main Function**	**Features**
	E-mail	**AutoPreview** The first few lines of each message can be displayed without requiring the user to open the message in a separate window. This allows users to quickly view the contents of messages.
		MessageFlags Users can place *flags* (i.e., notices) on messages to aid in sorting and prioritizing messages. Flags include reply, read, "for your information," or any custom text.
		Hyperlinks to URLs If a message includes a Web URL address (Uniform Resource Locator), Outlook will recognize that address. If the user clicks on the address, Outlook will start the user's Web browser and connect to that location.

T A B L E 6.5 Groupware features of Microsoft Outlook	**Main Function**	**Features**
	Group scheduling	**Browsing free/busy information** Users can browse other users' free/busy schedule information. **Meeting request processing** If a user sends another user a meeting request, that request is automatically copied from the inbox to the Calendar as a tentative meeting. **Delegate access** Users can grant other users the right to read and modify their schedules.
	Group calendars, contact lists, and task lists	**Public folder use** Calendars, contact lists, and task lists can all be published to public folders to allow group access to that information.
	Group task management	**Task tracking** Users can send tasks to other users and the status of those tasks can be automatically tracked. **Status reports** An automatic status report on a task containing details such as whether the task has been started, the percentage complete, the hours spent working on the task, and the task owner's name can be sent as a mail message.
	Forms and Office 97 objects	**Inclusion of Office 97 objects** Microsoft Office 97 applications can be used to create both presentation material and executable material for Outlook forms. For instance, Microsoft Word can compose the text of a form, and Microsoft Excel can add a spreadsheet to a form.

TABLE 6.6	**Main Function**	**Features**
PIM features of Microsoft Outlook	Functional integration within Outlook	**Outlook Bar** This navigation tool permits the creation of shortcuts to a user's e-mail inbox, calendar, contacts, tasks, and folders. **AutoCreate** Outlook can automatically convert one Outlook item into another. For example, if an e-mail message represents a task a user needs to complete, the user can drag-and-drop the e-mail message into the Task folder and Outlook will automatically convert it to a task.
	Document browsing and retrieval	**Outlook Journal** This feature maintains a log of users' actions, what they did and when they did it. Users can then search for items based on when they were created, not just on what they are named or where they were saved. **Outlook Views** Outlook comes with dozens of standard views of information, and users can create their own customized views.
	Calendar/Schedule features	**AutoDate** Outlook understands natural language input for dates, and can convert loosely worded dates into discrete calendar dates. For example, if a user types "the third Wednesday of October," Outlook will automatically convert that to " Wednesday 10/15/97 5:00 PM."
	Contact Manager Features	**Single address book** The lists of contacts in Contact Manager can be used to address e-mail or a fax, and even jump to a Web site or dial a phone.
	Functions for portable computer users	**Local replication** Information users input into Outlook while on the road with the portable computer can later be easily replicated back to their Exchange server. **Time switching** Outlook can change the system time and time zone as mobile users move from one location to another.
	Microsoft Office 97 integration	**Office 97 interface** Outlook shares many user interface elements with the other Office 97 applications, such as command bars, menus, shortcut menus, tabbed dialog boxes, and toolbars. **Single address book** The other Office 97 applications can use the Outlook Contact Manager address book.

T A B L E 6.6 (cont.)	**Main Function**	**Features**
PIM features of Microsoft Outlook	Microsoft Office 97 integration	**Attachments** Users can attach any Office 97 document to any Outlook item, such as an e-mail, contact, or task. **Mail merge** Users can perform a mail merge between the Outlook Contact Manager and Microsoft Word. **Word 97 and e-mail** Word can be used as the text editor for creating e-mail content. **Drag-and-drop** Users can drag-and-drop information between Office 97 applications and Outlook modules. **Outlook Journal** Office files can be located using Outlook Journal. **Office 97 objects and forms** As stated earlier, objects created in Office 97 applications can be included in Outlook forms.
	Importing and exporting data	**Import and export of data** Microsoft Outlook can import and export data from and to all Microsoft calendar and mail products, as well as many third-party PIM and messaging products.
	Visual Basic for Applications (VBA)	**VBA integration** Outlook includes Microsoft object technology and therefore can be used with Microsoft's Visual Basic for Applications to create compound applications.

Interoperability and Upgrading

Microsoft Outlook can interoperate with the other Exchange MAPI-clients such as Microsoft Exchange Client and Schedule+. There are some compatibility issues relating to the use of electronic forms. These issues will be addressed in Chapter 8.

Exchange Client and Schedule+ can also be upgraded to Microsoft Outlook. Remember, however, that Outlook is only supported on Windows 95 and Windows NT.

Installing Microsoft Exchange Clients

In this section, you will review the information necessary to install the Microsoft Exchange client programs. You can work through a hands-on exercise detailing the steps to install Microsoft Outlook. Our main topics of discussion will be:

- Installation requirements

- Two main installation options

- Additional installation tools

- Troubleshooting a client installation

Installation Requirements

The hardware requirements for the different Exchange client programs vary depending on the operating system platform. Table 6.7 lists the hardware requirements for each scenario. The numbers in the table are minimum requirements, not recommendations. The requirements for optimal performance will vary depending on the deployment scenario. Also, the numbers in the table for free disk space are only for the storage of the program files. They do not relate to any local storage needed for data files (e.g., stored messages, large address book, etc.). The chart references minimum and maximum disk space. The difference will depend on the optional modules you load during installation (e.g., how many information services you choose). Microsoft Schedule+ is included in the requirements for the Exchange Client.

T A B L E 6.7 Hardware requirements for the Microsoft Exchange clients	**Client Software**	**Operating System**	**RAM Required**	**Disk Space (minimum/ maximum)**
	Microsoft Exchange Client	MS-DOS	1MB	2MB/3MB
	Microsoft Exchange Client	Microsoft Windows 3.x	8MB	12MB/22MB
	Microsoft Exchange Client	Microsoft Windows 95	8MB	12MB/22MB

T A B L E 6.7 (cont.) Hardware requirements for the Microsoft Exchange clients	**Client Software**	**Operating System**	**RAM Required**	**Disk Space (minimum/ maximum)**
	Microsoft Exchange Client	Microsoft Windows NT	16MB Intel 20MB Alpha	12MB/22MB Intel 15MB/22MB Alpha
	Microsoft Exchange Client	Apple Macintosh	8MB	14MB
	Microsoft Outlook	Microsoft Windows 95 or NT	8MB Windows 95 16MB NT	26MB/46MB

All of the table's scenarios, with the exception of the Macintosh client, require the client to have a connection to the Exchange server that will support RPC communication. That means the network connection needs to be at LAN speeds, or a permanent WAN connection of at least 128Kbps (a much higher speed would be recommended). It also means that the client machine needs to use a network protocol that is also being used on the Exchange server. Options are TCP/IP, IPX/SPX, or NetBEUI. Macintosh clients are the exception. These clients use the AppleTalk File Protocol (AFP), and require the Windows NT Services for Macintosh to be run on the Exchange server.

Two Main Installation Options

The installation of the Exchange clients is very similar across the Windows platforms. They all start by executing SETUP.EXE and following the on-screen instructions. But there are two main installation options relating to where the client files will be installed to, whether all on the local machine, or most of them on a network share point. Those two options are referred to as:

- Local installation
- Shared installation

Local Installation

In a local installation, the client program files are loaded on the client's local workstation. This option can be used on all client platforms, assuming the required amount of disk space is available. There are three types of local installations:

- **Typical**   This option installs the components required by the typical user. It is available for Microsoft Exchange Client, Schedule+, and Outlook.

- **Custom**   This option allows the installer to choose the components to install. This option is also available for Microsoft Exchange Client, Schedule+, and Outlook.

- **Laptop**   This option installs only the minimum components necessary. It is only available for Microsoft Exchange Client and Schedule+.

Exercise 6.1 will walk you through a local installation of Microsoft Outlook. The exercise assumes that the computer being used for the installation is running Microsoft Windows 95 or Windows NT, and has a CD drive.

EXERCISE 6.1

A Local Installation of Outlook

1. Log on as administrator to a machine on which you want to install Outlook.

2. Once logged on, click the Start button, and then click Run.

3. In the Open box, type:
   <drive letter of CD disc>:OUTLOOK\SETUP.

   A Microsoft Outlook 97 Setup dialog box will appear.

4. Click Continue.

   The Name and Organization Information dialog box will appear.

5. In the Name box, type **<your name>**.

6. In the Organization box, type **<your organization name>**, and then click OK.

7. Click OK to confirm the registration information.

   A dialog box will appear and ask for the CD Key number.

---

8. Enter the CD Key number that came with your Outlook product, then click OK.

   A dialog box will appear, confirming your CD Key number.

9. Click OK.

   A dialog box will appear, showing the default directory path for the installation of the Outlook files.

10. Click OK.

    A dialog box will appear, displaying installation options.

11. Click Custom.

    The Custom dialog box will appear.

12. Click Continue to accept the default selections.

    Files will now be copied to your local hard drive.

    A message box will appear, indicating that Setup completed successfully.

13. Click OK.

14. The next steps are to run Outlook and configure a profile. We will cover these topics in Chapter 7.

Shared Installation

In a shared installation, most of the client program files are placed on a network *share point,* and the client computer reads them from the remote disk when the program is run. This option requires the least amount of disk space on the client computer. To perform a shared installation, the installer must first create a network share point. The procedure is slightly different depending on the operating system of the client computer. We will discuss creating a shared installation for MS-DOS clients and Windows-based clients next.

MS-DOS Clients   On the machine that will hold the shared installation, the installer executes the SETUP program for the MS-DOS version of the client program and then chooses the Shared option. The installer will be prompted for the directory path where the shared files are to be copied. This location is called the Install Point For Shared Mail. The SETUP program will then copy all the necessary files for a shared installation to this location.

Windows-Based Clients   On the machine that will hold the shared installation, the installer executes the SETUP /A command. The /A switch tells the SETUP program to perform a shared installation.

This scenario is complicated slightly if the client computers are using a shared copy of their operating system. If this is the case, the installer must also be running that same shared copy of the operating system WHEN the shared installation of the Exchange client software is performed. If there are multiple locations of the shared operating system, the Exchange client installer must do a shared installation of the Exchange client software at every one of those locations. These steps ensure that all of the necessary Exchange client files are copied to the shared operating system locations.

The Microsoft Exchange Client for Macintosh does not support a shared installation.

Performing the Shared Installation   Once the shared installation point has been created, the installation on the client computer is the same as a local installation, with a few exceptions. The installer will be presented with an installation choice called "Workstation." This option should be chosen. A dialog box asking for the location of the shared Microsoft applications, like the spell checker, may also appear.

Postinstallation Issues

The installation of an Exchange client program makes changes to the client computer configuration. These changes depend on the client operating system in use. This information is summarized in Table 6.8.

TABLE 6.8 Client configuration changes from the Exchange installation	Operating System	Configuration Changes
	Microsoft Windows 3.x	The WIN.INI file is modified to include a section called Mail that contains the path and file names of the OLE and MAPI settings. The installation program also creates an EXCHNG.INI file in the Windows directory. This file contains the settings used by some of the client processes, such as the RPC binding order.

T A B L E 6.8 *(cont.)* Client configuration changes from the Exchange installation	**Operating System**	**Configuration Changes**
	Apple Macintosh	The setup program creates an Exchange folder that contains the following items:
		■ **Exchange Settings** Used to manage profiles.
		■ **Inbox Repair Tools** These tools can scan and perform diagnostics on a user's personal storage.
		■ **Microsoft Exchange and Schedule+** Includes the e-mail and scheduling programs.
		The setup program also creates a folder, called Exchange Temp Items, that contains temporary data the client program might access during a session. The setup program also writes configuration information to the Preferences folder.
	Microsoft Windows 95 and NT	All configuration information is written to the Registry.

Additional Installation Tools

Three additional installation tools can be used when installing the Exchange clients:

- Setup Editor

- Auto Profile Generator

- Microsoft Office 97 Resource Kit

Setup Editor

An administrator can pre-determine the options that will be used in a client installation. This is done by using a utility called Setup Editor to modify the two script files that will be used during the installation of the Exchange client software. Those two script files are EXCHNG.STF and DEFAULT.PRF.

EXCHNG.STF contains the installation options that will be used by the client SETUP.EXE program. Installation options include the client directory where program files will be copied (e.g. c:\ExchangeClient\ ), the services that will be installed (e.g. Microsoft Exchange Server, MSN, Internet), the network protocols the client's RPC protocol will use (e.g. TCP/IP, IPX), and many other options.

DEFAULT.PRF ("PRF" stands for PRofile descriptor File) contains the configuration information that will be used when a user's messaging profile is created at installation. As discussed earlier, a messaging profile is a collection of configuration information relating to how the Exchange client application should operate (or, in more technical jargon, the messaging profile is read by the MAPI subsystem for instructions on how to implement the MAPI environment). Examples of parameters that can be placed in the DEFAULT.PRF file are whether receipts will be required for outgoing mail, how the spell checker will work, the home server of the mailbox, and many other options.

When the client setup program is run, it checks for a PRF file (which is the default). If there is a PRF file, the setup program automatically starts a program called the Automatic Profile Generator (NEWPROF.EXE) that will read the PRF file and automatically create a messaging profile based on the information in the PRF file. If there is no PRF file, the setup program will automatically run a utility called the Profile Wizard that will prompt the user with a series of questions relating to how the profile should be configured.

Many of these topics, such as messaging profiles, PRF files, and the Automatic Profile Generator, will also be discussed in Chapter 7.

Both of the script files, EXCHNG.STF and DEFAULT.PRF, can be modified in order to standardize client installations. The easiest way to do this is through the Setup Editor (STFEDTF.EXE). This utility is found on the Microsoft Exchange client CD, and it could also have been installed in the Microsoft Exchange program group. Setup Editor has three main steps:

1. **Select a client installation point**   This is the network directory containing the client installation files, two of which are the script files (DEFAULT.PRF is actually created during the execution of the Setup Editor). Because the Setup Editor will be writing changes to the two script files, the client installation point cannot be a CD-ROM or a directory where the administrator does not have write permission. The client installation files should be copied to a network share point where the script files can be modified and where users can connect to and run the SETUP.EXE program. Users will need to have at least Read permission at this directory.

2. Modify Setup program options   These options control how the setup program will function. The options the administrator chooses will be stored in EXCHNG.STF. When a user runs SETUP.EXE from this client installation point, SETUP.EXE will operate based upon the settings in EXCHNG.STF, also located at this client installation point.

3. Set user options   These options are written to the DEFAULT.PRF and will be used when each user's message profile is created at installation.

After an administrator has created a network share directory, copied the client installation files to that directory, and run the Setup Editor to create the standard setup and profile options, they would inform the relevant users of the location of the share directory and the program (SETUP.EXE) to execute in order to install the Exchange client software. Each installation from this directory would have the same basic configuration. This is called a *scripted installation*.

The Setup Editor is not applicable to the Microsoft Exchange Client for DOS or Microsoft Outlook.

Auto Profile Generator

As stated above, the Microsoft Exchange Client comes with a utility that can automatically create *user profiles*. A profile is a collection of information relating to how a user wants the MAPI client applications to look and behave. This utility, NEWPROF.EXE, can read the file DEFAULT.PRF and based upon that information create user profiles. This topic will be addressed in Chapter 7, when profiles are fully covered.

Microsoft Office 97 Resource Kit

The setup program for Microsoft Outlook uses a file called OUTLOOK.PRF. This file can be modified to customize the installation of Outlook. For more information, refer to the Microsoft Office 97 Resource Kit.

Troubleshooting a Client Installation

If you encounter problems with a client installation, check the following items first:

- Have the user and server names been entered correctly?

- Is the Directory Service running on the user's intended home server?

- If Windows for Workgroups is installed on the client, is the necessary patch installed as directed by Microsoft Exchange Server Installation Guide?

Other items to verify include the network connection to the server, and the hardware and software requirements for the client software.

Summary

Microsoft Exchange client applications are programs that can access Exchange mailboxes and public folders. These client applications include MAPI-based programs, such as Microsoft Exchange Client, Schedule+, and Outlook. Some Internet applications can be clients to Microsoft Exchange Server. These include Internet mail applications that support Post Office Protocol 3 (POP3), and Web browsers like Microsoft Internet Explorer.

The MAPI architecture provides a standard architecture for client-server messaging. It includes three architectural layers, the client application layer, the MAPI subsystem layer, and the service provider layer. There are three main types of service providers: address book providers, message store providers, and message transport providers.

The Exchange MAPI client applications share many features, such as a universal inbox, single address book, hierarchical storage, custom views, and rich-text message formatting.

Microsoft Outlook is a 32-bit client program that can be used with Microsoft Exchange Server. It is tightly integrated with Microsoft Office 97 and includes many very powerful personal, group, and messaging features.

Installing the Microsoft Exchange client applications is a relatively straightforward procedure. For most of the client applications, the installer has the option to perform a local or shared installation.

Review Questions

1. Which of the following is NOT a MAPI-based application?

   A. Internet mail with POP3

   B. Microsoft Schedule+

   C. Microsoft Exchange Client

   D. Microsoft Outlook

2. A Web browser cannot be used to access an Exchange mailbox.

   A. True

   B. False

3. The term used to describe the collection of MAPI configuration settings is:

   A. MAPI subsystem

   B. Service provider

   C. API

   D. Profile

4. A PST file is also known as what type of message storage?

   A. Personal folder

   B. Private folder

   C. Offline folder

   D. Macintosh folder

5. An inbox assistant is a:

A. Secretary

B. Temporary employee

C. Permissions set on a mailbox

D. Software agent that can apply rules to a mailbox

6. The MAPI-based clients that access an Exchange server require a client access license.

A. True

B. False

7. Which of the following is NOT true for the Microsoft Exchange Client?

A. Has remote mail features

B. Has a delegate access feature

C. Only runs on Windows 95

D. Can work with electronic forms

8. There is NO Exchange Client version for MS-DOS or Apple Macintosh.

A. True

B. False

9. Which of the following is true for Microsoft Schedule+?

A. Has an alarm feature

B. Is shipped with Microsoft Office 97

C. Will not work with Apple Macintosh

D. Will only run on 32-bit platforms

10. Which of the following features enables a Microsoft Outlook user to place notices on messages to help prioritize them?

    A. Message recall

    B. AutoNameCheck

    C. Voting

    D. Message flags

11. Microsoft Outlook enables schedules, contact lists, and task lists to be published to a public folder.

    A. True

    B. False

12. Which of the following are two navigational aids in Microsoft Outlook?

    A. Outlook Bar

    B. Tabbed Windows

    C. AutoDate

    D. Message recall

13. The following relate to the integration of Microsoft Outlook with Microsoft Office 97:

    A. Office 97 interface

    B. Use of Office 97 attachments

    C. Use of Office 97 objects in Outlook forms

    D. All of the above

14. The Microsoft Exchange Client for MS-DOS does NOT support a shared installation.

   A. True

   B. False

15. The Microsoft Exchange Client for Macintosh does NOT support a shared installation.

   A. True

   B. False

16. The following line would be used to set up a shared installation point for Windows-based clients:

   A. SETUP /A

   B. INSTALL /N

   C. INSTALL /A

   D. SETUP /A /N

17. Microsoft Schedule+ enables the grouping of tasks into a:

   A. Task commune

   B. Task group

   C. Project

   D. Task community

18. Which of the following does NOT relate to a scripted installation?

   A. Setup Editor

   B. Client installation point

   C. PROFILE.PROF

   D. DEFAULT.PRF

19. If you wanted all new client installations to be configured to use IPX and not use of TCP/IP, you would perform which action?

A. Use Setup Editor to remove TCP/IP from the RPC binding order

B. Do nothing, that is already the default

C. This can not be done

D. Run SETUP.EXE /A

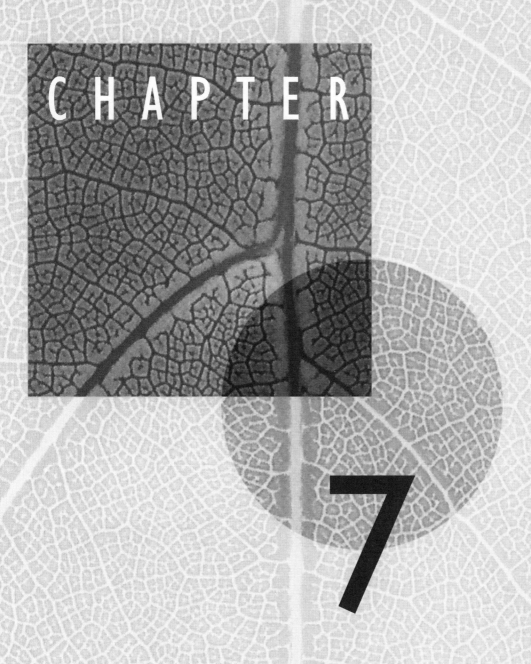

CHAPTER

7

Configuring Microsoft Exchange Clients

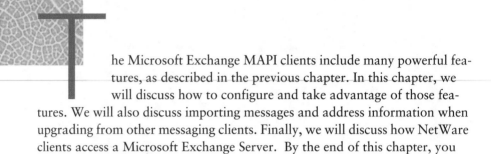

he Microsoft Exchange MAPI clients include many powerful features, as described in the previous chapter. In this chapter, we will discuss how to configure and take advantage of those features. We will also discuss importing messages and address information when upgrading from other messaging clients. Finally, we will discuss how NetWare clients access a Microsoft Exchange Server. By the end of this chapter, you will be familiar with:

- Messaging profiles

- Configuring the RPC transport

- Remote mail

- Importing messages and address information

- Microsoft Exchange clients in a NetWare environment

Messaging Profiles

As you learned in the previous chapter, a messaging profile is a collection of configuration information used by the MAPI components. In this chapter, you will learn more about:

- Messaging profile information

- Creating messaging profiles

- Editing messaging profiles

- Optional profile settings in Microsoft Outlook

- Profiles and roving users

Messaging Profile Information

The information in a messaging profile relates to much of the operation of a MAPI client application. Information found in a profile includes how to connect to back-end systems, where to store messages, and how to handle messages. Table 7.1 summarizes some of this information and indicates the default configuration. This table gives an overall view of a profile. The details of each item will be discussed after the table.

TABLE 7.1 Some information in a messaging profile	Category	Options
	Information services	■ Microsoft Exchange Server (default) ■ Personal folders (PST) ■ Personal Address Book (PAB) (default) ■ Outlook Address Book (default when Outlook is installed) ■ Microsoft Mail (default) ■ Internet Mail (default) ■ Microsoft Network (MSN) ■ Microsoft Fax ■ CompuServe Mail
	Information storage	■ Where to deliver incoming mail ■ Offline folders (OST) (if the Microsoft Exchange Server information service is being used) ■ Message handling settings
	Delegate access	■ Additional Exchange Server mailboxes to which to connect
	Remote mail	■ Phone book entry to dial ■ Dial-up schedule ■ Items to retrieve when using remote mail

Information Services

A profile specifies the information services to be used. Information services are collections of MAPI providers that permit access to back-end messaging systems (see the previous chapter for details on MAPI providers).

When an information service is added to a profile, additional information specific to the information service needs to be provided. For example, when the Microsoft Fax information service is added, the fax telephone number must be specified.

Here are some more details on the information services that are included with the Exchange clients:

- **Microsoft Exchange**   Choose this information service if the user has a mailbox account on an Exchange server. When this information service is included in a profile (it is by default), the user will be prompted to enter the following information:

  - Name of the user's Exchange server (also known as the user's home server)

  - Name of the user's Exchange mailbox (the alias name or display name as configured on the Exchange server can be specified)

- **Personal folders**   Personal folders can be used for storage instead of or in addition to a user's mailbox private folders in the Exchange Server Private Information Store. A profile can be configured to deliver mail to the Inbox folder of a personal folder store. In this case, messages are still delivered to a user's mailbox on the Exchange server first, but will then be automatically downloaded to the user's personal folder store when the user logs on with the Exchange client. Some reasons to use personal folders are:

  - To backup folders and messages

  - To copy a portion of your server-based mailbox to a portable computer for access when not on the network

  - To archive old messages

- **Microsoft Mail**   Provides access to a mailbox account on a Microsoft Mail post office. This information service is included in new profiles by default.

- **Microsoft Network**   This information service is only loaded with the MSN online service and is only supported on Windows 95.

- **Microsoft Fax**   This information service is included with Windows 95 and is only supported on Windows 95.

- **Internet Mail**   This information service enables a user to send and receive mail over the Internet using the SMTP and POP3 protocols.

- **CompuServe Mail**   This information service is included with Windows 95 and is only supported on Windows 95.

Information Storage

Information storage options in a profile include the following:

- **Where to deliver incoming mail**   As mentioned previously, a personal folder store can be specified as the location to where incoming mail is delivered. When the Microsoft Exchange Server information service is included in a profile, incoming mail is kept in the Exchange Server mailbox by default.

- **Offline folders**   When the Microsoft Exchange Server information service is included in a profile, users may download their mail messages to offline folders on their local machines. These folders are useful for doing work away from a network. When users connect again to their Exchange server, any changes they made offline are synchronized with that server. Any server-based folder can be specified for offline use. To make an offline folder copy of a public folder, the public folder must first be designated as a Favorite folder by the user. Offline folders are stored in an OST file.

- **Message handling settings**

  Options for when a new message arrives:

  - Play a sound

  - Briefly change the pointer

  - Display a notification message

  Options for deleting messages:

  - Warn before permanently deleting items

  - Empty the Deleted Items folder upon exiting

Options after moving or deleting an open message:

- Open the item above it

- Open the item below it

- Return to the main window

Additional options will be covered later in this chapter under "Optional Profile Options in Microsoft Outlook" and in Table 7.2.

Delegate Access

The Exchange MAPI clients enable a user to make another user a delegate for a mailbox or schedule. The delegate can then access the mailbox or schedule and, depending on the level of permissions granted, perform various functions. This feature is useful if a user is going out of town and wants another person to read his or her messages. The mailbox owner could assign a delegate and give the delegate the ability to read mail. Another scenario is when a manager has an assistant who handles scheduling. The assistant would need to access the manager's mailbox, read messages pertaining to scheduling requests, and respond to those requests on behalf of the manager. The manager could accomplish this by making the assistant a delegate and granting the necessary permissions to read and send mail on the manager's behalf.

Mailbox Owner Assigning Delegate Access   One way to make another user a delegate to your mailbox is to give them *permissions* to your mailbox. Individual permissions include create items, read items, create subfolders, edit items, and delete items. Any combination of these permissions can be assigned. Predefined groupings of permissions, called roles, can also be used. Exercise 7.1 outlines the steps to assign permissions.

Users can also delegate authority by giving another user the ability to send mail *on behalf of* them, or send mail *as* them. These two permissions are discussed here:

- **Send On Behalf Of**   A delegate who has this permission can send mail on behalf of the delegator. When a recipient gets the message, the header indicates that the message was sent from the delegate *on behalf of* the delegator. This permission can be assigned from either an Exchange MAPI client or from the Exchange Administrator program. Exercise 7.2 covers granting the Send On Behalf Of permission.

EXERCISE 7.1

Assigning Read Permission

1. For this exercise to be performed, there must be other users with NT accounts and Exchange mailboxes different from your own. You will delegate access to your mailbox to one of these other users.

2. While in Microsoft Outlook, right-click on your Inbox, then click on Properties. The Properties dialog box will appear.

3. Click the Permissions tab.

4. Click Add. The Add Users dialog box will appear.

5. Choose the user to whom you want to delegate access to your mailbox.

6. Click Add, then click OK. The Properties dialog box will now appear.

7. In the Name box, select the delegate's name, then in the Roles list select Reviewer. This role will permit the delegate to view the contents of your Inbox folder.

8. Click OK. The user you chose in Step 5 now has permission to open your Inbox and view messages.

EXERCISE 7.2

Assigning Send On Behalf Of Permission

1. In Microsoft Outlook, select Tools ➤ Options. The Options dialog box will appear.

2. Select the Delegates tab. The Delegates box will be empty.

3. Select Add. The Add Users dialog box will appear.

4. Select the user you want to designate as a delegate, then click Add, and then click OK. The Delegate Permissions dialog box will appear.

5. Click OK again. The user you selected now has the ability to send mail on behalf of this mailbox owner.

- **Send As** This permission allows the delegate to send mail and have it appear as if it were sent by the mailbox owner. When a recipient gets the message, the header indicates that the message was sent from the delegator with no indication of the delegate's name at all. Recipients do not know of the delegate's involvement. This permission can only be assigned from the Exchange Administrator program. Exercise 7.3 outlines the steps for assigning the Send As permission.

EXERCISE 7.3

Assigning Send As Permission

1. On the Exchange server, start the Exchange Administrator program.

2. Choose Tools ≻ Options. Choose the Permissions tab on the Options dialog box. Ensure that the Show Permissions Page for All Objects checkbox is selected. Click OK.

3. Select the Recipients container in the left pane. Then, in the right pane, double-click a recipient whose mailbox is to have a delegate with the Send As permission. The Properties page containing all the tabs for this mailbox will appear.

4. Select the Permissions tab.

5. Click Add. Now select the user you want to give Send As permission. After doing this, click Add and then OK.

6. Click the down-arrow in the Roles box. Select the Send As role.

7. Click OK. The user you chose in Step 2 now has the ability to send mail as if they were the owner of this mailbox.

Using Delegate Access To operate as a delegate user of a mailbox, the delegate must add the other mailbox to the active profile. When this is done, the other mailbox will appear in the delegate's folder list. Depending on the permissions given, the delegate can then read, edit, create, and delete messages in folders. Exercise 7.4 shows the steps for opening a mailbox as a delegate user.

A delegate who has been granted Send On Behalf Of permission can send a message for the other user by choosing the From field on the View menu of a Compose Message window. In the From field, the user can enter the name of the user they want to Send On Behalf Of.

EXERCISE 7.4

Opening a Mailbox as a Delegate User

1. Log on as the user you chose in Exercise 7.1, Step 5.

2. Start Microsoft Outlook.

3. Choose Tools ➤ Services. The Services dialog box will appear.

4. Select Microsoft Exchange Server and then click Properties. The Microsoft Exchange Server dialog box will appear.

5. Select the Advanced tab.

6. Click Add.

7. In the Add Mailbox box, type the name of the mailbox to which you have been assigned permissions. Then click OK. Click OK on the Microsoft Exchange Server properties dialog box. The Services dialog box will appear.

8. Click OK. Notice that the other mailbox to which you have been assigned delegate access appears in the folder list (click the Folder List toolbar button to display the folder list if it is not shown).

Creating and editing a messaging profile will now be covered in more detail.

Creating Messaging Profiles

There are three primary methods to create a profile:

- Setup program and DEFAULT.PRF or OUTLOOK.PRF

- Setup program and the Profile Wizard

- Control Panel

Setup Program and DEFAULT.PRF or OUTLOOK.PRF

During the Exchange Client installation, the SETUP program will look for a file named DEFAULT.PRF. This file contains default information that the SETUP program will use to create a profile during installation. The

DEFAULT.PRF file can be created using the Setup Editor program or by using a text editor to modify the DEFAULT.PRF file in the Exchange Client installation point. The process for Outlook is the same, but the file Outlook Setup looks for is named OUTLOOK.PRF. Administrators can use these files to eliminate the need for the installer to create profiles and ensure that all clients installed are using a consistent profile.

Setup Program and the Profile Wizard

If the DEFAULT.PRF does not exist, the Setup program will automatically start the Profile Wizard, which prompts the installer for the profile information. The installer may accept or change the defaults the Profile Wizard presents. The defaults are noted by parentheses in Table 7.1.

Control Panel

After an installation, a new profile can be created using the Mail and Fax applet in the Control Panel. After launching the applet, click Show Profiles, and then click Add. The Profile Wizard will start up and guide you through creating a new profile.

Editing Messaging Profiles

Profiles can be edited any time after the client is installed. If you want to edit an existing profile, you can use the Mail and Fax applet in the Control Panel. Also, the profile that is currently in use can be edited from within the Exchange client or Outlook by choosing the Services option on the Tools menu. We will discuss these two scenarios in greater detail next.

Editing an Existing Profile

The Mail and Fax applet in the Control Panel can be used to edit an existing profile. This applet can be used after a messaging product has been installed on a user's computer. Sometimes information needs to be manually added to a profile before a newly installed messaging product is fully configured for use. If there are applications using the MAPI subsystem at the time the profile is edited, they will all need to be stopped and restarted before the changes made to the profile will take effect.

Editing a Current Profile

If a user wants to make profile changes without having to log off and back on again to make those changes effective, the user can edit the current profile through the Services option on the Tools menu. Any changes made to the profile in this way become effective immediately, but some settings cannot be changed while the profile is in use.

Optional Profile Settings in Microsoft Outlook

MAPI applications have the functionality to allow users to set some of their messaging profiles within the application. For example, choosing Options from the Tools menu from within Outlook (see Figure 7.1) will bring up a dialog box containing numerous tabs, also called property pages, that allow users to set various options pertaining to their messaging environment. Table 7.2 provides a description of each property page.

FIGURE 7.1

The Microsoft Outlook Options screen

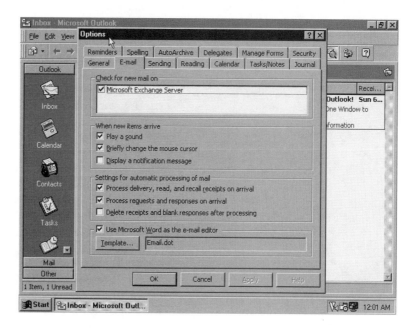

T A B L E 7.2	Property Page	Description

Microsoft Outlook property pages	General	■ When starting Outlook, prompt the user for the profile to use, or always use a designated profile, or start in a particular folder.
		■ Deleting message options:
		  Warn before permanently deleting
		  Empty the Deleted Items folder on exit
		■ Dialing options:
		  Settings for speed dialing
		  Settings for phone number formatting
		  Settings for phone number dialing
		  Add-In Manager

	E-mail	■ Where to check for new mail
		■ Notification of new mail options:
		  Play a sound
		  Briefly change the mouse cursor
		  Display notification message
		■ Settings for automatic processing of mail

	Sending	■ Sending mail options:
		  Use a particular font
		  Set importance of mail
		  Set sensitivity of mail

	Reading	After moving or deleting an open message, options:
		  Open the message above it
		  Open the message below it
		  Return to the Outlook window
		■ When replying or forwarding a message, options:
		  Include and indent the original text
		  Close the original message
		  Set the font or color settings

	Calendar	■ Define the work week ■ Define working hours ■ Appointment defaults ■ Set Microsoft Schedule+ as the primary calendar

	Property Page	Description
TABLE 7.2 (cont.) Microsoft Outlook property pages	Tasks/Notes	■ Define task working hours ■ Define task color options ■ Define task and note defaults
	Journal	■ Define items and contacts for journal entries
	Reminders	■ Define actions to initiate when a reminder comes due
	Spelling	■ Always suggest replacements for misspellings ■ Always check spelling before sending Ignore words in uppercase ■ Ignore words with numbers ■ Ignore original message text in a reply or forward
	AutoArchive	■ Define settings for when and where to perform automatic archiving
	Delegates	■ Define others who may send mail on your behalf
	Manage Forms	■ Install and manage forms from the various forms libraries
	Security	■ Set up advanced security

Profiles and Roving Users

Roving users are people who use multiple computers on the network. Because messaging profiles are stored on users' local workstations, a problem arises when roving users move to different computers but still want to use the same profile. Solutions to this situation vary depending on the operating system used by the client. The following sections discuss these solutions.

MS-DOS Clients

The Exchange Client for MS-DOS normally stores its messaging profile in the user's Exchange directory in a file named EXCHANGE.PRO. For a roving user, the Exchange directory and the EXCHANGE.PRO file can be copied to the user's home directory on a server. Then, regardless of the machine being used, the user accesses his or her home directory on the server and runs the

Exchange Client from that directory. The Exchange Client will automatically look for the profile in the same directory.

If a roving user wants to run a local copy of the Exchange Client, the profile in the home directory on the server can still be used. This is done by using the -P switch on the command line when executing the Exchange Client. This switch takes an argument that specifies the path to the profile, for which the roving user can provide his or her home directory on the server.

Windows 3.x Clients

To support roving users on Windows 3.x, the file containing the user's profile, EXCHNG.INI, can be placed on a server, and the Exchange Client on each computer the roving user uses can be configured to find the profile on that server. The WIN.INI file must be modified to do this.

Modifying WIN.INI The Exchange Client looks for the EXCHNG.INI file in a directory path specified in the WIN.INI file. The keyword for the path is found under the MAPI section in WIN.INI as follows:

```
[MAPI]

ProfileDirectory16=<path>
```

The user can specify the path to the network directory where the messaging profile has been placed.

Windows 95 and Windows NT Clients

Windows 95 and Windows NT maintain user configuration information in user environment profiles (not to be confused with the messaging profiles discussed in this chapter). Environment profiles can be stored on a local machine or on a server. Because a messaging profile is included within the environment profile, Windows 95 and Windows NT have built-in support for roving users. The roving user only needs to use a server-based user environment profile to be able to use more than one machine on the network.

Configuring the RPC Transport

The Exchange MAPI-based clients use the RPC protocol to perform client-server interactions. The RPC protocol uses other protocols to establish a connection with the server and to physically move its information. Table 7.3 describes the protocols that RPC can use.

	Network Protocol	Description
T A B L E 7.3 Protocols available for RPC use	Local RPC (LPC)	This communication method is used when the client and the server are on the same machine. No network traffic is generated.
	TCP/IP	RPC can use the Windows Sockets interface and TCP/IP to communicate with an Exchange server.
	Sequenced Packet Exchange (SPX)	RPC can use the Windows Sockets interface and the Novell IPX/SPX protocol to communicate with an Exchange server.
	Named Pipes	RPC can use Named Pipes.
	Network Basic Input/ Output System (NetBIOS)	NetBIOS is a protocol that creates a two-way conversation between a client and a server. NetBIOS uses network protocols to physically carry its information. It will work with TCP/IP, IPX/SPX, and NetBEUI. RPC can use NetBIOS to communicate with an Exchange server.
	Vines IP	Vines IP is a network protocol used in Banyan Vines networks. RPC can use this protocol to communicate with an Exchange Server. This protocol is only supported on the Windows 95, Windows NT, and Windows for Workgroups platforms.

Any one of the scenarios in Table 7.3 will allow a MAPI client using RPC to perform client-server interactions with an Exchange Server. RPC will try these different scenarios until it establishes a session with the server. The order that RPC uses to establish a connection depends on the operating system of the client. Table 7.4 shows the protocol order.

T A B L E 7.4 Protocol order used by RPC	**Windows 95,** **Windows NT**	**Windows 3.x**	**MS-DOS**
	Local RPC	Named Pipes	Local RPC
	TCP/IP	SPX	Named Pipes
	SPX	TCP/IP	SPX
	Named Pipes	NetBIOS	TCP/IP
	NetBIOS	Vines IP	NetBIOS
	Vines IP		

Although each of the protocols listed are automatically attempted until one succeeds, if a protocol is not supported on the system it may take an extended time for that protocol to time-out before the next protocol is attempted. This can cause an unwanted delay every time a user logs on. Therefore, it may be necessary to reorder the protocols so that those supported by your network are at the top of the list.

The connection orders in Table 7.4 can be modified before a client installation. This can be done using the Setup Editor utility or by manually editing lines in the configuration file (STF or INI) that Setup uses. After an installation, manual editing is the only way to change the order. The following two sections explain how to manually modify the connection order before and after an installation.

The phrases "RPC connection order" and "RPC binding order" are synonymous.

Preinstallation Modification of the RPC Connection Order

As mentioned, the RPC connection order that will be used in an installation can be determined before setup. This can be done by manually editing certain files and certain parameters in those files. That information is presented below and organized by operating system platform.

Windows 95 and Windows NT Clients

The SETUP program reads instructions from the EXCHNG.STF file. To change the RPC connection order, modify the following lines:

```
61  AddRegData  """LOCAL""",

""Software\Microsoft\Exchange\Exchange Provider""",
""Rpc_Binding_Order""",

""ncalrpc,ncacn_ip_tcp,ncacn_spx,ncacn_np,net-
bios,ncacn_vns_spp"""
```

As you can see in the previous line, the default order is LPC, TCP/IP, SPX, Named Pipes, and NetBIOS (this can also be seen in Table 7.4).

Windows 3.x Clients

The file EXCHNG.STF is also the file that SETUP reads for Windows 3.x clients. The following lines can be modified to change the RPC connection order:

```
62 AddIniLine """exchng.ini""", ""Exchange Provider""",
""RPC_Binding_Order""cacn_np,ncacn_spx,ncacn_ip_tcp,net-
bios,ncacn_vns_spp"""
```

MS-DOS Clients

For MS-DOS clients, SETUP reads configuration information from the file MLSETUP.INI. To change the RPC connection order, you must edit the following line in that file:

```
RPC_BINDING_ORDER=ncalrpc,ncacn_np,ncacn_spx,ncacn_ip_tcp,netbios
```

Postinstallation Modification of the RPC Connection Order

After installation is completed, the RPC connection order can only be changed by manually editing the appropriate files or the Registry. The method varies depending on the operating system. The following sections give the details.

Windows 95 and Windows NT Clients

To modify the RPC connection order on Windows 95 or Windows NT, the Rpc_Binding_Order value in the Registry must be modified. This value is found in the following key in the Registry:

```
\HKEY_LOCAL_MACHINE
    \Software
      \Microsoft
        \Exchange
          \Exchange Provider
```

Windows 3.x Clients

The RPC connection order can be modified on Windows 3.x clients by editing the Rpc_Binding_Order value in the EXCHNG.INI file.

MS-DOS Clients

When the MS-DOS Exchange client application is installed, the environment variable, RPC_BINDING_ORDER, is set in the AUTOEXEC.BAT file. This variable contains the RPC connection order and can be edited after the installation.

Remote Mail

As discussed previously, remote mail gives a user the ability to access and use his or her mailbox through a remote connection to the Exchange server. Certain technologies at the client and the server make this access possible. Our discussion will divide these technologies into the following four categories:

- Remote connection options

- Protocols supported

- ShivaRemote installation and configuration

- Remote mail features

Remote Connection Options

The remote connection method used to connect Exchange MAPI clients to an Exchange server depends on the operating system the client is using. The three remote connection options that can be used are:

- Microsoft Remote Access Service (RAS)

- Microsoft Dial-Up Networking (DUN)

- ShivaRemote

Microsoft Remote Access Service (RAS)

RAS is a subsystem included with Windows NT that enables dial-up access to a remote computer. By using RAS client software and a supported modem, a user can establish a dial-up connection to an RAS server and an Exchange server running on that RAS server or on its network. This allows a remote user to access his or her mailbox on an Exchange server. RAS client software is also included with Microsoft Windows for Workgroups.

Microsoft Dial-Up Networking (DUN)

DUN is a subsystem included with Windows 95 that enables dial-up access to a remote computer. A remote Exchange client can use DUN to connect to an Exchange server. Some of the remote access servers that a remote DUN client can connect to are Windows 95 dial-up server, RAS server, Shiva LanRover, and Shiva NetModem.

ShivaRemote

ShivaRemote is dial-up client software from the Shiva Corporation that is included with Exchange Server. It permits dial-up access to remote computers. ShivaRemote can run on MS-DOS, Windows 3.*x*, and Windows for Workgroups clients.

Protocols Supported

RAS, DUN, and ShivaRemote all use the *Point-to-Point Protocol* (*PPP*) to physically transfer information between the remote client and the server. PPP plays a role similar to a LAN adapter driver. PPP takes *datagrams*, which are chunks of data that are to be transferred, and frames them for network transfer. The remote user's modem takes the place of a LAN adapter.

The datagram protocols, also called network protocols, that can be used with these three remote connection options are TCP/IP, IPX, and NetBEUI. ShivaRemote only supports the Novell IPX implementation, not the Microsoft implementation.

In the next section, we will discuss the installation and configuration of ShivaRemote. RAS and DUN will not be discussed because they are covered in other Microsoft courses and exams.

ShivaRemote Installation and Configuration

Exchange Server comes with two versions of ShivaRemote, one for MS-DOS clients and one for Windows 3.*x* and Windows for Workgroups clients. The installation procedure for each is different.

MS-DOS Clients

During the normal installation of the MS-DOS Exchange client, a check box option is used to specify ShivaRemote installation. The ShivaRemote files are placed in the Exchange client directory. There is no separate installation program for ShivaRemote. If the initial installation of the Exchange client did not include ShivaRemote, but it is desired at a later time, the Setup can be run again to add ShivaRemote.

Each time a user wants to use ShivaRemote, CONNECT.EXE must be run to establish the physical connection to the server. This must be done before the user runs the MS-DOS Exchange client. Note that the MS-DOS clients do not have the capability to download only message headers during a remote connection to an Exchange server.

Windows 3.*x* and Windows for Workgroups Clients

When the Typical setup option is specified during a Windows 3.*x* Exchange client installation, a setup icon for ShivaRemote is created in the Microsoft Exchange program group. To utilize remote dial-up functionality, the user must run this ShivaRemote setup program. The program will copy all the

ShivaRemote files to the specified setup directory, except the files VNB.386 and CTL3D.DLL, which are copied to the <Windir>\SYSTEM directory. The setup program will also add the DIAL.386 driver to the SYSTEM.INI file, add the Shiva directory to the PATH statement in the AUTOEXEC. BAT file, and make some changes to the WIN.INI file. Before the setup program makes these changes it will back up the original files with .000 extensions to the Shiva directory.

The user must manually add the following lines to the CONFIG.SYS file:

```
device=c:\<Windir>\protman.dos /i:c:\<windir>
```

```
device=c:\<Shiva_dir>\dialndis.exe
```

The user must also add the following line, if it is not already present, to the AUTOEXEC.BAT file:

```
net start
```

If Windows for Workgroups is being used, the SYSTEM.INI file must also be modified by including the following line:

```
LoadRMDrivers=Yes
```

If a client is using Protected Mode Networking, the user must install the Shiva dial-in driver using the Network Application program found in the Network program group. In the list of adapters, the user must choose Unlisted and then enter the path to the Shiva files. The user will then have the option to install the protected mode dial-in driver and must configure it for the appropriate protocols. The computer must be restarted for the changes to take effect.

Remote Mail Features

Exchange MAPI clients have an option on the Tools menu named Remote Mail. This option enables a user to view new messages on an Exchange server, select specific messages to download to the offline Inbox, and send messages waiting in the Outbox. Downloading only the new messages is much faster than synchronizing the entire mailbox, as is done when using offline folders. All of these remote client features are only possible when connecting to Exchange Server.

Remote mail can be scheduled to automatically dial in to an Exchange server at specified times. This option can be used to take advantage of off-peak telephone rates.

Another feature of remote mail is the ability to create filters relating to retrieving remote mail. Rather than being forced to retrieve all your remote mail, you can designate conditions (i.e. filters) that must be met for a message to be downloaded. Conditions could include only retrieving messages sent by certain users, or only messages with a certain value in the subject field. There are even advanced filters such as message size and the date the message was received by your server mailbox.

Importing Messages and Address Information

Exchange MAPI clients can import messages and address books from the Microsoft Mail environment. This is useful for former users of Microsoft Mail who have upgraded to Exchange. Microsoft Mail messages are imported to Exchange folders and are not deleted from the original location.

Importing Messages

Microsoft Mail messages are stored in a file with the MMF extension, which can be password protected. A user must know the password to perform the import. MMF files also contain a copy of the user's Personal Address Book (PAB). When importing, the user is given the option to import either the messages, the address entries, or both. The imported messages must be placed in an Exchange personal folder store (PST). This can be an existing folder, or a folder can be created during the import procedure.

Messages can be imported from within an Exchange MAPI client. When the Import option on the File menu is chosen (the option is named Import and Export in Outlook), the user is prompted for the MMF password, what to import, and the folder to import messages to. Imported messages cannot be exported back to the Microsoft Mail environment.

The MS-DOS Exchange Client does not have the Import option.

Importing Address Book Information

Microsoft Mail Personal Address Books (PAB) can also be imported into the Exchange client environment. The imported address entries will be added to the current Exchange Personal Address Book entries. If any conflicts or errors occur during the import, the user will be notified. The address book import process is started the same way as the message import process, by choosing Import from the File menu (Import and Export in Outlook).

Exchange Clients in a NetWare Environment

Exchange Server is an application server—specifically, a messaging server. As such, it can be used in a Novell NetWare environment. NetWare clients can run the Exchange client software and connect to an Exchange server (see Figure 7.2). The Exchange server will still run on the Windows NT Server operating system, but there are some configuration parameters that must be met to enable the NetWare clients to access the Exchange server. Those configuration parameters are:

- NWLink installed on the Exchange server

- SAP running on the Exchange server

- NetWare clients correctly configured

In the following sections, we will discuss the NetWare environment.

NWLink Installed on the Exchange Server

Most Novell NetWare networks use the Internetwork Packet Exchange (IPX) and Sequenced Packet Exchange (SPX) network protocols. If NetWare clients are to be clients to an Exchange server, then the Exchange server must also use these network protocols. This is enabled by loading and binding the Microsoft NWLink protocol on the Exchange server. NWLink is Microsoft's 32-bit implementation of the IPX/SPX protocols. NWLink supports RPC communication between the NetWare clients and the Exchange server over the IPX/SPX protocols. Running NWLink on the Exchange server does not preclude using other network protocols simultaneously.

FIGURE 7.2

NetWare clients acting as
Exchange clients

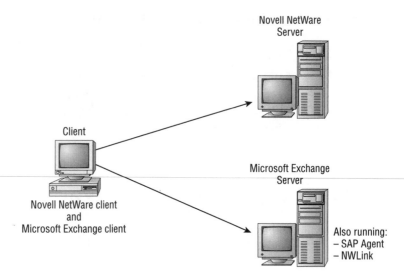

If the NetWare clients are not using IPX/SPX, but are instead using TCP/IP, then the Exchange server needs to be running TCP/IP.

Various configuration parameters for NWLink relate to how NetWare clients can communicate with the Exchange server. These parameters are:

- **Frame type** A frame is the information carrying package created by Data Link protocols, such as Ethernet, Token Ring, or FDDI. Frames carry the datagrams created at the Network Layer, such as IPX/SPX or TCP/IP. These protocols can use different formats when creating *frames*. The different formats are called frame types. For communication to take place, both sides need to use the same frame type. Consequently, the Exchange server must use the same frame type as the NetWare clients.

- **Internal network number** If the Exchange server has multiple network cards or is using multiple frame types, the network card and frame type being used by the NetWare clients must be assigned the network address of the Novell network. This address is referred to by Microsoft as the *internal network number*. The Exchange administrator can get this number from the NetWare system administrator. The number must have a value other than 0.

SAP Running on the Exchange Server

SAP stands for Service Advertising Protocol, a Novell protocol used by servers to advertise their services to clients and other servers. Information in the advertisement, called an SAP broadcast, consists of the name and location of the server. NetWare clients learn of the presence of servers by listening to the SAP broadcasts sent from servers. After learning of a server, a NetWare client can then access and use its services. Therefore, if an Exchange server wants to service NetWare clients, it too must utilize SAP.

An Exchange server can utilize SAP by having the Microsoft Gateway Service for NetWare (GSNW) component loaded and configured. Once this is done, the Exchange server is what Microsoft refers to as an SAP agent and can advertise its services by sending out SAP broadcasts.

If a *router* exists between the Exchange server and the NetWare/Exchange clients, the router must be configured to pass SAP broadcasts. Exchange Server uses SAP server type 0x640 to identify itself. This is the unique number that identifies the type of server that is advertising.

NetWare Clients Correctly Configured

There are also some steps that need to be done to the NetWare clients to enable them to access an Exchange server. Logging on to an Exchange server involves being authenticated in a Windows NT domain. This poses a challenge because Novell's NetWare client software does not support RPC communication, and therefore does not permit a client to be authenticated in a Windows NT domain (i.e. logon to the NT domain). Microsoft has solved this by providing various client programs. The Microsoft software that implements this depends on the operating system used by the NetWare client.

NetWare clients using Windows 95 and wishing to access an Exchange server would need to run the Client for Microsoft Networks program. If using Windows NT Workstation, a NetWare client would need to use the Windows NT Workstation service, which is included with this operating system. Both of these programs serve as a redirector, redirecting Exchange client requests to a Windows NT domain controller or Exchange server. Obviously, one of the Microsoft Exchange client applications, such as Outlook or the Exchange Client, would also need to be running on the NetWare client.

NetWare clients using Windows 3.*x* or MS-DOS and wishing to access an Exchange server use special RPC components to participate in a Microsoft network. These RPC components are automatically installed when the Exchange client software for Windows 3.*x* or MS-DOS is installed.

Summary

A messaging profile is the collection of configuration information used by a MAPI application, such as Microsoft Exchange Client or Microsoft Outlook. Some of the information contained in a profile indicates the information services to be used, such as Microsoft Exchange Server, Microsoft Fax, or Internet Mail. Other information in the profile relates to information storage, delegate access, and remote mail. Profiles can be created at the time of the client software installation. They can also be created and edited after the installation.

Exchange MAPI applications use the RPC protocol to perform client-server interactions. The RPC protocol uses a network protocol to physically transport its information. The order in which RPC attempts to use network protocols can be configured.

The Exchange MAPI clients support remote mail features that enable users to dial in to an Exchange server and access their mailboxes.

Some users will be upgrading from Microsoft Mail to Exchange. The Exchange MAPI clients permit a user's existing Microsoft Mail messages and address book entries to be imported into Exchange.

Review Questions

1. Which of the following is NOT a default information service in a messaging profile?

   A. Microsoft Fax

   B. Microsoft Mail

   C. Microsoft Exchange

   D. Both A and B

2. Remote mail supports Dial-Up Networking in Windows 95 clients.

   A. True

   B. False

3. A Personal Address Book is configured in a profile as an information service.

   A. True

   B. False

4. Delegate access is a feature of Microsoft Outlook only.

   A. True

   B. False

5. From which programs can the Send On Behalf Of permission be assigned?

   A. Microsoft Exchange Client

   B. Microsoft Outlook

   C. Microsoft Exchange Administrator program

   D. All of the above

6. Which of the following information files does SETUP look for when building a messaging profile?

   A. DEFAULT.PRF

   B. PROFILE.DAT

   C. PROFILE.PRF

   D. DEFAULT.DAT

7. What file contains the profile for an MS-DOS client?

A. PROFILE.DOS

B. PROF-MS.DOS

C. EXCHANGE.PRO

D. DOS.PRO

8. Which of the following is NOT a feature of remote mail?

A. PCMCIA cards

B. Downloading only new messages

C. Offline folders

D. Working offline

9. Which of the following relates to remote mail?

A. Offline address book

B. Scheduled connections

C. ShivaRemote

D. All of the above

10. Which of the following file types can be imported by the Exchange Client?

A. MMX

B. GIF

C. MMF

D. Both B and C

11. A Microsoft MAPI application can use only ONE information service.

    A. True

    B. False

12. The profile currently in use can be edited from within Exchange MAPI clients.

    A. True

    B. False

13. A user can designate their mailbox in the Private Information Store as the storage location of their messages.

    A. True

    B. False

14. Exchange clients have which of the following as notification options for new mail?

    A. Play a sound

    B. Blinking screen

    C. Briefly change the pointer

    D. Both A and C

15. Which of the following programs can be used to edit a messaging profile?

    A. WordPad

    B. PaintBrush

    C. Server Monitor

    D. The Mail and Fax applet in the Control Panel

16. Which of the following is required for a folder to be designated for offline use?

A. It must have a size limitation

B. It must have a password

C. It must not have a size limitation

D. It must be designated as a Favorite folder

C H A P T E R

8

Microsoft Exchange Forms

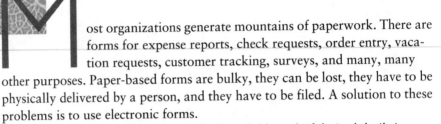

ost organizations generate mountains of paperwork. There are forms for expense reports, check requests, order entry, vacation requests, customer tracking, surveys, and many, many other purposes. Paper-based forms are bulky, they can be lost, they have to be physically delivered by a person, and they have to be filed. A solution to these problems is to use electronic forms.

Electronic forms are e-mail with built-in fields and, if desired, built-in actions. They can be used instead of paper-based forms to automate and streamline organizational functions. Each of the forms mentioned in the previous paragraph can be implemented as an electronic form (see Figure 8.1 for a typical electronic form). Electronic forms can be easily stored, backed up, transported through e-mail, and even configured for automation. An example of e-form automation is a check request form that is automatically routed to the correct, check signature authority depending on the amount of the check request. Electronic forms can be used in place of just about any paper-based form or any process that requires the acquisition of structured data (i.e., the data in the fields of a form). The completely paperless office is not quite a reality today, but electronic forms are a key technology for realizing this goal.

This chapter discusses how to create forms to be used in stand-alone and folder-based applications. The following main steps to create an Exchange form will be covered:

- Creating forms libraries

- Designing forms

- Installing forms

The term "electronic forms" will often be shortened to simply "forms" throughout the rest of this book.

F I G U R E   8.1

A typical electronic form

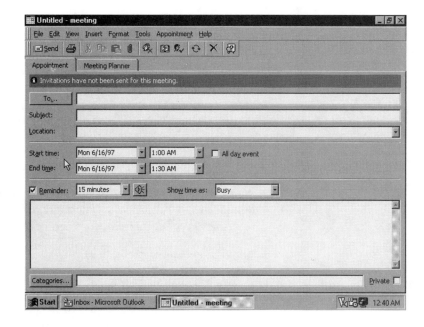

F I G U R E   8.1

A typical electronic form

Electronic Forms

Two powerful programs that design and create forms, Microsoft Outlook Forms Designer and Microsoft Exchange Forms Designer (EFD), are included with Exchange Server.

Microsoft Outlook Forms Designer is a 32-bit program that creates 32-bit forms. The forms it creates can only be accessed using the Microsoft Outlook client. Microsoft Exchange Forms Designer (EFD) is a 16-bit program that creates 16-bit forms. Forms created by EFD can be accessed using any of the Windows 16-bit or 32-bit Exchange clients (including Outlook).

These two form design tools and the forms they create will not run on the MS-DOS or Macintosh operating systems.

Both programs provide a visual, nonprogrammatic method to design and create forms. To design a form, users simply drag-and-drop objects (like text entry fields, checkboxes, and drop-down lists) onto a form. Users can also assign properties to these objects, such as font size, color, alignment, and even actions. The form design process is further simplified by the inclusion of numerous premade forms, called sample forms or applications. These sample forms can be used without modification, or they can be easily customized through the drag-and-drop interface.

Both the Outlook Forms Designer and the EFD are front-end programs to a specialized version of Microsoft Visual Basic. While the user is creating a form through the visual nonprogrammatic interface, Visual Basic is running "under the hood." This means the source files of both sample forms and new forms can be loaded into Visual Basic for further customization. Specialized forms that send data to a database, or forms that include multimedia, can be created by modifying forms in Visual Basic. Therefore, Exchange forms are extensible.

Two primary types of applications can be built using Exchange forms:

- Stand-alone applications

- Folder-based applications

Stand-alone form applications are forms that are sent from one person to another (for example, an expense report form that is filled out and sent to the user's manager). When forms are used in this manner, they are referred to as *Send forms*.

Folder-based applications utilize folders that have forms associated with them. Forms provide an easy and effective way to send and view data in a folder. Forms used this way are referred to as *Post forms*. Using folder-based applications can solve some problems that arise when using simple Send forms. For example, if a team of people is working on the same project, they are probably going to send many electronic messages between themselves. Some messages are even going to be sent to several people via carbon copies, forwarded messages, and reply messages. The result is a long list of unstructured information that takes a long time to sift through, and takes up unnecessary space. One solution is to create various forms for submitting, reading, replying, and modifying data. These forms can be associated with a public folder for the members of the team to use. Information becomes centralized and organized. Using forms in a public folder offers increased security and a more efficient use of space.

Creating Forms Libraries

Forms libraries are groups of forms. There are three types of forms libraries:

- **Organization Forms Library**   Forms in this library are available to everyone in the Exchange organization. This library makes it easy to distribute forms to a large number of people. The organization forms library is actually a public folder that is stored on an Exchange server, and it can be replicated to multiple Exchange servers in the same way any other public folder can. The Exchange administrator can give the organization library an arbitrary name, or keep the default name, Organization Forms. An Exchange organization may cover multiple locales around the world, so different language translations of the same forms may need to be made available. The Exchange administrator can create individual organization forms libraries for each language that is required. Each of these libraries is maintained as a separate public folder. Forms stored in the organization forms library are usually Send forms.

- **Personal Forms Library**   A personal forms library is stored in a user's mailbox and holds forms used by that user only. Forms stored in a personal forms library are usually Send forms.

- **Folder Forms Library**   Forms can be saved in a public folder for group access, a private folder, or even in a personal folder in a personal folder store (PST). Forms stored in a folder forms library are usually Post forms.

The Exchange administrator creates the organization forms library using the Exchange Administrator program. Because this library is actually a public folder, permissions on the library can be assigned to Exchange users (see Chapter 9 for information on public folder permissions). This enables the administrator to decide who can access the library and what they can do with it. A user must have the Folder Owner permission to install a form in a library. Exercise 8.1 walks you through the procedure to create the organization forms library.

Once form libraries have been created, forms can be designed and installed in these libraries. This will be discussed in the next two sections.

EXERCISE 8.1

Creating the Organization Forms Library

1. While in the Exchange Administrator program, choose Tools ➢ Forms Administrator. The Organization Forms Library Administrator dialog box will appear.

2. Click New. The Create New Forms Library dialog box will appear.

3. Keep the default Library folder name, Organization Forms. Next, choose the relevant language, such as English (USA), and click OK. The Organization Forms Library Administrator dialog box will reappear.

4. Click Permissions. The Forms Library Permissions dialog box will appear.

5. Click Add. Highlight the user George Washington and then click Add. Click OK. The Forms Library Permissions page will reappear with George Washington assigned the Reviewer role.

6. Highlight the user George Washington. Click on the down-arrow next to the Roles list box. Choose the role Owner. You can now log on as George Washington and publish the forms you will create later in this chapter. Click OK.

7. Click Close.

Designing Forms

Exchange provides two tools that can be used to design forms, the Outlook Forms Designer and the Exchange Forms Designer. Neither of these tools require programming to create a form, and both come with sample forms that can be used with or without customization. In this section, we will discuss these tools and the interoperability of the forms they create with client applications.

Microsoft Outlook Forms Designer

Sometimes the best way to explain something is to start at the end and work back. We will do this by first discussing the characteristics of an Outlook form, then covering the features that assist in the creation of an Outlook form, and finally outlining the actual steps to design and create a form.

Outlook Form Characteristics

The Outlook Forms Designer creates full-featured, yet small (average size 10K), 32-bit forms that can be quickly loaded and sent. The forms created are not *compiled*, meaning they are not translated into machine code (1s and 0s). Instead the source code is interpreted every time the form is loaded. This is an advantage because it allows forms to be easily modified. Forms can be linked to other Office 97 documents. For example, a chart created in Microsoft Excel could be used in an Outlook form. Also, a Web page can contain a link to an Outlook form. When the Web page is viewed in a browser, the link accesses an Outlook form and the user can input the requested information.

Microsoft Outlook Forms Designer Features

As stated earlier in this chapter, Outlook Forms Designer provides a visual, nonprogrammatic interface for forms creation. A user can simply choose a sample form, and then drag-and-drop the sample objects or new objects around on the form. The user can also assign properties and events to objects by accessing an object's property pages.

Outlook Sample Forms   Users are not relegated to creating forms from scratch. Outlook Forms Designer comes with numerous sample forms that can be used unchanged, or easily modified without any programming. They can also be modified using Visual Basic. Table 8.1 lists and describes these sample forms. More sample Outlook forms can be downloaded from the Microsoft Web site, `http://www.microsoft.com`.

TABLE 8.1 Outlook Forms Designer sample forms	Sample Form	Description
	Expense Report	Contains fields for various expense report information, such as name, date, expense categories, and subtotals. This form is patterned after a Microsoft Excel spreadsheet.
	Help Desk	Contains fields for making requests to a help desk, such as fixing or ordering equipment. This form also enables status tracking of the help desk request.

TABLE 8.1 (cont.)	Sample Form	Description
Outlook Forms Designer sample forms	Job Candidate	Contains fields for an interviewer to enter various information about a job candidate so this information can be posted in a public folder. Several interviewers can post their comments on a candidate, and then a supervisor can view this information.
	Sales Management	Contains fields relating to contact management (e.g., name, address, phone) and sales processes (e.g., meeting schedules). Permits sales management to store and view structured information.
	User Group	This form is part of an online discussion folder, where users can post, read, and respond to user-generated topics. Topics can be grouped by *discussion thread* to make a discussion easy to follow.
	Vacation Report	Contains fields relating to vacation requests and approvals.
	While You Were Out	Enables someone to take a message for another person, and to send the message to that person's mailbox.

Form Types   When designing a form from scratch, a user can choose from various standard types of forms. These form types are described in Table 8.2.

TABLE 8.2	Form Type	Description
Form types	Mail Message	Used to create Send forms, which can be used to send and receive information between recipients. Use this form type to create stand-alone form applications.
	Post	Used to create Post forms, which can be used to post information to a folder. If posted in a public folder, a group of users can view and respond to the postings. Folder-based applications are created by adding Post forms to a public folder and then customizing the permissions, views, and rules on that folder.

	Form Type	Description
TABLE 8.2 *(cont.)* Form types	Office 97 Document	Forms can include Office 97 documents. For example, a Microsoft Excel spreadsheet could be used in a form. The Outlook form, in a sense, wraps around the Office 97 document, allowing the document to be sent to other recipients.
	Contact, Task, and Calendar	Standard forms in Outlook are used to create new contacts, tasks, appointments, and meetings. These standard forms can be modified using Outlook Forms Designer.

Standard Design Features   Table 8.3 summarizes the features that help a user design a form.

	Feature	Description
TABLE 8.3 Standard design features	Alignment	Various alignment options assist the user when placing items on a form. Alignment options include left, center, right, top, middle, bottom, and snapping to a grid.
	Adjustable grid size	Enables the accurate positioning of items on a form.
	AutoLayout	Outlook Forms Designer can automatically position items on a form. For example, if a new item is placed below an existing item, AutoLayout will automatically left-align the new item with the existing item.

Figure 8.2 shows a design window in Outlook Forms Designer.

Advanced Design Features   Outlook Forms Designer includes design features that can be used to create advanced forms. Two of these features are described in Table 8.4.

FIGURE 8.2

A design window in
Outlook Forms Designer

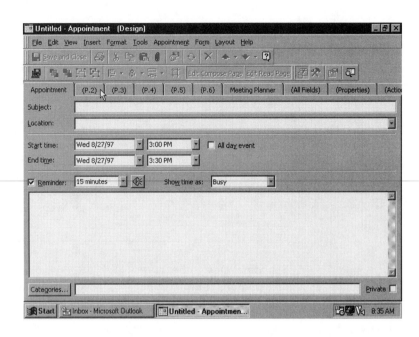

TABLE 8.4	**Feature**	**Description**
Advanced design features	Access Expression Service	A user can design a form that includes formula-based fields or validated or calculated fields. For example, a calculated field might total the number of days requested for vacation or a validated field might enforce a check request amount to be less than a certain ceiling.
	Visual Basic Scripting	Although Outlook Forms Designer is a nonprogrammatic forms-creation tool, the source code of the forms it creates is in Visual Basic format. Consequently, the source code of a form can be modified using Visual Basic or Visual Basic Scripting Edition (VBScript).

Designing and Creating an Outlook Form

You now have the necessary knowledge to proceed with the steps to create an Outlook form. The Outlook Forms Designer is started from within Outlook. Under the File menu, choose the New option, and then choose an Outlook component that will serve as the basic building block of the form. After the form is loaded, choose the Tools menu on the form window, and select the Design Outlook Form option. This option runs the Outlook Forms Designer.

Exercise 8.2 will walk you through the basic steps to create a form with the Outlook Forms Designer. Figures 8.3A and 8.3B depict the form that you will create in this exercise.

EXERCISE 8.2

Creating a Customer Tracking Form with Outlook Forms Designer

1. While in Outlook, choose File ➢ New ➢ Contact. You will see a window titled "Untitled-Contact." This loads the Outlook contact form which will serve as a building block for our form.

2. From the Untitled-Contact window, choose the Tools menu, then choose Design Outlook Form. The window will now be titled "Untitled-Contact (Design)." The Outlook Forms Designer is now running. Maximize the window.

3. Click the tab labeled "(Properties)." In the Form Caption box, enter **Customer Tracking for Widget, Inc**.

4. Click the tab labeled "(P.2)." Under the Form menu, choose Rename Page. The Rename Page dialog box appears. In the Page Name box, enter **More Info**. Click OK. Now we will begin dragging-and-dropping objects onto the new form.

5. In the Field Chooser palette window, click Full Name and drag it to the upper-left corner of the form. A text entry field labeled "Full Name" will be added.

6. Click the down-arrow on the Field Chooser palette, and click Personal fields. From the options that now appear, drag Anniversary, Children, Hobbies, Referred By, and Web Page to the area below the Full Name field.

EXERCISE 8.2 (CONTINUED FROM PREVIOUS PAGE)

7. Click the New button at the bottom of the Field Chooser palette. The New Field dialog box appears. In the Name box, enter **Key Customer**. In the Type list, choose Yes/No. Click OK.

8. Drag the Key Customer field to the area under the Web Page field. You should notice that the Yes/No option is displayed as a check box.

9. On the File menu, choose Save As. The Save As screen will appear. In the File name field, type **cust-track-form**. Select Outlook Template in the Save type field. Click Save. The form will be saved with this name.

10. The form is now created, but it is not available for use. It must be installed in a forms library. The installation is performed in Outlook, but this step will be covered in the section "Installing Forms" and in Exercise 8.4.

FIGURE 8.3A

The form created in Exercise 8.2

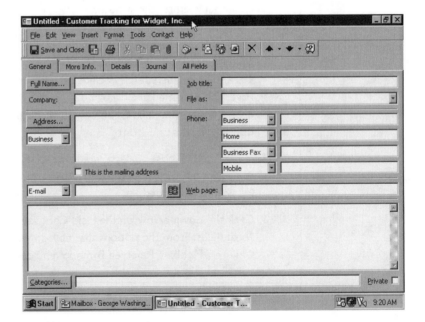

FIGURE 8.3B

The form created in
Exercise 8.2

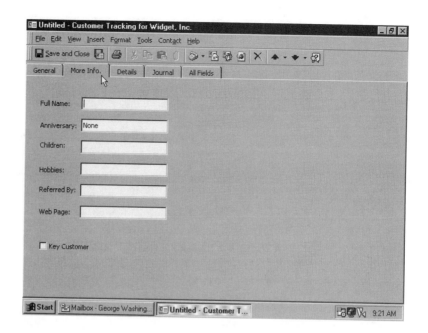

Now you need to create a Task Form. Exercise 8.3 will help you get
started. Use your creativity to design and finish the form yourself.

EXERCISE 8.3

Creating a Task Form with Outlook Forms Designer

1. In Outlook, choose File ➢ New ➢ Task. You will see a window titled
   "Untitled-Task." This loads the Outlook task form which will serve as
   a building block for our form.

2. From the Untitled-Task window, choose the Tools menu, then choose
   Design Outlook Form. The window will now be titled "Untitled-Task
   (Design)." The Outlook Forms Designer is now running. Maximize
   the window.

3. Click the tab labeled "(Properties)." In the Form Caption box, enter
   Task Form, Accounting Dept.

4. Design the form any way you would like.

EXERCISE 8.3 (CONTINUED FROM PREVIOUS PAGE)

5. When you have finished designing the form, save it by choosing the File menu, and Save As option. Name it **task-form**. Select Outlook Template in the Save as type field.

6. As with the last exercise, this form is created, but is not available for use. The form must be installed in a forms library while in Outlook. You will perform this procedure in Exercise 8.4.

Exchange Forms Designer

We will now discuss the characteristics of an EFD form, the features that assist in the creation of a form using EFD, and the steps to create a form using EFD.

EFD Form Characteristics

Whereas Outlook forms are 32-bit and not compiled, EFD forms are 16-bit and compiled. After an EFD form has been created, it is installed in a forms library. For EFD forms, forms are compiled into executable files at the moment they are installed in a library (there is more on this process in the section Installing Forms).

Exchange Forms Designer Features

Some EFD features are similar to those in Outlook Forms Designer. Both tools enable a drag-and-drop manipulation of objects, like text entry fields and checkboxes, in order to design a form. Both tools include sample forms that can be used immediately or customized. Forms created with both tools can be extended with Visual Basic programming.

Two of the main differences between EFD and Outlook Forms Designer are that EFD builds compiled forms, and EFD cannot use Office 97 objects as part of a form because EFD is a 16-bit application. Also, EFD and Outlook Forms Designer include different sets of sample forms.

Exchange Forms Designer Sample Forms   Exchange Forms Designer comes with many useful sample forms. These forms can simplify record keeping, enhance office communication, and increase staff efficiency. Table 8.5 lists and describes the sample forms that come with Exchange Forms Designer.

T A B L E 8.5	**Sample Form**	**Description**
Exchange Forms Designer sample forms	Anonymous Submissions	Enables anonymous information to be posted to a public folder.
	Charity Donation	Includes fields for a charity name and amount to donate.
	Classified Ads	Enables classified ads to be posted to a public folder.
	Chess	A demonstration form showing how Visual Basic, Active Messaging, and Exchange can be used to create a form-based application. Users can play chess via e-mail, complete with a view of the board, using this nifty sample.
	Customer Tracking	Includes fields relating to various customer information. Can be used to track customer contacts and information.
	Discussion and Response	This form is part of an online discussion folder, where users can post, read, and respond to user-generated topics. Topics can be grouped by *discussion thread* to make a discussion easy to follow.
	Help Desk	Includes fields for help desk requests, such as fixing or ordering equipment.
	Hot Topics	Enables moderator approved news items to be submitted.
	Interpersonal Forms	A collection of forms that are appropriate for inclusion in the organization forms library. Includes the following forms: Answer, Bug Report, Charity Donation, Purchase Offer, and Vacation/Sick-Day.
	Schedule Time Away	Includes fields for submitting vacation or sick-day requests.
	Survey	Includes fields that can be customized to create polls or surveys.

Exchange Forms Designer Interface   EFD includes a toolbox palette which permits a user to drag-and-drop text entry fields, drop-down lists, and other elements onto a form. EFD also includes a toolbar that allows easy access to functions such as changing colors, creating tables, and saving forms. The sample forms mentioned earlier can be used as a starting point for creating a custom form. EFD also includes the Forms Design Wizard. The Wizard guides the user through the process of creating a new form. When the Wizard is complete, the user can further customize the new form using the tools in EFD.

Designing and Creating an EFD Form

The Exchange Forms Designer can be launched from within the Exchange Client application. Start EFD by choosing Application Design, Forms Designer from the Tools menu. When EFD starts, it prompts the user to choose the Form Template Wizard, a sample form from the Template List, or another existing form. After a form has been created, it can be saved by choosing Save from the File menu, or by clicking the Save toolbar button. When an EFD form is saved, it is stored in an Exchange Forms Project (EFP) file. This is a Microsoft Access 2.0 database file containing all the information about the form's structure and functionality. The EFP file is used to generate Visual Basic source code during the installation of the form (see "Installing Forms.")

Interoperability Issues

Outlook users can use forms created by either the Outlook Forms Designer or EFD, but Exchange Client users cannot use forms created by the Outlook Forms Designer. Microsoft Mail and other foreign mail system users cannot use forms created in either the Outlook Forms Designer or EFD. This is an important issue to keep in mind when designing an Exchange organization. If all users will be using Outlook, then the Outlook Forms Designer is the obvious choice for forms creation. But if some users are using Outlook and some are using the Exchange Client, then EFD should be used until all users have been upgraded to Outlook.

Comparing Outlook Forms Designer and EFD

Table 8.6 summarizes and compares the two forms creation programs.

T A B L E 8.6 Comparison of Outlook Forms Designer and EFD	**Outlook Forms Designer**	**Exchange Forms Designer (EFD)**
	32-bit forms	16-bit forms
	Visual, nonprogrammatic design method	Visual, nonprogrammatic design method

	Outlook Forms Designer	Exchange Forms Designer (EFD)
T A B L E 8.6 (cont.) Comparison of Outlook Forms Designer and EFD	Forms not compiled	Forms compiled
	Send and Post forms	Send and Post forms
	Microsoft Office 97 integration	No Microsoft Office 97 integration
	Sample forms included	Sample forms included
	Form code can be extended using Visual Basic	Form code can be extended using Visual Basic
	Can be read by Outlook, but not by the Exchange Client	Can be read by Outlook or the Exchange Client

Installing Forms

After a form is created, it must be installed in a forms library before it can be used. Installation in a library makes a form available to a specific user or a group of users. The installation process puts a form in the necessary format and location for use. Outlook, EFD, and the Exchange Client can each be used to install (or *publish*) a form.

Installing a Form Using Outlook

After a form has been created using the Outlook Forms Designer, the user can install it from within Outlook. Choose Options from the Tools menu and select the Manage Forms property page on the Options dialog box that appears. Click the Manage Forms button to open the Forms Manager. The Forms Manager is used to install forms into libraries and move forms between libraries. Forms can also be installed directly from the form window when they are created. A user installing a form into a folder needs the Folder Owner permission on that folder. Exercise 8.4 outlines the steps for this process.

EXERCISE 8.4

Installing a Form Using Outlook

1. If you still have the task form loaded, you can install it by choosing File ➤ Publish Form As. The Publish Form As dialog box will appear (if this form is not loaded, go to Step 5).

2. Click Publish In. The Set Library To dialog box will appear.

3. In the Forms Library list, click Organization Forms, and then click OK.

4. Click Publish.

5. If the task form is not loaded, go to the Outlook Bar (the icon and options on the far-left side of your Outlook window), and click on the Other option. This will bring up the icons for My Computer, My Documents, and Favorites. Click on My Documents or navigate to the folder in which you saved the task form.

6. In the right content pane, locate and double-click on the TASK-FORM.OFT file. This will bring up the task form. To see the information that you designed, choose Tools ➤ Design Outlook Form.

7. To publish this form, choose File ➤ Publish Form As. The Publish Form As dialog box will appear.

8. Click Publish In. The Set Library To dialog box will appear.

9. In the Forms Library list, click Organization Forms, and then click OK.

10. Click Publish.

11. Choose File ➤ Close.

12. You also need to publish the Customer Tracking for Widget, Inc. form. We saved this form, so use the procedure outlined in Steps 5 – 10 to retrieve it.

Installing a Form Using EFD

Immediately after creating and saving a form in the EFD program, the form can be installed. To do this, choose the Install option from the File menu.

When this option is selected, three processes occur automatically, and a fourth process requires user input. The four processes are listed here:

1. **Generation of source code** The EFD program takes the information in the Exchange Forms Project (EFP) file and generates Visual Basic source code in a file with a VBP extension. The EFP file was created when the form was saved.

2. **Compiling into an executable file** The EFD program compiles the Visual Basic source code into an executable file (EXE).

3. **Creation of a configuration file** The EFD creates a text file containing configuration information about the compiled form. Information includes the form's executable name, message type (i.e., Send or Post form), and a list of fields on the form. The configuration file has a CFG extension and is stored in the <form_name>.vb directory. This file is used in the next step.

4. **Install in a forms library** The user now specifies the forms library where the form is to be installed. After Step 3 is complete, the Set Library To dialog box will appear. The user selects the destination forms library in this dialog box.

Installing a Form Using the Exchange Client

If a form has already been compiled in EFD, it can be installed through the Exchange Client. To do this, choose Options from the Tools menu and select the Exchange Server tab from the Options dialog box that appears. Click the Manage Forms button on this tab to invoke the Forms Manager. The Forms Manager can be used to install new forms and move forms between forms libraries. A user installing a form into a folder needs the Folder Owner permission on that folder.

Summary

Electronic forms can be used instead of most paper-based forms to provide a more efficient method of communication. Send Forms can be used to send information to other users. Post Forms can be used to post information to a personal, private, or public folder. Forms posted in public folders can be used as the foundation for a folder-based application.

Exchange Server ships with two forms design programs, Outlook Forms Designer, and Exchange Forms Designer (EFD). Outlook Forms Designer is a 32-bit program that creates small, fast-loading, uncompiled 32-bit forms. It integrates very tightly with Microsoft Office 97. EFD is a 16-bit program that creates compiled forms. Both programs provide a visual, nonprogrammatic method to create forms. They also both provide sample forms that can be used immediately or customized.

After forms have been created, they are installed, or published, in a forms library. This makes the form available for use to a user or group of users. Security can be applied to a forms library to configure who can install and use forms.

Both forms design programs use a specialized version of Visual Basic. The forms that are created can therefore be further customized or extended by loading the form file into Visual Basic and adding further program code.

Users send and receive forms through their normal Exchange client programs, such as Outlook and the Exchange Client.

Review Questions

1. A form that is used to directly input information into a public folder is called:

   A. A Send form

   B. An Input form

   C. A Folder form

   D. A Post form

2. The Exchange Client can send and receive Outlook forms.

   A. True

   B. False

3. Outlook forms are not compiled.

   A. True

   B. False

4. The following procedure makes forms available for use:

   A. Installing or publishing forms

   B. Customizing in Visual Basic

   C. Saving in the FRM format

   D. Saving to the Access database

5. EFD forms are compiled into an executable format.

   A. True

   B. False

6. A Microsoft Office 97 object could be used in an Outlook form.

   A. True

   B. False

7. If a form needed wide availability, it would be installed in this location:

   A. Personal folder

   B. Organization forms library

   C. Administrator's mailbox

   D. A public mailbox

8. Outlook can send and receive forms created in EFD.

   A. True

   B. False

9. Which of the following is NOT a design feature of Outlook Forms Designer?

A. AutoLayout

B. Alignment

C. Visual Basic scripting

D. Lotus Notes formatting

10. EFD saves form information in this database format:

A. Microsoft Access

B. SQL

C. Paradox

D. DB2

CHAPTER

9

Public Folders as a Client Resource

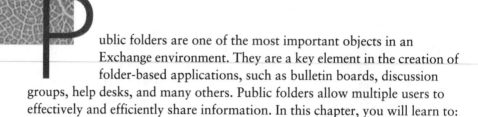

ublic folders are one of the most important objects in an Exchange environment. They are a key element in the creation of folder-based applications, such as bulletin boards, discussion groups, help desks, and many others. Public folders allow multiple users to effectively and efficiently share information. In this chapter, you will learn to:

- Create public folders

- Configure public folders

- Use public folders

The tasks described in this chapter can all be performed by client users. Chapter 12 will cover public folders from the perspective of an Exchange administrator. Topics covered will include public folder replication, storage limits, creating dedicated public folder servers, and many others.

Creating Public Folders

Public folders are created using Exchange MAPI-based clients. They cannot be created from the Exchange Administrator program. It is a very simple process for users to create new public folders, assuming they have been granted the necessary permissions by the administrator and have a basic understanding of public folder functionality.

Public Folder Hierarchy

Public folders are organized hierarchically, like a directory structure. Every user in the organization views the same hierarchy (see Figure 9.1). The root, or highest level, is called the *top-level*. By default, all users may create folders at this level, but the Exchange Administrator program can be used to modify the list of users who have permissions to create top-level folders. It is important to have this administrator control so that users don't clutter up the root of the tree and make it difficult to navigate. Exercise 9.1 outlines the steps to modify the permissions.

FIGURE 9.1

Public folder hierarchy

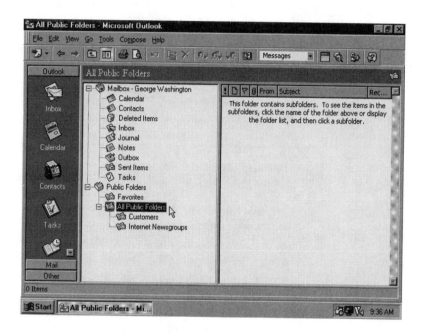

Subfolders can be created within the top-level folders. Subfolders can also have subfolders, and those subfolders can also have subfolders...and so on (see the sidebar). Subfolders are like subdirectories in a directory structure. A folder's owner (who is, by default, the user who created the folder) determines who may create subfolders in a folder by assigning the necessary permissions. Create Subfolders is the name of the permission that must be granted (permissions are discussed in the section "Configuring Public Folders").

EXERCISE 9.1

Modifying the Top-Level Permissions

1. Start the Exchange Administrator program and connect to the Exchange server.

2. In the left pane, click to expand your site object, then click on the Configuration object within it.

3. In the right pane, double-click on the Information Store Site Configuration object. This will bring up the property pages for Information Store Site Configuration.

4. Click on the tab labeled "Top Level Folder Creation." You will see two list box fields that allow you to specify who may or may not create public folders at the top-level of the public folder hierarchy. For our purposes, do not change the default.

Turtles All the Way Down

The following story may not be true, but it is funny. Some years ago, a famous professor of astronomy at an Ivy League college went on a speaking tour of small, out-of-the-way towns. He would speak and show slides of planets, solar systems, and the rest of the universe. At the end of his presentations, he would answer questions. At one meeting, a little old man got up and thanked the professor for coming and talking. But he made it quite clear that he thought everything the professor had said was bunk because the Earth rested on the back of a big turtle. After hearing this, the professor smiled and wanted to know what the turtle rested on. The little old man replied that the turtle rested on the back of another bigger turtle. As the professor began to ask what that turtle rested on, the little old man interrupted him by saying, "Oh no, you can't trick me. The answer is turtles all the way down!"

Programs and Procedures

The Exchange Administrator program can be used to manage public folders, but not create them. Both Outlook and the Exchange Client programs can be used to create public folders. In Outlook, a public folder can be created by choosing Folder, Create Subfolder from the File menu. The Create New Folder dialog box will appear, prompting you for various information. Exercise 9.2 will walk you through these steps.

EXERCISE 9.2

Creating a Public Folder with Outlook

1. Log on to the Windows NT domain as GeorgeW.

2. Start Outlook, click on the File menu, choose Folder ➤ Create Subfolder. The Create New Folder dialog box will appear.

3. In the Name field, enter a name for the public folder you are creating. For this exercise, enter the name **Customers**.

4. In the Make this Folder a Subfolder Of field, expand the Public Folders object, and then select the All Public Folders object within it.

5. Type the following in the Description field: **This folder contains various information relating to customers of Widget, Inc.** Click OK.

6. If the Folder List is not visible, click the Folder List tool button on the toolbar, or choose Folder List from the View menu. The folder hierarchy will be displayed in a new pane. Maximize Outlook, and if necessary, enlarge the Folder List by grabbing its right border and resizing it to a suitable viewing width.

7. Notice the Customers public folder directly under the All Public Folders object. Click on the Customers folder to see that there are no items in it yet.

Configuring Public Folders

The key configuration elements of public folders are:

- Permissions

- Forms

- Rules

- Views

Public folders have a set of property pages that are used for configuration. There are two ways to display these property pages. One way is to highlight the public folder, click the right mouse button, and choose Properties from the pop-up menu that appears. Another way is to highlight the public folder and then choose Folders, Properties for <public folder name> from the File menu.

Permissions

By assigning permissions, a public folder owner can choose which users have access to the folder, and what actions those users may perform. There are eight individual permissions and nine groupings of permissions, called roles, that can be assigned. Table 9.1 describes the permissions, descending from the permission with the most capabilities to the permission with the fewest capabilities. The word "items," as used in this table, refers to the contents of the public folder, such as e-mail messages, forms, documents, and other files.

T A B L E   9.1

Public folder permissions

Permission	Description
Folder Owner	Can change permissions in a folder and perform administrative tasks, such as adding rules and installing forms on a folder
Create Items	Create new items in a folder
Create Subfolder	Create a subfolder within a folder
Edit Items	Edit (modify) items in a folder
Delete Items	Permanently delete items in a folder

T A B L E 9.1 (cont.) Public folder permissions	**Permission**	**Description**
	Read Items	Open and view items in a folder
	Folder Contact	Receive e-mail notifications relating to a folder. Notifications include replication conflicts, folder design conflicts, and storage limit notifications. (There is more on this in Chapter 12.)
	Folder Visible	Whether the folder is visible to the user in the public folder hierarchy

Table 9.2 lists the predefined groupings of permissions into roles.

T A B L E 9.2

Predefined roles and their permissions

Role	Folder Owner	Create Items	Create Subfolder	Edit Items	Delete Items	Read Items	Folder Contact	Folder Visible
Owner	✓	✓	✓	✓ (all)	✓ (all)	✓	✓	✓
Publishing Editor		✓	✓	✓ (all)	✓ (all)	✓		✓
Editor		✓		✓ (all)	✓ (all)	✓		✓
Publishing Author		✓	✓	✓ (own)	✓ (own)	✓		✓
Author		✓		✓ (own)	✓ (own)	✓		✓
Nonediting Author		✓			✓ (own)	✓		✓
Contributor		✓						✓
Reviewer						✓		✓
None								✓

Custom roles consisting of any combination of individual permissions may also be assigned.

When a public folder is created, three users are included on the permissions list by default: the user who created the public folder, a special user called Default, and another special user called Anonymous. The user who created the public folder is assigned the Owner role by default. Other users may also be assigned this role. The special user called Default represents all users who have access to the public folder store. On top-level folders, the Author role is assigned to the Default user by default. But on subfolders, the default role assigned to the Default user is the same role that is assigned to the Default user on the parent folder. The Anonymous user represents permissions that users logged on anonymously using a Web browser or newsgroup reader will have. All users can be removed from the access list except the Default user, Anonymous user, and the folder owner. See Figure 9.2 for a view of the Permissions property page of a public folder.

If the Windows NT user account that is the owner of a public folder is deleted, the Exchange administrator can designate themselves as the owner of the public folder.

FIGURE 9.2

The Permissions property page of a public folder

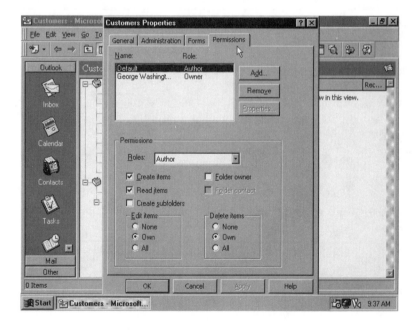

Exercise 9.3 outlines the steps to configure the permissions on the Customers public folder.

EXERCISE 9.3

Configuring the Permissions on a Public Folder

1. In Outlook, highlight the Customers public folder. Click the right mouse button and choose Properties from the pop-up menu. The Customers Properties dialog box will appear.

2. Click on the Permissions tab. Notice that (because this is a top-level folder) the Default user has the Author role. Notice that the user who created this public folder, GeorgeW, has the Owner role.

3. Highlight the Default user, then click on the down-arrow in the Roles field. Choose the None role from the list.

4. Click Add and highlight the user Thomas Jefferson. Then click Add and click OK. The user Thomas Jefferson is added to the access list for the public folder with the role of None. This role was automatically assigned because the Default user's role is None. Change Thomas Jefferson's role to Author. Notice that Thomas Jefferson now has the Create items and Read items permissions. This role also allows him to edit and delete his own items.

5. Click OK to save the configuration. These permissions will be tested in the section "Using Public Folders" later in this chapter.

Hiding Public Folders

Public folders can be hidden from the GAL and the public folder hierarchy. Hiding public folders can be part of your security plan. The following bullet points contain information about the different aspects of this topic:

- **Hiding a public folder from the GAL**   By default, each public folder is hidden from the GAL. A public folder can be made visible by clearing the "Hide from address book" checkbox found on its Advanced property page.

- **Hiding a public folder from the public folder hierarchy**   By default, all public folders and their content is visible in the public folder hierarchy to all other recipients. To make the contents of a particular public folder hidden, you must revoke the Read Items permission for the recipient or recipients at that particular folder. If you wanted to hide not merely the contents of a public folder, but also its very listing in the hierarchy you can revoke the Read Items permission at the parent folder of the folder you want hidden. Since a subfolder is considered part of the content of its parent folder, revoking this permission at the parent folder can prevent the viewing of that subfolder in the hierarchy.

Since top-level folders, also called root folders, do not have a parent, they cannot be hidden from the hierarchy. But their content can be hidden. Many times an organization will create a top-level folder (e.g. Hidden Folders) that will contain all the folders they want hidden from the majority of their users. The Author role will be revoked from the Default user at this top-level folder, and instead they will be assigned the None role. The top-level folder will still be seen, but all the subfolders will be hidden. To enable the recipients who do need to access those subfolders, a distribution list can be created with those recipients as members and that DL can be assigned the Read Items permission at that root folder.

Forms

Forms can be associated with a public folder, allowing users to submit structured data into the folder. The list of forms associated with a public folder is found in the folder's property pages. Exercise 9.4 walks through the steps to associate a form with a public folder.

EXERCISE 9.4

Associating a Form with a Public Folder

1. In Outlook, highlight the Customers public folder in the hierarchy in the Folder List. Choose File ➢ Folders ➢ Properties for "Customers." The Customers Properties dialog box will appear.

2. Click on the Forms tab. Notice that there are currently no forms associated with this public folder, but that the Allow These Forms in This Folder field is set to Any Form. You are going to associate a specific form with this folder and configure it as the only form to be used with this folder.

3. Click Manage. The Forms Manager will appear listing the forms published in the Organization Forms library. In Chapter 8 you created the Customer Tracking for Widget, Inc. form. This form will appear in the list box under the Organization Forms library.

4. Click on the Customer Tracking for Widget, Inc. form, then click Copy. Because this form was already installed, all you have to do now is click Close. Notice that this form is now associated with this public folder.

5. Under the Allow These Forms in This Folder field, choose Only Forms Listed Above. Then click OK. The form installation performed in this exercise will be tested in the section "Using Public Folders."

Rules

Rules consisting of conditions and actions can be configured on public folders. Rules allow a public folder to automate certain procedures. The following is a list of some of the conditions (or *criteria*) that can be used to determine if a rule will be activated when messages arrive in a public folder:

- **From**   Message from specified recipients.

- **Sent To**   Message sent to specified recipients.

- **Subject**   Specified text in the Subject heading of a message.

- **Message Body**   Specified text or phrase in the body of a message.

- **Size**   A specified size of a message, "At least" x size, or "At most" x size.

- **Received**   A specified date range that a message was received within.

The following actions can be triggered if the preceding conditions are met:

- **Delete**   Delete the message.

- **Reply With**   Reply to the message's sender with a specified message template.

- **Forward To**   Forward the message to specified recipients.

Rules are added to public folders by clicking the Folder Assistant button on a folder's Administration property page. Clicking this button displays the Folder Assistant dialog box which enables you to add, edit, delete, and order rules for a public folder. Exercise 9.5 outlines the steps to create a rule on a public folder.

EXERCISE 9.5

Creating a Rule on a Public Folder

1. In Outlook, highlight the Customers public folder. Click the right mouse button and choose Properties from the pop-up menu. The Customers Properties dialog box will appear.

2. Click on the Administration tab.

3. Click Folder Assistant. The Folder Assistant dialog box will appear.

4. Click Add Rule. The Edit Rule dialog box will appear. In the Subject field type **Acme**, and in the Message Body type **Acme** again. This is the condition part of the rule.

5. Now we will set the action part of the rule. Click the Forward check box, and then click To. The Choose Recipient dialog box will appear. In the Show Names from The field, choose Global Address List. Then, choose the user Andrew Jackson and click To. Click OK. Then click OK successively on the next three dialog boxes. The rule is now saved within the properties of the Customers public folder. This rule will be tested in the "Using Public Folders" section.

Views

Outlook and the Exchange Client include many powerful features to view items in a folder. Some of the features in Outlook are listed in Table 9.3.

TABLE 9.3 Outlook features	Feature	Examples
	Sort	Sort items by who they are from, who they are to, importance, subject text, sensitivity, or other properties.

T A B L E 9.3 (cont.) Outlook features	**Feature**	**Examples**
	Filter	Filter items by words of phrases contained in the subject text or message body, who they are from, who they are to, what time they were sent, or other properties. Only items that pass through the filter are displayed in the contents pane.
	Group By	Group items by when they are due, who they are from, who they are to, importance, subject text, sensitivity, or other properties.

The next section will cover using some of the features discussed earlier in this chapter.

Using Public Folders

This section and its exercises cover how to add content to a public folder.

Adding Content to a Public Folder

The two primary methods to add content to a public folder are:

- Posting forms
- Mail messages

Posting

If a public folder is configured to accept postings, which is the default, users who have the necessary permissions can post data to the public folder. To post, a user must highlight the public folder and either click the Post tool on the Toolbar, or choose New Post in This Folder from the Compose menu. Posting is an easy and efficient method of adding content to a public folder because the user does not have to address the message as they do when sending a mail message to a public folder. Exercise 9.6 outlines the steps for this procedure.

EXERCISE 9.6

Posting Information to a Public Folder

1. In Outlook, highlight the Customers public folder.

2. Choose File ➢ New ➢ Choose Form. The New Form dialog box will appear.

3. Highlight the Customer Tracking for Widget, Inc. form. Click OK. The form will appear.

4. Enter the following in the Full Name field: **Dolly Madison**.

5. Enter the following in the Company field: **Acme**.

6. Enter some text in the body.

7. Click on the More Info. tab to view the page you designed. Enter some information.

8. When you are finished entering information, click the Save and Close toolbar button.

9. Notice the new entry in the Customers public folder. If you double-click that entry, you will see the information you just entered.

10. To test our configuration of the forms associated with this public folder, try to use the Task Form, Accounting Dept. form to post information to this public folder. You should not be able to do so because we configured this public folder to use only the Customer Tracking form.

11. To test Thomas Jefferson's permission assignments at this folder, log on as Thomas Jefferson and post some information to the Customer folder. Use the Post button on the Toolbar to enter information into this folder. We gave Thomas Jefferson the Author role, so you should be able to post.

12. Log on as Andrew Jackson. Can you enter information into the Customer folder? Did we give Andrew Jackson any permissions to the folder?

13. Log back on as George Washington to prepare for the next exercise.

Another method of adding content to a public folder is to drag-and-drop a Microsoft Office 97 object directly into the folder. This method is equivalent to posting an item to the folder.

Mail Messages

A mail message can be sent to a public folder. As you will remember from Chapter 4, a public folder is a recipient, and can therefore receive and send messages. Exercise 9.7 outlines the steps to send a mail message to a public folder.

EXERCISE 9.7

Sending a Mail Message to a Public Folder

1. In order for someone to send a mail message to a public folder, the public folder must be visible in the address book. By default, public folders are not visible in the address book. To perform this exercise, we must make the Customers public folder visible. While in Exchange Administrator, navigate to and highlight the Customers public folder under the Public Folders container. Click File ➢ Properties. The Customers Properties pages appear. Click the Advanced page. Notice the checkbox labeled "Hide from address book." It is checked. For this exercise, clear this checkbox. Click OK. This public folder will now be visible in the address book.

2. Make sure you are logged on as George Washington. In Outlook, choose Compose ➢ New Message. An untitled mail-message window will appear.

3. Click To. In the Show Names from The field, choose Global Address List. Find the Customers public folder in the Global Address List.

4. Select the Customers public folder and click To. Click OK.

5. In the Subject field, type **Acme Proposal**.

6. In the body of the message enter the following: **I think we can lower our unit price and increase the units shipped in regard to the Acme proposal. What are your thoughts?**

---

7. Click the Options tab. In the Importance field, choose High. For Tracking options choose Tell Me When this Message Has Been Read.

8. Click the Send tool in the Toolbar.

9. To test the rule we assigned to the Customer folder, log on as Andrew Jackson and see if the Folder Assistant automatically sent Andrew Jackson the information about Acme that was posted to the Customer folder.

Summary

Public folders are an efficient and effective way to share data among several people. Permissions, forms, rules, and views can be configured on public folders to create folder-based applications. Users can easily create public folders using Outlook or the Exchange Client.

Permissions enable a folder owner to specify who can access a folder, and what users can do in that folder. Associating a form with a public folder assists users in submitting structured information into the folder. Rules on public folders can perform automated actions when the appropriate conditions are met. Public folders can hold a large quantity and variety of information, so views can be leveraged to display the pertinent items in a desired way.

Adding content to public folders is very easy. It can be done by posting directly to a public folder, or by sending the public folder regular e-mail messages.

Exercise Questions

1. Public folders can be assigned the user rights used in Windows NT.

   A. True

   B. False

2. By default, no users can create folders at the top-level of the public folder hierarchy.

    A. True

    B. False

3. Which of the following relate to assigning rules to a public folder?

    A. Conditions

    B. Actions

    C. Folder Assistant

    D. All of the above

4. Public folder permissions are grouped into predefined:

    A. Hives

    B. Clone sets

    C. Roles

    D. Sets

5. There can be only one user with the Owner role on a public folder.

    A. True

    B. False

6. Which of the following cannot be done?

    A. Hide a public folder from the hierarchy

    B. Hide the contents of a public folder

    C. Hide a top-level public folder

    D. Hide a public folder from the GAL

7. If the recipient who is the owner of a public folder is deleted, what can be done in order to allow the administrator to grant permissions to other recipients?

    A. Delete the public folder, and recreate it

    B. Designate the recipient used by the administrator as the owner

    C. Give the administrator account the "right to logon as a service"

    D. Restore a backup tape that was made before the previous recipient was deleted

8. What must you do to hide a subfolder from a particular recipient?

    A. Revoke the Read Items permission from that recipient at the parent folder

    B. Revoke the Read Items permission from that recipient at that subfolder

    C. Hide the root folder above that subfolder

    D. A subfolder cannot be hidden, only its contents

9. By default, all public folders can be seen in the GAL.

    A. True

    B. False

10. By default, all public folders are visible in the public folder hierarchy.

    A. True

    B. False

CHAPTER

10

Advanced Security

As computer networking has become more and more pervasive, the information transported over networks has become more important and valuable. As a result, some unscrupulous people try to steal information and disrupt business affairs. E-mail messages are susceptible to eavesdropping, tampering, and forgery. These and other security threats can be prevented by implementing advanced security measures.

Theft, tampering, and forgery can be countered through *cryptology,* which is the study and implementation of hiding and revealing information. The word cryptology comes from two Greek words, *kryptos*, which means "hidden," and *logos*, which means "word." A cryptological method can take information in standard format, called *plaintext* or *cleartext,* and hide it by scrambling it to make it unintelligible. This is called *encryption.* Encrypted information is sometimes called *ciphertext.* Most methods of hiding information do so by rearranging patterns or substituting characters with other characters (see the sidebar "The Caesar Code"). The procedure used to scramble information is called an *encryption.* The procedure used to unscramble the information back to plaintext, so that it can be read, is called *decryption.* Cryptology provides for confidentiality by preventing stolen data from being read or altered, making it useless to the thief.

Encryption methods are also used to authenticate the identity of the sender of a message. They verify that a message was really sent by the person from whom it indicates it was sent. Authentication discourages forgeries and data tampering.

Advanced security is not enabled by default in Exchange Server or the Exchange client programs. But if a network environment requires this level of security, it can be configured and implemented. This chapter provides a brief background on advanced security methods and standards, and describes how Exchange uses them. In this chapter, we will discuss:

- Encryption methods and standards

- Installation and architecture of Exchange advanced security

- Configuring advanced security

- Operation of advanced security

- Managing advanced security

- Multiple sites and advanced security

The Caesar Code

One early form of cryptology was the Caesar code:

a b c d e f g h i j k l m n o p q r s t u v w x y z

D E F G H I J K L M N O P Q R S T U V W X Y Z A B C

To encrypt a message, its letters are taken one by one and substituted with the letters appearing below them. The message "Send spears" would be encrypted as "VHQG VSHDUV." The substitution method used today is much more complicated.

Encryption Methods and Standards

Modern encryption methods scramble information by running a mathematical algorithm (i.e., a formula) involving a randomly chosen number, on the data to be encrypted. The random number is called a *key*. The key is added to the algorithm by a user or by software. Because the algorithm can remain constant, and may even be published, the keys are what add the variations and secrecy to the encryption. For example, a sender encrypts data using an agreed upon algorithm and a secret key. The recipient, using the same algorithm, must supply the same secret key for the algorithm to decrypt the data.

The length of a key determines the difficulty of breaking the encryption. Each bit in a key can be in one of two states, a one or a zero. A key of 4 bits would have only 16 (2^4) unique combinations. If the algorithm were known, it would be simple to try every possible key with the algorithm and decrypt any message. But a key of 56 bits would have 2^{56} unique combinations, which is 72 quadrillion possible keys. Keys do not make encryption unbreakable, but they make it costly, time consuming, and impractical to break. With the computer hardware available in the 1970s, it would take over 2,000 years to decrypt a message encrypted with a 56-bit key. Recently, a network of computers working together was able to decrypt a message with 56-bit encryption in less than 6 months. Therefore, as computers get more powerful, more bits are needed to keep encryption strong. We will discuss the two basic types of key mechanisms: public/private key pairs and secret keys.

Public/Private Key Pairs

Some encryption methods assign each user a key which is divided into two mathematically related halves, called a *key pair*. One half of the key is made public and is called the *public key*. The other half is known only by one user and is called the *private key*. Some encryption protocols have the sender encrypt a message using the recipient's public key. The only key that can be used to decrypt the message is the other half of the key, the private key, which is known only to the recipient. Because there are two different keys, this method is referred to as being asymmetrical. Figure 10.1 illustrates the use of public/private key pairs. This technique is often called simply *public key encryption*. One of the most frequently used public key protocols is called RSA.

FIGURE 10.1

Public key encryption

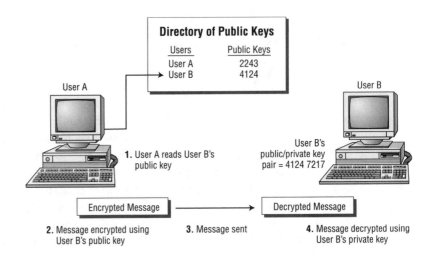

RSA Public Key Protocol

The RSA protocol was developed in the late 1970s by Ron Rivest, Adi Shamir, and Leonard Adleman. They used the first letters of their last names, RSA, to name the protocol. The RSA protocol is computationally intense and slower than other methods, so it is not usually used to encrypt large amounts of data. However, it *is* used for secure user authentication.

Just as a fingerprint or retinal pattern can be used to uniquely identify a person, a key pair can be used to identify a message sender. When keys are used in this manner they help to create what are called *digital signatures*. A digital signature is added to a message by a sender. When the recipient receives the message, they use the digital signature to authenticate (i.e. prove) the sender's identity. Digital signatures help protect against message forgeries.

The following lists the main procedures and protocols used in the Exchange digital signature mechanism:

1. A sender's security software performs a set mathematical formula on a message, which produces a unique 128-bit value (the message is not affected). This process is called *hashing,* and the value produced by the hashing is called a *message digest,* or simply a *digest* (this is similar in concept to a checksum). The protocol used to perform the hashing is Message Digest 5 (MD5).

2. The message digest is then encrypted by using a 512-bit RSA algorithm and the sender's private signing key. The encrypted message digest is the digital signature.

3. The digital signature, along with a certificate that contains the sender's public key, are sent along with the message (certificates are discussed later in this chapter).

4. The recipient's security software reads the plaintext message to learn the identity of the sender (i.e. the name in the From field).

5. The recipient's security software then uses the sender's public signing key to decrypt the encrypted message digest (i.e. the digital signature). If this operation is successful, it authenticates the identity of the sender, because only the public signing key of the sender could decrypt the encrypted message digest. A forger could place someone's name in the From field, but they would not be able to forge that person's digital signature because the forger does not know that person's private signing

key, because it is secret. When a recipient tries to decrypt an encrypted message digest using the forged sender's public signing key, it will not work. The two key halves will not be mathematically related. The recipient will know the message is not authentic.

6. The recipient's security software, which now knows the message digest that the sender calculated, performs its own hash on the message. If the two values are the same, this proves the message was not tampered with during transit. Conversely, if someone captured a message and modified it before sending it back on its way, the message digest the recipient will arrive at and the one sent by the sender will not be the same. This is because the recipient is performing the hash on a different message than the sender.

Figure 10.2 summarizes the main steps in this process.

FIGURE 10.2

Public key method used for authentication

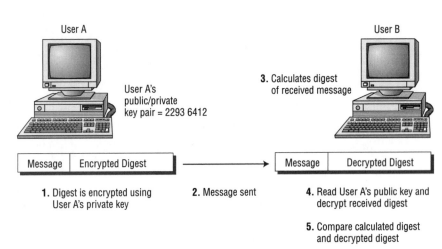

Certification Authority

A public key protocol relies on a central authority to create, distribute, publish, and validate keys. The server that performs these roles is called the Certification Authority (CA). The CA is a key distribution center that responds to requests for new key assignments by creating new public/private key pairs and delivering them to clients. The CA also publishes public keys in a directory for user access.

A CA also keeps a list of expired keys and revoked keys called the Certificate Revocation List (CRL). When client software attempts to use a public key, it checks the CRL to determine if the public key is still valid. If not, the key cannot be used.

One CA implementation standard, published in 1988, is ITU X.509. The Exchange Key Management (KM) server component conforms to this standard. Figure 10.3 illustrates the roles of the KM server CA.

FIGURE 10.3

The roles of the Exchange KM server Certification Authority

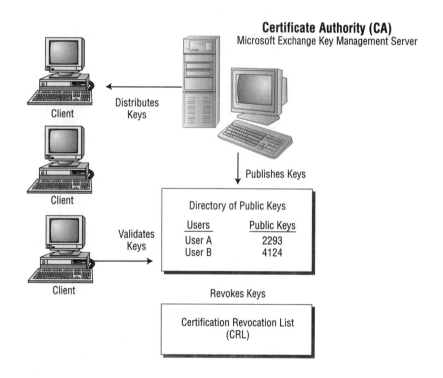

Secret Keys

Authentication only provides proof of identification and proof of data integrity. It *does not* encrypt the message data. Encryption is normally achieved with *secret keys*. A secret key mechanism uses the same key to both encrypt and decrypt information. When a message is encrypted, the key used by the algorithm is sent along with the message. The recipient uses the single secret key to decrypt the information. To prevent someone from simply reading the secret key appended to the message, the secret key must be securely transferred between the sender and recipient. This is usually done by encrypting the secret key so that the recipient, and only the recipient, can decrypt it. After decrypting the secret key, the recipient uses it to decrypt the message.

Because there is only one key, the secret key scheme is a symmetrical method, and sometimes referred to as the *shared-secret* method. Data Encryption Standard (DES) uses the secret key method.

Data Encryption Standard (DES)

DES was developed by IBM and in 1977 was accepted by the United States government as an official standard. DES is extremely secure and is used by many financial institutions for electronic fund transfers. DES uses a 64-bit key. The only method of cracking a DES-encrypted message is the brute-force approach of attempting every possible key.

Software-based DES encryption can be performed about 100 times faster than RSA encryption. Because of its speed, DES is suited for encrypting and decrypting large amounts of data.

When a message is encrypted in Exchange using DES, the secret key is encrypted with RSA and sent in a *lockbox* with the message. This type of hybrid system leverages the speed advantages of DES, and the strength of 512-bit public key RSA. When the message is received, the recipient's private key is used to decrypt the secret key lockbox, and the secret key is used to decrypt the message. Figure 10.4 illustrates this type of hybrid system.

United States export law allows Exchange's DES implementation to be sold only in the United States and Canada.

CAST

Another protocol that uses a secret key mechanism is the CAST protocol. CAST derives its name from the initials of its developers, Carlisle Adams and Stafford Tavares, who worked at Northern Telecom Research. CAST uses a variable-length key between 40 and 128 bits. Exchange can use CAST 40, which uses a 40-bit key, and CAST 64, which uses a 64-bit key. A 64-bit key is 16 million times more secure than a 40-bit key.

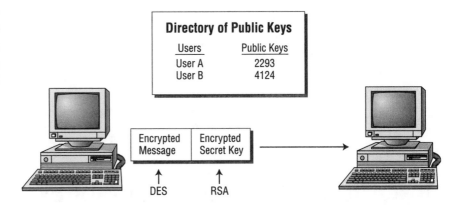

FIGURE 10.4

A hybrid encryption system using both RSA and DES

United States export law allows CAST 64 to only be sold in the United States and Canada. Only the CAST 40 option can be used in the international version of Exchange. In addition, France prohibits the import of any encryption implementations. Table 10.1 provides a summary of the encryption protocols Exchange supports, and the locales where they can be used.

512-bit RSA is legally exported to all international locations because it is used only to digitally sign messages and encrypt lockboxes. Only technology that encrypts message content is prohibited for export.

TABLE 10.1

Summary of encryption protocols

Protocol	Use	Key Length	Locations
RSA	Authentication (digital signatures)	512-bit	All
DES	Data encryption	64-bit	U.S. and Canada
CAST 64	Data encryption	64-bit	U.S. and Canada
CAST 40	Data encryption	40-bit	International, except France

The terms "encryption" and "authentication" are often substituted with the terms "sealing" and "signing" respectively in Exchange Server and its documentation.

Now that you have an adequate understanding of the appropriate security protocols, we can fully discuss using Exchange Server's advanced security.

Installation and Architecture of Exchange Advanced Security

Various components implement advanced security in an Exchange environment. Some of them run on an Exchange server and some run on client workstations.

Installing Advanced Security

This chapter focuses primarily on the KM server installation because client-side security components are automatically installed during a client installation.

KM Server Installation

To deploy advanced security in an Exchange organization, one and only one Exchange server in the organization must be configured as the Key Management (KM) server. In this section, you will learn about the following:

- KM server setup

- KM components

- Security administration

- KM database

KM Server Setup   To install a KM server, an installation program separate from Exchange Server Setup is used. At the end of this section, Exercise 10.1 will step through a KM server installation.

The Setup program for KM server is on the Exchange Server compact disc in the directory SETUP\\<processor_type>\\EXCHKM (where <processor_type> is Alpha or I386). During KM Server Setup the following occurs:

1. Setup checks whether KM server is already installed on any other Exchange server in the organization.

2. Files are copied to the server from the compact disc.

3. The Key Manager service is installed, but not started.

4. A password is created for the KM server. This password must be supplied each time the KM server is run. The installer has the option of allowing the setup program to write the password to a floppy disk, where it will be automatically read at each startup of the KM server. The password is written to a file named KMSPWD.INI on the floppy disk. If the floppy disk option is not chosen, the setup program will display the password to the installer, who will need to write it down, because it will need to be manually entered at each startup of the KM server.

5. Two objects are created in the site Configuration container in the Exchange DS, named "CA" and "Encryption."

After installation, the Microsoft Exchange Key Manager service must be manually started using the Services applet in the Control Panel.

KM Components   The following components are installed during setup:

- **Key Manager Service**   This is the core component of advanced security. It enables the KM server to function as a Certification Authority (CA). As a CA, the KM server creates and assigns keys, maintains the Certificate Revocation List (CRL) in the Exchange Directory database, and creates and manages the KM database which holds users' public keys and other security information.

- **KM Security DLL (SECKM.DLL)**   Security-enabled client programs call functions in this library. When a client needs a new key assigned, a function in the KM Security DLL is called and the key request is passed to the Key Manager service.

Security Administrator Program   KM Setup copies the file SECADMIN .DLL to the \\Exchsrvr\\bin directory. This library is used by the Exchange Administrator program when advanced security elements are configured (e.g., when advanced security is enabled on a mailbox).

KM Database   The KM database contains a master copy of an organization's private sealing keys, public signing keys, and certificates. This database is comprised of the directories and files in the SECURITY\MGRENT directory.

- **Private keys**   While a user's private keys are stored in a file on his or her workstation, all users' private *sealing* keys are stored in the KM database. By centrally storing private sealing keys, an organization can access and revoke keys for employees who have left the organization. Public sealing keys are stored in the DS because they need to be accessed by client programs.

- **Certificates**   Security-enabled clients request key assignments from the KM server. The KM server acts as a CA and generates the requested keys, places them in packets called certificates, signs the packets to authorize them, and sends them to the client. The information contained in a certificate includes:

  User's identity

  Private signing key (in a signing certificate)

  Private sealing key (in a sealing certificate)

  Algorithms to be used

  Expiration date of keys

Because all of the organization's private keys and certificates are stored in the KM database, it is secured with a master encryption key and can only be accessed with a password.

- **Master encryption key**   The KM database is encrypted with a special key called the master encryption key. This key can only be accessed with a KM password.

- **KM password**   Administrators access the KM database with passwords. The default password, "password," should be changed during the first use. Different passwords can be given to each user account that is assigned the KM administrator role. See Figure 10.5 for a summary of the role of the KM database and the DS.

Now that you are familiar with the KM server, components, and database, Exercise 10.1 will walk you through the KM server installation.

FIGURE 10.5

The role of the KM database and the DS

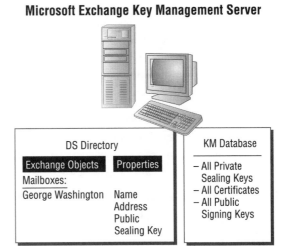

Microsoft Exchange Key Management Server

DS Directory

Exchange Objects   Properties
Mailboxes:
George Washington   Name
Address
Public
Sealing Key

KM Database

– All Private
  Sealing Keys
– All Certificates
– All Public
  Signing Keys

EXERCISE 10.1

Installing the Key Management Server

1. Choose an Exchange server that will act as the KM server. Navigate to the following folder on the Exchange Server compact disc using Windows NT Explorer, \SETUP\<processor_type>\EXCHKM (where <processor_type> is either Alpha or I386). Double-click the file Setup.exe. The Key Management Server Setup dialog box will appear.

2. Click Continue. The Name and Organization Information dialog box will appear, prompting you for registration information. Input the correct information and click OK. Click OK again to confirm the information.

3. The Key Management Server Setup dialog box will reappear. You can select the installation directory for the KM server files. Choose the default or select a different directory and click OK.

4. You are prompted to choose the installation type. Click Typical.

5. The Key Management Server Services Account dialog box will appear. The user account you chose for the Exchange Server site services account will be supplied for you. Enter the account's password in the Account Password field. Click OK.

6. You are prompted for a country code. Accept the default or select a different code. Notice that the Create KM Server Startup Floppy Disk check box is selected. If you leave this check box selected, Setup will write the KM server password to the disk in floppy drive A. Click OK.

7. A message box will appear, asking you to put a disk in drive A. Insert the disk and click OK. Information will be copied to the disk, and a message box will appear indicating that the file has been written to the disk in drive A. Click OK.

8. A message box will appear indicating that Setup has completed successfully. Click OK. Although the KM server is installed, it has not yet been started.

9. In the Control Panel, double-click the Services icon. In the Services applet window, click on Microsoft Exchange Key Manager and click the Start button. After a moment, the Key Manager service will be started. Exit out of the Services applet and close the Control Panel window.

10. To confirm the KM server installation, run Exchange Administrator and view the objects in the site Configuration container. There will be two new objects, CA and Encryption.

Client Advanced Security Installation

During the Exchange client setup, the necessary advanced security programs are copied to the client workstation. Depending on the client operating system, the main function library will be either:

- ETEXCH.DLL (16-bit Windows – Windows 3.*x* and Windows for Workgoups)

- ETEXCH32.DLL (32-bit Windows – Windows 95 and Windows NT)

Advanced security is available only for Windows-based clients. Other platforms such as MS-DOS are not supported.

Before security can be enabled and used, the KM administrator must configure each user's mailbox for advanced security and create certificates.

Exchange Advanced Security Architecture

When configuring Exchange advanced security, it is helpful to have an understanding of the communications that take place among the integral components. The following components will be discussed:

- **Client Components**   Functions in the client security libraries, ETEXCH.DLL and ETEXCH32.DLL, communicate with the Exchange Server System Attendant service (SA) during the initial configuration of advanced security. Client requests for keys and certificates are directed to the SA. Thereafter, the client security functions communicate with the DS to read public keys. The SA communication is illustrated in Figure 10.6.

FIGURE 10.6

Client security communication with the System Attendant

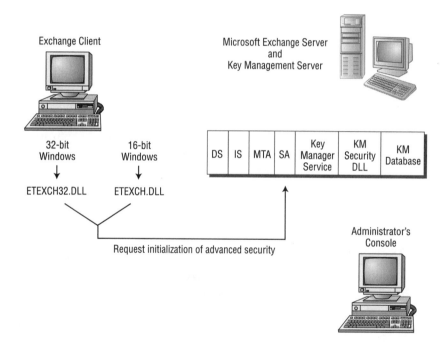

- **System Attendant (SA)**   After receiving a client request for advanced security initialization, the SA passes the request message to a function in the KM Security DLL. The SA essentially acts as middleware between the client and the KM server. This is illustrated in Figure 10.7.

F I G U R E 10.7

System Attendant
communication with the
KM Security DLL

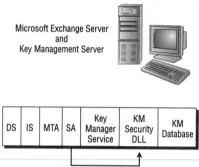

Exchange Client

Microsoft Exchange Server
and
Key Management Server

DS	IS	MTA	SA	Key Manager Service	KM Security DLL	KM Database

Transfer of security messages

Administrator's
Console

- **KM Security DLL**   When the KM Security DLL receives client messages via the SA, it passes the security requests to the Key Manager service for processing. This is illustrated in Figure 10.8.

F I G U R E 10.8

The KM Security DLL calls
on the Key Manager
service

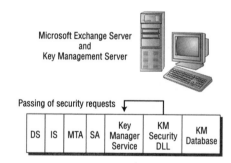

Exchange Client

Microsoft Exchange Server
and
Key Management Server

Passing of security requests

DS	IS	MTA	SA	Key Manager Service	KM Security DLL	KM Database

Administrator's
Console

- **Key Manager Service**   The Key Manager service creates keys and certificates for the client, and communicates this information to the following three places (see Figure 10.9):

  - **SA**   The System Attendant delivers keys and certificates to clients.

  - **KM database**   This database is where keys and certificates are centrally stored.

  - **DS**   Public keys used for sealing messages are made publicly available in the DS. The Key Manager service also stores the CRL in the DS.

FIGURE 10.9

The Key Manager service distributes keys and certificates

- **Security Administration DLL**   The Exchange Administrator program uses the security administration DLL for advanced security configuration and management. This DLL communicates directly with the Key Manager service as illustrated in Figure 10.10.

Now that you have installed advanced security and understand its architecture, we will discuss its configuration.

FIGURE 10.10

The Security
Administration DLL
communicates with the
Key Manager service

Exchange Client

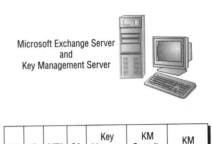

Microsoft Exchange Server
and
Key Management Server

DS	IS	MTA	SA	Key Manager Service	KM Security DLL	KM Database

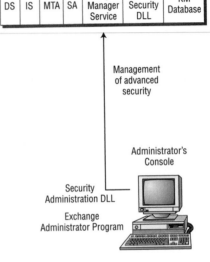

Management
of advanced
security

Administrator's
Console

Security
Administration DLL

Exchange
Administrator Program

Configuring Advanced Security

Advanced security must be configured on both the KM server and the client workstations. This section covers both configurations. The KM server must be configured first.

Configuring the KM Server

A KM administrator uses the Exchange Administrator program to configure advanced security. Organization-wide and individual mailbox configurations must be made.

Organization-Wide Configurations

A KM administrator can configure the preferred encryption algorithm for the organization. This is configured on the Security property page of the Encryption object in the Configuration container. The options for North America are CAST-64 (the default) and DES. Locales outside of North America can only use the CAST-40 algorithm.

Another organization-wide configuration is the selection of users to be KM administrators. This configuration is also performed in the Security property page of the Encryption object. Exercise 10.2 outlines the steps for configuring the organization-wide settings.

EXERCISE 10.2

Organization-Wide Configuration of Advanced Security

1. In the Exchange Administrator program, expand the site object and choose the Configuration container. In the Configuration container, double-click on the Encryption object. The Encryption Properties dialog will appear.

2. Click on the Security tab. The top section of this page, labeled "Preferred encryption algorithm," allows you to configure the message encryption algorithms that will be used when sending to sites in North America and sites in other locales.

3. To modify the list of KM administrator accounts, click the Key Management Server Administrators button.

4. The Key Management Administrator Password dialog box appears. Type **Password** and click OK. The Key Management Server Administrators dialog box will appear. If you would like to add another KM administrator, click Add Administrators. If you would like to change the KM password, click Change Password. If you change the password, do not forget the new one.

Individual Mailbox Configuration

The mailbox object of each user that is to use advanced security must be enabled for advanced security. To enable a mailbox, the KM administrator must click the Enable Advanced Security button on the mailbox's Security property page and provide the mailbox user with the token displayed. When advanced security is enabled, the following actions automatically take place:

1. The Security Administration DLL (SECADMIN.DLL) transfers the mailbox security information to the Key Manager service on the KM server. This information is accompanied with the KM administrator's password in order to access the Key Manager and KM database.

2. The Key Manager service generates a sealing key for this mailbox and writes it to the KM database. This will be used by either the DES or CAST protocol for data encryption.

3. The Key Manager creates a random, 12-character security token. This is a password that the client will show to the KM server in order to receive its mailbox's keys and certificates. This prevents user B from asking and receiving user A's private keys.

4. The Security Administration DLL displays the secret token in the dialog box in the Exchange Administrator program. A KM administrator needs to convey this token to the user.

Exercise 10.3 outlines the steps to configure advanced security on individual mailboxes.

EXERCISE 10.3

Configuring Advanced Security on Individual Mailboxes

1. In the Exchange Administrator program, expand your site object and choose the Recipients container. Double-click on the George Washington mailbox recipient. The George Washington Properties dialog will appear.

2. Click on the Security tab. The Key Management Server Password dialog box will appear. Enter the correct password. If you did not change it in Exercise 10.2, the password is still "password."

---

3. Click Enable Advanced Security. An information dialog box will appear stating that advanced security has been enabled. At the bottom of this dialog box will be the security token that the user George Washington will need to enter when he configures his client software. Write this value down. Click OK. Then click OK again.

4. Configure advanced security for the Andrew Jackson mailbox. We will use these two mailboxes to send secure messages back and forth later in this chapter.

After the administrator configures a user's mailbox, that user can configure the client security components on his or her local workstation.

Configuring the Client

The user configures the client security components through the Exchange client software, either Exchange Client or Outlook. In both of these programs, configuration is performed by choosing Options from the Tools menu, and selecting the Security property page (see Figure 10.11). The user can choose to encrypt messages and attachments, and to add digital signatures to messages. Also, the name of the file that will hold private keys and signing certificates can be specified (it must have an .EPF extension). Because of the sensitivity of the information in this file, it is encrypted and can only be accessed with a password.

Before a user can configure advanced security, they must request and receive their keys and certificates from the KM server. To do this the user must click the Set Up Advanced Security button and enter the security token they received from the KM administrator. This will prove to the KM server that they have permission to receive the keys and certificates for this mailbox. The following step is performed by the client security DLL:

1. The client security DLL (either ETEXCH.DLL or ETEXCH32.DLL) generates the user's public and private signing keys. The private signing key is stored and encrypted in the user's local .EPF file. The public signing key is encrypted with the user's security token and sent as a mail message to the SA. The SA transfers this message to the SA on the KM server if it is not the local server.

FIGURE 10.11

The Security property
page in the client software

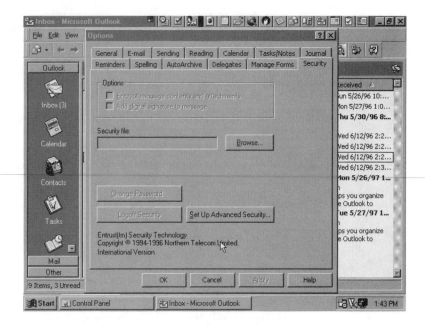

The following steps take place on the KM server.

2. The SA on the KM server passes the user's mail message to the KM Security DLL, which passes it to the Key Manager service. The user is notified of a successful submission.

3. The Key Manager service decrypts the message using the user's security token that was assigned earlier, and then writes the user's public signing key to the KM database. The Key Manager then creates two certificates, one for sealing and one for signing, and sends them to the client.

Step 4 is performed by the user, and Step 5 is performed by the client's security DLL.

4. When the user receives the certificates, he or she must supply the user account password. This verifies that this user is the one who made the advanced security request in Step 1.

5. The client security DLL takes the user's public sealing key and communicates it to the DS on the client's home server. The server will replicate this information in the normal course of DS replication.

When mailboxes and client software has been configured, the KM server does not need to be online for advanced security to function. Private keys and certificates are available from the local .EPF file, and public keys and certificates are available from the DS. The KM server only needs to be running to initialize new advanced security clients.

Exercise 10.4 outlines the steps to configure the client security components.

EXERCISE 10.4

Configuring the Client Security Components

1. At the client workstation, log on with the GEORGEW user account. Then run Outlook.

2. In Outlook, choose Tools ➢ Options. The Options dialog will appear. Choose the Security tab.

3. Click Set Up Advanced Security. The Setup Advanced Security dialog will appear.

4. In the Token field, enter the security token that was generated in Exercise 10.3 Step 3.

5. In the Password and Confirm Password fields, type **dollar.** This new password will be used to access the certificates that contain your keys for signing and sealing messages. Click OK. An informational dialog box will appear stating that you will be notified when your security request has been processed by the Key Management server. Click OK. On the Options dialog box, click OK.

6. Check your Inbox, you will soon receive a message from the System Attendant. Notice that the envelope icon for this message has a lock on it.

7. Double-click on the message from the System Attendant. A dialog box will appear prompting you for your password. This is the password you entered in Step 5 **(dollar)**. Enter **dollar** and click OK. An informational dialog box will appear stating that you are now security enabled and can sign and encrypt messages. Click OK.

EXERCISE 10.4 (CONTINUED FROM PREVIOUS PAGE)

8. Log on with the Andrew Jackson user account and configure the security components. Remember, Andrew Jackson has a different security token than George Washington. Also remember to write down Andrew Jackson's personal security password. Both user accounts need to be configured so we can send and receive secure messages in Exercises 10.5 and 10.6.

Now that the KM server, mailboxes, and client security components are configured, advanced security operations can commence.

Advanced Security Operation

Advanced security is very straightforward to use. Most of the operation is automatic and transparent to the user. This section will discuss the steps involved in signing and verifying a message, and sealing and unsealing a message. Exercises 10.5 and 10.6 will provide an opportunity to use these features. This section will conclude with a description of some advanced security operational scenarios.

Signing/Verifying a Message

As explained earlier in this chapter, the RSA public key method is used for digital signatures. The following two sections outline the procedures for signing a message and verifying a signature on a message.

Signing a Message

The steps for signing an outgoing message are:

1. The client security DLL calculates an SHA1 digest from the outgoing message.

2. The user is prompted for the security file password. When the correct password is entered, the client security DLL decrypts the user's private signing key.

3. The private key is used to encrypt the message digest, thereby creating a digital signature.

4. The client software appends the digital signature and the user's signing certificate (which contains his or her public signing key) to the plaintext message. The message is then sent.

Verifying a Message

The steps for verifying a digital signature on a received message are:

1. The client security DLL checks the CRL in the DS for the sender's signing certificate. If it is on the list, the recipient is notified that the sender certificate cannot be trusted. If it is not on the list, the client software uses the sender's public signing key to decrypt the message digest.

2. The recipient's client software calculates the SHA1 digest of the message and compares its value with the one decrypted from the message. If they are not the same, the recipient is warned that the message has been altered since it was signed. Otherwise, the message has arrived intact and the sender's identity has been authenticated.

Sealing/Unsealing a Message

Exchange can use either the DES or CAST protocol to seal messages. These mechanisms were discussed earlier in this chapter. The following two sections outline the steps performed by the Exchange software when sealing and unsealing messages.

Sealing a Message

The steps that occur when sealing an Exchange message are:

1. The sender's security DLL generates a random secret key, also called the *bulk encryption key*. This key is used to seal the message with DES or CAST depending on the Exchange server configuration.

2. The sender's security DLL accesses the DS to obtain each recipient's public sealing key.

3. Each recipient's public sealing key is used to encrypt the secret key in lockboxes which will be sent along with the sealed message. One lockbox is attached for each recipient. If the message is being sent to distribution lists (DLs), the DLs are expanded on the client and a lockbox is attached for each DL member. One copy of the actual message content is included (in sealed form).

4. The message containing sealed content and lockboxes is sent to the recipients.

Unsealing a Message

The steps to unseal a message are:

1. The recipient's security DLL retrieves the recipient's private sealing key from the .EPF file, and uses this key to unseal the lockbox.

2. The unsealed secret key is then used to unseal the message contents.

Now that you have learned about signing and sealing messages, Exercise 10.5 will walk you through the steps. Exercise 10.6 will take you through the necessary steps to verify and unseal a message.

EXERCISE 10.5

Sending a Signed and Sealed Message

1. Log on as GeorgeW and start Outlook.

2. Click the New Mail Message tool button on the toolbar. A new message window appears.

3. Click To. The Select Names dialog box appears. In the Show Names From The drop-down list, choose Global Address List. Find and select Andrew Jackson in the leftmost listbox. Click To and then click OK.

4. In the Subject field, type **Advanced Security Test**.

5. Type a short message in the body.

6. Click the Seal Message with Encryption toolbar button. This tool button is found on the right side of the toolbar and appears as an envelope with a lock attached.

7. Click the Digitally Sign Message toolbar button directly to the right of the Encryption button.

8. To send the message, click the Send button on the toolbar. The Microsoft Exchange Security Logon dialog box will appear (see Figure 10.12).

9. In the Security password box, type GeorgeW's security password, **dollar**. This will permit your private key to be used to digitally sign the message, and your secret key to be used to seal the message. Click OK. The message is now sent.

FIGURE 10.12

Microsoft Exchange
Security Logon screen

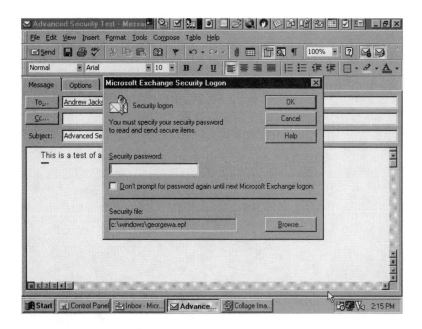

EXERCISE 10.6

Verifying and Unsealing a Message

1. Log on as AndrewJ, and start Outlook.

2. If your Inbox is not already visible, open it. Notice the message from GeorgeW. The envelope icon has a lock on it, signifying that it is sealed (see Figure 10.13).

3. Double-click on the sealed message from GeorgeW. The Microsoft Exchange Security Logon dialog box will appear.

4. In the Security password box, enter AndrewJ's security password. Click OK. The message content will appear.

5. When you are done, close the message.

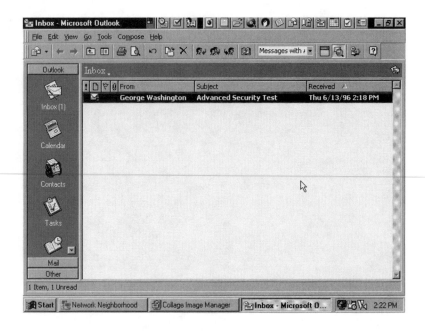

Advanced Security Scenarios

This section describes some scenarios you may encounter with your deployment of advanced security.

Using Different Sealing Protocols

If a user sends a message to multiple recipients that are enabled for different sealing protocols, the weakest sealing protocol of the lot will be used to seal the message. For example, if some recipients are enabled for CAST-64 and others are enabled for CAST-40, Exchange will use CAST-40 to seal the message.

Changing the Preferred Encyption Algorithm

The KM administrator may change the preferred encryption algorithm of a site. This is done through the Encryption object and the Security property page. After changing the site configuration, the administrator would then have to recover the security keys for all security-enabled mailboxes in that site.

Sending Messages to Recipients Not Configured for Advanced Security

If a user attempts to send a sealed message to a recipient that is not advanced security enabled, the message cannot be delivered. The sender will be presented with the following two options:

- Send the message as plaintext

- Cancel the delivery

If a user attempts to send a sealed message to a number of recipients, some that are advanced security enabled and some that are not, the sender will be presented with the following three options:

- Remove the recipients who are not advanced security enabled, and send the message only to the advanced security enabled recipients

- Send the message as plaintext to the entire list of recipients

- Cancel the delivery

Forwarding a Sealed Message

Recipients who can unseal a message can modify the message and forward it to other recipients. It may seem obvious, but users should remember that once sensitive data is received and unsealed, it is up to the recipients to preserve the confidentiality of the information.

Managing Advanced Security

Once advanced security is installed and configured, administrative duties are minimal. KM administrators will primarily perform the following three tasks:

- Key and certificate management

- KM database and server management

- Batch creation of security tokens

Key and Certificate Management

Certain scenarios require key and certificate management. When users leave the organization, their advanced security capabilities need to be disabled. The KM administrator does this by revoking user key and certification information. When a user password is forgotten or an .EPF file is corrupted or lost, the KM administrator can save the day by recovering key and certificate information. Also, keys and certificates expire after a certain amount of time elapses. Client software can request a renewal when the expiration date approaches. Revocation, recovery, and renewal procedures are discussed next.

Revocation

To revoke advanced security keys and certificates from a mailbox, a KM administrator uses the Exchange Administrator program. In the procedure outlined here, the KM administrator performs Step 1 and the remaining steps occur automatically.

1. In the Exchange Administrator program, the KM administrator chooses the mailbox that is to have advanced security revoked, and clicks the Revoke Advanced Security button on the Security property page. After the administrator provides the KM password, the process to revoke the user's security keys and certificates begins.

2. The security DLL locates the KM server and tells it which mailbox is to have its security configuration revoked.

3. The KM server adds the user's signing and sealing keys to its revocation list.

4. The KM server informs the DS to add the user's sealing certificate to the CRL. The user's ability to sign and seal messages is now revoked.

5. A dialog box appears in the Exchange Administrator program indicating the revocation is complete.

The revocation process does not delete keys from the KM database, but rather makes them unusable for future sealing. The revoked keys are still available for a KM administrator to use to unseal any messages still signed and sealed by those keys.

Recovery

Users' private keys are stored on their computers in their .EPF file. The user must provide the correct password to access these keys. If a user forgets this password, or the .EPF file becomes corrupted or gets accidentally deleted, the user will not be able to unseal messages, or send signed or sealed messages. The KM administrator can fix this situation by performing a recovery.

A recovery is similar to enabling advanced security. To do a recovery, the KM administrator clicks the Recover Security Key button on the Security property page of the affected user's mailbox. The KM server then sends the user a history of the keys associated with the mailbox, including the current keys and certificates. The user must then reconfigure advanced security on his or her workstation to create a new .EPF file.

Renewal

New certificates are valid for 18 months. At the end of this period, the certificate must be renewed, or "rolled over." When certificates near expiration, the Exchange client software sends a request for renewal.

KM Database and Server Management

Because the KM database contains the master copy of all private sealing keys and all public signing keys, its maintenance is important. Three maintenance activities will be discussed in this section:

- Backing up and restoring the KM database

- Moving the KM server

- Creating additional KM administrators

Backing Up and Restoring the KM Database

It is important to back up the KM database on a regular basis. This can be done with the Windows NT Backup utility. The directories and files that need to be backed up are under the SECURITY\MGRENT directory. These files can be backed up while the KM server is online, but to guarantee a valid backup, the Key Manager service should be temporarily stopped.

The entire KM database can be restored from a backup. The Key Manager service needs to be stopped during the restore.

Moving the KM Server

The KM server may need to be moved to another Exchange server to keep it segregated, or to upgrade or replace the hardware on which it is running. The KM server can only be moved to another Exchange server within the original site.

Moving the KM server is simple. The steps to do so are outlined here:

1. Using Control Panel/Services, stop the Key Manager service.

2. Back up the KM database on the current KM server.

3. Remove the Key Manager service by running KMSERVER -U.

4. Remove the directory containing the KM database. The default directory is SECURITY\MGRENT.

5. On the server that will be the new KM server, run the KM server setup program from the Exchange Server compact disc.

6. Restore the backed-up KM database to the new KM server.

Creating Additional KM Administrators

The user account that performs the installation of a KM server, is by default the initial KM administrator. The default password that this user must initially use to perform KM functions is "password." This password should be changed as soon as possible. Additional users can be assigned KM administrator rights through the Encryption object in the Configuration container. Each additional KM administrator should have his or her own password.

Batch Creation of Security Tokens

It is often inconvenient to configure advanced security one mailbox at a time. If a large batch of users need advanced security configured, the Security Import utility (SIMPORT.EXE) can be used.

The Security Import utility can create security tokens for multiple users in a batch process (i.e., processing a group of mailboxes at one time). This process must be performed one server at a time. When the Security Import utility is run, it will prompt the administrator for the following information:

- Site name

- Home server

- KM administrator password

- KM server name

The program will create the user keys and certificates and write each user's security token information to a file called SRESULTS.TXT. Here is an example of the format of this file:

```
/o=widget/ou=chicago/cn=recipients/cn=jwilson, ISLIWXIWLELE
```

```
/o=widget/ou=chicago/cn=recipients/cn=gwashington, RRXOWQMTPCJF
```

The KM administrator reads the security token at the end of each line and securely passes it to the corresponding user.

Multiple Sites and Advanced Security

While there is only one KM server for an organization, each site must have an object in the DS that points to the KM server. To create this object, run the KM server Setup program on one Exchange server in each site. KM Setup will detect an existing KM server in the organization and just install the appropriate object in the local site instead of installing an additional KM server. To determine if a KM server already exists in the organization, KM Setup reads the DS on the local server, so be sure DS replication to this server is complete before running KM Setup.

The DS object pointing to the KM server enables each Exchange server in the organization to receive security requests from clients and forward them to the KM server.

If a KM server has been installed in another site, but DS replication to the local site has not yet been completed, KM server Setup will create a KM server in the local site.

Summary

Advanced security facilitates the authentication of a message sender's identity and the privacy of message data. Authentication is accomplished using digital signatures and message privacy is maintained using encryption. In Exchange terminology, "signing" refers to authentication and "sealing" refers to encryption.

The RSA protocol is used by Exchange to implement digital signatures. RSA uses a key pair that includes a public key that can be accessed by anyone, and a private key that is only known by one user. While these two keys are different, they are mathematically related and information is unlocked with the opposite of the key that was used to lock it.

The protocols that Exchange uses for sealing data are DES and CAST. These protocols utilize a single secret key that is used to both seal and unseal message content. This secret key is itself sealed using RSA and sent along with the message.

The components that make up the advanced security subsystem in Exchange include the Key Manager service, the KM Security DLL, the System Attendant, and the Security Administration DLL. There is also a KM database, which contains a master copy of all users' keys and certificates.

One Exchange server in the organization acts as the KM server. Other Exchange servers have a DS object pointing to the single KM server.

The Exchange Client running on any Windows platform and the Outlook client support advanced security. The 16-bit client security library is named ETEXCH.DLL and the 32-bit version is named ETEXCH32.DLL.

KM server management duties include key and certificate revocation and client security information recovery and renewal. The KM database can be backed up, restored, or moved across servers. The KM server can be configured to support multiple administrators. The Security Import utility allows you to configure batches of users for advanced security at one time.

Review Questions

1. There can be only one KM administrator.

   A. True

   B. False

2. Client software must be configured before a user's mailbox can be configured.

   A. True

   B. False

3. The KM database is made up of the directories and files under which directory?

   A. DATA

   B. KM\DATA

   C. DATA\KM

   D. SECURITY\MGRENT

4. Which program can create security tokens in a batch manner?

   A. SIMPORT.EXE

   B. BATCH.BAT

   C. BATCH.EXE

   D. SECADMIN.DLL

5. What program is used to revoke a user's keys and certificates?

   A. Exchange Administrator

   B. SIMPORT.EXE

   C. KM database

   D. REVOKE.EXE

6. The MS-DOS-based Exchange client, although slow, can perform signing and sealing operations.

   A. True

   B. False

7. CAST-64 cannot be used in the United States.

   A. True

   B. False

8. What core Exchange component is involved in the initialization of advanced security for a client?

   A. MTA

   B. IMS

   C. POP3

   D. System Attendant

9. What is the extension of the client-side file that stores a user's security information?

   A. .EPF

   B. .EFP

   C. .KMS

   D. .KM

10. Which extension enables the Exchange Administrator program to interface with the Key Manager service?

   A. SECADMIN.DLL

   B. KM.DLL

   C. ADMIN.SEC

   D. KMSEC.DLL

11. Which of the following must an administrator do to enable advanced security for a user?

A. Enabled advanced security on the Security property page of that user's mailbox

B. Have the user first install and configure advanced security on their computer, then have the user inform the administrator of their configuration

C. Inform the user of their security token which will be used to configure their client software

D. Both A and C

12. What must an administrator do to change the preferred encryption algorithm of a site?

A. Reinstall the Microsoft Exchange Key Manager service

B. Change the preferred encryption algorithm on the Encryption object

C. Recover the security keys for all security-enabled mailboxes

D. Both B and C

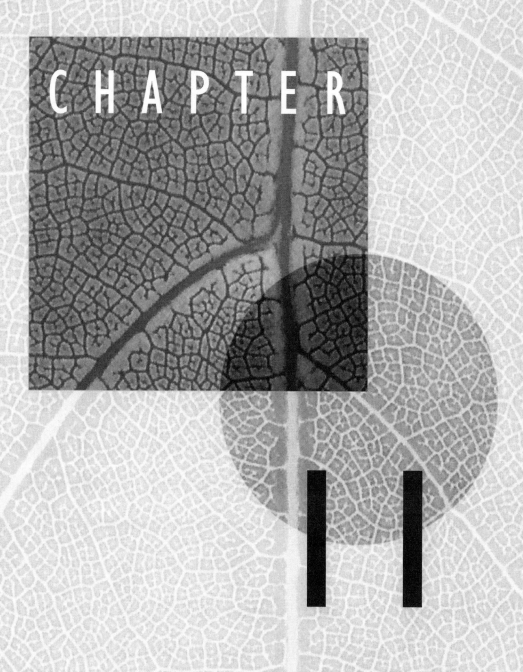

CHAPTER

11

Internet-Based Exchange Clients

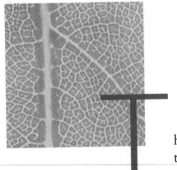

he Microsoft Exchange Client and Microsoft Outlook applications (which were discussed in Chapters 6 and 7) use the MAPI protocol to access Exchange resources such as mailboxes and public folders. This chapter discusses four Internet protocols that can also be used to access Exchange resources:

- **Post Office Protocol (POP3)**   Retrieves mail from a remote server mailbox.

- **HyperText Transfer Protocol (HTTP)**   Handles data transfer between World Wide Web servers and browsers.

- **Lightweight Directory Access Protocol (LDAP)**   Provides access to directory information.

- **Network News Transfer Protocol (NNTP)**   Transfers data between newsgroup servers and newsgroup reader programs.

Exchange Server's support for these four protocols permits a large number of Internet client applications to act as Exchange clients. This chapter provides a brief background on each protocol and then discusses specifics of the use of each protocol within Exchange Server and on the clients. All of these protocols are configured in a common manner in Exchange Server, so we begin with an overview of Internet protocol configuration.

Protocol Configuration Overview

POP3, LDAP, and NNTP are built into the core components of Exchange Server. POP3 and NNTP are part of the Information Store, and LDAP is part of the Directory Service. But while they are built in to Exchange

Server, they can also be disabled. HTTP is not built in to the core components, and is only present if the Active Server Components were installed during the Exchange setup.

Each protocol is configured using the Exchange Administrator program. Some of the settings for HTTP must be configured on the Microsoft Internet Information Server (IIS). This is because the Active Server Components that Exchange uses are installed on an IIS computer.

This section will provide an overview of topics that relate to configuring any of the Internet protocols mentioned above. Following this overview, the properties and configuration of each individual protocol will be discussed.

Protocols Container

Each site and server object in the Exchange hierarchy contains a Protocols container. An administrator can set protocol defaults and configure related functions by configuring the container's four property pages.

General Property Page

The General property page is used to change the display name of the container and enter an administrative note. This page also shows the directory name of the container in a read-only field.

Permissions Property Page

This page is visible only if the Exchange Administrator program has been configured to display permission pages for objects (see Step 2 of Exercise 7.3 in Chapter 7). Permissions determine which users or groups have management access to the protocol objects in this container, and what type of access they have. Roles or individual rights can be assigned to users or groups.

Connections Property Page

The Connections property page enables an administrator to accept or reject POP3, LDAP, and NNTP connections to Exchange servers based on client IP addresses. By default, any client can connect. HTTP connections are not affected by this property page, but they can be restricted using the Microsoft IIS Internet Service Manager program.

MIME Types Property Page

MIME (Multipurpose Internet Mail Extensions) is a standard that allows non-textual content types to be included in an SMTP message. MIME content types include audio, image, HTML (HyperText Markup Language), and video. An administrator can use the MIME Types property page to associate MIME attachment content types to file name extensions. For example, the text/html MIME content type is by default associated with the .HTML file extension. This identification allows the client's operating system to select the appropriate application to access an attachment.

Protocols and the Exchange Hierarchy

The POP3, LDAP, and NNTP protocols can be configured at the site and server levels of the Exchange hierarchy. The HTTP protocol can be configured at the site level. In addition, POP3, NNTP, and HTTP can be configured on individual mailboxes and POP3 and HTTP can be configured on individual custom recipients. Therefore, an Exchange administrator has great flexibility in configuring the Internet protocols.

By default, each protocol is enabled at every hierarchical level. An administrator can enable or disable protocols at various levels to provide users with the necessary functionality. The following are some example configurations:

- A protocol can be enabled at the site level, but disabled on some servers in the site. To do this, the administrator would enable the protocol at the site level and selectively disable the protocol at individual servers. Then, clients using the protocol can only connect to those servers that have not had the protocol disabled.

- A protocol can be disabled at the site level, yet enabled at specific servers in the site. Clients using the protocol can only connect to those servers that have the protocol enabled.

- A protocol can be enabled at both the site and server level, but disabled at certain mailboxes. Clients that have not had the protocol disabled at their mailboxes can connect to the server using the protocol.

If a protocol is disabled at the server level, the settings on the mailboxes and custom recipients on that server are irrelevant. Users on that server will not be able to connect using the protocol.

> You may have wondered when all that stuff in Chapter 2 about X.500, parent-child, and inheritance would come into play. That information may come in handy now.

Post Office Protocol (POP3)

The Post Office Protocol version 3 (POP3) enables a client to retrieve mail from a remote server mailbox. POP3 is commonly used on home computers to download mail from servers run by Internet Service Providers (ISPs). Because home computers are not always connected to mail servers (and are not always turned on), user mailboxes are stored on POP mail servers. These POP servers have permanent Internet connections, so incoming messages can be successfully delivered to users' server mailboxes. Basically, POP servers provide mail-drop service. When users connect to their ISP POP servers, POP routines in their e-mail programs interface with the POP server to download mailbox content. POP is used only to retrieve mail, not send it.

The remainder of this section covers these POP-related topics:

- POP3 architecture

- Exchange Server POP3 Overview

- Configuring POP3 on Exchange Server

- Configuring a POP3 client

- Troubleshooting POP3

POP3 Architecture

POP works through a simple request-response mechanism. A POP client sends request commands, and a POP server sends responses back to the POP client. These client-server interactions can be divided into three main states:

- Authorization

- Transaction

- Update

Authorization, also called *greeting,* is the client logon to the POP server. The POP username and password are sent to the POP server. After a successful authorization, transactions can take place between the POP client and server. The POP client can request the number and size of messages in its mailbox, and messages can be downloaded and deleted. After the POP server has responded and the POP client is finished, the POP client issues a QUIT command. This ends the POP session and causes the POP server to enter the update state for the user's mailbox. Messages may be deleted during the update state.

POP uses TCP/IP as its transport protocol. The session, or *conversation,* between the POP client and server takes place on TCP port 110. A *port* is a numeric identifier assigned to an application or protocol and is used to route incoming packets to the correct application. Just because a packet has arrived at the correct computer, it still has to be delivered to the correct application on that computer. POP clients address the requests to port 110 on the POP server. The POP server listens to port 110 for those requests (this same principle is applicable to LDAP, HTTP, and other Internet protocols). The third revision of the POP standard, POP3, is documented in RFC 1939.

You may be familiar with Ethernet or Token Ring addresses, which are used to deliver a frame to a specific computer. You may even be familiar with network addresses, such as IP addresses, which are used to route packets to the correct networks and computers. Ports are yet another type of address that are used to route packets to the correct applications on a machine.

Exchange Server POP3 Overview

POP3 is integrated into the Information Store (IS) component of Exchange Server. Although it is not a separate service, the POP3 functionality is sometimes referred to as the Exchange POP3 Service. It permits any POP3-enabled e-mail program to connect to an Exchange server and retrieve mail (see Figure 11.1). Only messages in the Inbox folder of a mailbox can be accessed. Messages in other folders are not accessible. The POP3 Service does not permit access to encrypted messages.

As mentioned previously, POP3 retrieves mail, but does not send it. The Simple Mail Transfer Protocol (SMTP) is used to send mail. SMTP functionality can be added to an Exchange server by using the Exchange Internet Mail Service (IMS). The IMS enables an Exchange server to send and receive SMTP messages

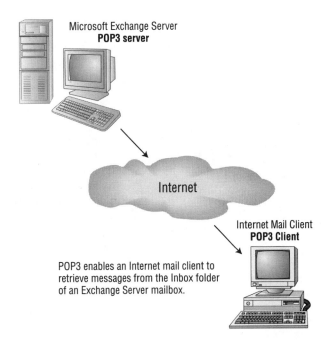

FIGURE 11.1

Exchange and POP3

Microsoft Exchange Server
POP3 server

Internet

Internet Mail Client
POP3 Client

POP3 enables an Internet mail client to
retrieve messages from the Inbox folder
of an Exchange Server mailbox.

through port 25. When POP3 and the IMS are running, a remote client can connect to the Exchange server, retrieve mail using POP3 on port 110, and send mail using SMTP on port 25. The IMS passes incoming SMTP messages to the IS for delivery. Chapter 14 covers the IMS in detail.

Configuring POP3 on an Exchange Server

POP3 can be enabled or disabled at the site, server, and mailbox levels. The properties of a parent object can be inherited by its child objects (e.g., settings at the site level can be inherited by the site servers). Inherited values can be overridden. For example, if POP3 is enabled and configured with certain properties at the site level, an administrator can override those properties at a particular server in that site. The same can be done with mailboxes to override the home server settings. Therefore, POP3 can be configured on a mailbox-by-mailbox basis. These configurations are covered next. We will also discuss how to set up an IMS so that Internet e-mail clients can send mail.

POP3 Site and Server Configuration

The site and server level POP3 objects have four property pages in common (five if the Permissions page is displayed). Table 11.1 lists and describes these property pages.

T A B L E 11.1 Property pages on the site and server POP3 objects	**Property Page**	**Description**
	General	This page contains a checkbox to enable or disable the POP3 protocol. The default is enabled. You can also set the display name of the POP3 object and view its directory name in a read-only field. An administrative note field is also available. At the server level, this page contains a checkbox to specify whether the site level settings should be used for the server. The default is to use the settings from the site object.
	Authentication	This page is used to select the authentication protocols that POP3 clients are allowed to use. The options are: ■ Basic (Cleartext) ■ Basic (Cleartext) using Secure Sockets Layer ■ Windows NT Challenge/Response ■ Windows NT Challenge/Response using Secure Sockets Layer
	Message Content	This page is used to set the encoding protocol and character set to be used for messages. The encoding options are: ■ MIME ■ UUENCODE ■ BINHEX Many international character sets are available. The default is US-ASCII. You can also specify whether Microsoft Exchange rich-text format can be used in POP3 messages.
	Idle Time-out	This page is used to configure how long an idle POP3 connection will be held open before automatically closing. Options include: ■ Do not close idle connections ■ Close idle connections after a specified number of minutes The default is to close idle connections after 10 minutes.

The server level POP3 object also contains a Diagnostics Logging property page that can be used to specify the type and amount of information the POP service logs to the Windows NT application event log. Exercise 11.1 outlines the steps for accessing the POP3 property pages and attributes.

EXERCISE 11.1

Configuring POP3 at the Site Object

1. In Exchange Administrator, navigate to the Protocols container by expanding the site object and its Configuration container. Click on the Protocols container in the left pane to display the individual protocol objects in the right pane.

2. Double-click on the POP3 (Mail) Site Defaults object. The property pages for this object will appear. A checkbox on the General page allows you to enable or disable POP3 for the site.

3. Select the Message Format page. Examine the options on the drop-down menu. Click the Help button for information on the message encoding formats.

4. Feel free to examine any of the other property pages. When you are finished, click OK to save any changes you made, or click Cancel to discard them.

POP3 Mailbox Configuration

An administrator can override server level settings at the mailbox level using the Protocols page of a mailbox object. A mailbox can independently have POP3 enabled or disabled or have unique POP3 settings. As mentioned earlier, if a protocol is disabled at the server level, the settings at the mailbox level have no effect.

Internet Mail Service (IMS) Configuration

POP3 only enables clients to retrieve mail. If a client needs to send mail, the Exchange server must have an Internet Mail Service (IMS) providing SMTP support. The POP3 client does not have to actually forward messages to the Internet but can instead rely on the IMS for the delivery of submitted messages. Chapter 14 discusses the role of an IMS within an SMTP mail system.

Users of TCP/IP-based applications like POP3 and SMTP normally use friendly computer names when performing actions (e.g., SEND joesmith@widget.com) rather than IP addresses (e.g., SEND joesmith@131.54.23.48). Somewhere, a database that maps friendly names to IP addresses must exist so that information can be routed to the correct computer over the network. A Domain Name System (DNS) server is the database that fills this role. In most configurations, the IMS requires that a DNS server be designated. The DNS server's location is specified using the Network Control Panel applet to configure the DNS property page of the TCP/IP protocol.

Configuring a POP3 Client

The following information must be configured on a POP3 client in order to connect to a POP3 server (in this case, the POP3 server is an Exchange server running the Exchange POP3 Service):

- **POP3 server name**   The computer name of the home server of the Exchange mailbox.

- **SMTP server name**   The computer name of the Exchange server that is supporting SMTP by running the IMS.

- **POP3 account name**   The name the POP3 client must use when being authorized by a POP3 server. The Exchange POP3 Service requires a Windows NT domain and user account that has read permissions on the Exchange mailbox, followed by the alias name of the mailbox in the format *domain\account\alias*. If the account name and alias are the same, the alias name can be left off.

- **POP3 account password**   The Exchange POP3 Service requires the password of the Windows NT user account that is specified in the POP3 account name field.

- **POP3 client e-mail address**   The SMTP address of the POP3 client. For an Exchange mailbox, this is the SMTP address found on the E-mail Addresses property page of the mailbox.

Table 11.2 provides sample information and shows how that information can be used to configure a POP3 client.

T A B L E 11.2	**Sample Information**	**POP3 Client Configuration**
An example of a POP3 client configuration	Computer name running the Exchange POP3 Service= Education	POP3 server name=Education
	Computer name running the Exchange IMS= Education	SMTP server name=Education
	Window NT account with read permission on the mailbox=NTDomain\GeorgeW Alias name of mailbox= GeorgeW	POP3 account name=NTDomain\GeorgeW\GeorgeW or simply NTDomain\GeorgeW
	Password of GeorgeW=woodenteeth	POP3 account password=woodenteeth
	Domain name=Chicago.com Alias name of mailbox=GeorgeW	POP3 client e-mail address=GeorgeW@Chicago.com

Troubleshooting POP3

When a POP3 client connects to a POP3 server but encounters problems during the session, protocol logging can be turned on to help troubleshoot. Protocol logging records the entire conversation between the POP3 client and server by writing that information to a log file.

By default, protocol logging is turned off. It can be enabled and configured in the Registry of the Exchange POP3 server. Two settings, both under HKEY_LOCAL_MACHINE\System\CurrentControlSet\Services\MSExchangeIS\ParametersSystem, are used to control logging. This one is used to enable logging:

```
POP3_Protocol_Logging_Level= <numeric value of 0, 1, or 4>
```

A value of 0 configures no logging. A value of 1 configures minimum logging, and 4 maximum logging.

This setting specifies the directory and file name that will contain the logging information:

```
POP3_Protocol_LogPath= <directory_path>
```

A potential problem involves upgrading Exchange Server and its effect on POP3. If you upgrade an Exchange server from version 4.0 to 5.0 and then enable POP3, users will not be able to use POP3 to access their mailboxes. This is because the Exchange POP3 service needs to use the site service account to impersonate the POP3 client and to log on to the Exchange Server. The POP3 service can then retrieve mail messages for the POP3 client. For this operation to work, the site service account must have the Windows NT right of "Act as part of the operating system." When upgrading Exchange Server from version 4.0 to 5.0, this right must be manually granted the site service account. After this is done, the POP3 clients will be able to access their mailboxes.

HyperText Transfer Protocol (HTTP)

The World Wide Web (WWW) has become one of the most pervasive networks in the world. Servers all over the world are added to the Web daily, and the number of Web users is skyrocketing. Two standards used in the implementation of the WWW are HyperText Markup Language (HTML) and HyperText Transfer Protocol (HTTP). HTML is used to create hypertext and multimedia documents on the WWW. Hypertext is used to link one WWW object to another. For example, a word in a Web document can have a link to a Web document on another server. The other server could be anywhere else on the Web. Clicking on that word transfers the user to the linked document. Words, phrases, buttons, pictures, and other objects can have links. Multimedia (sound, video, and animation) can also be included in an HTML document. HTTP is the protocol used to connect a Web client program, called a Web browser, to a Web server. HTTP handles application-to-application communication.

Microsoft has developed technology that enables Web clients to access Microsoft BackOffice applications, like Exchange Server. The term Active Platform describes the collection of technologies that makes this possible. Simply put, Active Platform technology turns a Microsoft Internet Information server (IIS) into a Web gateway to BackOffice applications. This makes it possible for a Web client using a standard Web browser to access Exchange resources like the DS, mailboxes, public folders, and schedules. Active Platform technologies translate between HTML and the various BackOffice application formats such as MAPI. Figure 11.2 depicts the Active Platform architecture.

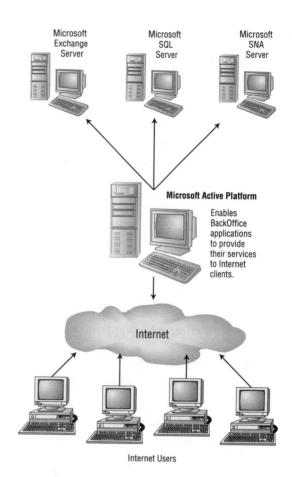

The remainder of this section discusses:

- The Active Platform

- Installing HTTP on Exchange Server

- Configuring HTTP on Exchange Server

- The HTTP client and Exchange Server

The Active Platform

Active Platform refers to the collection of technologies that enable Web clients to access BackOffice applications. In this context, the term "platform" is synonymous with the term "architecture." The best way to explain this architecture is to start at the client-side and work through to the server-side.

Active Platform is designed to interoperate with the Web standards. The only requirement for a Web browser to communicate with an Active Server is that it must support JavaScript and frames. Microsoft Internet Explorer 3.0 and later, and Netscape Navigator 3.0 and later meet this requirement.

In this section, we will examine the following technologies:

- ActiveX

- Active Server

- Active Messaging

- Active Server Pages

- Exchange Web Client

ActiveX

All of the Active Platform technologies are based on *ActiveX*. ActiveX is a Microsoft specification for software objects. The term *control* refers to an object. A control is a self-contained software component that has properties (e.g., size, color, content) and methods (e.g., the code to print or edit content). An example of an ActiveX control might be a graphic control. A program could send the ActiveX control that contains that graphic to another program on a different computer. The second program would have all the necessary information to access and manipulate the graphic. A control or object is like a container, containing both content and programming code. ActiveX is part of the Microsoft programming architecture called the Component Object Model (COM). Figure 11.3 illustrates the role of ActiveX in the Active Platform.

Active Server

Active Server is a set of specifications and components that provide a gateway for Web clients to Microsoft BackOffice applications, such as Microsoft Exchange Server. The collection of programs that make up the Active Server are referred to as the Active Server Components. Examples of Active Server Components are Active Messaging and the Exchange Web Client. Figure 11.4 illustrates Active Server and some of its components.

FIGURE 11.3

The role of ActiveX in the
Active Platform

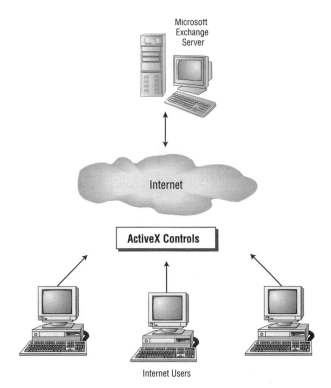

Active Messaging

Active Messaging includes all the specifications and components that implement messaging services for all Active Server applications. Two main components comprise Active Messaging:

- **Active Messaging Library**   This library contains functions that could be used in a Active Server application and that allow that application to interface with Microsoft BackOffice functions and resources. Some of this library's functions are Windows NT authentication (i.e. logon services), access to Exchange mailboxes, public folders, and the Exchange Directory. Through an Active Server application containing these functions, Web clients can access the many resources of an application like Microsoft Exchange Server.

FIGURE 11.4

The Active Server
components of Exchange
Server

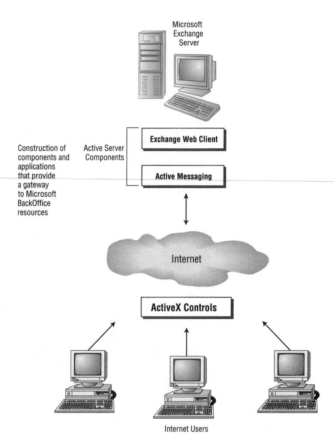

- **Active Messaging Rendering Library**   This library contains functions that can translate the various Microsoft formats into the HTML format. For example, just as a MAPI-based Exchange client can view information by using various columns, groupings, and filters, so too can a Web client using HTML. This is accomplished through an Active Server application and the functions of this library to translate those views into HTML.

As mentioned, the Active Messaging Library provides Windows NT authentication services. This functionality provides security for the Exchange resources being accessed from the Web. An Active Server application can be configured to allow access to two types of users:

- **Windows NT account name** If this option is chosen, a Web client must log on with a Windows NT account by providing a domain, account name, and password. The logon information that is passed from the Web client to the Active Server can be protected using the Secure Sockets Layer (SSL) protocol. Once authenticated, the Web client can access an Exchange mailbox or public folders.

- **Anonymous user** This option allows users without Windows NT accounts to access Exchange resources. Restrictions can be set to limit which resources anonymous users can access.

Figure 11.5 depicts Active Messaging in the Active Platform.

FIGURE 11.5

Active Messaging in the Active Platform

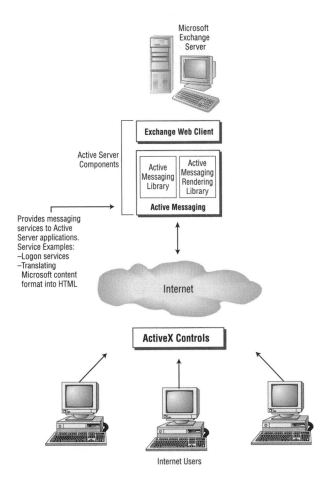

Internet Users

Active Server Pages (ASP)

Active Server Pages (ASP) is the Microsoft phrase for the server applications running on the Active Server. They are made up of standard HTML documents and ActiveX code that calls the functions in the Active Server Components.

ASPs are developed by writing a script that includes the HTML code for interfacing with the Web clients, and the ActiveX code that will interface with the various Active Platform components. The ActiveX code can be written using any number of tools (such as C++, Visual Basic or VBScript, and Java or JavaScript). ASPs are compiled automatically as necessary by IIS, so developers only need to modify and save scripts to quickly try them out.

Exchange Web Client

Microsoft's Active Server Pages provide Web access to Microsoft Exchange Server. These ASPs, along with their supporting .GIF and .HTM files, are collectively referred to as the Exchange Web Client, and are shipped with the Exchange Server product. As with the other ASPs, they must be installed on the Active Server running on the Microsoft Internet Information Server (IIS).

Figure 11.6 illustrates the place of the Active Server Pages in the Active Platform architecture.

Installing HTTP on Exchange Server

HTTP is not built-in to the core components of Exchange Server, as are the other three protocols discussed in this chapter. It is an installation option during the setup of Exchange Server (the default option), and is referenced on the setup screen as the "Active Server Components." If chosen, this option will install components to a Microsoft Internet Information Server (IIS), version 3.0 or greater. This necessitates that you have IIS on your network. An additional requirement is that the Active Server Pages be installed on the IIS computer. Once the setup is complete, the Exchange hierarchy will have an object in the site Protocols container labeled "HTTP (Web) Site Settings."

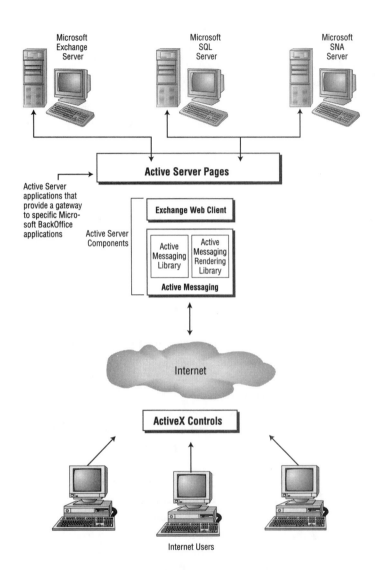

FIGURE 11.6

Active Server Pages in the Active Platform architecture

Configuring HTTP on Exchange Server

HTTP can be configured in Exchange Server using the HTTP (Web) Site Settings object. This object has the three property pages listed in Table 11.3 (the standard Permissions page is also shown if Exchange Administrator is configured to display it on all objects).

TABLE 11.3	**Property Page**	**Description**
The property pages of the HTTP object	General	This page contains the display name and directory name for the HTTP object. There is also a checkbox to enable or disable anonymous access to published public folders and the Global Address List.
	Folder Shortcuts	This page is used to define which public folders are displayed to anonymous users logging on with a Web browser.
	Advanced	You can use this page to set the number of address book entries that will be sent to Web clients when they perform an address lookup. The default is 50 entries. If a number is not specified on this page, then the entire address book will be sent to a Web client (which is not desirable for large directories).

After a public folder has been published, the folder's owner can determine which users, including anonymous Web clients, can access their folder, and what level of access they will have. This is done through an Exchange client application, such as Microsoft Exchange Client or Outlook, and through the Permissions property page of a public folder. If a folder owner wanted anonymous Web clients to read the contents of their public folder, that owner would grant the Read permission to the "anonymous" user on the Permission property page of that folder (that folder would also have to be on the Folder Shortcuts list).

Some configuration issues relating to this topic can only be accomplished on the IIS computer and through its Internet Service Manager program. For example, if an Exchange administrator wanted to prevent certain IP addresses from accessing any Exchange resources, this would have to be accomplished through the Internet Service Manager. The other three protocols discussed in this chapter, POP3, LDAP, and NNTP, can all be configured through Exchange Administrator to reject designated IP addresses.

The HTTP Client and Exchange Server

There is no special configuring of the HTTP client for it to connect to an Exchange server. The Web user must enter the Exchange server's Web address, called a Uniform Resource Locator (URL), in the following format:

```
http://<IIS_name>/exchange
```

The *IIS_name* is the name of the server running the Exchange Active Server Components.

Lightweight Directory Access Protocol (LDAP)

The Lightweight Directory Access Protocol (LDAP) provides client access to a directory service. An LDAP conversation can take place between an LDAP-enabled client and a server that responds to LDAP requests. LDAP supports actions such as reading, sorting, and deleting directory objects.

Exchange Server integrates LDAP directly in the DS component, and LDAP support is enabled by default. An administrator can disable this protocol at the site and server levels. Even though it is part of the DS component, LDAP is configured using objects in the site and server Protocols containers.

The LDAP object under the Protocols container has five property pages (the standard Permissions page is also shown if Exchange Administrator is configured to display it on all objects). They are explained in Table 11.4.

TABLE 11.4 The property pages of the LDAP object	**Property Page**	**Description**
	General	This page shows the display name (which can be modified) and the directory name (which is only informational) of this object. The most important attribute of this page is the ability to enable or disable LDAP. This page also provides an administrative note field.
	Authentication	This page is used to set the authentication protocol that must be used by an LDAP client when accessing an Exchange server. By default, basic cleartext with or without SSL is permitted.
	Anonymous	This page is used to enable or disable anonymous user LDAP access to Exchange. The default is enabled. If disabled, all LDAP clients need to log on with a valid Windows NT user account and password.
	Search	This page is used to configure how substring directory searches are handled and the maximum number of search results to return (default is 100).
	Idle Time-out	This page is used to configure how long an idle LDAP connection will be held open before automatically closing. Options include: ■ Do not close idle connections ■ Close idle connections after a specified number of minutes The default is to close idle connections after 10 minutes.

Another Exchange object that relates to LDAP operations is the DS Site Configuration object. One of the property pages of this object, the Attributes page, enables an Exchange administrator to determine what attributes can be seen by anonymous users. For example, an organization might not want anonymous Web clients to see the telephone numbers associated with Exchange mailboxes. To hide this information, the Exchange administrator would access the Attributes page of the DS Site Configuration object and clear the checkbox for the Telephone-Number attribute for any anonymous requests.

Exercise 11.2 outlines some of the steps to configure the LDAP protocol at the site object.

EXERCISE 11.2

Configuring the LDAP Protocol at the Site Object

1. In Exchange Administrator, navigate to the site object. Choose the Protocols container within the site Configuration container. Double-click on the LDAP (Directory) Site Defaults object in the right pane. The properties pages for this object will appear.

2. The General page is where you enable or disable the LDAP protocol.

3. Select the Anonymous page. This page is where you enable or disable anonymous LDAP client access.

4. Feel free to investigate other properties of this object. When you are finished, click OK or Cancel.

Network News Transfer Protocol (NNTP)

USENET is a network within the Internet that is comprised of numerous servers containing information on a variety of topics. Each organized topic is called a *newsgroup*. A newsgroup can be thought of as a discussion group or a bulletin board. The USENET servers are also referred to as newsgroup servers. Users access these newsgroups to post information or to read other people's postings.

Clients and servers use the Network News Transfer Protocol (NNTP) to transfer information across USENET. When a client reads or posts information to a newsgroup server, NNTP is used for this exchange. The NNTP client application is frequently called a *newsgroup reader program*.

NNTP is also used to transfer newsgroup content between servers. This function is referred to as a *newsfeed*. A newsgroup server can be configured to send all or some of its newsgroups to other servers. When one server actively sends information to another server, it is referred to as a *push feed* (it is also referred to as *publishing*). A server also can be configured to request that information be sent to it from another server. This is referred to as a *pull feed*. Push feeds are usually used with large newsfeeds. A pull feed allows a local administrator to specify which and when newsgroups are received.

NNTP is included with Microsoft Exchange Server by being incorporated in the Information Store. Even though it is a part of the IS, NNTP has its own object in the Exchange hierarchy, under the Protocols container (POP3 and LDAP, while part of Exchange components, also have their own objects). While NNTP does not have its own installation, the newsfeeds between an Exchange server and the USENET do need to be setup. This is done through the Newsfeed Configuration Wizard (see the section "Newsfeed Configuration Wizard," later in this chapter). When a newsfeed is configured between an Exchange server and the USENET, this functionality is referred to as the Internet News Service (INS). INS enables an Exchange server to function as a newsgroup server. It can push (i.e., publish) public folder content as newsfeeds to other USENET servers. It also can receive newsfeeds from the USENET and place newsgroups in public folders. To receive newsfeeds, INS can either pull a newsfeed or receive a push. See Figure 11.7 for an illustration of INS.

The remainder of this section covers the following topics:

- Newsfeed Configuration Wizard

- Newsfeed property pages

- Publishing a public folder

- Configuring newsgroup public folders

Newsfeed Configuration Wizard

Exchange Server includes a Wizard for newsfeed configuration. The Wizard leads an administrator through first time INS setup and additional newsfeeds that are added thereafter. The Wizard presents a series of questions and places the administrator's input into the necessary configuration object. Some of the configuration options that are configured by the Wizard are found in Table 11.5.

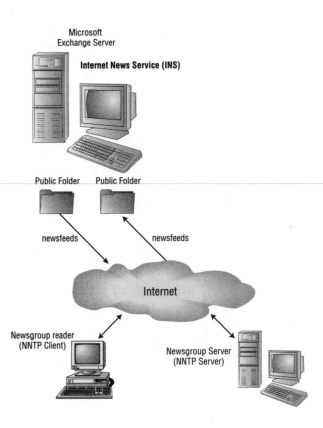

FIGURE 11.7

Internet News Service (INS) and the USENET

TABLE 11.5	**Wizard Dialog Box**	**Description**
Newsfeed Configuration Wizard	Installed Server	This is the name of the Exchange server that will receive the newsfeed. The default is the server on which the administrator is currently logged.
	Type of Newsfeed	Specifies the type of newsfeed. Options include inbound and outbound, inbound only, and outbound only. If an inbound newsfeed is chosen, the type of newsfeed must also be configured as either push or pull.
	Connection Type	Specifies the type of network connection to be used for connection to the USENET. The options include LAN and Dial-Up Networking (DUN).

TABLE 11.5 (cont.) Newsfeed Configuration Wizard	**Wizard Dialog Box**	**Description**
	Schedule	Permits the administrator to configure the connection frequency to another newsgroup server (this can't be set on push newsfeeds). Once setup is complete, the administrator can create a custom schedule through the Schedule property page on the newsfeed object the Wizard creates.
	Host Computer	Specifies the computer that sends newsfeeds to this Exchange server. Identified by either a host name or an IP address.
	Security	Provides for the following security configurations: ■ How the Exchange server logs on to another newsgroup server (pull feed). ■ How another newsgroup server logs on to the Exchange server (push feed).
	Administrator	Selects the newsgroup administrator that will receive any Exchange newsgroup management messages. This account also becomes the owner of all public folders configured for INS.
	Active File	Allows the configuring of the active file. This file contains a list of what newsgroups are to be published to this newsfeed.

After INS has been initially set up with the Wizard, it can be further configured through the property pages of the NNTP and newsfeed objects.

Newsfeed Property Pages

After the INS is installed, a newsfeed object appears under the Connections container in the Exchange hierarchy. This object contains the nine property pages explained in Table 11.6.

TABLE 11.6 Newsfeed property pages	**Property Page**	**Description**
	General	Provides fields for the newsfeed name and administrator mailbox. This is where you enable or disable the newsfeed.
	Messages	Controls the inbound and outbound message sizes.

TABLE 11.6 (cont.) Newsfeed property pages	**Property Page**	**Description**
	Hosts	Specifies the names of the remote newsgroup servers being sent newsfeeds. Specifies the hosts sending newsfeeds to this Exchange server.
	Connection	Controls the type of connection used to connect to remote hosts. The options are LAN and DUN.
	Security	Provides the selection of the outbound user name and password and the inbound user name.
	Schedule	Controls the frequency of inbound pull feeds and outbound feeds.
	Advanced	Used to mark all newsgroup messages as being delivered. This is normally used to cancel processing of queued messages when a backlog occurs.
	Outbound	Specifies what public folders will be published to a remote host.
	Inbound	Specifies the newsgroups to publish to this Exchange server. The list of newgroups to choose from is determined by the active file.

Publishing a Public Folder

After INS installation, the USENET connection you configure is represented in the Exchange hierarchy as a newsfeed object located in the Connections container. If you run the Newsfeed Configuration Wizard for each USENET connection, you will have multiple newsfeed objects. On the Outbound property page of newsfeed objects, you can select the Exchange public folders to be published to the USENET host.

Configuring Newsgroup Public Folders

A published public folder can be configured by an administrator using the Exchange Administrator program. Each published folder has an NNTP property page. This page is where the character set used for MIME and non-MIME messages is configured.

Published public folders can be configured by users in the same manner as other public folders by accessing the public folder property pages in the Exchange Client or Outlook programs.

Summary

Exchange Server support for the POP3, HTTP, LDAP, and NNTP Internet protocols expands the number of client applications that can access Exchange.

POP3 enables an e-mail program to retrieve messages from a remote server mailbox. Internet users who have Exchange mailboxes can use POP3 to retrieve mail from their Inbox folders.

HTTP is the primary protocol used for client-server interactions on the World Wide Web. Exchange Server supports HTTP using the Microsoft Active Platform architecture, and thereby allows Web users to access Exchange resources such as mailboxes, public folders, and calendars using a standard Web browser.

LDAP is used to give client applications access to directory information. LDAP support is integrated in the Exchange DS, allowing Internet client programs using LDAP to access the Exchange DS.

Exchange Server supports NNTP, and can therefore operate as part of the USENET. Exchange can both publish public folders to the USENET, and receive newsfeeds from the USENET. Newsgroups received from newsfeeds are published in public folders.

Review Questions

1. The POP3 protocol can be used to both retrieve and send messages.

   A. True

   B. False

2. The following can be accessed through the POP3 protocol:

   A. Public folders

   B. Inbox

   C. Public folders and Inbox

   D. Calendars

3. Web access to an Exchange server requires a Microsoft Internet Information Server (IIS).

   A. True

   B. False

4. The following is one of the roles of the Active Server:

   A. Creates Windows NT accounts

   B. Holds public folders accessed by Web users

   C. Translates Visual Basic code into C++

   D. Translates Exchange content to HTML

5. An Exchange server can publish data to the USENET using NNTP, but cannot receive it.

   A. True

   B. False

6. The POP3 protocol is configured on an Exchange server using this object:

   A. Information Store

   B. Global Address List

   C. POP3

   D. Site addressing

7. After an Exchange server has upgraded from 4.0 to 5.0, what could be the reason POP3 clients can no longer access the server?

   A. The site service account does not have the "Act as part of the operating system" right.

   B. The POP3 Service needs to be stopped and restarted.

C. The IS needs to be upgraded.

D. POP3 does not work with Exchange Server 5.0.

8. If you wanted to prevent anonymous users using LDAP from seeing a particular Exchange attribute, like telephone numbers, where in the Exchange hierarchy would you have to go to prevent this?

A. Information Store Site Configuration

B. Encryption object

C. Directory Replication object

D. DS Site Configuration

9. If you wanted to reject certain IP addresses of Web clients from accessing your Exchange server, what program would you use?

A. Microsoft Exchange Administrator

B. Network applet in Control Panel

C. Internet Service Manager

D. Link Monitor

10. Which of the following is a reason why POP3 clients could not see e-mail messages in subfolders of their Inbox?

A. POP3 can only access messages in the Inbox, not subfolders of the Inbox.

B. LDAP is not enabled at the mailbox object.

C. NNTP is not enabled at the mailbox object.

D. The IIS computer is down.

11. Which of the following would have to be configured for an anonymous Web client to be able to read a public folder?

    A. The Web client would have to log on using a Windows NT account.

    B. The public folder would have to be listed in the Folders Shortcuts.

    C. The folder owner would have to grant the Read permission to the anonymous user type.

    D. Both B and C

12. For POP3 clients to be able to send Internet mail from their mailbox, what other component must be operation on the Exchange server?

    A. LDAP

    B. NNTP

    C. Active Server Components

    D. Internet Mail Service (IMS)

CHAPTER

12

Managing an Exchange Environment

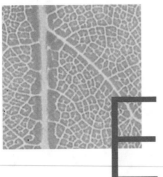

Even after an Exchange Server environment is operational, it still requires "care and feeding." Databases must be maintained and backed up. Storage limits might need to be set. Message transfer parameters might need to be modified. These are just some of the management tasks in an Exchange environment. One nice thing is that most of these tasks are automatically performed while a server is online. However, administrators still have the ability to modify settings and, in some instances, manual and offline maintenance is required.

This chapter covers these and other management tasks and the programs and procedures used to accomplish them. In this chapter, you will learn about:

- Windows NT Server tools

- Exchange Administrator

- Managing public folders

- Managing user storage

- Managing Exchange databases

- Managing message delivery

- Troubleshooting

Windows NT Server Tools

Exchange Server is tightly integrated into Windows NT Server and leverages the management tools built into the operating system. In this section, we will discuss these tools:

- Control Panel/Services

- Event Viewer

- Performance Monitor

- Registry Editor

- Server Manager

- Task Manager

Control Panel/Services

Control Panel/Services can be used to check the status of the Exchange Server services. It can be used to start, stop, and pause a service. It can also be used to configure the startup parameters of a service.

Event Viewer

All Exchange services write event information to the NT Event Log. Administrators should regularly (daily is recommended) view the event log for management and troubleshooting purposes using the Event Viewer application. Exchange services can be configured to log different amounts and types of events for diagnostic logging (this will be discussed further in the "Server Management" section). The vast majority of Exchange information is written to the Application Event Log. The administrator may want to increase the maximum size of this log (the default is 512KB) if logging levels are turned up for troubleshooting or just to maintain the events that have occurred over a longer period. Event Viewer can also be used to view the event logs of a remote server.

Performance Monitor

The Exchange Server SETUP program adds Exchange-related counters to Performance Monitor, making it possible to view the performance of various Exchange activities. Setup also adds a number of preconfigured Performance Monitor counter configurations to the Microsoft Exchange program group. For example, the configuration "Microsoft Exchange Server Load" tracks items such as messages submitted and delivered, and the number of times the Directory is read.

The following is a case study of using Performance Monitor to manage Exchange Server. An administrator is receiving reports from users that the Exchange server response time is slow. A quick examination shows that the server's disk is almost constantly active. The administrator decides to take a deeper look and, using Performance Monitor, collects the following information about that particular Exchange server:

%Processor time=70

%Disk free space=60

Pages/sec=40

Avg. Disk sec/Transfer= 0.02

The administrator then compares these statistics to the "rule of thumb" thresholds that their organization has determined. The following are those thresholds, which when exceeded, have been associated with performance problems:

%Processor time >80%

%Disk free space <10%

Pages/sec >5

Avg. Disk sec/Transfer >.3

Comparing the current statistics with the thresholds, the administrator sees that the Pages/sec number is over the threshold. This suggests that there is not enough memory to cache information, therefore leading the system to page data to the disk. The administrator decides to add memory to this server and continue to monitor the situation.

Registry Editor

Like all Windows 95 and NT applications, Exchange Server stores some configuration information in the registry. This information can be read and modified using the Registry Editor application (regedit.exe). All the registry settings for Exchange Server are stored under the keys HKEY_LOCAL_MACHINE\ SOFTWARE and HKEY_LOCAL_MACHINE\SYSTEM. You normally will not need to edit the registry directly. Most configurations are made through the Exchange Administrator program and are automatically written to the registry.

Server Manager

Server Manager can be used to view and manage the services of a server, and to send messages to connected users. These functions can be performed for any server, local or remote.

Task Manager

Task Manager displays the programs and processes running on a computer. It also displays various performance information, such as CPU and memory usage. An Exchange administrator can use this tool to view the overall health of a server. Task Manager is accessed by right-clicking on the Task bar and choosing the Task Manager menu option.

Exchange Administrator Program

The Exchange Administrator program (ADMIN.EXE) is the primary tool for managing an Exchange environment. We have already seen, in Chapter 5, how it is used to create and manage recipients. This section discusses how it can be used to manage other Exchange activities relating to site and server management. In this section, you will learn about:

- Installation and implementation

- General features

- Site management

- Server management

Installation and Implementation

Exchange Administrator runs on Windows NT and can be installed on the Exchange Server computer or an administrator's computer (assuming it is running Windows NT). To install it, run the Exchange Server SETUP program, select the Custom installation option, and then select Microsoft Exchange Administrator. Exchange Administrator is also installed when the Typical installation option is selected. Connections are made to other servers through the File menu and "Connect to server" option. The dialog box that appears allows you to browse the network and choose the server to connect to, or you may type the server's computer name (i.e., the NetBIOS name) or IP address.

If an organization's network infrastructure supports RPC connections between sites, Exchange Administrator can perform *single-seat administration*. This means an administrator can connect and manage every Exchange server in an organization from one workstation.

General Features

Before we discuss the specific uses and details of Exchange Administrator, we need to examine some of the general features of the program—features relating to the interface, who can use the program, and what functions they can perform.

Administration Window

The Administration window displays a graphical representation of the Exchange hierarchy. The display is divided into two parts:

- **Container pane**   The left pane displays all the container objects in the Exchange hierarchy.

- **Contents pane**   The right pane displays all the objects in the container selected in the container pane. The contents pane can display both container and leaf objects. Both of these are discussed next.

Types of Objects

As you learned in Chapter 2, Exchange entities like sites, servers, and mailboxes are represented as objects. There are two types of objects:

- **Container objects**   A container object contains or groups other objects. The recipients object, which contains mailboxes, DLs, custom recipients, and public folders is an example of a container object.

- **Leaf objects**   A leaf object does not contain any other objects. A mailbox is a leaf object.

Figure 12.1 shows the two panes and two types of objects displayed in Exchange Administrator.

Customizing Exchange Administrator

Exchange Administrator can be customized to meet the needs of a particular administrator or organization. Some of the ways in which it can be customized are listed in Table 12.1. The first two options in Table 12.1 are settings that are saved for the particular administrator who sets them. The remaining options are in effect for all administrators who run Exchange Administrator from the same workstation.

FIGURE 12.1

The two panes and two types of objects in Exchange Administrator

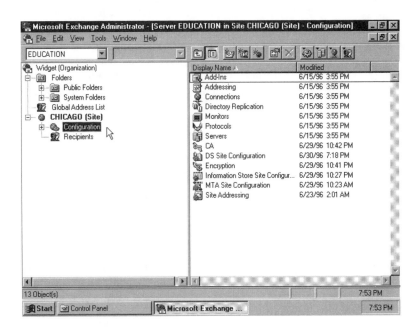

TABLE 12.1	**Custom Option**	**Purpose**
Exchange Administrator custom options	Views	The View menu contains a Sort by option that can be used to sort recipients either by Display Name (the default) or by Last Modified Date.
	Columns	The View menu also contains a Columns option that can be used to choose which columns to display in the contents pane and the order in which to display them.
	Auto naming	An administrator can determine how the display name and alias name attributes of a new recipient will be defaulted. Preset or custom naming options can be selected for display name and alias name independently. The default setting for display names is *FirstName LastName*. The default setting for alias names is *FirstNameLastInitial* (no space between them). These settings are accessed by selecting Options from the Tools menu and configuring the Auto Naming property page.

T A B L E 12.1 (cont.) Exchange Administrator custom options	**Custom Option**	**Purpose**
	Permission settings	An administrator can configure whether the Permissions property page is displayed for all objects and whether the specific rights that make up security roles are displayed. These settings are accessed by selecting Options from the Tools menu and configuring the Permissions property page.
	Windows NT domain settings	An administrator can set which Windows NT domain will be used when Windows NT account information is displayed. The administrator can also configure whether or not the primary Windows NT account associated with a mailbox is deleted when the mailbox is deleted. This domain is also used to search for the default primary Windows NT account when a mailbox is created. These settings are accessed by selecting Options from the Tools menu and configuring the Permissions property page.

One of the new features of Exchange Server 5.0 is "Address Book View" containers. This feature permits the organizing of addresses from the GAL into groups. Rather then the flat structure of the normal GAL (i.e., a long list containing everybody), this new feature can be used to create address containers based upon such attributes as title, department, city, and state. For example, if your Exchange organization contained 5000 recipients in 20 different cities, you could create an address book view that groups recipients based upon their city. These views can also be made available to Exchange clients. The only way to accomplish this type of organization had been to create separate Recipient containers and create recipients in the correct container.

To create an address book view, click the Address Book View container found in the Organization container. From the File menu in Exchange Administrator, click New Other and then the Address Book View option. A dialog box will appear enabling you to create address book views.

Permissions in Exchange Administrator

Administrative access to Exchange objects can be configured. An administrator can assign permissions to specific users or groups at different levels of the Exchange hierarchy in order to determine who has what type of access to what information. To understand how permissions are assigned, you must understand context levels and roles.

Context Levels   The three main tiers of the Exchange hierarchy are the organization, sites, and servers. But for the purpose of assigning administrative permissions, the hierarchy is divided into three levels:

- Organization

- Sites

- Configuration

The organization object is at the top of the hierarchy and contains public folders, the Global Address List, and the site objects. The next level, the site object, contains recipient containers and the configuration object. The last level, the configuration object, contains other containers and objects that facilitate configuration specific to the site. Objects in this level include addressing, MTA site configuration, protocols (e.g., LDAP, NNTP, and POP3), and several others.

These three levels are called *context levels*, or simply *contexts*. Administrative permissions assigned to an object are inherited by all of its child objects within its context. However, permissions are not inherited across context boundaries. Therefore, contexts are self-contained areas that require independently assigned permissions.

Roles   Permissions are granted to users or groups by giving them a group of rights, called a *role*. There are two types of roles: *predefined roles* that consist of a fixed set of rights, and *custom roles* that consist of any combination of individual rights that the administrator desires.

The predefined roles are:

- Admin.

- Permissions Admin.

- Send As

- Service Account Admin.

- User

- View Only Admin.

Rights are listed and described in Table 12.2.

T A B L E 12.2 Exchange rights	Right	Function
	Add Child	Creates child objects, like a mailbox within a recipients container.
	Modify User Attributes	Modifies user-level attributes, like the membership of a DL.
	Modify Admin. Attributes	Modifies administrator-level attributes, like the display name of a mailbox.
	Delete	Deletes objects.
	Logon Rights	Allows access to the Directory. A user must have this right in order to use Exchange Administrator.
	Modify Permission	Modifies permissions on an object.
	Replication	Replicates directory information with other servers. The site service account uses this right to carry out replication with other servers.
	Mailbox Owner	Logs on, reads, creates, and deletes messages in a mailbox. This right is also given to the site service account at the site and configuration objects so service processes can send messages to each other.
	Send As	Sends messages with the recipient object's display name as the return address. This right is also given to the site service account at the site and configuration objects so service processes can send messages to each other.

Not all roles and rights are available on all types of objects.

The predefined roles and their associated rights are listed in Table 12.3.

TABLE 12.3

Exchange roles and associated rights

			Roles			
Rights	**Admin.**	**Permissions Admin.**	**Service Account Admin.**	**View Only Admin.**	**User**	**Send As**
Add Child	✓	✓	✓			
Modify User Attributes	✓	✓	✓		✓	
Modify Admin. Attributes	✓	✓	✓			
Delete	✓	✓	✓			
Logon Rights	✓	✓	✓	✓		
Modify Permissions		✓	✓			
Replication			✓			
Mailbox Owner			✓		✓	
Send As			✓		✓	✓

Site Management

Site-wide parameters are inherited by all servers in a site (some of these parameters can be overridden at the server level). To manage a site, objects are configured under the Configuration and Recipients containers. Chapter 5 covered recipient objects, so this discussion focuses on the objects in the Configuration container (see Figure 12.2). Table 12.4 summarizes these objects. Additional details on some of these objects are provided in the discussion of management tasks later in this chapter.

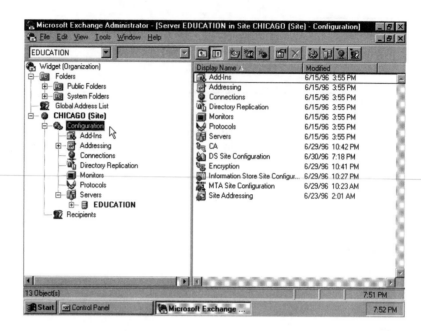

FIGURE 12.2

Configuration container objects

	Object	Contents
TABLE 12.4 Configuration objects summary	Add-Ins	Contains add-ins that offer additional administrative user interfaces.
	Addressing	Holds containers containing programs for generating e-mail addresses and information used to customize the fields and controls viewed in client programs. More information on this container follows this table.
	Connections	Holds the connector objects used to connect a site to other sites and non-Exchange mail systems. (See Chapter 13.)
	Directory Replication	Contains configuration information used for directory replication to other sites. (See Chapter 13.)
	Monitors	Contains configuration information used by Link Monitors and Server Monitors. These features are covered later in this chapter.

T A B L E 12.4 (cont.) Configuration objects summary	**Object**	**Contents**
	Protocols	Contains Protocol objects such as LDAP, NNTP, and POP3.
	Servers	Contains all the server objects for the site.
	DS Site Configuration	Contains properties used by the Directory Service in managing the Directory.
	Information Store Site Configuration	Contains properties for the private and public information stores in the site, such as the list of users who can create top-level public folders.
	MTA Site Configuration	Contains properties used by the MTA for message delivery. This is covered in more detail later in this section.
	Site Addressing	Contains properties related to site-wide addressing, such as the format of a site's Internet address, and properties used for message routing, such as route costs. Administrators can also use this object to enable or disable the foreign addresses that are created for each Exchange recipient. For example, if an organization did not want Microsoft Mail addresses automatically created for their Exchange recipients, the administrator would access this object and disable the "MS" address space entry.
	CA	Contains general information and permissions to the Certification Authority. This object is part of advanced security (see Chapter 10).
	Encryption	Contains general information, permissions, encryption algorithm preferences, and key manager administrator permissions properties. This object is part of advanced security (see Chapter 10).

The DS Site Configuration object warrants a brief summary of its properties.

DS Site Configuration Object

The DS Site Configuration object contains configuration information for operating the Directory Service databases in a site. The five property pages for this object are described in Table 12.5 (the standard Permissions page is also shown if Exchange Administrator is configured to display it on all objects).

T A B L E 12.5 DS Site Configuration property pages	**Property**	**Description**
	General	Two properties on this page relate to how the DS components in a site handle deleted directory objects, such as a deleted mailbox or public folder. The two properties are: ■ **Tombstone lifetime** Whenever an object is deleted in a Directory, that fact is noted in a piece of information called a *Tombstone*. Tombstones are replicated to the other servers in a site to notify them to also delete these objects. The Tombstone Lifetime property sets the life span of a tombstone. ■ **Garbage collection interval** The number of hours between the removal of expired tombstones (garbage).
	Offline Address Book	The Offline Address Book (OAB) is a list of recipient addresses that can be downloaded to a client computer. This page lets you specify which recipients are in the OAB, generate the OAB, and specify which server will store the OAB.
	Offline Address Book Schedule	Because recipients may be added, deleted, or modified, the OAB needs to be regenerated periodically. This page lets you schedule when to perform the regeneration.
	Custom Attributes	This page permits the creation of custom attributes that are associated with recipient objects. An administrator can add attributes for Social Security numbers or employee numbers, for example. Up to 10 custom attributes can be created.
	Attributes	This page contains properties relating to what attributes will be replicated to other sites, and what attributes can be accessed by anonymous and authenticated LDAP client access.

Exercise 12.1 walks through the steps in managing site-level objects and properties.

EXERCISE 12.1

Managing Site-Level Objects

1. In Exchange Administrator, expand the site object, and then click the Configuration container object. You will see seven container objects directly under the Configuration object in the left pane (the container pane) and the same seven objects along with six additional leaf objects in the right pane (the contents pane).

2. In the contents pane, double-click on the DS Site Configuration object. This will bring up the property pages of this object.

3. Click on the Custom Attributes page. In the Custom Attribute 1 dialog box, type **Employee Number**. In the Custom Attribute 2 dialog box, type **Job Class Level**. Click OK.

4. View the Custom Attributes page of George Washington's mailbox. You will see the two custom attributes you just created. Click OK or Cancel.

Server Management

Exchange servers can be individually configured with server specific settings. To do this, configure the properties of a particular server container and configure the objects within that server container.

The server configuration objects are described in Table 12.6. The first seven objects in Table 12.6 will appear in every server. The last two will appear only if certain components are installed on that server (those components are noted in Table 12.6). Figure 12.3 shows the objects within the EDUCATION server object.

T A B L E 12.6 Server configuration objects	Object	Description
	Private Information Store	Use to set storage limits for mailboxes, view resources such as Windows NT accounts accessing mailboxes, and configure diagnostic logging for the Information Store such as storage limit information. This object is discussed in more detail in the Managing User Storage section later in this chapter.

TABLE 12.6 (cont.) Server configuration objects	**Object**	**Description**
	Protocols	Contains protocol objects, such as LDAP, NNTP, and POP3.
	Public Information Store	Use to set storage limits for public folders, age limits for items in public folders, replica locations, the replication schedule, and diagnostic logging. This object is discussed in more detail in the Managing User Storage section later in this chapter.
	Server Recipients	Contains the recipients homed on this particular server.
	Directory Service	Use to manually initiate DS functions, such as directory replication with other servers in a site. Diagnostic logging for the DS can be configured using this object.
	Message Transfer Agent	Contains MTA message size limits. Can be used to manually recalculate the routing table. Use to view and change priorities of queued messages. Diagnostic logging for the MTA can be configured using this object.
	System Attendant	Use to configure automatic deletion of message tracking log files after a specified number of days.
	Directory Synchronization	This object will only be present if the Microsoft Mail Connector is installed. Contains the properties of the Directory Synchronization service. Chapter 15 discusses this object in more detail.
	MTA Transport Stack	This only appears if an MTA Transport Stack was installed. This is transport protocol information used by intersite connectors. Stacks are installed by choosing File, New Other, MTA Transport Stack. For example, the TP/4 protocol stack could be installed and then used by the X.400 Connector for intersite communication. More on this is found in Chapter 13.

A server object itself has property pages that are accessed by selecting the server object and choosing Properties from the File menu (see Figure 12.4). Table 12.7 describes these property pages.

FIGURE 12.3

Server configuration
objects

FIGURE 12.4

The Diagnostic Logging
property page

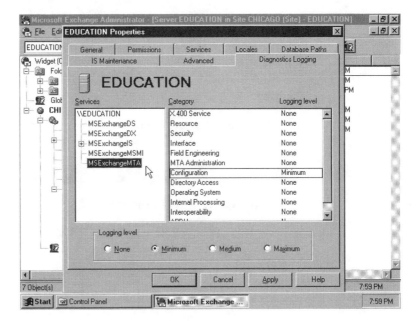

TABLE 12.7	Property Page	Description
Property pages on the server object	Services	Displays installed services on this server, and the services to be monitored by server monitors.
	Database Paths	Displays and allows modification to the directory locations for the Exchange database files, such as the DS, the Private Information Store, the Public Information Store, and the various transaction log files. Transaction log files will be discussed later in this chapter.
	IS Maintenance	Contains the schedule for online maintenance of the IS, which includes the defragmenting of the Public and Private Information Stores. (See the "Managing Exchange Databases" section.)
	Advanced	Contains settings related to consistency between the DS and IS, and the Exchange transaction logs. (See the "Managing Exchange Databases" section.)
	Diagnostic Logging	Used to configure the collection of log information for Exchange components. The log information is written to the Windows NT Event Log. For example, information regarding the modification of the MTA service can be logged. If any administrator reconfigures the MTA service, an event will be logged. See Figure 12.4 to view the Diagnostics Logging property page.

Exercise 12.2 reviews managing a server object with Exchange Administrator.

EXERCISE 12.2

Managing a Server Object

1. In Exchange Administrator, double-click on the Servers container object. An object with your server name will appear under this container.

2. Double-click on your server object. Four container objects will appear in the left pane. Those four objects and three or more additional leaf objects will appear in the contents pane.

EXERCISE 12.2 (CONTINUED FROM PREVIOUS PAGE)

3. With your server object selected in the container pane, choose File ➤ Properties. This brings up the eight property pages for this server.

4. Click on the Database Paths page. You will see the directory paths where the database and transaction log files are stored.

5. When you are done looking, click OK or Cancel.

Managing Public Folders

While public folders can be one of the most important resources in an Exchange environment, they must be properly managed to be effective. This section will examine some of the more important issues of public folder management. These issues will be covered under the following headings:

- Creating dedicated public folder servers

- Public folder replicas

Creating Dedicated Public Folder Servers

A dedicated public folder server is an Exchange server that is used to store public folders and has no mailboxes. Dedicating a server for this purpose can increase client access to public folder data and can make for a more central backup strategy.

Implementing a dedicated public folder server involves the following steps:

1. Move public folders to the designated server. This can be done through the Replicas property page of a public folder object, or through the Instances property page of the target Public Information Store.

2. If there are any mailboxes on the designated public folder server, move them to another server. One way to do this is through the Advanced property page of a mailbox object.

3. Configure the servers that will contain only mailboxes, sometimes called private servers, to use the designated server as the location for future public folder creation. This is done on the General property page of the Private Information Store object.

4. Remove the Private Information Store from the dedicated public folder server, and the Public Information Store from the private servers. This is done through the Exchange Administrator program and by deleting the Private Information Store object and Public Information Store object on their respective servers.

Dedicated public folder servers can be an appropriate part of an Exchange environment when there are large amounts of public folder data, a need to off-load processing and disperse the workload, and for a more central backup strategy.

Public Folder Replicas

Public folders can be replicated to other Exchange servers. Each copy of a public folder is called a replica. Each replica contains the same information as the original public folder, but resides on a different Exchange server. Replicas can reside in the same site as the home server of the original public folder, and they can reside on servers in different sites.

Reasons for using public folder replicas include:

- **Load balancing**   If a large number of users access a particular public folder, access times could be slow. A solution is to create public folder replicas and disperse user access to the various replicas.

- **Fault tolerance**   Having a public folder replicated eliminates a possible point of failure.

- **Easier access for remote users**   If sites are geographically separated and users are accessing public folders in a remote site, it can make sense to distribute those public folders to the other sites through the use of replicas.

Creating Replicas

An Exchange administrator creates replicas through the Replicas property page of a public folder object. A server, or servers, are chosen to house a copy of that particular public folder. When an Information Store detects that it has been chosen to hold a replica, the IS sends a request for the contents of that public folder to a server containing that folder. The request is called a *backfill request,* and the process is called *backfilling* (for more on backfilling see the section "Synchronizing Replicas").

Configuring Replicas

Two important properties of a replica are its replication schedule and affinity number. Both are discussed below.

Replication Schedule   Configuring the times at which a public folder will replicate its content is the primary configuration task. Two important criteria for choosing a schedule are the available bandwidth and the time-sensitiveness of the data. For example, if a replica is located over a slow WAN and contains data that is only periodically changed, the replication schedule could be set for once a day and late at night.

Two methods can be used to set a replication schedule. Each public folder object has a Replication Schedule property page that can be used to set a schedule. To set one replication schedule that would be inherited by all public folders on a server, you would use the Replication Schedule property page of the Public Information Store object. If an individual public folder has its own replication schedule, the server-level configuration would be overridden.

Exchange servers replicate public folders by taking new, modified, or deleted content, and sending it to all the other servers on the replica list. These updates are sent in the form of messages.

If a replica detects that it is not synchronized with the other replicas, it will initiate the backfill process. This entails sending a request for the missing data to another server containing an updated replica. Three circumstances can cause the backfill process to be initiated:

- A new replica is created and needs to receive the public folder content.

- A message containing updated data was lost in transit.

- A server was restored from backup.

Backfilling helps ensure the integrity of a replica.

Affinity Number   When a client selects a public folder to view its contents, the IS must decide where that folder resides. If there are replicas of that folder, the IS uses a series of criteria to choose the folder to connect the client with. These criteria are listed below:

1. If the public folder resides on the client's public folder hierarchy server, that server is connected.

2. If the above criterion is not applicable and there are multiple replicas in the site, the IS uses an algorithm to generate a random number that is used to choose the replica to connect to. This mechanism distributes connections among a number of replicas and produces load balancing.

3. If the IS cannot connect to the random number server, the remaining replicas in the site are tried. Servers that the IS server already has RPC connections with are tried first.

4. If replicas in the local site cannot be connected, the IS will attempt to connect the client to a replica in another site. To help the IS choose the site to connect to, sites can be assigned a public folder affinity number. This is similar to a cost value. The IS uses affinity numbers to determine the order in which different sites are attempted. The site with a remote replica and with the lowest affinity number is attempted first. If two sites have the same affinity number, the IS views them as one logical site and attempts connection to a random replica. Sites without affinity numbers are not attempted.

After a site is connected, the replicas within that site are tried in a random order.

Affinity numbers are applied at the site-level through the Information Store Site Configuration object, and the Public Folder Affinity property page.

Managing User Storage

Anyone who has ever had a personal computer knows how fast a hard drive fills up. No matter how much storage you have, it is not enough. This is even more true for a server, because of its "one to many" relationship with clients. Exchange administrators can maximize the space available by managing mailbox storage and public folder storage.

Managing Mailbox Storage

User mailboxes are stored in the Private Information Store (PRIV.EDB) database on their home Exchange server. Server-based mail storage has the advantages of central administration and central backup. All Exchange storage functions are managed by the IS service. An administrator can manage and monitor mailbox storage by configuring and viewing the Private Information Store object. Exchange Administrator also contains a utility that can delete messages in mailboxes to recover storage space. These topics are discussed under the following headings:

- Setting mailbox storage limits

- Monitoring mailbox storage

- Cleaning mailboxes

- Diagnostic logging and mailbox storage

Setting Mailbox Storage Limits

Storage limits for mailboxes can be configured by setting a general default that applies to all mailboxes, or by setting limits on a per-mailbox basis.

Default Storage Limit   The Private Information Store object contains the storage limit attribute. This attribute configures the storage limit default for all mailboxes on the server. The storage limit attribute has two features. One, called "Issue warning," allows you to set a limit for the amount of data allowed in a mailbox before the system sends the user a warning message. The warnings are sent at the times specified on the Storage Warnings page of the Information Store Site Configuration object. The other feature, called "Prohibit send," allows you to set a limit for the amount of data allowed in a mailbox before a user is prohibited from sending mail. The mailbox can still receive mail, but the mailbox user cannot send mail until items are deleted from the mailbox.

Per-Mailbox Storage Limits   An administrator can also set mailbox storage limits on an individual mailbox. This setting overrides the default setting at the Private Information Store object. This configuration is made on the Advanced property page of a mailbox.

Monitoring Mailbox Storage

An administrator can monitor mailbox storage using the Mailbox Resources object under the Private Information Store object. This object displays various information about a mailbox including the total space it uses, and the total number of items it contains.

Cleaning Mailboxes

"Cleaning" in this context refers to deleting data. Exchange Administrator has a cleaning utility that is invoked by choosing Clean Mailbox from the Tools menu. Criteria is selected to determine which messages will be deleted. An administrator can highlight one or more mailboxes and then use this utility to delete messages in those mailboxes.

Diagnostic Logging and Mailbox Storage

The Private Information Store has a Diagnostic Logging property page where the administrator can activate and configure event logging. One of the categories that can be logged is storage limits. Event logs can be viewed using the Windows NT Event Viewer.

The single-instance storage of the IS contributes greatly to keeping storage levels lower than they would be otherwise. If a 10 MB message is sent to a distribution list of 10 users, all on the same server, the IS only stores a single instance of the message and gives each of the 10 members a pointer to the message. Rather than 100 MB of storage being used, only 10 MB is used. If some of the members of a DL are on another server, a copy of the message is sent to that server and recipients. The single instance storage would also apply to that server.

Managing Public Folder Storage

Public folders are the repository for shared information in an Exchange organization and they can grow to be quite large. Exchange includes many features to help manage public folder storage. These features are exhibited in the following management procedures:

- Setting public folder storage limits

- Setting age limits for data

- Monitoring public folder storage

- Diagnostic logging and public folder storage

Setting Public Folder Storage Limits

Storage limits can be set on public folders at the server level and on individual public folders. Limits on public folder storage can assist in keeping the Public Information Store database from growing too large.

Default Storage Limit   The Public Information Store object can be configured with a storage limit that applies to all public folders on the server. If the limit is reached, warning messages are sent to public folder contacts. The warnings are sent at the times specified on the Storage Warnings page of the Information Store Site Configuration object.

Per-Folder Storage Limits   As with individual mailboxes, you can configure a particular public folder with its own storage limit. This is set on the Advanced property page of the public folder. If the storage limit is reached, a warning message will be sent to the folder contacts.

Setting Age Limits For Data

Another method that can help control public folder storage is to set a maximum length of time an item can be in a folder. This is called an *age limit*. Age limits can be set for all public folders in an IS, or on a per-folder basis. The replicas of a public folder can also be separately configured. Age limits can keep a public folder from growing out of control.

Monitoring Public Folder Storage

Periodically, an administrator will want to check the storage level of public folders. This can be done using the Public Folder Resources object found under the Public Information Store. Clicking on the Public Folder Resources object displays all the folders on the server in the contents pane. Information including the total space used and the number of items in a folder will be displayed. This information can also be accessed through the Public Folder Resources property page of the Public Information Store.

Diagnostic Logging and Public Folder Storage

The Public Information Store can be configured for different levels of event logging. Various categories can be logged, including storage limits.

Managing Exchange Databases

All Exchange data, such as messages and directory information, is stored in various database files. Because of the extreme importance of the files, Exchange has many automatic and online maintenance processes. There are also various programs that can be run by an administrator to manage these files. Before we cover these programs and processes, we will explore the database technology that Exchange uses. This will serve as a background to the managing of the databases. This section will cover:

- Database technology and files

- Managing the Directory database

- Managing the Information Store databases

- Backing up the databases

Database Technology and Files

There are three primary Exchange database files. The IS component manages PRIV.EDB for the Private Information Store and PUB.EDB for the Public Information Store. The DS component manages DIR.EDB which holds all directory information. Each database also has its own transaction log files, which have a .LOG extension. Some additional files that pertain to the databases will be discussed in the following section. Table 12.8 summarizes this information.

TABLE 12.8 The main Exchange database and transaction log files	**Exchange Component**	**Default Directory Path and Filename**	**Transaction Log File**
	Directory Service	\EXCHSRVR\DSADATA\DIR.EDB	EDB.LOG
	Information Store	\EXCHSRVR\MDBDATA\PRIV.EDB \EXCHSRVR\MDBDATA\PUB.EDB	EDB.LOG EDB.LOG

The location of these database files can be modified using the Database Paths property page of a server object (also see Table 12.7). If a server has multiple drives, database files can be located on different drives to improve performance.

The Exchange databases are based on a 32-bit, multithreaded, transaction-based database engine. The engine is specially tailored for Exchange to be fast, compact, and optimized for message databases that experience constant record creation and deletion. One of the reasons the engine is fast is because it uses transaction log files.

Transaction Log Files

When data is to be written to one of the Exchange databases, the database engine does not write the data directly to the database file. The data is first written to a transaction log file, and then later written (or *committed*) to the database through a background process. This method has two advantages. One advantage is performance. When data is written to a transaction log file, it is entered sequentially, always at the end of the file. This can be done very fast. When data is committed to a database file, however, the database engine must search for the appropriate location to place the data. This is much slower than the simple sequential method. The second advantage is fault tolerance. If a database file becomes corrupt, a transaction log file can be used to recreate the database file.

As transactions in transaction log files are committed to the database files, a *checkpoint file* (EDB.CHK) is updated. The checkpoint file keeps track of which transactions in the sequential list still need to be committed to a database by maintaining a pointer to the last information that was committed. This tells the engine that everything after that point still needs to be committed to a database. If a server shuts down abnormally, Exchange can read the checkpoint file to learn where in the transaction logs it needs to start recovering data. The checkpoint file therefore assists in the fault tolerance of Exchange.

Transaction log files can contain up to 5MB of transactions. However, the log files are always 5MB in size no matter how many transactions they contain because the engine creates them as 5MB files and then proceeds to fill them with transactions. The current log file being written to is named EDB.LOG. When it is filled with 5MB of transactions, it is renamed to EDB*nnnnn*.LOG where *nnnnn* is a hexadecimal number, and a new, empty EDB.LOG file is created. The log files will, therefore, accumulate on the hard disk. A way to minimize this is to perform regular full or incremental backups of the databases. During a full or incremental backup, fully committed log files are automatically deleted because the data in them is backed up. This prevents the number of log files from growing until they take up the entire disk.

Transaction log files can also be configured to recycle themselves to prevent constant accumulation on the hard disk. This process is called *circular logging*. Instead of continually creating new log files and storing the old ones, the database engine "circles back" to the oldest log file that has been fully committed and overwrites that file. Circular logging minimizes the number of transaction log files on the disk at any given time. The downside is that these logs cannot be used to re-create a database because the logs do not have a complete set of data. They only have the data not yet committed. Another disadvantage of circular logging is that it does not permit a differential or incremental backup of the databases. Circular logging is the default setting and can be enabled or disabled on the Advanced property page of a server object (see Table 12.7).

A summary and comparison of circular logging enabled and disabled is found below:

Circular Logging Enabled (default)	Circular Logging Disabled
Transaction log files recycled	Old transaction log files stored
Does not permit the recreation of a database	Does permit the recreation of a database
Does not permit differential or incremental backups	Does permit differential and incremental backups
	A full or incremental backup automatically deletes old transaction log files

One other feature of the transaction-based databases is the use of reserve log files. Exchange creates two reserve log files (RES1.LOG and RES2.LOG) for each database. They are used if the system runs out of disk space. If that happens, Exchange shuts down the database service, logs an event to the event log, and writes any outstanding transaction information into these reserve log files. These two files reserve an area of disk space that can be used after the rest of the disk space is used.

Managing the Directory Database

Some maintenance of the Directory database occurs online while the DS service is started, and other maintenance is performed offline while it is stopped.

Online Maintenance of the Directory Database

Whenever a directory object is deleted, the deletion needs to be replicated to the other servers in the site (remember, there is only one logical directory for a site). The unit of information that says an object has been deleted is called a *tombstone*. Tombstones are replicated to other servers. By default, Exchange lets tombstones live for 30 days to ensure that this information is replicated.

The 30-day setting can be modified through the General property page of the DS Site Configuration object (see Table 12.5).

A related setting is the Garbage collection interval. This is the time interval at which the expired tombstones are permanently deleted and the space they take is reclaimed. Exchange automatically collects garbage when the system is online. The Garbage collection interval defaults to 12 hours. (You should not change the default under normal circumstances.) This configuration is also found on the General property page of the DS Site Configuration object.

Offline Maintenance of the Directory Database

Offline maintenance of the Exchange Directory (or Information Store) databases can be performed using the EDBUTIL.EXE utility (Exchange Database Utility). To use this utility, the database service (DS or IS) must be stopped. EDBUTIL.EXE performs the following functions:

- **Defragments a database** Over time, databases can become *fragmented*, which means that the data stored on the disk is noncontiguous. This can be caused by retaining deleted items. A data item may be logically marked as deleted, but physically kept on the disk for possible recovery. When a file is updated, the new data is stored in available free space, which may not be contiguous. Accessing a noncontiguous file causes extra head movement and therefore slower disk access. EDBUTIL can be used to defragment a database and decrease the database file size.

- **Consistency check** Compares related information in a database to make sure it agrees. For example, pointers in the database that reference other pages of data can become *orphaned* and actually point off to nowhere. If these pointers are ever accessed, erratic behavior may occur. A Consistency check will fix this problem.

- **Recover a database** In a rare case when a database becomes badly damaged and cannot be repaired through the database consistency process, EDBUTIL can attempt to recover the database by reconstructing each entry in the database.

Managing the Information Store Databases

Some maintenance of the Information Store database occurs online while the IS service is started, and other maintenance is performed offline while it is stopped.

Online Maintenance of the Information Store Databases

Exchange Server automatically performs the following maintenance functions on the IS databases:

- Defragments the Private and Public Information Stores

- Expires messages based on configured age limits

- Deletes indices created to cache folder views

The defragmenting of the IS can recover a fair amount of disk space. In situations that are approaching the limit of available disk space and that require a quick fix, performing an online IS maintenance can be the answer.

You can schedule when these maintenance functions are performed by configuring the IS Maintenance property page of a server. Nonpeak hours are the best time to schedule this because server performance may degrade during maintenance.

Offline Maintenance of the Information Store Databases

ISINTEG (Information Store Integrity) is an offline utility that can be used to repair the IS database. To execute it, the IS service must be stopped. If an IS database encounters enough errors to prevent it from starting or to prevent users from logging on to it, ISINTEG can be run to find and eliminate these errors. This utility is found in the \EXCHSRVR\BIN directory.

One scenario that requires the use of ISINTEG is after an offline backup and restore of Exchange. An offline backup is a file-level backup of the IS while Exchange Server is offline (the two files that would be backed up are PRIV.EDB and PUB.EDB). An offline restore is a file-level restore of the IS while Exchange Server is offline.

After the offline restore of the IS, you must execute ISINTEG to patch the IS before it can be used. This is done by executing the following command line:

```
ISINTEG -PATCH
```

Other scenarios that could require the use of ISINTEG is a server's disk becoming full and stopping the IS service, or a power failure shutting down the server and after the restart the IS service will not work. In both of these scenarios, Exchange should automatically roll back to the last checkpoint and be operational. But if that does not occur, you would need to execute ISINTEG with the following parameter:

```
ISINTEG -FIX
```

The EDBUTIL program discussed earlier also can perform offline maintenance of the IS. While ISINTEG only works on the IS databases, EDBUTIL operates on the DS database and the IS databases.

Because IS database maintenance is automatic, manually using ISINTEG or EDBUTIL is not regularly required.

Backing Up the Databases

Because of the importance of the Exchange databases and transaction logs, backup is essential. When Exchange Server is installed, a new version of Windows NT Backup, one that is Exchange-aware, replaces the existing version. This program can be used to back up Exchange data.

Although there are many backup strategies, three basic strategies will serve as an introduction to this topic. Table 12.9 describes these three basic strategies, along with some of their advantages and disadvantages (a five day work week is assumed).

TABLE 12.9

Three basic backup strategies

Backup Strategy	Description	Advantages	Disadvantages
Full Daily	A full (i.e., complete) backup is performed every day.	Only one tape is needed to perform a restoration.	Longest amount of time needed to perform the backup.
One full, and four incremental	A full backup is done on day 1. An incremental backup (using a new tape) is performed every day for the next four days. This procedure only backs up the new and changed data since the last full or incremental backup (whichever is more recent).	Takes the least amount of time to back up.	Could require up to five tapes to perform a restoration.
One full, and four differential	A full backup is done on day 1. A differential backup (using a new tape) is performed every day for the next four days. This procedure only backs up the new and changed data since the last full backup.	No more than two tapes, the full and the last differential, are required to perform a restoration.	This strategy takes progressively longer each day.

The Exchange databases and transaction logs can be backed up while an Exchange server is online. If the full backup strategy is used, the following Exchange files are backed up:

PRIV.EDB

PUB.EDB

Transaction log files

Checkpoint file (EDB.CHK)

If a differential or incremental backup is performed, the *.EDB files are not backed up, and only these files are backed up:

Transaction log files

Checkpoint file (EDB.CHK)

For a differential or incremental backup to be performed, circular logging must be turned off.

In a perfect world, you would perform a full backup of Exchange every night. But if your databases are large, you might not have enough time in one night to do a full backup. One solution to this scenario is to combine backup strategies. For example, a Full (i.e., Normal) backup can be performed every weekend, and a Differential backup every weekday evening.

Standby Servers

Part of a backup and restore strategy could involve using standby servers, also called recovery servers. These are computers that you have prepared to take the place of your Exchange server should it have a catastrophic failure. A standby server would have installed Windows NT Server and Exchange Server. Since you want this server to be operational as soon as possible after the failure of your primary server, you need to have the Exchange database files loaded on the standby server, or on media that would facilitate loading on that server. Some organizations create a batch file that stops the Exchange services on the primary server and copies the relevant files to the standby server. Those files are the directory file, transaction log files, checkpoint file, and the Private and Public Information Store files. These files could also be copied to removable media and then uploaded to the standby server when needed.

It is not recommended that you install Exchange Server on a primary domain controller (PDC) in a domain with no backup domain controllers (BDCs). Exchange clients need to be authenticated by a domain controller in order to access Exchange resources. If a computer serving as both the Exchange server and the PDC has a major failure, the standby server will not do you much good. Even though all the Exchange files are still present, the Exchange clients would not be able to be authenticated.

Problems can occur when you back up or restore servers. Table 12.10 lists some problems (and possible causes) that you may encounter when you perform two common procedures.

TABLE 12.10	Situation	Problem	Casue
Backup and restore problems and causes	Restored the Information Store to a different server.	After the restore, users cannot access the Information Store.	The restore was performed on a server in a different Windows NT domain than the original server.
	Backed up an Exchange server that was running on a primary domain controller. Restored the Information Store to a different server.	After the restore, users cannot access the Information Store.	The organization and site names on the new server are not the same as the original server.

You can also use the backup log file, BACKUP.LOG, that resides in your Windows NT directory (e.g., \WINNT) as a diagnostic tool when you troubleshoot.

Managing Message Delivery

Ensuring the efficient delivery of messages is central to an administrator's job. To accomplish this job, an administrator needs to understand the role of the MTA and its properties. As you learned in Chapters 2 and 3, the role of the MTA is to manage the transfer of data. The transfer can be between servers in the same site, or even between servers in different sites. This chapter covers the former scenario, and Chapter 13 covers the latter. In this section, you will learn about:

- Message tracking

- MTA messaging settings

- The MTACHECK utility

Message Tracking

MTA properties are accessed through the MTA Site Configuration object in the Configuration container. One of these properties is message tracking, which can be enabled or disabled. The MTA component manages the delivery of messages to remote servers. If you enable message tracking, the System Attendant will keep a log of routing information for every message the MTA processes. The log file is an ASCII text file that is stored in the directory EXCHSRVR\ TRACKING.LOG. The file naming convention is YYYYMMDD.LOG, where YYYY is the year, MM is the month, and DD is the day. For example, a log file created on February 1, 1997 is called 19970201.LOG.

To use tracking logs, choose Track Message from the Tools menu in Exchange Administrator. You will be able to search for and select the message you want to track.

MTA Messaging Settings

Other properties of the MTA Site Configuration object relate to the defaults used when sending messages. These properties are found on the Messaging Defaults property page (see Figure 12.5). Four categories of properties are found on this page. Each will be described along with its individual attributes.

RTS (Reliable Transfer Service) values are properties that indicate how often you want to verify information being sent, how long you want to wait after an error has occurred to resend a message, and how often you want verification from another server that it has received a message. The specific attributes that relate to these settings are described in Table 12.11.

Another set of attributes is grouped under the heading "Connection retry values." These values determine how many times you want to try to open a connection, how many times to try to send a message, how long to wait after an error to reopen a connection, and how long to wait to resend a message after an error. The specific attributes that relate to these settings are described in Table 12.12.

FIGURE 12.5

Messaging Defaults
property page

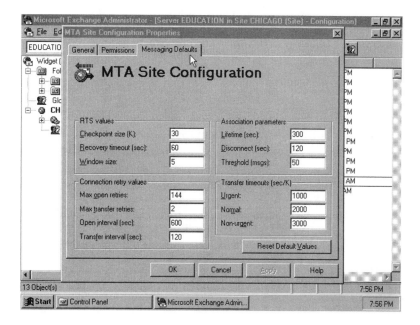

FIGURE 12.5

Messaging Defaults
property page

	Attribute	Description
TABLE 12.11 RTS values attributes	Checkpoint size (K)	The amount of data to be sent before a *checkpoint* is inserted. A checkpoint is like a bookmark placed in the stream of data being sent. If there is an error in the transfer of a message, the MTA will go back to the last checkpoint and resend data from that point. Using checkpoints causes message transfers to be slightly slower. If a connection is considered unreliable, the checkpoint size should be decreased.
	Recovery timeout (sec)	The length of time the MTA waits for a reconnection after an error has occurred. When this time is reached, the MTA will delete the checkpointed information and restart the data transfer from the beginning. If a reconnection is made before this time period is reached, the MTA resends only from the checkpoint forward.
	Window size	The window size indicates the number of checkpoints that can be sent before an acknowledgment must be received from the destination. If the window size is reached with no acknowledgment, the data transfer is suspended. The greater the window size, the faster the transfer rate.

TABLE 12.12	**Attribute**	**Description**
Connection retry value attributes	Max open retries	The maximum number of times the MTA tries to open a connection before it sends an NDR (Non-Delivery Report) to the sender.
	Max transfer retries	The maximum number of times the MTA tries to transfer a message over an open connection.
	Open interval (sec)	The length of time the MTA waits after an error has occurred before it attempts to reopen a connection.
	Transfer interval (sec)	The length of time the MTA waits after a failed transfer before it tries to resend a message over an open connection.

Three attributes are grouped under the heading "Association parameters." An *association* is an open pathway to another system. An association is a subset of a connection. While there may be only a single connection between two systems, there can be multiple associations in that single connection. Association parameters relate to how long to keep an association open, how long to wait for a response before closing the association, and the number of queued messages that will trigger an additional association. The specific attributes that relate to these settings are described in Table 12.13.

TABLE 12.13	**Attribute**	**Description**
Association parameters	Lifetime (sec)	The length of time the MTA keeps an association open after it has finished sending messages.
	Disconnect (sec)	The length of time the MTA waits after it sends a disconnect request before it will close the connection.
	Threshold (msgs)	The maximum number of queued messages before the MTA opens another association.

The final group of message defaults is called Transfer timeouts. These attributes specify how long to wait after a transfer failure before sending a Non-Delivery Report (NDR) to the sender. Different transfer timeouts can be assigned for each message priority.

The MTACHECK Utility

The MTA Check utility (MTACHECK) scans a MTA queue looking for corrupted messages that could prevent the MTA from sending messages. MTACHECK will attempt to remedy that situation by rebuilding the MTA queue. This program can run only when the MTA service is stopped. MTACHECK is found in the \EXCHSRVR\BIN directory and can be run from a command prompt.

Troubleshooting

An administrator has many tools and resources to help troubleshoot an Exchange environment. This section discusses some of these, including:

- Client troubleshooting tools

- Diagnostic logs

- Monitors

Client Troubleshooting Tools

Two tools are used to troubleshoot an Exchange client. One repairs personal folder storage, and the other tests connections to a server.

- **Inbox Repair Tool**   SCANPST.EXE tests and repairs a personal folder store (*.PST). It scans for bad blocks and attempts to rebuild them. If a .PST file is corrupted beyond repair, this program will try to evacuate the good blocks of data and remove the corrupted blocks. This program does not need to be run unless there are operational problems with personal folders. On rare occasions, if an Exchange client application is abnormally terminated, a personal folder can become corrupted. You will be notified of the corruption on the next startup of the client application. The Inbox Repair Tool is found in the Exchange client program group.

- **RPC Ping**   The RPC Ping utility is used to test RPC connections between two computers. It can be used to test the RPC connection between a client and a server. The RPC Ping Server component (RPINGS.EXE for the Intel platform) is run first on the Exchange server. The RPC Ping Client component (e.g., RPINGC32.EXE for 32-bit clients) is then run on the client computer and sends a request to the server. This procedure tests the existence and quality of that connection. There are RPC Ping client versions for Windows 3.x, Windows 95, Windows NT, and MS-DOS. Both the client and server side programs are on the Exchange Server compact disc in the SUPPORT\RPCPING directory.

Diagnostic Logs

Many Exchange objects have a Diagnostics Logging property page. This page is used to configure the types and levels of events logged to the Windows NT Event Log. The logs are viewed with the Event Viewer application. This topic was already discussed earlier in this chapter, but because of its use in troubleshooting it is also mentioned here.

Monitors

Exchange Server includes two monitoring features that can be used in the management of an Exchange environment. These features are:

- **Server Monitor**   Can be used to monitor the Exchange services running on a server.

- **Link Monitor**   Can be used to test the message link (i.e., connection) between two Exchange servers. A link is tested by sending a message to a designated remote server, or a designated recipient on a remote server.

Multiple monitors can be configured to provide different views, but each monitor can also track multiple servers. The remainder of this section covers the two types of monitors in more detail.

Server Monitor

Server Monitors are a straightforward, yet powerful feature. In addition to monitoring the services running on an Exchange server, server monitors can automatically send notifications and perform specified actions.

A Server Monitor is created by choosing File, New Other, Server Monitor in Exchange Administrator. This brings up the property pages of a new Server Monitor. The five main property pages and their primary attributes are found in Table 12.14 (the standard Permissions page is also shown if Exchange Administrator is configured to display it on all objects).

TABLE 12.14 Server Monitor property pages	**Property Page**	**Primary Attributes**
	General	▪ Directory name ▪ Display name ▪ Log file ▪ Polling interval
	Servers	Monitored servers Services to monitor
	Notification	**When** Indicates the time delay after a server goes into an alert or warning state before the notification occurs. **How** Specifies the type of notification event. Options include launch a process, mail message, and Windows NT Alert. **Who** States where the notification will be sent. It is possible to have a series of escalation steps.
	Actions	Attributes include the actions to perform when a service has stopped. Options include take no action, restart the service, and restart the computer. Actions can also be configured separately for the first, second, and subsequent attempts.
	Clock	Attributes include issuing warnings and alerts if the system clocks of the server running the Server Monitor and the server being monitored are not synchronized within a specified range. Clocks can also be automatically synchronized.

Link Monitor

A Link Monitor can be used as an early warning system for problems with links between servers. A Link Monitor is created by choosing File, New Other, Link Monitor in Exchange Administrator. This brings up the property pages of a new Link Monitor.

A Link Monitor has many of the same attributes as a Server Monitor, such as polling interval, notifications, and servers to monitor. One unique attribute of a Link Monitor is *bounce*. Bounce is the longest acceptable round-trip time for a test message to travel between the monitor's home server and the target server. An administrator can set the bounce warning and alert time thresholds.

Starting and Stopping Monitors

After a monitor has been created and configured, administrators are responsible for starting and stopping it. These two actions are discussed in the following text.

Starting Monitors   Monitors can be started two ways:

- Exchange Administrator

- Command prompt

Exchange Administrator can be used to start a monitor. To do so, highlight the particular monitor you want started and choose Start Monitor from the Tools menu. Next, select the server on which to run the monitor. The monitor then starts and the Server or Link Monitor window is displayed.

Monitors can also be started automatically when Exchange Administrator is started. To configure this, leave a monitor started when you exit Exchange Administrator. The monitor will be started automatically the next time Exchange Administrator is launched.

An administrator can also run Exchange Administrator from a command prompt with certain parameters to start a monitor. This is done by accessing a command prompt and changing to the \EXCHSRVR\BIN directory, which contains ADMIN.EXE. The following line is an example of the command line format to use to start a monitor. In this example, *serverA* is the server to which Exchange Administrator will connect and *serverB* is the server on which the monitor *monitor_name* will be run.

```
admin /s serverA /m monitor_name/serverB
```

Stopping Monitors   Stopping a monitor using Exchange Administrator is as simple as clicking on the Close button of the monitor window. Monitors can also be temporarily stopped at a command prompt using the command:

```
admin /t
```

Exercise 12.3 will walks through the steps to create, configure, start, and test a Server Monitor.

EXERCISE 12.3

Server Monitor

1. Highlight the Monitors object in the Configuration container. Choose File ➤ New Other ➤ Server Monitor. This will bring up the property pages of a new Server Monitor.

2. Go to the General page. In the Directory name and Display name fields, type **ServerMonitor1**.

3. In the Polling interval for Normal, enter 1 minute.

4. Choose the Notification page. Click New. This will bring up the New Notification dialog box.

5. Choose the Notification type of Windows NT Alert and click OK. The Escalation Editor dialog box will appear.

6. Enter the number 1 in the Time delay box. In the "Computer to alert" field, enter the name of your Exchange server. Click OK. Click OK on the alert concerning notifications.

7. Choose the Servers page. Highlight your Exchange server name in the left listbox and click Add.

8. Click the Services button. In the Installed services list box, highlight the Microsoft Exchange Key Manager. Then click Add and click OK.

9. Click OK to save and exit from the Server Monitor you just created.

10. Before you start your Server Monitor, access Control Panel/Services, and make sure the Microsoft Exchange Key Manager service is running. If it is not, start it (you will need to supply the KM password or a floppy disk with the password on it—see Chapter 10 for details).

11. Back in Exchange Administrator, highlight the Server Monitor you just created and choose Tools ➤ Start Monitor. The Connect to server dialog box will appear.

12. Make sure your Exchange server name is in the dialog box, then click OK. The Server Monitor window will now appear.

EXERCISE 12.3 (CONTINUED FROM PREVIOUS PAGE)

13. Use Control Panel/Services to stop the Microsoft Exchange Key Manager service.

14. After a moment, your Server Monitor will generate a Windows NT Alert stating "The service MSExchangeKMS is not available. Its status is Stopped." Click OK. You will also see this information written to the Server Monitor window.

15. To stop the Server Monitor, click the Close box on the Server Monitor window.

Summary

Many tools are included with Exchange Server to help manage an Exchange organization. Various Windows NT Server tools, like Event Viewer, can be used by an Exchange administrator. The main tool in an administrator's arsenal is the Exchange Administrator program, which manages objects at the organization, site, and server levels of the Exchange hierarchy.

Exchange Server stores messages and configuration data in various database files. To increase system performance and to facilitate fault tolerance, Exchange Server first writes data to transaction log files. The data is then later committed to the relevant database during a background process.

Server and Link Monitors provide an early warning system for service status and links between servers.

Review Questions

1. Configuring circular logging for transaction log files increases fault tolerance.

   A. True

   B. False

2. Which of the following is NOT true for a differential backup of a database?

   A. Backs up new data since the last full backup

   B. Backs up modified data since the last full backup

   C. Takes progressively longer each day

   D. Takes less time than the incremental strategy

3. Control Panel/Services should NOT be used to start or stop an Exchange service.

   A. True

   B. False

4. The diagnostic logging performed by Exchange services is written to this location:

   A. Windows NT Event Log

   B. \BIN

   C. \exchsrvr\bin

   D. \logging

5. Which of the following relates to information about a deleted Directory object?

   A. RTS values

   B. Retry timeouts

   C. Bounce

   D. Tombstone

6. Some site-level configuration properties can be overridden at a server object.

   A. True

   B. False

7. Which of the following is required for single-seat administration of multiple Exchange sites?

   A. RPC connections between sites

   B. NNTP

   C. POP3

   D. X.400

8. Which of the following procedures could help recover significant disk space on an Exchange server?

   A. MTACheck

   B. Server Monitor

   C. Online IS Maintenance

   D. Performance Monitor

9. How would you use Exchange Administrator to group Exchange recipients by city?

   A. Create an address book view container

   B. Autonaming

   C. You cannot group recipients

   D. Delete the GAL and create Personal Address Books

CHAPTER

13

Connecting Exchange Sites

An organization can have more than one Exchange site for various reasons, including geographical layout, administrative needs, and network infrastructure. Sites must be linked with site connectors to facilitate message transfer from one site to another. Communication between sites (*intersite* communication) is somewhat different than communication within a site (*intrasite* communication).

For intrasite communication, servers communicate directly with each other using either the MTA or DS. Messages are delivered through MTA-to-MTA communication, and directory information is exchanged through DS-to-DS communication. Both types of communication use the RPC protocol for component interaction. Manual configuration is not necessary for intrasite communication. All the servers on a site "know" each other through directory replication. They can communicate directly with each other because of the availability and speed of network connections required within a site.

Intersite communication requires configuration, but high-speed connections between sites are not mandatory. A software component, called a *connector,* must be installed at each site in order for messages to be passed between sites. When the connector software is in place, the MTAs of each site can send messages to the other sites. The MTAs handle the packaging and routing tasks, while the connector software manages the transportation of the messages to the other sites. Figure 13.1 illustrates intrasite and intersite communication.

There are two types of connectors: messaging connectors and the directory replication connector. Messaging connectors, as you may have guessed, manage the transport of messages. There are four messaging connectors:

- Site Connector

- X.400 Connector

- Dynamic RAS Connector

- Internet Mail Service (IMS)

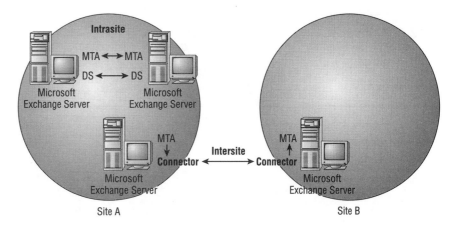

FIGURE I3.I

Intrasite and intersite
communication

The directory replication connector manages the transfer of directory information between sites. This connector can use any of the messaging connectors to transport its directory information to another site.

Some connectors can be used to provide interoperability between Exchange and non-Exchange systems (i.e., foreign systems). Examples of these connectors are the X.400 Connector and the Internet Mail Service (IMS). In this role, a connector can take an Exchange message and translate it into a foreign-system format for delivery to a foreign client. If the message is from the foreign system, a connector can translate it into the Exchange format (see Figure 13.2). Chapters 14 and 15 will focus on connectors used in this role.

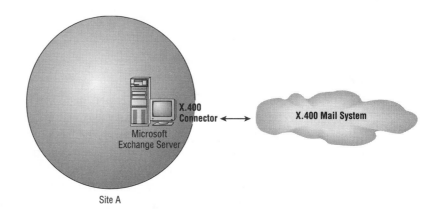

FIGURE I3.2

Connectors used for
interoperability with non-
Exchange systems

When an X.400 or an IMS connector is used to connect two Exchange sites, messages are still translated into the foreign format, but only for passage through the foreign system and for ultimate delivery to the other Exchange site. This temporary translation is illustrated in Figure 13.3.

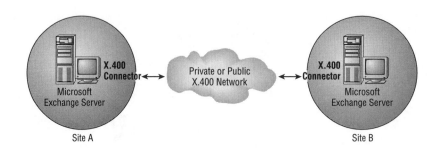

FIGURE 13.3

Connectors used for site connection

This chapter discusses some of the common properties of connectors. Then, each of the four messaging connectors and message routing are discussed. Finally, the directory replication connector is covered. In this chapter, you will learn about:

- Connectors and their properties

- Message routing and tracking

- Design scenarios

Connector Properties

This section examines two connector properties:

- Address space

- Connector cost

Address Space

Each connector has a property called an *address space*. The address space is the set of addresses to remote mail systems, and even remote recipients, to which the connector can send messages. Simply put, these addresses are the remote addresses that can be reached through the connector. A connector must have at least one entry in its address space. An address space entry is in the format of the remote messaging system. For example, if an Internet Mail Service connector is attached to a remote site named Detroit, which is a sub-domain of Sales.com, the address space would include the entry:

Type	Address
SMTP	*@Detroit.Sales.com

If the MTA receives a message addressed to a user at `Detroit.Sales.com`, the MTA could route it to that destination through the connector configured with the previous address space.

A connector can also have address space entries to messaging systems of different types from the one used by the connector. For example, the IMS connector used in the previous example, can also be used to send messages to a remote X.400 mail system. In this scenario, the address space would look like:

Type	Address
SMTP	`*@Detroit.Sales.com`
X.400	`c=us; a= ; p=Sales;` `o=Detroit;`

Connector Cost

Two sites can have multiple connectors configured between them (see Figure 13.4). The connectors can be the same type (e.g., all Site Connectors) or different types (e.g., a Site Connector and a Dynamic RAS Connector). Multiple connectors between two sites can use the same network connection (e.g., a Token Ring network), or different connections (e.g., one connector can use a Token Ring network while another connector uses a RAS connection).

Multiple connectors can be used to increase fault tolerance and balance the load. When two or more connectors are configured between sites, messages can be delivered as long as any one of the connectors is available.

When the physical network is not a bottleneck, but message queues are backing up, multiple connectors on the same network can alleviate the traffic jam. Site-to-site traffic can be divided to balance the load among the connectors. When multiple connectors are used to balance the load, all of the connectors must have the same *cost*.

One criterion the MTA uses when choosing which connector to use is cost. A connector can have a cost value of 1–100. The lower the cost, the more frequently the MTA will select it for message transfer (see Figure 13.5).

FIGURE 13.4

Multiple connectors between two sites

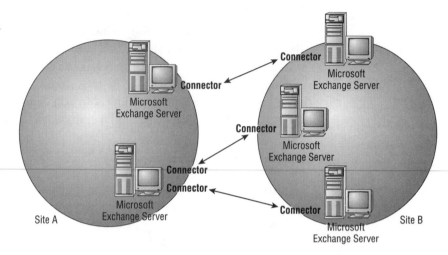

FIGURE 13.5

Connector costs

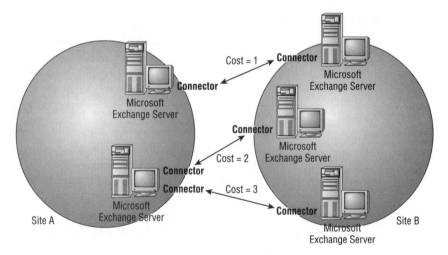

The MTA uses cost values of different connectors as a factor in making routing decisions.

In this chapter, *local site* refers to your own site, and *remote site* refers to the site to which you are connecting.

Site Connector

The Site Connector is the most unique of the four site connectors. The Site Connector is essentially a set of parameters that tell the MTA component how to transfer messages to another site. The Site Connector adds another role to the MTA. With a Site Connector installed, an MTA can perform inter-site communication in addition to intrasite communication.

Requirements

There are two primary requirements if the Site Connector is to be used:

- There must be a permanent, LAN-grade network connection between the two sites.

- The bridgehead server of the local site must be able to authenticate the bridgehead server of the remote site (bridgehead servers are discussed in a later section).

These requirements are discussed in the following sections.

Network Connection between Sites

Because the Site Connector uses RPC for intersite communication, it requires a permanent, LAN-grade network connection between sites.

This is the same mechanism used within a site. The Site Connector can also use any network protocol that supports RPC, including TCP/IP, IPX/SPX, and NetBEUI.

Service Account

When a Site Connector is used to transport information between two sites, an MTA in the local site must bind to an MTA in the remote site. To do this, the local MTA must use an account that is authenticated by the remote site server (in effect, the local MTA logs on to the remote site server). The account used for this procedure will depend on the cross-site authentication abilities of the two sites. Some common configurations are explained here.

Single Account / Same Windows NT Domain or Two Windows NT Domains with a Two-Way Trust Relationship

If both sites are in the same Windows NT domain, both sites can use the same Exchange site service account for intersite communication. If the sites are in different domains, the same account can be used only if the domains have a two-way trust relationship.

Single Account / Two Windows NT Domains with a One-Way Trust Relationship

If two sites are in different Windows NT domains, a remote account can be granted the Service Account permission at the local site's Organization, Site, and Configuration objects. The local site's Windows NT domain must "trust" the remote site's Windows NT domain.

Designated Remote Account / Different Windows NT Domains

If an administrator does not want to use the same account or does not want to set up trust relationships, he or she can configure the Site Connector to use a designated remote account when connecting to the remote site. The designated remote account is specified on the Override property page of a Site Connector.

Messaging Bridgehead Servers

Certain servers in the local site can be defined as the servers that deliver messages to the remote site. These servers are called *messaging bridgehead servers* (see Figure 13.6). By default, all local site servers are bridgehead servers, which means they will all connect directly to the remote site. But the Site Connector can be configured to use specific servers as bridgehead servers. Use this configuration when not all local site servers have a network connection to the remote site. Non-bridgehead servers route messages destined for the remote site to the bridgehead servers in the local site. A bridgehead server takes responsibility for intersite routing so the non-bridgehead servers do not have to.

Target Server

A Site Connector will only connect to designated servers in the remote site, called *target servers*. By default, one server in the remote site is designated as a target server, but the target server list can be configured to have any combination of the servers in the remote site act as target servers (see Figure 13.7).

FIGURE 13.6

Bridgehead server

FIGURE 13.6

Bridgehead server

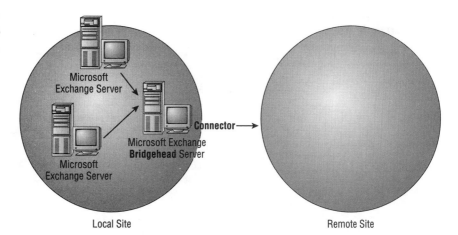

Local Site   Remote Site

FIGURE 13.7

Target server

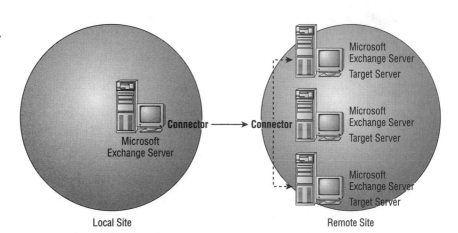

Local Site   Remote Site

Because there can be several target servers in a remote site, you must set preferences for which server will be selected. Target servers are assigned costs between 0 and 100. The value 0 means that the target server is always to be used if it is available, and 100 means that the target server is to be used only if no other target servers are available. The remaining numbers, 1–99, provide a weighted average that the MTA uses when selecting a target server. For example, if one target server has a cost of 1, and another target server has a cost of 2, the first target server will be used approximately twice as much as the second one. Figure 13.8 illustrates the use of target server costs.

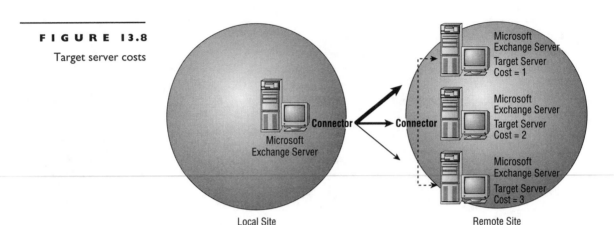

Connector

Connector

Microsoft
Exchange Server

Microsoft
Exchange Server
Target Server
Cost = 1

Microsoft
Exchange Server
Target Server
Cost = 2

Microsoft
Exchange Server
Target Server
Cost = 3

Local Site

Remote Site

Do not confuse *connector cost* with *target server cost.* The MTA uses connector costs to choose between multiple connectors between two sites. Once a Site Connector is chosen, the MTA can use the target server costs to determine to which particular remote server to send messages.

Site Connector Advantages

Two advantages of the Site Connector are its efficiency and its performance. High-speed network connections and the use of RPC permit information to be sent to another site without being converted to a different message format. Data can be sent directly to an MTA on the other site (just like it would be for intrasite communication). This is approximately 20% faster than the X.400 Connector, which must convert messages into a different format for transportation. The IMS also must convert information from the Exchange format (to SMTP format) to transfer data. Also, with the X.400 connector and the IMS, the connector at the other end must convert messages back to the Exchange format. Because both ends of a Site Connector connection use the Exchange format, no conversion is necessary, so performance is optimal.

The Site Connector is also the easiest connector to configure. Most of its configuration is automatic. It automatically uses the currently configured network protocol for message transportation. If both sites use TCP/IP, the Site Connector automatically uses TCP/IP to move messages. Other connectors (like the X.400 Connector) require a manual configuration of this setting. Both sides of a Site Connector connection can be configured at once. You do not have to go to the other site and manually configure it before site-to-site communication can take place.

Site Connector Disadvantages

The Site Connector does have disadvantages. It does not allow some of the configuration options that other connectors do. The Site Connector cannot be configured to make scheduled connections to another site, to restrict message size, or to prohibit specific users from using its connection.

Site Connector Summary

Table 13.1 summarizes the properties and requirements of the Site Connector.

	Category	Site Connector
TABLE 13.1 Site Connector summary	Network connection required	High bandwidth (above 128 Kbps; LAN-grade connection, such as Ethernet or Token Ring)
		Permanent connection
	RPC mechanism or message delivery	RPC
	Transport protocols supported	Any protocol that supports RPC. Examples are TCP/IP, IPX/SPX, and NetBEUI.
	Message format	Exchange format
	Amount of configuration required	Minimal
	Cost associated with a connector (1–100)	Yes
	Messaging bridgehead servers	Yes (optional)
	Target servers	Yes (optional)
	Cost associated with a target server (0–100; 0=always use if available; 100=never use, unless no others available)	Yes
	Connection scheduling	No
	Delivery restriction/Control of user access	No

	Category	Site Connector
TABLE 13.1 *(cont.)* Site Connector summary	Delivery restriction/Maximum message size	No
	Override of account used for connector authentication in remote site	Yes (default is site service account)
	Automatic configuration of remote site	Yes (optional)

Trip Analogy

Another way to explain the properties of a connector is to compare it to a trip. A trip takes you where you want to go, and a connector gets your information where you want it to go. This comparison will help you understand how to configure a connector. Table 13.2 compares a site connector to some of the aspects of a trip. The table also lists connector attributes and the property pages on which they are found.

	Trip Analogy	Connector Equivalent	Connector Attribute	Property Page
TABLE 13.2 Site Connector and the trip analogy	Name of this particular trip	Name of this instance of the connector	Display name; Directory name	General
	Destination of the trip	Name of the remote site	Target site	General
		Address of the remote site	Type; Address	Address Space
	Trip starting point	Name of the local bridgehead server	Messaging bridgehead in the local site	General
	Trip chaperon	User account used by connector to be authenticated by the remote site	The default is to use the Site Service Account	Override

T A B L E 13.2 *(cont.)* Site Connector and the trip analogy	**Trip Analogy**	**Connector Equivalent**	**Connector Attribute**	**Property Page**
	Cost of the trip	Cost of this connector	Cost	General
	Trip restrictions	(not applicable)	N/A	N/A
	Vehicle used for trip	Transport stack	The network protocol currently being used.	(Not applicable)

Exercise 13.1 walks through the steps for configuring a Site Connector. To perform these steps, you need another site to which you can connect.

EXERCISE 13.1

Configuring a Site Connector

1. In Exchange Administrator, navigate to and select the Connections container under the Configuration container.

2. Choose File ➤ New Other ➤ Site Connector. The New Site Connector dialog box will appear.

3. Enter the name of a server in the remote site. Click OK. Exchange Server will use that server to obtain information necessary to configure the Site Connector. When the connection is complete, all servers in the remote site will be target servers by default. You can later reconfigure any subset of the remote servers to be target servers. The Site Connector Properties dialog box will appear, displaying information about the remote site.

4. Click OK. A message box will appear asking if you want to create the Site Connector at the remote site. Click Yes. If you click No, you will have to connect to that site and configure that end of the connection.

X.400 Connector

The X.400 Connector is based on the CCITT X.400 standard. It includes many of the features the Site Connector has, such as the use of:

- Address space

- Connector cost

- Option to override the account used to make the connection

Each end of an X.400 connection must be configured with the name of one remote MTA to which it will connect. The local MTA name is assigned when an MTA transport stack is installed. Typically, this name is the same as the server name.

X.400 and Site Connector Differences

The X.400 Connector has several differences from the Site Connector:

- **Network bandwidth required** The X.400 Connector requires only a low to medium network bandwidth.

- **All data is transferred through messages** The Site Connector uses RPC to transfer data directly between servers. The X.400 Connector (because it was designed for use in large, multirouted network environments) always puts data into a message format for transportation.

- **Different transport stacks used** In addition to supporting the TCP/IP protocol, the X.400 Connector supports two other transport stacks: TP0/X.25 and TP4/CLNP. Each must be installed and configured through Control Panel/Network, and defined as an MTA transport stack in Exchange. Stacks are created using Exchange Administrator by choosing File, New Other, MTA Transport Stack. After a stack is created, an X.400 Connector can be installed and configured.

- **Remote site configuration is not automatic** Unlike the Site Connector, both sides of an X.400 Connector link must be manually installed and configured.

Additional Features of the X.400 Connector

The X.400 Connector has two main features that are not present in the Site Connector:

- Connection scheduling

- Delivery restrictions

Connection Scheduling

The X.400 Connector and the Dynamic RAS Connector allow connections to the remote site to be scheduled. This feature has four options:

- **Remote Initiated**   This option prevents the local connector from initiating a connection to the remote connector, but instead waits for the remote connector to initiate the connection. After the remote connector has finished sending messages to the local site, the local connector can send all queued (stored) messages to the remote site.

- **Never**   This option disables the connector.

- **Always**   Approximately every 15 minutes, the local connector initiates a connection to the remote connector and sends all queued messages.

- **Selected times**   The connector operates according to the schedule on the Schedule property page. Time intervals can be either 1 hour or 15 minutes.

Delivery Restrictions

The X.400 Connector has two delivery-restriction properties that give an administrator additional control over the connector's use:

- **Which users can use the connector**   The Delivery Restrictions property page allows an administrator to specify which users can use the connector and which users cannot use the connector. The defaults are:

  - "Accept messages from" all

  - "Reject messages from" none

- **Maximum message size allowed over the connector**   The maximum size of messages that can be sent through the connector can be set on the Advanced property page. The default is:

  - No limit

Figure 13.9 provides a graphical summary of the X.400 Connector.

FIGURE 13.9

X.400 Connector
properties

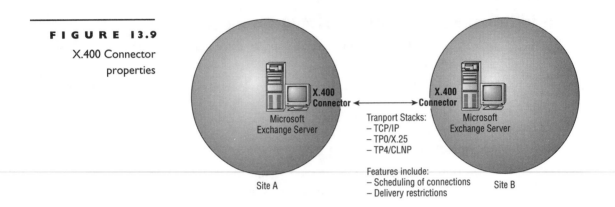

X.400 Connector Advantages

Advantages to using the X.400 Connector include its additional configuration options and its ability to connect to large multirouted networks. An organization can use a public X.400 network, or even the Internet, as its messaging backbone. Figure 13.10 illustrates this scenario.

FIGURE 13.10

Using the X.400
Connector as a messaging
backbone

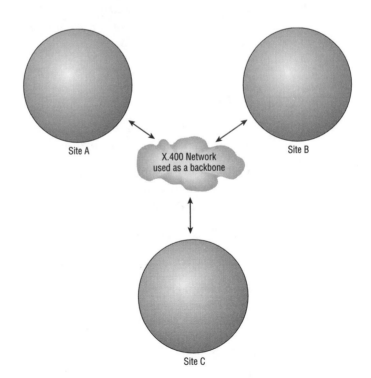

X.400 Connector Disadvantages

One of the X.400 Connector's disadvantages is the increased amount of configuration you may have to do. This is a "good news, bad news" situation. "Good" in the sense that you have a lot of options, "bad" in the sense that you must figure out how to configure them. Another disadvantage is the possibility of a message bottleneck at the bridgehead server. Because the X.400 connector must have a single, messaging bridgehead server at each site, bridgeheads can become bottlenecks if message traffic is heavy.

Summary and Comparison

Table 13.3 summarizes and compares the X.400 Connector and the Site Connector.

T A B L E 1 3.3 X.400 Connector summary and comparison	**Category**	**Site Connector**	**X.400 Connector**
	Network connection required	High bandwidth (above 128 Kbps; LAN-grade connection, such as Ethernet or Token Ring)	Low to medium (64 Kbps to 2 Mbps)
		Permanent connection	Does not require permanent connection
	RPC mechanism or message delivery	RPC	Messages
	Transport protocols supported	Any protocol that supports RPC. Examples are TCP/IP, IPX/SPX, and NetBEUI.	TCP/IP TP0/X.25 TP4/CLNP
	Message format	Exchange format	X.400 format
	Amount of configuration required	Minimal	Medium to high
	Cost associated with a connector (1–100)	Yes	Yes
	Messaging bridgehead servers	Yes (optional)	Yes (required)

T A B L E 13.3 (cont.) SX.400 Connector summary and comparison	**Category**	**Site Connector**	**X.400 Connector**
	Target servers	Yes (optional)	Yes (defines remote connector)
	Cost associated with a target server (0–100; 0=always use if available; 100=never use, unless no others available)	Yes	Not applicable
	Schedules connections	No	Yes
	Delivery restriction/ Control of user access	No	Yes
	Delivery restriction/ Maximum message size	No	Yes
	Override account used for connector authen- tication in remote site	Yes (default is site service account)	Yes
	Automatic configuration of remote site	Yes (optional)	No

Dynamic RAS Connector

The Dynamic RAS Connector utilizes Microsoft's Remote Access Service (RAS) to connect sites. RAS is software that, along with the necessary hardware, enables dial-up network connections. The dial-up connections include modem connections over the normal telephone system, Integrated Services Digital Network (ISDN), and X.25. The Dynamic RAS Connector can be used to connect two sites that both have RAS servers (see Figure 13.11).

In Figure 13.11, the RAS server is running on the same computer as the Exchange server and the Dynamic RAS Connector. A computer other than the Exchange server can be used to create a dedicated RAS server that processes calls from the remote site.

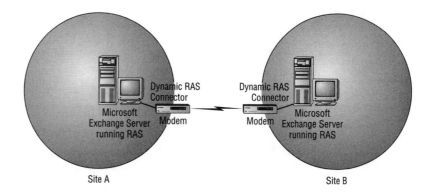

FIGURE 13.11

Dynamic RAS Connector

The Dynamic RAS Connector has many of the same features as the Site Connector and X.400 connectors, including:

- Address space

- Connector cost

- Option to override the account used to make the connection

The Dynamic RAS Connector has many features in common with the X.400 Connector. It can use temporary, scheduled connections between sites. It supports restrictions, such as which users have access to a connection. The Dynamic RAS Connector must be manually configured at both sites it is connecting.

Unique Aspects

The RAS Connector uses a unique security feature called "MTA Callback." If MTA Callback is enabled, the local server initiates a call to the remote server. After the remote server answers the call, the local server terminates the connection. The local server then waits for the remote server to call back the telephone number defined in the MTA callback number field. For this connector feature to be used, RAS callback security must be enabled on the RAS server.

Another unique aspect of the Dynamic RAS Connector is its use of low-bandwidth network connections. Although performance will be compromised, this connector can work with a modem connection running at 64Kbps or less.

RAS Connector Advantages

The RAS Connector's main advantages are its use of temporary and low-bandwidth network connections and its additional configuration options (like scheduled connections and delivery restrictions). You probably will not use it for your main intersite connections. However, you can use it as a backup connection to provide fault tolerance.

RAS Connector Disadvantages

The RAS Connector's main disadvantage is that message transfer will be slow because it uses a low-bandwidth network connection.

Other disadvantages are that it needs a lot of configuration, and that both sides of a connection must be manually configured.

Summary and Comparison

Table 13.4 summarizes and compares the Dynamic RAS Connector to the Site Connector and X.400 Connector.

T A B L E 13.4 Dynamic RAS Connector summary and comparison	Category	Site Connector	X.400 Connector	Dynamic RAS Connector
	Network connection required	High bandwidth (above 128 Kbps; LAN-grade connection, such as Ethernet or Token Ring)	Low to medium (64 Kbps to 2 Mbps)	Low (less than 64 Kbps for a modem connection; also can use ISDN and X.25 connections)
		Permanent connection	Does not require permanent connection	Does not require permanent connection
	RPC mechanism or message delivery	RPC	Messages	Messages
	Transport protocols supported	Any protocol that supports RPC. Examples are TCP/IP, IPX/SPX, and NetBEUI.	TCP/IP TP0/X.25 TP4/CLNP	RAS supported protocols, such as TCP/IP, IPX/SPX, and NetBEUI.

	Category	Site Connector	X.400 Connector	Dynamic RAS Connector
TABLE 13.4 *(cont.)* Dynamic RAS Connector summary and comparison	Message format	Exchange format	X.400 format	X.400 format
	Amount of configuration required	Minimal	Medium to high	Medium to high
	Cost associated with a connector (1–100)	Yes	Yes	Yes
	Messaging bridgehead servers	Yes (optional)	Yes (required)	Yes (this is inherent, because of the point-to-point topology of RAS)
	Target servers	Yes (optional)	Yes (defines remote connector; called Remote MTA Name)	Yes (because of point-to-point topology of RAS)
	Cost associated with a target server (0–100; 0=always use if available; 100=never use, unless no others available)	Yes	Not applicable	Not applicable
	Connection Scheduling	No	Yes	Yes
	Delivery restriction/ Control of user access	No	Yes	Yes
	Delivery restriction/ Maximum message size	No	Yes	Yes

	Category	Site Connector	X.400 Connector	Dynamic RAS Connector
TABLE 13.4 (cont.) Dynamic RAS Connector summary and comparison	Override account used for connector authentication in remote site	Yes (default is site service account)	Yes	Yes
	Automatic configuration of remote site	Yes (optional)	No	No

Internet Mail Service (IMS)

The Internet Mail Service (IMS) can be used for intersite communication. If there is an SMTP mail system between two or more Exchange sites, each site can use IMS to connect through that SMTP system to the other Exchange sites (as illustrated in Figure 13.12). The IMSs in two sites can also connect directly to each other.

FIGURE 13.12

Using IMS to connect Exchange sites

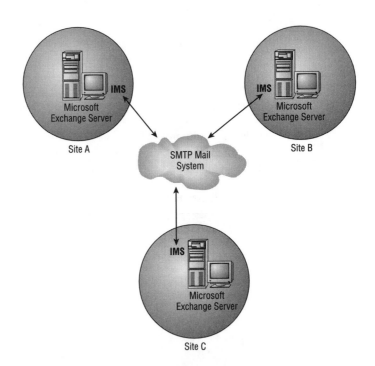

The IMS has many of the same properties seen in the other connectors, such as address space entries, connector costs, delivery restrictions, and configurable security for the remote-site authentication account.

Both ends of a connection must use TCP/IP. Using TCP/IP and an SMTP mail system is advantageous because these protocols are standards-based.

Using IMS to connect Exchange sites also has disadvantages. Data must be converted from the Exchange message format to the SMTP format to be transported over the SMTP mail system, and then reconverted back at the remote Exchange server. These conversions negatively affect performance. Another disadvantage is that the IMS does not allow the scheduling of connections unless a dial-up connection is being used.

Installation and configuration of the IMS is covered in Chapter 14.

Summary and Comparison

Table 13.5 summarizes and compares the IMS to the Site Connector and the X.400 Connector.

T A B L E 13.5 Internet Mail Service summary and comparison	Category	Site Connector	X.400 Connector	Internet Mail Service
	Network connection required	High bandwidth (above 128 Kbps; LAN- grade connection, such as Ethernet or Token Ring)	Low to medium (64 Kbps to 2 Mbps)	Low to medium (64 Kbps to 2 Mbps)
		Permanent connection	Does not require permanent connection	
	RPC mechanism or message delivery	RPC	Messages	Messages (SMTP)
	Transport protocols supported	Any protocol that supports RPC. Examples are TCP/ IP, IPX/SPX, and NetBEUI.	TCP/IP TP0/X.25 TP4/CLNP	TCP/IP

TABLE 13.5 (cont.)	Category	Site Connector	X.400 Connector	Internet Mail Service
Internet Mail Service summary and comparison	Message format	Exchange format	X.400 format	SMTP
	Amount of configuration required	Minimal	Medium to high	Medium to high
	Cost associated with a connector (1–100)	Yes	Yes	Yes
	Messaging bridgehead servers	Yes (optional)	Yes (required)	Yes
	Target servers	Yes (optional)	Yes (defines remote connector; called Remote MTA Name)	Not applicable
	Cost associated with a target server (0–100; 0=always use if available; 100=never use, unless no others available)	Yes	Not applicable	Not applicable
	Connection scheduling	No	Yes	No, except for dial-up connections
	Delivery restriction/ Control of user access	No	Yes	Yes
	Delivery restriction/ Maximum message size	No	Yes	Yes
	Override account used for connector authentication in remote site	Yes (default is site service account)	Yes	Yes, optional security allows an NT account in the remote site to be specified
	Automatic configuration of remote site	Yes (optional)	No	No

Message Routing

The MTA is responsible for delivery of all messages that are destined for a server other than the one upon which they originated. (The IS is responsible for local server delivery.) Remote message delivery can be intrasite or intersite. For intersite delivery, the MTA will choose a message connector to transport the message.

If there is only one connector between the local site and the remote site, routing is obviously simple. If however, there are several connectors, the MTA will go through a selection process to choose a connector through which to send messages. During the selection process, the MTA reads a routing table called the *Gateway Address Routing Table (GWART)*.

Gateway Address Routing Table (GWART)

Every connector installed on an Exchange server has an address space, which is the set of addresses that can be reached through the connector. The System Attendant (SA) on each server collects the address space entries for all the connectors on the server and places them in a routing table, called the Gateway Address Routing Table (GWART). Each server in the site exchanges its local GWART information with the other servers in the site, to compile one big site-wide GWART. This means that each site server, even if it does not have a connector homed on it, knows about the connectors it can use in the site.

The GWART can be viewed on the Routing property page of the Site Addressing object which is found in the site Configuration container. The Routing property page also contains a Recalculate Routing button that triggers a GWART rebuild. However, the routing table is automatically rebuilt whenever a change is made to a connector, so you should not need to use the Recalculate Routing function very often.

Each entry in the GWART displays the type of messaging system used at the remote destination, the address of the remote destination, and the cost to reach that destination. Some examples of GWART entries are listed here:

Type	Value	Cost
EX	/o=Widget/ou=Cleveland	2
SMTP	*@Detroit.Widget.com	1
X.400	c=us;a= ; p=Widget; o=Miami	2

The EX type is the native Exchange Server address format which uses Distinguished Names (DNs). (Refer back to Chapter 2 for the discussion of DN addresses.) An SMTP or Microsoft Mail destination will have an address using the format of those foreign systems. An X.400 destination will have an Originator/Recipient (O/R) address (see Chapter 2 for a discussion of O/R addresses).

The GWART text file is stored in the \EXCHSRVR\MTADATA directory. The second most recent GWART is always available in a file named GWART1.MTA. If GWART0.MTA gets corrupted, GWART1.MTA can be used for a recovery.

Route Selection Process

The basic steps of the route selection process are outlined here:

1. A local MTA component receives a message for delivery to another site. The MTA temporarily stores the message in a queue while it determines a route for the message.

2. The MTA reads the destination address of the message and queries the GWART for an entry to that destination. If there is only one connector for that destination, the MTA passes the message to the MTA on that connector's server. If there are several entries, the MTA goes through a selection process. Although there are several criteria involved in this process (see note), a key factor is the cost of the route via each connector.

Various criteria may be used to select the route, including the precision of the address space match, delivery restrictions, and message size restrictions on eligible connectors. Also, if the MTA service of a connector's server is stopped, that connector will be bypassed during route selection.

3. After the MTA passes the message to the relevant connector and it is successfully sent, the MTA deletes the message from its queue and notifies the SA component of the successful delivery. The SA writes that information to the tracking log file.

If the message is passed to a Site Connector and there are multiple target servers in the remote site, the Site Connector uses target server cost (a value used to weigh the frequency of target server use) to choose to which target server to send the message.

4. If the message cannot be delivered, the local MTA sends the message back to the sending object with a Non-Delivery Report (NDR).

As you know, the MTA and connectors work together to move data between sites. Therefore it is not only the connector and its properties that must be taken into account when designing intersite communication, but also the properties of the MTA. Please see Chapter 12 for some of the properties of the MTA that relate to intersite design.

Connectors and Message Tracking

Chapter 12 discussed message tracking in an intrasite environment. Message tracking in an intersite environment is very similar from the viewpoint of an administrator. For intrasite message tracking, the MTA Site Configuration object must have message tracking enabled to allow administrators to use the Message Tracking Center to view the routes of messages (the Information Store Site Configuration object can also have message tracking enabled to track local server deliveries). For intersite message tracking, the connectors used to deliver messages must have message tracking enabled. An administrator can then use the Message Tracking Center to track message routing. The tracking utility is accessed through Exchange Administrator, by choosing Track Message from the Tools menu. After selecting a message to track, the Message Tracking Center will display the message's path from its origin to destination, as well as detailed information such as the message size and the time of day it reached each stop along the way.

Directory Replication Connector

In order for users to view the resources of a remote site (like mailboxes and public folders), directory information must be exchanged between sites. Unlike intrasite directory replication which is automatic and performed by direct DS-to-DS communication, intersite directory replication is performed by the Directory Replication Connector and must be manually configured. The Directory Replication Connector uses an existing messaging connector to send directory information to a remote site.

The four primary steps to setting up directory replication between sites are listed here and then described in more detail in the following text.

1. Configure the messaging connector to be used for intersite directory replication.

2. Install a Directory Replication Connector for both sites.

3. Identify the directory replication bridgehead at each site that will be responsible for transferring directory updates.

4. Configure a replication schedule to determine how often directory updates will occur.

Message Connector Configuration

If the messaging connector to be used for intersite directory replication is the X.400 Connector, Dynamic RAS Connector, or IMS, the messaging connector must be configured for intersite directory replication. Specifically, it must be "informed" that the remote site it is connecting to is an Exchange Server site. If this is not done with these messaging connectors, the directory replication connection will not be able to use that connector for intersite directory replication. This information is specified on the Connected Sites property page of the messaging connector. Only the site directly at the remote end of a connection needs to be defined. The Site Connector does not need this particular information because it is only used to connect two Exchange sites (so you do not have to tell it that it is connected to another Exchange site).

Directory Replication Connector Installation

The Directory Replication Connector is installed using Exchange Administrator by choosing File, New Other, Directory Replication Connector. The instance of the connector that you have created will be stored in the Directory Replication container within the site Configuration container.

If the Directory Replication Connector will use the X.400 Connector, Dynamic RAS Connector, or IMS for its messaging connector, both sites must have their Directory Replication Connector manually configured. The information that will need to be supplied includes:

- Local bridgehead server

- Remote site name

- Remote bridgehead server

- E-mail address of the remote bridgehead server

When configuring directory replication between two sites on the same network that are connected with a Site Connector, the only information required is the name of the remote site. This option also allows you to automatically configure the remote site for intersite directory replication.

Directory Replication Bridgeheads

When you configure directory replication between two sites, you must choose one server in each site to be the *directory-replication bridgehead server*. All the servers in a site send their directory changes to their local bridgehead server. The local bridgehead server sends the directory information to the remote directory-replication bridgehead server. Only one server in a site can be assigned the duty to replicate with a given remote site. Several servers in one site may be responsible for directory replication with other sites, but no two can replicate with the same remote site. One server can, however, perform directory replication to more than one remote site. These scenarios are illustrated in Figure 13.13.

Intersite Directory Replication

Bridgehead servers must request directory replication information from remote bridgehead servers. Directory information is never automatically pushed to a remote site. The remote bridgehead responds to the request by sending the directory changes. This is in contrast to intrasite directory replication, where servers send a notification of new directory information to the other servers of their site. Those servers then request the new information.

Scheduling Intersite Directory Replication

By default, intersite directory replication occurs every three hours. You can modify the frequency on the Schedule property page of the Directory Replication Connector object. This page allows you to configure the schedule that will be used to request directory updates from the remote bridgehead server. The requests can be sent Never (disabling the Directory Replication Connector), Always, or at Selected times. Because the Directory Replication Connector uses a messaging connector to transport directory information in the form of a mail message, it is important to take into account the schedule configured on the messaging connector.

Transitive Connections

Directory information can be passed between two sites that do not have a direct
connection, if those two sites have a third site in common. In Figure 13.14, Site A
and Site C do not have a direct connection between them. But because they each
share directory information with Site B, which shares its directory information
with both Site A and Site C, all three sites will share the same directory information.

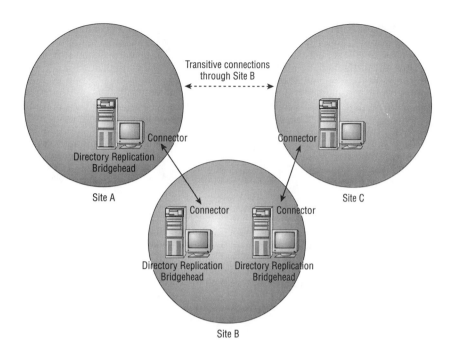

FIGURE 13.14

Transitive connections

Forcing Directory Replication

Directory replication between sites takes place every three hours or during the configured schedule. When new directory information is created, you may need to force the update of the other directories. Use the Sites property page of a configured directory replication connector. All of the remote sites that this local site receives updates from are listed in the Inbound site listbox on this page. The Outbound sites listbox lists the remote sites that receive updates from the local site. To force a remote site to send its new directory information, highlight the remote site in the Inbound sites listbox and click the Request Now button.

Design Scenarios

After gaining an understanding of connectors (and all the other earlier topics in this book), you now have much of the knowledge necessary to design intersite solutions. This section will describe some sample organizational scenarios and then present a viable intersite design for that scenario.

Scenario 1

Your company has ask you to design an Exchange environment. The company is in two buildings connected by a 33.6 Kbps dial-up connection. There are 20 users in one building, and 25 users in the other building. You find out that the vast majority of messaging will take place among users in their own buildings. What design would you use?

Option A: Single-site, one server

Option B: Single-site, a server in each building

Option C: Two sites, one server in each site

Since intrasite communication requires high-speed connections for RPC communication, Options A and B are out. Option C would work because of the localized traffic patterns and that the Directory Replication Connector can use a slower link.

Scenario 2

Your company has already implemented a multisite Exchange environment. You find out from the network administrator that Exchange is using an excessive amount of the network bandwidth between the two Exchange sites. That administrator also tells you they have noticed fairly large messages being sent between the sites. What could you configure to help solve this problem?

Option A: Limit message size for the MTA.

Option B: Limit outgoing message size for each mailbox.

Option C: Limit incoming message size for the IS.

Options B and C would have an affect on local delivery of messages, which is not the problem. Option A, however, would directly affect the intersite communication.

Scenario 3

Your Exchange environment consists of multiple remote sites. These sites are connected by an unreliable WAN that experiences a high packet loss. You want to configure Exchange to adjust to this reality. One possible adjustment is to decrease the amount of redundant data that is transferred because of a failed or interrupted WAN connection. You access the MTA Site Configuration object and its Messaging Defaults property page. You set a low checkpoint size that is greater than zero, and you set a high recovery timeout (see Chapter 12).

Scenario 4

You manage a multisite Exchange environment. The sites are connected over a high-cost third-party WAN that charges you for connection time. Even though it is high-cost, there are a lot of line errors that result in transfer delays. The long delays hurt performance and increase connection costs. Until you can find a new WAN vendor, you decide to adjust the amount of time Exchange waits after a line error before it attempts to reopen a connection. As in Scenario 3, you do this on the Messaging Defaults page.

Scenario 5

Your company has just installed 20 new Exchange sites. All of the sites are geographically dispersed but attached to a permanent WAN TCP/IP network. The physical infrastructure of the network is not reliable. Because bandwidth is at a premium, you decide you will schedule the intersite transfer of data at off-peak periods of network traffic. What connector type would you choose?

Option A: Internet Mail Service

Option B: X.400

Option C: Site Connector

Most people will probably choose Internet Mail Service. But that would not meet the design criteria because IMS cannot use scheduled connections (except for dial-up connections). The Site Connector also cannot use scheduled connections. X.400 would meet all the above design criteria. It can use TCP/IP as a transport stack. It can use scheduled connections. And it was designed to operate in a large network.

Summary

Connectors are software that can be used to connect Exchange sites. There are two main types of connectors: messaging connectors, and the directory replication connector. Messaging connectors include the Site Connector, X.400 Connector, Dynamic RAS Connector, and the Internet Mail Service.

Each connector contains a property called an address space, which is the set of addresses of remote systems that can be reached through that connector. Some of the other properties that a connector can have are cost, messaging bridgehead servers, target servers, and target server costs.

The connectors installed in a site are part of the site-level configuration and therefore can be used by all the servers in the site. When an MTA on a server receives a message for remote delivery outside the site, it references the Gateway Address Routing Table (GWART) to locate a connector that can be used to deliver the message.

The Directory Replication Connector is used to share directory information between sites. It uses a messaging connector for the actual information transfer.

Review Questions

1. The IMS permits the scheduling of message transfer over permanent and dial-up connections.

A. True

B. False

2. Which of the following statements is NOT true for the X.400 Connector?

A. Requires a high-speed network connection

B. Can use TCP/IP

C. Can be assigned costs

D. Can connect through a public backbone

3. Which of the following is true for the Site Connector?

A. Sends information between sites in a message format

B. Can schedule connections

C. Permits delivery restrictions

D. Uses RPC

4. Using multiple messaging connectors between two sites can provide:

A. Fault tolerance

B. Load balancing

C. A foundation for multiple directory replication connectors between the two sites

D. Both A and B

5. The IMS uses the Exchange message format with no conversion required.

A. True

B. False

6. When there are multiple connectors between two sites, the primary factor used by the MTA to select a connector is:

A. Target server costs

B. Connector cost

C. Versions of Exchange

D. Both A and B

7. The Exchange component that makes routing decisions is:

A. RAS

B. SA

C. IS

D. MTA

CHAPTER

14

Internet Mail Service (IMS)

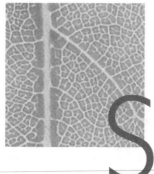

Simple Mail Transfer Protocol (SMTP) is an important part of the Internet protocol suite. Many mail systems, including the Internet, are based on the SMTP standard, which defines message formats and determines transfer methods.

The Internet Mail Service (IMS) is a component that enables an Exchange server to also function as an SMTP server. An Exchange server with an IMS can send and receive SMTP messages just like any other SMTP server. The IMS converts and transfers messages between the Exchange and SMTP environments. To participate in an SMTP environment, the IMS must also work with other Internet protocols such as TCP/IP and Domain Name System (DNS). Figure 14.1 illustrates some of the protocols that are involved with the IMS.

The terms *server*, *computer*, and *host* are equivalent.

FIGURE 14.1

IMS and Internet protocols

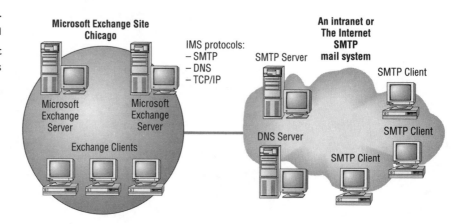

In this chapter, you will learn about:

■ Domain Name System

■ Simple Mail Transfer Protocol

■ How the IMS works

■ Deploying the IMS

■ Troubleshooting IMS

Domain Name System

In a TCP/IP environment, every computer is uniquely identified by a numeric identifier called an IP (Internet Protocol) address. To address a computer, a user needs to know that particular computer's IP address (e.g., 196.112.20.9). Remembering IP addresses is fairly easy in a small network, but it can be very difficult in a large network. Another way to identify computers (and one that is easier for humans) is to give them symbolic names, like SALES-HOST or ACCT-Server. A computer's symbolic name is also referred to as the *host name* or *domain name*.

Although it is easier for humans to work with domain names, the network still requires IP addresses to package and route data. DNS is used to bridge these two addressing schemes. DNS defines a database of domain names and information about those domain names, such as their IP addresses. The computers that hold this database are called DNS server. Programs, like client applications, can have the DNS protocol written into them to allow them to query a DNS server. Programs that query a DNS server are called DNS clients. For example, a user could use a domain name in an address, such as widget.com. This is convenient for the user, but the networking software on the client's computer needs an IP address for widget.com. Not to worry. The DNS client software will automatically query its designated DNS server for the IP address of widget.com. When the DNS client has received that information, the client's networking software can package and send the data.

The next three sections discuss the DNS hierarchy, distribution, and name resolution.

DNS Database Hierarchy

DNS uses a hierarchical structure to organize domain names, which makes it easy to locate and distribute database items. The top-level domains are high-level categories (not specific computers) used to organize the database. Examples of top-level domains are:

GOV	A government body
EDU	An educational institution
COM	A commercial enterprise

The subdomains (under the top-level domains) can be specific hosts (like ACME.COM). You can use another domain name to categorize and group several subdomain names. Using `Chicago.Widget.com` and `Detroit.Widget.com` as examples, COM is the top-level domain and Widget is a subdomain which contains the specific domain names of the computers in that organization (Chicago and Detroit). All three examples are illustrated in Figure 14.2. The DNS naming convention uses a bottom-up hierarchy, meaning that the most specific portion of a name (i.e., the lowest name in a hierarchy) is given first, the next most specific is given second, and so on, finally ending with the top-level domain name (also called a *DNS root*). Each name in the path is separated by a period. The full domain path (bottom to top) to a specific host is called a *fully qualified domain name* (*FQDN*).

F I G U R E   14.2

Examples of domain names

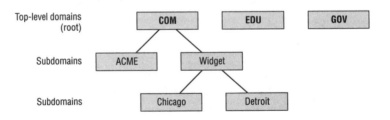

In the DNS hierarchy, a domain name that is directly under another domain is called a *subdomain*.

Each entry in a DNS database has information associated with it. Most entries contain the IP address of that domain name. An entry may state the role of that particular host, such as DNS server, DNS client, or *mail exchanger* (MX). A mail exchanger is another name for an SMTP mail server. An MX record can have a weight value. Because a single domain can have several mail exchangers, DNS clients use the MX weight number to choose which MX to use for mail delivery. If there are multiple MXs, a DNS client will choose the MX with the lowest weight value. If that MX is unavailable, the DNS client will choose the MX with the next lowest weight value.

The Exchange server running the IMS will be configured in the DNS database as an MX entry. The IMS can receive SMTP messages sent to Exchange recipients; therefore, it is a mail exchanger.

The DNS hierarchy of domain names is referred to as the *domain name space.*

DNS Database Distribution

In a large environment like the Internet, storage restraints, administrative costs, and performance requirements make it impractical to store the entire global DNS database on a single machine. Various organizations store and administer different parts of the DNS hierarchy. Many DNS servers store parts of the DNS hierarchy, but do not perform administrative tasks.

Each DNS server has a list of other DNS servers it can query. Because an individual DNS server does not have the entire DNS hierarchy, it may receive client queries that it cannot resolve. When that happens, the DNS server queries other DNS servers until it obtains the required information. This procedure is called DNS *name resolution*.

DNS Name Resolution

When DNS client software is installed, it is configured with the location of a DNS server. The DNS client software uses this DNS server whenever a TCP/IP-based application addresses a remote computer using its domain name, to map the domain name to its IP address. This process is called *name resolution*. The basic process is outlined in the following steps:

1. A TCP/IP-based application addresses a remote computer using its host name.

2. The DNS client software (also called a *resolver program*) queries its DNS server for the IP address of that domain name.

3. If that DNS server does not contain the needed information, it will query another DNS server on behalf of the DNS client.

The IMS functions as a DNS client by querying a DNS server on behalf of Exchange clients sending messages to SMTP recipients. The presence of the IMS is established on the Internet because the Exchange server will have a DNS entry registered on DNS servers. This allows SMTP users to locate the Exchange server so messages can be sent to its recipients. Figure 14.3 illustrates using DNS in an Exchange environment with IMS.

FIGURE 14.3

IMS and DNS

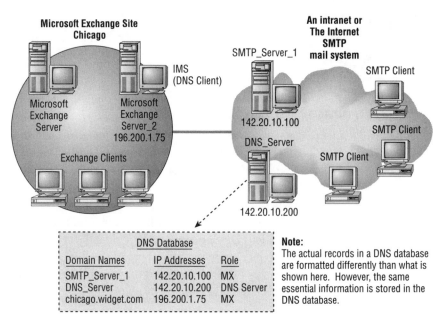

DNS Database		
Domain Names	IP Addresses	Role
SMTP_Server_1	142.20.10.100	MX
DNS_Server	142.20.10.200	DNS Server
chicago.widget.com	196.200.1.75	MX

Note:
The actual records in a DNS database are formatted differently than what is shown here. However, the same essential information is stored in the DNS database.

Simple Mail Transfer Protocol (SMTP)

The Simple Mail Transfer Protocol (SMTP) defines the methods for exchanging mail messages between applications. The protocol addresses mail transfer between an SMTP client and an SMTP server (the client may itself be another SMTP server). This section discusses SMTP and outlines how it works.

SMTP Process

The SMTP process involves a TCP connection, a series of client-server commands and replies, and the use of spooling. We will discuss each of these in the following sections.

TCP Connection

When an SMTP client application sends mail to an SMTP server, it uses TCP to establish a connection with port 25 on the SMTP server. Port 25 is the application doorway on the SMTP server for mail activity. Once that connection is established, a series of commands and replies are exchanged between the client and the server. The connection is similar to a telephone connection, and the commands and responses are similar to verbal communication over a telephone connection.

SMTP Commands and Replies

Now we will examine the steps in the SMTP process (including the TCP connection). In this example, we will send a message. You do not need to remember the reply code numbers. They are included here merely to provide a complete picture.

1. A client establishes a connection with the server at port 25.

2. The server confirms the connection by replying with a 220 reply code, which means "ready for mail."

3. The client computer identifies itself to the server by sending the HELO command with the computer's identity (for example, HELO server1.acme.com).

4. The server confirms the HELO by responding with the 250 reply code (which means "all is well") and its identity. The server may also require a password or some other form of authentication.

5. The client sends the MAIL FROM command that contains the identification of the sender.

6. The server responds with the 250 reply code ("all is well").

7. The sender then sends the RCPT TO command (Recipient To) with the identity of a recipient of the mail message.

8. The server responds with either a 250 reply code or a 550 reply code (which means "no such user here").

9. After all the RCPT TO commands are sent (one command is sent per recipient), the client sends the DATA command indicating that it is ready to send the actual mail message.

10. The server responds with a 354 reply code (which means "start mail input").

11. The client, upon receiving the 354 reply, sends its outgoing mail messages line by line. The data must be in 7-bit ASCII format. If the data is in 8-bit format, it must be translated into 7-bit format using either Multipurpose Internet Mail Extensions (MIME) or UUencode (UNIX-to-UNIX encode).

12. After the data has been sent, the sender sends a special sequence of control characters (e.g., CRLF.CRLF) to signal the end of the transfer.

13. The client sends a QUIT command to end the session.

14. The server responds with the 221 reply code (which means that it "agrees with the termination"). Both sides of the communication close the TCP connection.

When you first read this process, it may seem complicated. However, after you review it, you will begin to see why it is called the "Simple" Mail Transfer Protocol.

SMTP and Spooling

The word "spooling" in this context means "storing." SMTP uses spooling to delay message delivery. For example, when a client sends a message addressed to another user, that message is spooled on the sender's SMTP server. The SMTP server will periodically check its spooled messages and try to deliver them to the relevant users. If it cannot deliver a message, the SMTP server will keep the message spooled and try to deliver it at a later time. When the recipient's server comes online, the SMTP server can deliver the message. If a message cannot be delivered within a time period set by the administrator, the spooled message is returned to the sender with a non-delivery message.

The advantage of the spool mechanism is that the message sender does not have to establish a connection with a recipient's computer in order to send a message. After sending a message, the sender can proceed with other computing activities because he or she does not need to wait online for the message to reach the recipient. The recipient does not have to be online in order for mail to be sent to him or her.

IMS and SMTP

The IMS uses SMTP to send and receive mail from SMTP servers and clients. For example, an Exchange user, using Outlook, addresses a mail message to an Internet user (that Internet user might be represented in the Exchange address book as a custom recipient). The message leaves the Exchange client in the Exchange format. The IMS on the Exchange server uses the DNS protocol to resolve the recipient's domain name to its IP address. IMS translates the message to the SMTP format, and using SMTP, sends the message to the relevant SMTP server for spooling and delivery to the recipient. In this case, the IMS assumes the role of an SMTP client.

If another SMTP host sends mail to the IMS for delivery to an Exchange recipient, the IMS assumes the role of an SMTP server. After receiving the SMTP message, the IMS resolves the recipient address to the relevant Exchange address, translates the message to Exchange format, and hands off the message to the IS for delivery to the recipient. Both IMS roles are illustrated in Figure 14.4.

FIGURE 14.4

IMS and SMTP

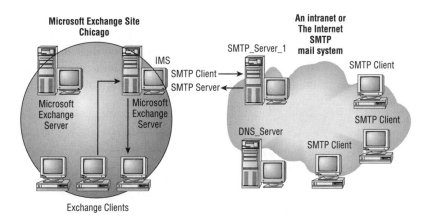

We have discussed how the IMS uses DNS and SMTP to participate in a TCP/IP-based mail system. We have seen how the IMS enables an Exchange server to perform as a DNS client, an SMTP client, and an SMTP server. We have also seen how the IMS acts as a gateway between Exchange and an SMTP system. In that role, it can translate messages sent from one system to another. In the next section, we will see how the IMS integrates with the other Exchange components.

How the Internet Mail Service Works

In this section, you will learn how the IMS interacts with other Exchange components so that Exchange recipients and SMTP users can exchange messages. Then you will learn about *address encapsulation,* which is the process of creating an SMTP return address for an Exchange sender who does not have one.

Sending Exchange Messages to SMTP Users

In order for an Exchange message to be sent to an SMTP user, the IMS and the other Exchange components complete the following process:

1. An Exchange user creates, addresses, and sends a message to an SMTP user. The user might address the message to an SMTP custom recipient in the GAL, or use a *one-off* address by typing the SMTP address directly into the message window before sending.

2. The Information Store (IS) on the Exchange server receives the message. The IS reads the DS and determines that the recipient is not local to that server. The IS then passes the message to the MTA for routing purposes.

3. The MTA compares the recipient's address with the Gateway Address Routing Table (GWART) and determines that the message must be delivered by the IMS component in that site.

4. If the IMS is local to the MTA, the MTA places the message in a folder in the IS specially designated for the IMS. If the IMS is on a different server than the MTA, the MTA sends the message to the remote MTA on the IMS server. The remote MTA then delivers the message to the IMS folder in the local IS.

5. The IMS picks up the message from the IS, and translates the message and any attachments from Exchange format to SMTP format. During the translation, the IMS references the DS to obtain the SMTP address of the Exchange sender. It uses the address in the FROM field in the header of the outbound message (this field is used by a receiving SMTP server to send back a message receipt or error message). The Exchange sender's SMTP address must be used because the native Exchange address, which is in the form of a Distinguished Name (DN), is not understood by SMTP software. If no SMTP address is available for the sender, the IMS will use a process called address encapsulation (which is explained in the next section).When the translation is completed, the IMS places the message in a subdirectory of the EXCHSRVR/IMCDATA directory, which serves as a temporary holding area for all outbound messages.

6. The IMS now acts as a DNS client, mapping the destination domain name to its IP address. It also acts as an SMTP client by establishing a TCP connection to the relevant SMTP server and participating in the SMTP mail exchange process by using SMTP commands and replies.

When an Exchange recipient is created, a number of foreign addresses (including an SMTP address) are automatically generated for that recipient. To refresh your memory, refer to Chapter 5.

Address Encapsulation

Along with the Exchange Client and Outlook, there are foreign clients that could use the IMS to send and receive messages from SMTP users. An example is a Microsoft Mail user connecting to an Exchange server through the Microsoft Mail Connector. If there is an IMS in the Exchange organization the MS Mail user is connecting to, this user could use the IMS to send messages to SMTP users.

Because the Microsoft Mail user does not have an associated SMTP address (assuming directory synchronization with Microsoft Mail is not being used, so there is no custom recipient representing the user), there is no SMTP return address for this user. The client's native address cannot be used in the FROM field of the message because the SMTP system would not understand that address format. To work around this problem, the IMS uses a process called *address encapsulation*.

The IMS takes a sender's native address and encapsulates it inside a valid SMTP address. The encapsulated address is placed in the FROM field of the message. If a reply or report message is returned from the SMTP system, the IMS can strip the original native address from the encapsulated address and deliver the reply or report message to the sender. The following is an example of a native Microsoft Mail address and how it would be encapsulated by the IMS:

Native Microsoft Mail address:

MS:SPROCKETS/SERVER1/LJONES

> MS=address type of Microsoft Mail for PC
>
> SPROCKETS=network name
>
> SERVER1=post office name
>
> LJONES=mailbox name

Encapsulated address:

IMCEAMS-SPROCKETS_SERVER1_LJONES@CHICAGO.WIDGET.COM

> IMC=address type of Internet Mail Connector
>
> EA=Encapsulated address
>
> MS=address type of Microsoft Mail for PC
>
> SPROCKETS_SERVER1_LJONES=encapsulated username
>
> CHICAGO.WIDGET.COM=SMTP address of IMS server

If directory synchronization is enabled between the Microsoft Mail system and the Exchange system, Microsoft Mail users will be defined in the Exchange GAL and will automatically have SMTP addresses (making address encapsulation unnecessary).

Now that you understand the DNS and SMTP protocols and understand how the IMS works, we can deploy an IMS.

Deploying the Internet Mail Service

Once you understand the various protocols and processes, deploying an IMS is relatively simple. An IMS deployment can be divided into three stages:

- IMS preinstallation

- IMS installation

- IMS customization

Each of these stages will be explained in the following sections.

IMS Preinstallation

Before you install an IMS, you need to make some decisions, collect some information, and install and configure the TCP/IP protocol on the IMS server. You need to decide how many IMSs to install and which Exchange servers to install them on. You also need to decide what security to implement. You need to collect information about the SMTP network and the advertisement of the IMS server in DNS. Each of these topics will be covered in the following discussion:

- Using multiple IMS servers

- IMS security

- Connections to an SMTP network

- DNS information to be registered and collected

- TCP/IP protocol

Using Multiple IMS Servers

Although an IMS server can send and receive a large load of messages, some situations may require more than one IMS server in a site. You may need to balance the load or increase fault tolerance.

Load balancing can be accomplished by having one IMS handle all the outgoing messages, while another IMS handles the incoming messages. You may decide to have one IMS handle messages to and from a particular SMTP network, while another IMS handles messages to and from a different SMTP network.

Fault tolerance can be implemented by having two IMSs handle all message traffic to and from an SMTP network. If one IMS is taken offline for maintenance, the other continues messaging services.

Once the number and purpose of the IMSs in a site is determined, you can decide on which specific Exchange servers to install an IMS.

IMS Security

Four main areas of security can be configured on the IMS:

- **Accepting and rejecting SMTP connections**   By default, an IMS accepts incoming SMTP messages from any IP address. However, if the IMS only needs to accept messages from particular SMTP servers, those server IP addresses can be entered into the IMS configuration and all other connection attempts will be rejected.

- **Limiting message size**   The IMS allows message size limits to be set for both incoming and outgoing messages. If an incoming message exceeds the message size limit, the IMS will not accept it. This prevents large messages from filling up the disk on the IMS server and helps prevent a *"denial-of-service"* attack. A denial-of-service attack occurs when someone sends so many service requests or so much data to your server that your server is overwhelmed and effectively shuts down.

- **Disable delivery of automatic replies**   Many client applications can generate automatic replies to messages (for example, an out-of-office message). If you do not want this type of message to be sent outbound over the IMS, you can block them on a per-outbound-domain or global basis.

- **Restricting user access**   You can specify which Exchange users can and cannot send outbound messages through an IMS.

SMTP Network Connections

An IMS can connect directly to an SMTP server on an intranet or the Internet, or it can connect to an SMTP relay host that forwards mail to and from an intranet or the Internet. The connections between an IMS server and an SMTP network can be permanent TCP/IP connections, such as through a LAN. The connection can also be dial-up using the *Point-to-Point Protocol* (PPP) to encapsulate TCP/IP packets for transmission over a WAN. A dial-up connection can be made directly to an SMTP server, or it can be made through an *Internet Service Provider* (ISP) and then routed to the destination SMTP server. Dial-up connections may require additional hardware, such as ISDN equipment, and additional software, such as the Microsoft Remote Access Service (RAS). Some of the different connection options are illustrated in Figure 14.5.

FIGURE 14.5

IMS connection options

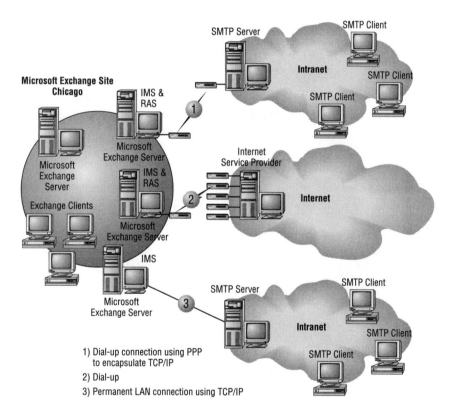

DNS Registration

An IMS server domain name must be registered with the intranet authority of an organization and with the InterNIC when connecting to the Internet. The InterNIC is an agency that registers domain names used on the Internet. By default, an Exchange site uses the following domain naming convention:

```
site.organization.com
```

The default domain name of a site can be modified on the Site Addressing object.

You need to know the IP address of the DNS server to be used before you install the IMS. The IMS will query this DNS server.

TCP/IP Protocol

Because SMTP and DNS are part of the TCP/IP protocol suite, they must use the TCP/IP transport stack to transmit and route data. A TCP/IP transport stack must be loaded and configured on the server on which the IMS will be installed (normally, the stack included with Windows NT is used). As part of the installation process of this stack, the IP address, host name, and domain name of that server (the Exchange server) will be defined. The DNS server (or servers) that will be used is also specified. The IP address of the IMS server can be obtained from an organization's intranet authority, from an ISP, or from the Internet authority, the InterNIC.

After you have made the necessary decisions and all your information is collected, you can install the IMS.

Installing an IMS

An IMS is installed using the Internet Mail Wizard. Once installed, an IMS can be stopped and started using Control Panel/Services.

The Internet Mail Wizard provides an easy way to install and configure the IMS. Access the Wizard in Exchange Administrator by choosing File, New Other, Internet Mail Service. The Wizard presents a series of dialog boxes containing questions, options, and input fields. When the Wizard is finished, the IMS will be installed and configured. Table 14.1 describes the dialog boxes that the Wizard presents (pages are referenced according to the information they contain).

	Wizard Dialog Box	Description
T A B L E 14.1 Internet Mail Wizard pages	Welcome page	This page describes what the Wizard will do.
	Information page	This page states that TCP/IP must be installed, tells what to do if the IMS will be using DNS, and gives information about using a dial-up connection. See Figure 14.6.
	Select the Exchange server	This page lets you specify the Exchange server on which to install the IMS. This page is also where you specify that Internet mail is to be sent through a dial-up connection.
	Dial-up	This page is only displayed if the dial-up connection option was chosen on the preceding page. The Remote Access Service must also be configured on the server that will be running the IMS. An RAS phone book entry for the connection to the remote SMTP server or ISP will need to be configured. The phone book entry must be enabled for TCP/IP.
	How IMS will send mail	There are two options for sending mail: ■ Use DNS to resolve recipient domain names to their IP addresses. ■ Use a single SMTP host, called a *relay host,* to send all outbound SMTP messages. The relay host resolves addresses and delivers messages. Figure 14.7 shows this page and Figure 14.8 illustrates the use of a relay host.
	Restrict connections to specified addresses	By default, the IMS will send messages to any SMTP addresses. But it can be configured to send messages to only selected SMTP addresses.
	Addressing for Exchange clients	Use this page to configure the SMTP naming convention that will be used for Exchange recipients. For example, the SMTP address for an Exchange recipient with the alias name Lisa, in an Exchange site named Chicago, in an organization named Widget, would be Lisa@Chicago.Widget.com. This address would be placed in the FROM address field in an outgoing SMTP message header.

TABLE 14.1 (cont.) Internet Mail Wizard pages	**Wizard Dialog Box**	**Description**
	Administrator mailbox	Notifications of SMTP Non-Delivery Reports will be sent to this mailbox. Note that a DL or public folder could be specified here instead of a mailbox.
	Site service account password	The password of the site service account.
	Install page	When the Finish button is selected on this page, the Internet Mail Wizard will install the IMS. The IMS Wizard will: ■ Create an IMS directory object in the site where the IMS is installed. ■ Trigger a recalculation of the routing tables in the site where the IMS is installed. ■ Configure the IMS to start automatically and start the service.

FIGURE 14.6

Information page of the Internet Mail Wizard

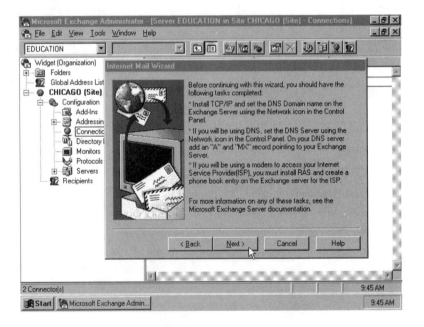

FIGURE 14.7

How IMS Will Send Mail page

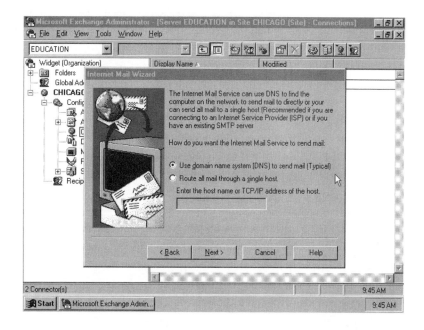

FIGURE 14.8

IMS using a relay host

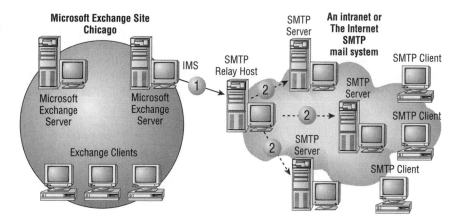

Microsoft Exchange Site Chicago

1) All outbound messages are sent to a relay host.
2) The relay host submits the messages to the appropriate recipient hosts.

Exercise 14.1 outlines the steps necessary to start the Internet Mail Wizard and proceed through its pages. If your Exchange server does not have TCP/IP installed or does not have a DNS server designated, you will not be able to perform the final step of the Wizard (the actual IMS installation).

EXERCISE 14.1

Executing the Internet Mail Wizard

1. In Exchange Administrator, choose File ➣ New Other ➣ Internet Mail Service. If the focus is not on the Connections container, an information dialog will appear asking if you would like to switch to the Connections container. If you see this dialog, click OK.

2. Read the Welcome page and click Next.

3. Read the next page, which provides information and describes preinstallation steps you may need to do. When you are done, click Next.

4. The next page lets you choose the Exchange server on which the IMS will be installed. Choose your server if it is not already selected. Click Next.

5. The next page asks you to designate how the IMS will deliver messages. For this exercise, leave the default (which is to use the domain name system (DNS) to send mail). Click Next.

6. Use the next page to restrict the SMTP addresses to which the IMS will send outbound messages. The default is to accept all outbound Internet mail. Leave the default setting, and click Next.

7. The next page lets you specify the domain name to be used in Exchange recipient SMTP addresses. Leave the default, and click Next.

8. The Internet Mail Wizard next prompts you for the Exchange mailbox to which the IMS will send notifications of Non-Delivery Reports. Choose the Select a mailbox or distribution list option. Then click Select. Choose one of the mailboxes you previously created, such as George Washington. Click OK, then click Next.

9. The next page will prompt you to enter the password for the Exchange site service account. If you used the password in Chapter 4, enter 12*12. If you used a different password, enter that password. Then click Next.

10. The final page will inform you that the Wizard is finished gathering information and is now ready to install the Internet Mail Service. Click Finish. If some of the necessary components were not installed or configured (like TCP/IP or a DNS server), an error message will appear.

Customizing the IMS

The Internet Mail Service is represented as an object in the Exchange hierarchy under the Connections container. It can be customized using the properties of this object. Table 14.2 lists the property pages of the IMS object and describes some of the attributes that can be customized on those pages.

	Property Page	Attributes
T A B L E 14.2 Property pages of the IMS object	General	Specifies the maximum message size of messages that can pass through this IMS.
	Connected Sites	Configures IMS connections to other Exchange sites. Lists the other Exchange sites that can receive SMTP messages from this IMS.
	Address Space	Lists the remote addresses (the address space) to which this IMS component can send messages.
	Dial-up Connections	Attributes for connection and schedule information for using RAS to connect the IMS to a remote SMTP server or an Internet Service Provider (ISP).
	Connections	Lists the attributes needed to send and receive messages, such as transfer mode, message delivery method, connections to accept, retry intervals, and message time-out options.
	Queues	Monitors the queues that hold inbound and outbound SMTP messages.
	Delivery Restrictions	Allows the administrator to select which users the IMS component will accept or reject messages from.
	Advanced	Allows the administrator to handle messages in the IMS outbound queue, such as number and length of time for queued but unsent messages, transfer timeouts, and the total allowable size of queued messages in the outbound queue.
	Diagnostic Logging	Sets which IMS events will be written to the Windows NT Event Log.

T A B L E 14.2 (cont.)	**Property Page**	**Attributes**
Property pages of the IMS object	Internet Mail	Includes the following attributes: ■ Message type (SMTP) ■ Administrator mailbox ■ Encoding method for attachments (e.g., MIME) ■ Character sets for MIME and non-MIME data ■ Enable message tracking

After any change is made to the IMS configuration, the IMS service must be stopped and restarted for the changes to take effect. In Exercise 14.2, you will use some of the property pages of the IMS object.

EXERCISE 14.2

Using the Property Pages of the IMS Object

1. In Exchange Administrator, highlight the Connections container. In the contents pane, you will see the IMS object you created in Exercise 14.1. Double-click on the IMS object. The property pages of the object will appear.

2. On the General page, set a maximum message size for messages traveling through the IMS.

3. Click on the Delivery Restrictions page, then restrict Andrew Jackson from using the IMS.

4. Click on the Internet Mail page, then change the administrator's mailbox from George Washington to James Madison.

5. Explore the other property pages. When you are finished, click OK to save and exit, or click Cancel to exit without saving.

Troubleshooting IMS

If problems occur when messages are sent or received through the IMS, one of the first troubleshooting steps you can take is to view the IMS queues. Information about a message can help you determine why it is not being properly sent or received. The IMS queues, details about messages in those queues, deleting a message, and forcing a retry will be covered in the following sections.

IMS Queues

The Queues property page of the IMS object permits you to access the three IMS queues:

- **MTS Out queue** This queue receives messages from the MTA on the Exchange server that is running the IMS. These messages are being sent from Exchange users to SMTP recipients.

- **OUT queue** Messages are sent from this queue to SMTP recipients.

- **IN queue** This queue receives messages from an SMTP system. These messages are converted to the Exchange format and passed to the Information Store. The MTA retrieves them from the IS and delivers them to the intended Exchange recipient.

After you have selected a queue, you can view details on any message in that queue.

Message Details

If you highlight a message, you can choose the Details button to view the following information about that message:

- Originator

- MTS-ID (Identifies the component that sent the message; it is only available in the MTS queue.)

- Destination host

- Submit time

- Size (in kilobytes)

- Next retry time (Appears only when an attempt to send the message has failed.)

- Retries (Number of times the IMS has attempted to send the message.)

- Expiration (When retries will stop.)

- Recipients (Includes the status of message delivery attempts.)

Detailed information about a queued message can help you track down the reason why it is not being delivered correctly.

Deleting a Message

If a message is hindering the operation of a queue, that message can be deleted. Highlight the message and click Delete. A Non-Delivery Report (NDR) will be sent to the sender of the message.

Forcing a Retry

An administrator can manually force the IMS to retry delivery of a message. To do so, highlight the message and click Retry Now.

Summary

The Domain Name System (DNS) protocol creates a hierarchical, distributed database of domain names and information. These distributed databases reside on computers called DNS servers. When addressing computers on a TCP/IP-based network, you can use domain names instead of IP addresses. DNS client software, also called a resolver program, can query the DNS server for the IP address of a particular domain name. The client's TCP/IP stack can then use the IP address to address and route data. The Exchange Internet Mail Service (IMS) can use DNS to resolve names in outbound SMTP messages and deliver them to the correct SMTP server.

Simple Mail Transfer Protocol (SMTP) defines the mechanism for applications to exchange mail messages. Part of the SMTP mechanism is a series of commands and replies between an SMTP client and an SMTP server. The IMS enables an Exchange server to be both an SMTP client when it sends messages to an SMTP network and an SMTP server when it receives SMTP messages for delivery to Exchange recipients.

The IMS works with the other Exchange components to process Exchange messages that are sent to SMTP users. These components also process messages sent from SMTP users to Exchange users. Translating message formats from one system to another is an important part of this process.

If a client sending through Exchange does not have an SMTP address that can be used in the FROM field of an outgoing message, the IMS will encapsulate the client's address into an SMTP address.

Implementing IMS involves three main stages:

- **Preinstallation**   In this stage, you gather information (such as the IP address of the DNS server that the IMS will use).

- **Installation**   In this stage, you execute the Internet Mail Wizard to install and configure the IMS.

- **Customization**   In this stage, you can modify IMS settings and set advanced options.

Review Questions

I. You can start the IMS by using which of the following?

   A. Internet Explorer

   B. Control Panel/Network

   C. DNS Administrator

   D. Control Panel/Services

2. The IMS must use a DNS server.

   A. True

   B. False

3. The MTA is involved in choosing a particular IMS component to deliver a message to a remote SMTP destination.

   A. True

   B. False

4. Which of the following is NOT a role of the IMS?

   A. Automatically generate SMTP addresses for new Exchange recipients

   B. Act as a DNS client

   C. Act as an SMTP server

   D. Act as a mail exchanger (MX)

5. The DNS hierarchical database is sometimes referred to as the domain name space.

   A. True

   B. False

6. The fully qualified domain name (FQDN) SALES.ACME.COM is in what root domain?

   A. COM

   B. SALES

   C. There is no way to tell

   D. ACME

7. The IMS relies on which component to resolve addresses of Exchange recipients on inbound messages?

   A. DNS

   B. SMTP

   C. Resolver program

   D. DS

8. The IMS component can be configured to use either a DNS server or to send all outbound messages to a designated host called a relay host.

   A. True

   B. False

9. After a change is made to the IMS configuration, the following should be done:

   A. The IMS should be paused and restarted

   B. The IMS should be reinstalled

   C. The IMS should be stopped and restarted

   D. The DNS server should be rebooted

10. Which of these connections to an SMTP server or ISP does the IMS support?

   A. Permanent connection using TCP/IP

   B. A dial-up connection using PPP

   C. A dial-up connection using POP3

   D. Both A and B

11. An Exchange site CANNOT have more than one IMS configured.

   A. True

   B. False

12. Which of the following must be true for the IMS to use RAS for a dial-up connection?

   A. A SAP agent must be configured

   B. RAS must be installed

   C. An RAS phone book entry must be created for the remote SMTP server or ISP

   D. Both B and C

13. Which of the following is the default Exchange naming convention for the domain name of a site?

A. site.organization.com

B. organization.site.com

C. com.organization.site

D. mailbox_name.site.organization

14. Which process maps domain names to IP addresses?

A. Address encapsulation

B. Name resolution

C. IP wrapping

D. Address spaces

15. Soon after the IMS is installed and started, an SMTP address space will be in the GWART.

A. True

B. False

CHAPTER

15

Connecting to
Microsoft Mail and Lotus cc:Mail

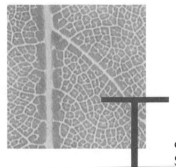

o provide interoperability and a path for migration, Exchange Server includes connectors for both Microsoft Mail (MS Mail) and Lotus cc:Mail systems. The connectors allow mail transfer and directory synchronization between Exchange and these foreign systems. Organizations can install Exchange and keep their current investment in MS Mail or Lotus cc:Mail, or they can use these connectors while migrating to Exchange. (Migration is the topic of Chapter 16.)

In this chapter, you will learn about:

- MS Mail

- Exchange and MS Mail interoperability

- Lotus cc:Mail Connector

MS Mail Overview

To understand the MS Mail Connector, you need to have a basic understanding of MS Mail. We will examine four elements of the MS Mail architecture:

- Postoffices

- MS Mail MTA

- Directory synchronization across postoffices

- Gateways from MS Mail to non-MS Mail systems

Postoffices

MS Mail is a *shared-file* mail system. The mail messages are stored as files in a shared directory on a designated computer, called a *postoffice*. An MS Mail system can have more than one postoffice.

MS Mail MTA

If an organization has several postoffices, the MS Mail MTA component routes messages between those postoffices. The MTA is implemented by either the External MTA or the Multitasking MTA.

Directory Synchronization across Postoffices

MS Mail postoffices exchange directory information through the MS Mail *Directory Synchronization Protocol*. A single postoffice is designated as a directory synchronization server (*dirsync server*). DISPATCH.EXE is the MS Mail program that executes the functions of a dirsync server. The dirsync server stores the master copy of a network's directory information (the Global Address List) and sends that list to the other postoffices. These other postoffices are designated as directory requestors (*dirsync requestors*). They send new, locally created directory information to the dirsync server, and they receive the Global Address List from the dirsync server.

Three primary events occur during synchronization: a requestor sends directory information to the server, the server compiles the Global Address List and sends it to requestors, and a requestor rebuilds its Global Address List. Each of these events is initiated at a certain timed interval configured through the following parameters:

- **T1** The interval used by dirsync requestors to send their postoffice address list to the dirsync server.

- **T2** The interval used by the dirsync server to compile a new Global Address List and to send that list to the dirsync requestors.

- **T3** The interval used by the dirsync requestors to rebuild their postoffice address lists.

The default setting for each of these events is once every 24 hours. Each event can also be manually initiated.

Gateways from MS Mail to Non-MS Mail Systems

MS Mail includes optional software that allows it to exchange messages with non-MS Mail systems. Gateways to the following foreign mail systems exist:

- AT&T EasyLink
- IBM PROFS, OfficeVision, and SNADS
- Novell Message Handling System (MHS)
- MCI Mail
- SMTP mail systems

In a typical MS Mail gateway configuration, a dedicated computer runs the gateway software and connects to the foreign mail system. Another postoffice (the *Gateway Postoffice*) is configured to receive all the messages destined for the foreign mail system. The rest of the postoffices send their foreign addressed messages to the Gateway Postoffice, which then sends them to the gateway computer. To send foreign addressed messages to the Gateway Postoffice, a postoffice must have a special software program (the MS Mail 3.*x Gateway Access Component*) installed. (See Figure 15.1 for an illustration.)

Figure 15.2 illustrates and summarizes the following four architectural elements of MS Mail:

- Postoffice
- MTA
- Directory synchronization
- Gateways

Exchange and MS Mail Interoperability

For an Exchange and MS Mail system to interoperate, they must be able to exchange messages, directory information, and client schedule information. Three Exchange components enable these operations: the MS Mail Connector, the Directory Synchronization Agent (DXA), and the Schedule+ Free/Busy Connector.

FIGURE 15.1

MS Mail gateway
configuration

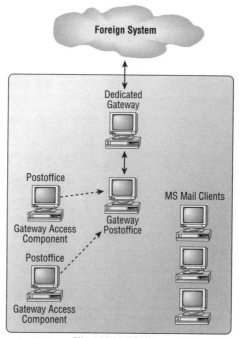

This section provides an overview of these components and their processes. You will learn about:

- MS Mail Connector architecture

- MS Mail Connector roles

- Directory Synchronization Agent (DXA)

- Schedule+ Free/Busy Connector

MS Mail Connector Architecture

The MS Mail Connector enables an Exchange server to function like an MS Mail postoffice. The MS Mail Connector translates Exchange messages addressed to MS Mail users into an MS Mail message format and sends those messages to MS Mail postoffices. It can also receive MS Mail messages addressed to Exchange recipients and translate them into the Exchange message format.

FIGURE 15.2

MS Mail

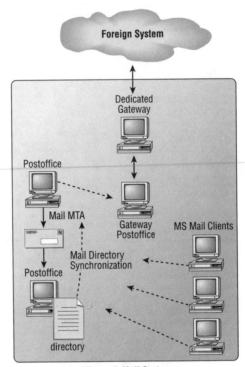

Microsoft Mail System

To understand how the MS Mail Connector functions, you need to understand its architecture. This section provides information on the following topics:

- MS Mail Connector Postoffice

- MS Mail Connector Components

- Message flow

- Physical connections

- Using multiple MS Mail Connectors

MS Mail Connector Postoffice

The MS Mail Connector Postoffice is an area on an Exchange server used to store MS Mail messages. This postoffice serves a slightly different purpose than an actual MS Mail postoffice. Rather than sending, receiving, and permanently storing MS Mail messages, this postoffice is only used to send and receive MS Mail messages. When an MS Mail message is received by the MS Mail Connector, it is temporarily stored before it is translated to the Exchange format and sent to the relevant Exchange recipients. When an Exchange message is to be sent to an MS Mail user, it is translated into the MS Mail format and temporarily stored before being transferred to the relevant postoffice. Because it is dedicated to message delivery and has no local mailboxes, this storage is sometimes referred to as a *shadow postoffice*, or as a *gateway postoffice*. Figure 15.3 illustrates the role of the MS Mail Connector Postoffice.

FIGURE 15.3

MS Mail Connector Postoffice

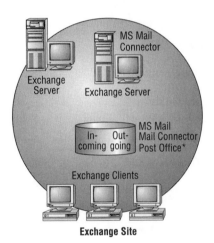
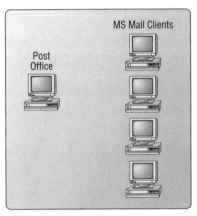

*Temporary storage of incoming and outgoing messages.

The component that submits and retrieves messages from the MS Mail Connector Postoffice and the component that sends and receives MS Mail messages will be discussed next.

MS Mail Connector Components

The MS Mail Connector is made up of two components:

- MS Mail Connector Interchange

- MS Mail Connector (PC) MTA

Both of these are Windows NT services. Both of them use the MS Mail Connector Postoffice to temporarily store MS Mail messages.

MS Mail Connector Interchange   The MS Mail Connector Interchange translates messages from the Exchange format to the MS Mail format, and vice versa. When an Exchange user sends a message to an MS Mail user, the Interchange receives the outgoing message, translates it to the MS Mail format, and submits it to the MS Mail Connector Postoffice. From there it will be sent to the MS Mail system.

If an MS Mail message that is addressed to an Exchange recipient is in the MS Mail Connector Postoffice, the Interchange reads the message, translates it to the Exchange format, and passes it to the other Exchange components for delivery to the Exchange recipients. Figure 15.4 illustrates both of these processes.

FIGURE 15.4

MS Mail Connector
Interchange

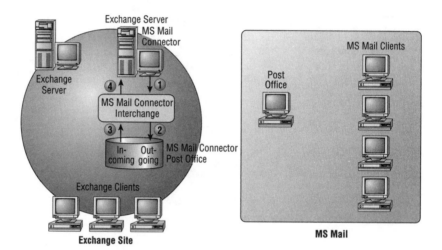

1) Exchange message
2) MS Mail message
3) MS Mail message
4) Exchange message

MS Mail Connector (PC) MTA   The MS Mail Connector (PC) MTA transfers MS Mail messages between an Exchange server and MS Mail postoffices. The MS Mail Connector (PC) MTA is similar to the Exchange MTA in that it routes and transfers messages.

While an Exchange server can have only one instance of the MS Mail Connector installed, the MS Mail Connector (PC) MTA can be configured with up to 10 instances, allowing a single MS Mail Connector to connect to more than one postoffice. Figure 15.5 illustrates the role of this component.

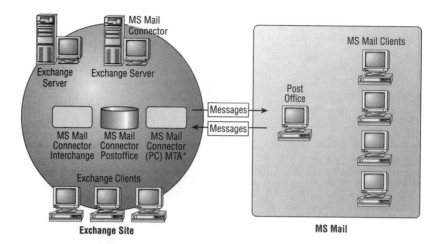

FIGURE 15.5

MS Mail Connector
(PC) MTA

*Sends and receives MS Mail messages.

The MS Mail Connector (PC) MTA can be configured to make direct or indirect connections to MS Mail postoffices. Both of these options are explained here:

- **Direct Connection to a Postoffice** When an MS Mail Connector (PC) MTA is configured to send messages directly to a postoffice, the connection is referred to as a *direct connection* to an external postoffice. Mail sent over a direct connection does not go through any other postoffices, and it is sent directly to the destination postoffice. Figure 15.6 illustrates a direct connection to an external postoffice.

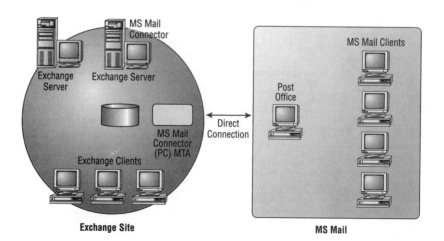

FIGURE 15.6

Direct connection to a
postoffice

- **Indirect Connection to a Postoffice** When an MS Mail Connector (PC) MTA has a direct connection to a postoffice that has connections to other postoffices, the MS Mail Connector can use its directly connected postoffice to forward messages to other postoffices. The connection to these "downstream" postoffices is referred to as an *indirect connection*. Figure 15.7 illustrates indirect connections.

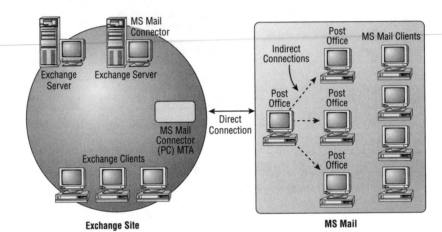

The next section explains how an Exchange server, with the MS Mail Connector, processes incoming and outgoing MS Mail messages.

Message Flow

This section describes the flow of a message through an Exchange server when the MS Mail Connector is used.

Receiving an MS Mail Message After an MS Mail user has created and sent a message addressed to an Exchange recipient, and after that user's postoffice has transferred the message to the Exchange server, the following processes occur:

1. The MS Mail Connector (PC) MTA receives the message and places it in the MS Mail Connector Postoffice.

2. The MS Mail Connector Postoffice temporarily stores the message until the MS Mail Connector Interchange processes it.

3. The Interchange reads the queued message, translates it to the Exchange format, passes it to the Exchange MTA for delivery, and then deletes the message that was temporarily stored in the MS Mail Connector Postoffice.

4. The Exchange MTA compares the message destination with the Exchange Directory. If the message recipient is on that server, the message is passed to the Information Store (IS) for local delivery. If the recipient is on a remote Exchange server, the MTA transfers the message to that remote server.

Figure 15.8 illustrates these steps.

FIGURE 15.8

An Exchange server receiving an MS Mail message

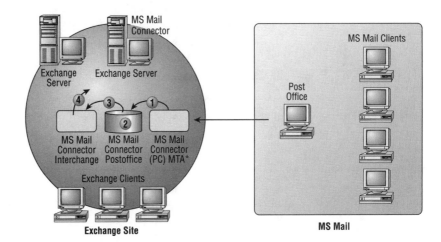

1) Mail message
2) Temporary storage, MS Mail message
3) Translates, Exchange message
4) Exchange MTA, Exchange message

Sending a Message to an MS Mail Postoffice　After an Exchange user has created and sent a message addressed to an MS Mail recipient, the following processes occur on the Exchange server with the MS Mail Connector:

1. The IS compares the destination address to the Exchange Directory and determines that this message is for remote delivery. Therefore, the IS passes the message to the Exchange MTA.

2. The Exchange MTA temporarily queues the message and then compares the destination address with the Exchange Directory. (This is to determine how the message is to be delivered.) In this case, the Exchange MTA determines that it must use an MS Mail Connector. It then passes the message to the MS Mail Connector Interchange.

3. The Interchange translates the message content from the Exchange format to the MS Mail format. It then passes the message to the MS Mail Connector Postoffice.

4. The MS Mail Connector (PC) MTA scans the MS Mail Connector Postoffice for outgoing messages. When it detects one, it sends the message to the MS Mail postoffice to which it is connected. After sending the message, the MS Mail Connector (PC) MTA deletes the message from the MS Mail Connector Postoffice.

Physical Connections

The MS Mail Connector can use any of three physical connection types to send and receive messages from an MS Mail postoffice. These three connection types are:

- LAN

- Asynchronous modem

- X.25

LAN The default and preferred connection option between an MS Mail Connector and an MS Mail postoffice is a LAN connection. This connection is the easiest to configure and performs the best. You must configure the network path to the shared directory that serves as the postoffice on the MS Mail server. After you enter that primary piece of information, the MS Mail Connector automatically configures almost everything else.

An advantage of using a LAN connection is that it enables automatic uploading of information about downstream postoffices. You will need to manually enter downstream postoffices when using asynchronous modem and X.25 connections.

Asynchronous Modem Asynchronous modems can be used to connect an MS Mail Connector and its external postoffice when they are not connected by a LAN. This connection option will normally be slower than a LAN connection, and it will require more configuration and administration on both sides of the connection. The remote network name, postoffice name, telephone number, and other information must be manually entered when configuring the MS Mail Connector.

The remote network containing the MS Mail postoffice must have a computer running either the MS Mail 3.*x* External MTA or Multitasking MTA. Use the External MTA on a computer running MS-DOS. Use the Multitasking MTA if the computer is running Windows NT. The MS Mail Connector will connect to the MS Mail MTA computer in order to deliver messages to the remote postoffice.

X.25   An X.25 connection is another WAN connection that can be used between an MS Mail Connector and an MS Mail environment. This connection can be slower than the LAN option and will require more configuration and administration. The LAN, asynchronous modem, and X.25 connections are illustrated in Figure 15.9.

FIGURE 15.9

Connection options between an MS Mail Connector and MS Mail

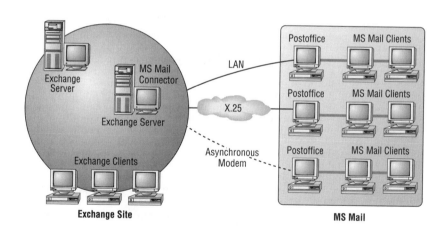

Using Multiple MS Mail Connectors

If your organization has a large number of MS Mail postoffices and a large number of messages passed between them and your Exchange system, you might need to configure multiple MS Mail Connectors to handle the load. Although an individual Exchange server can have only one instance of the MS Mail Connector, more than one Exchange server can be configured with an MS Mail Connector. Because all of the MS Mail Connectors in an Exchange site use the same address space, the site appears to the MS Mail environment as one big postoffice. Using multiple MS Mail Connectors is illustrated in Figure 15.10.

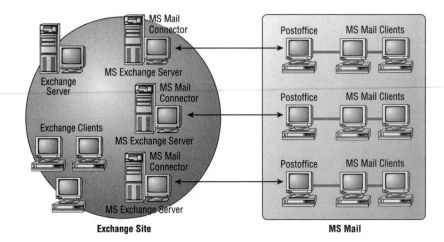

FIGURE 15.10

Using multiple MS Mail Connectors

Utilizing the MS Mail Connector

Network administrators and designers have several ways to utilize the MS Mail Connector in an organization. In addition to enabling message exchange between a single Exchange site and a single MS Mail postoffice, the MS Mail Connector can be used for:

- Backboning MS Mail through Exchange

- Accessing MS Mail gateways from Exchange

- Accessing Exchange connectors from MS Mail

Backboning MS Mail through Exchange

An Exchange site configured with the MS Mail Connector can be used as a messaging backbone for multiple MS Mail postoffices or even multiple MS Mail sites. To implement this, each postoffice must be configured to route messages through the Exchange MS Mail Connector. Each postoffice will have an indirect connection to the other postoffices through the MS Mail Connector backbone.

Directory synchronization can be configured to take advantage of the messaging backbone. Each postoffice passes new directory information to the Exchange site. The Exchange site contains, in effect, a master copy of the messaging system's directory, which it replicates to the individual postoffices. Figure 15.11 illustrates using an Exchange site as a messaging backbone for MS Mail.

FIGURE 15.11

Exchange as a messaging backbone for MS Mail

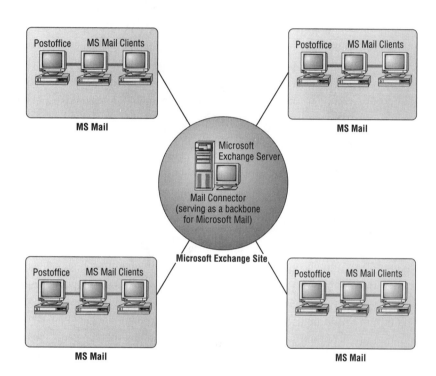

Accessing MS Mail Gateways from Exchange

As stated earlier, MS Mail includes optional software that enables an MS Mail system to exchange messages with foreign mail systems. That functionality can be leveraged by Exchange users. To do this, an Exchange server with the MS Mail Connector installed must also have the MS Mail Gateway Access Component installed. This setup allows Exchange users to send messages (through the MS Mail Connector) to an MS Mail gateway and to recipients on the foreign system. Figure 15.12 illustrates this process.

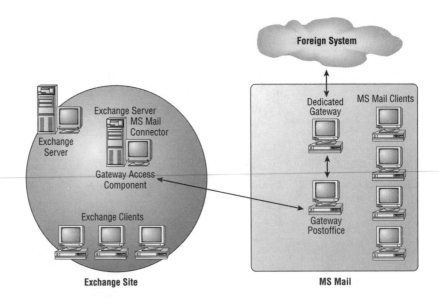

An Exchange server with the MS Mail Connector can also be configured to be the Gateway Postoffice. In this setup, all the other postoffices send foreign addressed messages to the Exchange server, which forwards them to the gateway computer. Figure 15.13 illustrates this procedure.

Accessing Exchange Connectors from MS Mail

Exchange users can utilize MS Mail gateways, and MS Mail users can utilize Exchange gateways (i.e., connectors). MS Mail users can address messages to X.400 or SMTP recipients and have those messages delivered through an X.400 Connector or Internet Mail Service installed in an Exchange site. The MS Mail messages enter the Exchange site through an MS Mail Connector, which passes them to the appropriate connector for delivery to the foreign mail system. MS Mail postoffices that need to send messages to the Exchange connectors must have the appropriate Gateway Access Component installed.

There are a couple of good reasons to use an Exchange connector instead of an MS Mail gateway to access foreign mail systems. The Exchange connectors are Windows NT services that are 32-bit, multithreaded programs. They can also run on a high-end server utilizing multiple processors and large amounts of RAM. Using Exchange connectors also eliminates the need to use a dedicated computer for the MS Mail gateway. Figure 15.14 illustrates the use of an Exchange connector as a gateway for MS Mail users.

FIGURE 15.13

FIGURE 15.13

An Exchange server
acting as the Gateway
Postoffice

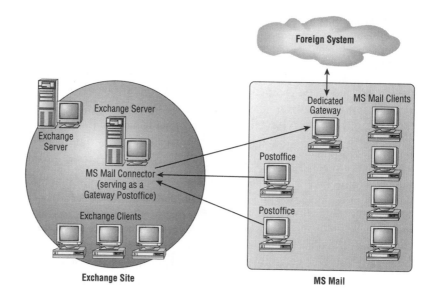

FIGURE 15.14

Using Exchange
connectors as gateways
for MS Mail users

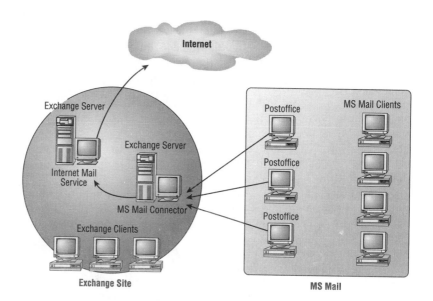

Directory Synchronization Agent (DXA)

The MS Mail Directory Synchronization protocol has been incorporated in other messaging products, like Exchange, permitting them to exchange directory information with MS Mail. The Exchange component that supports this protocol is the Directory Synchronization Agent (DXA). When this component is used, Exchange can automatically exchange directory information with an MS Mail system. Information about Exchange recipients is sent to the MS Mail system, and information about MS Mail recipients is sent to the Exchange Directory. MS Mail recipients are entered into the Exchange Directory as custom recipients. Although the MS Mail Connector provides for message transfer between the two systems, the DXA allows the users on each system to see the directory information (e.g., e-mail addresses) of the other system.

The DXA enables an Exchange server to function as either a dirsync server or dirsync requestor. Although it can assume either role, it can only perform one of these roles at a time (i.e., the Exchange server cannot be a dirsync server and a dirsync requestor concurrently). An Exchange site can have only one Exchange server designated as a dirsync server, but a site is not required to have a dirsync server. All Exchange servers in a site can be dirsync requestors using an MS Mail postoffice as the dirsync server.

When configured as a dirsync server, an Exchange server will receive the new directory information sent by the postoffices configured as dirsync requestors and compile the Global Address List. This master list of directory information is then sent to all requestor postoffices. Figure 15.15 illustrates this configuration.

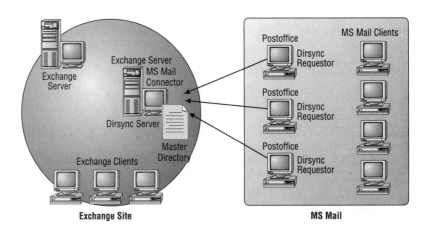

FIGURE 15.15

An Exchange server as a dirsync server

If configured as a dirsync requestor, an Exchange server will send its new directory information to the postoffice designated as the dirsync server and receive the Global Address List from that postoffice. Figure 15.16 illustrates this configuration.

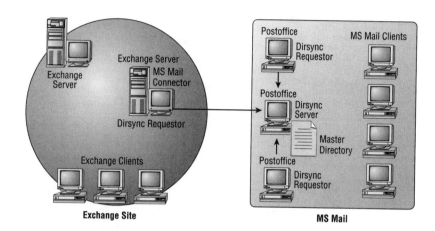

FIGURE 15.16

An Exchange server as a dirsync requestor

One of the most useful administrative features of Exchange directory synchronization is the ability to select which Exchange recipients to synchronize to an MS Mail system. An Exchange administrator can prevent certain Exchange recipients from being sent to the MS Mail global address list. This can be implemented at two levels.

Each Exchange recipient has a property called *trust level,* which holds a value of 1–100. An Exchange dirsync servers, or requestor can be configured to only synch recipient objects with trust levels less than or equal to a specified value. For example, if an Exchange recipient named Bob has a trust level of 10, and the Exchange dirsync requestor is configured to synch objects with trust levels less than or equal to 3, then information about Bob will not be sent to the MS Mail dirsync server.

This feature can be applied at another level, the recipient container level. If there are many Exchange recipients that do not need to be synchronized, a separate Exchange recipients container can be created to hold these recipients. That container would not be included in the list of containers to send to the MS Mail system.

Creating a Global Distribution List

You may need to create a global distribution list containing all the Exchange recipients and all the MS Mail users. One way to do this is to create an Exchange DL that contains two members, an Exchange DL with all the Exchange recipients, and a custom recipient synched from MS Mail that represents an MS Mail DL which contains all the MS Mail users.

Schedule+ Free/Busy Connector

Schedule+ is a personal and group scheduling program. One of its many features allows users to view the free/busy schedule information of other users. MS Mail ships with Schedule+ version 1.0 and Exchange ships with Schedule+ version 7.5. Exchange includes the Schedule+ Free/Busy Connector to allow users with one version to view information from users of the other version. In the following two sections, we will discuss the elements and processes for sending scheduling information in both directions (i.e., from Exchange to MS Mail and from MS Mail to Exchange).

Sending Information from Exchange to MS Mail

All Schedule+ 7.5 free/busy information is stored in an Exchange public folder called Schedule+ Free Busy (found under the System Folders container in Exchange Administrator). The Schedule+ Free/Busy Connector uses a special mailbox agent (ADMINSCH) to translate and address that information for delivery to a designated distribution list (DL) on the MS Mail network. (When Exchange Server is installed, ADMINSCH is automatically created.) The MS Mail DL contains the administrative user accounts that are used to distribute free/busy information to the users of that network.

Sending Information from MS Mail to Exchange

On an MS Mail network, a program called SCHDIST.EXE can be used to collect free/busy information and send it in the form of a message to the ADMINSCH mailbox agent on the designated Exchange server. The Free/Busy Connector then translates it and places it in the Schedule+ Free Busy public folder. This information is available to Exchange clients using Schedule+ 7.5. Figure 15.17 illustrates the Schedule+ Free/Busy Connector architecture.

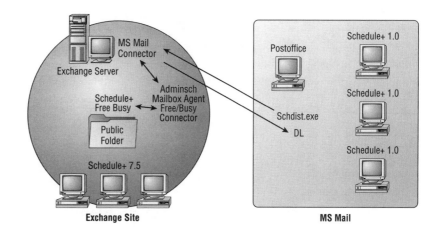

Now that we have covered the background for the Exchange components, we can move on to implementing these concepts and creating interoperability between Exchange and MS Mail environments.

Exchange and MS Mail Interoperability

This section discusses implementing the components necessary for the following types of interoperability between Exchange and MS Mail:

- Message exchange

- Directory synchronization

- Schedule+ information access

Message Exchange

The MS Mail Connector must be installed, configured, and started before messages can be exchanged between Exchange and MS Mail. MS Mail postoffices must be configured to route messages to the MS Mail Connector.

MS Mail Connector Installation

When you install Exchange Server, one of your options is to install the MS Mail Connector. If you choose this option, the MS Mail Connector will be installed and will appear in the Exchange hierarchy as an object in the site Connections container.

If the MS Mail Connector is not installed during the initial Exchange Server setup, it can be installed later by executing the Exchange Setup program (SETUP.EXE) and choosing the Add/Remove option. Highlight the Microsoft Exchange Server selection and click Change option. A dialog box appears permitting you to select the MS Mail Connector for installation.

MS Mail Connector Configuration

The MS Mail Connector configuration process can be organized into four main procedures:

1. Define and configure a physical connection to an external postoffice.

2. Define and configure message transfer.

3. Configure destination addresses.

4. Configure other settings.

These steps and procedures will be explained in the following sections. All of these procedures are executed through the Exchange Administrator program and configured on the MS Mail Connector object, found in the Connections container. You will configure an MS Mail Connector in Exercise 15.1.

Define and Configure a Physical Connection to an External Postoffice

To send and receive messages from an MS Mail postoffice, you must configure a physical connection on the Connections property page. As you learned earlier, three connection types can be used: LAN, Asynchronous, and X.25.

Some of the important attributes of each of these connections are listed here:

- **LAN Connection**   Only two pieces of information must be entered for this connection type:

  - **Postoffice path**   The network path to the shared directory on an MS Mail postoffice in which mail messages are stored. The path must be entered using the Universal Naming Convention (UNC). In a Microsoft networking environment, the path format would be \\computer_name\ share_name\directory_path. If the postoffice is located on a NetWare server, the path format would be \\server_name\volume_name\ directory_path.

- **Connection attempts**   The number of times the MS Mail Connector will attempt to send a message before it returns the message to the sender with a Non-Delivery Report (NDR). The default is 3.

- **Asynchronous Connection (Async)**   Asynchronous connections require more settings than LAN connections. The primary settings are:

  - **Network name**   The name of the MS Mail network to which the MS Mail Connector is attaching.

  - **Postoffice name**   The name of a specific postoffice to which the MS Mail Connector will connect.

  - **Sign-on ID**   The serial number of the external postoffice to which a connection is being made.

  - **Password**   The password used at the external postoffice. This is an optional attribute at the external postoffice.

  - **Connection attempts**   The number of times the MS Mail Connector will attempt to send a message before it returns the message to the sender with a Non-Delivery Report (NDR). The default is 3.

  - **Phone number**   The phone number to the external postoffice.

  - **Optional settings**   Accessed by clicking the Options button.

- **X.25 Connection**   For this connection option to be used, the X.25 protocol must already be installed and configured on the Exchange server. The X.25 option has many of the same properties as the async option, including network and postoffice name, sign-on ID, password, and connection attempts. The primary difference is that this connection type requires the X.121 address of the external postoffice. A 16-digit number identifies the computer on the X.25 network that contains the external postoffice.

Define and Configure Message Transfer   Once a physical connection has been configured, you can define and configure message transfer. You must create one or more instances of the MS Mail Connector (PC) MTA. As you learned earlier, only one instance of the MS Mail Connector can exist on an Exchange server. However, that single instance of the MS Mail Connector can use multiple instances of the MS Mail Connector (PC) MTA to transfer messages. The Connector MTAs property page is used to create and configure an MTA.

To create a new Connector MTA instance, click the New button on the Connector MTAs property page. The main attributes to configure are:

- **Service name**   The name that represents a particular instance of this MTA. This name is registered with the Windows NT operating system as a service which can be started and stopped with the Services applet in the Control Panel.

- **Polling frequency**   Can be set to indicate how long this instance of the MTA waits before checking the external postoffice for new mail to be picked up. The default is 5 minutes.

- **Connection parameters**   The MTA must use a physical connection to send and receive messages. That connection is chosen under Connection Parameters. The default is LAN.

After an MTA instance is created, you can determine the external postoffices with which it will exchange messages. This information can be entered after clicking the List button on the Connector MTAs property page.

If a particular MS Mail Connector (PC) MTA will use an async or an X.25 connection, additional properties need to be set for the MTA (such as the communication port and the modem timeout value).

Configure Address Spaces   Like other connectors, the MS Mail Connector is configured with the destination addresses to which it will route messages. These addresses are configured on the Address Space property page.

Four address templates can be used to enter addresses:

- X.400

- MS Mail

- Internet

- General (can be used to create any type of address)

Addresses can be to specific recipients on a foreign system, or they can be to an entire network of recipients. An example of an MS Mail address space is:

```
MS: Sprockets/Manufacturing/*
```

"MS" refers to the address space type (MS Mail in this example). "Sprockets" is the network name. "Manufacturing" is the postoffice name. The asterisk (*) is a wildcard, meaning all recipients.

Configure Other Settings   The General, Interchange, and Local Postoffice property pages contain other MS Mail Connector properties that can be configured:

- **General property page**   Use this page to set a maximum message size and indicate an administrative note for this connector.

- **Interchange property page**   Use this page to select an administrator's mailbox to receive information messages and alert notifications from this connector. Other properties on this page include the primary language used by clients accessing this connector and message tracking. If message tracking is enabled, information about messages sent through this connector will be written to the tracking logs.

- **Local Postoffice property page**   The MS Mail Connector allows an Exchange server to function as an MS Mail postoffice. As such, it must have a network and postoffice name. By default, the Exchange organization name is used as the network name, and the Exchange site name is used for the postoffice name. This page allows these values to be changed. The MS Mail Connector can also require a password to be used by external postoffices that are connecting to and sending messages to this connector. This page is where you enter this password.

Exercise 15.1 tells you how to configure the MS Mail connector. To perform this exercise, you must have an MS Mail system on your network.

EXERCISE 15.1

Configuring the MS Mail Connector

1. In Exchange Administrator, navigate to the Connections container and double-click on MS Mail Connector. The property pages for this object will appear.

2. On the Interchange page, designate one of your recipients as the administrator's mailbox.

3. On the Connections page, click Create to create a connection to an MS Mail postoffice. Choose the LAN connection parameter, and enter the UNC path to the MS Mail postoffice.

4. On the Connector MTAs page, click New to create a new Connector MTA instance. In the Service Name field, give this Connector MTA a name. Also choose the LAN option under Connection Parameters.

5. On the Address Space page, click New MS Mail to configure the addresses to which this connector will send messages. Enter the remote network and postoffice names in the template.

6. Click OK to save and exit these property pages.

7. In the Control Panel, run the Services applet. Scroll down until you see MS Mail Connector Interchange. Highlight that entry, and click Start. The MS Mail Connector will now start. (The service can also be stopped from this location.) Start the connector MTA service you created in Step 4.

MS Mail Postoffice Configuration

The previous procedures configured the MS Mail Connector to transfer messages to the external postoffices. Those postoffices also need to be configured to send messages to the MS Mail Connector. The primary information that must be entered at these postoffices is the network and postoffice name used by the MS Mail Connector. If the MS Mail Connector uses a password, it must also be configured on the MS Mail postoffices.

Directory Synchronization

The primary steps to implement directory synchronization between Exchange and MS Mail are:

1. Configuring and starting the DXA.

2. Use an Exchange server as a dirsync server,

   or

   Use an Exchange server as a dirsync requestor.

Each of these primary steps will be covered in the following sections.

Configuring and Starting the DXA

The Exchange DXA component is installed when the MS Mail Connector is installed. As a Windows NT service, it can be stopped and started through the Control Panel Services applet. It is represented by the Directory Synchronization object in the Exchange hierarchy. As with other Exchange objects, it has properties that can be configured.

Exchange Server as a Dirsync Server

To use an Exchange server as a dirsync server, the following procedures must be performed:

- **A dirsync server object must created and configured**   In Exchange Administrator, choose File, New Other, Dirsync Server. (When you create this object, make your hierarchy context the Connections container.) Some of this object's properties are:

  - **Name**   The directory name of this object.

  - **Dirsync administrator**   The Exchange recipient that receives administration notifications pertaining to this object.

  - **Server**   The name of the Exchange server that will function as the dirsync server.

  - **Schedule**   A schedule can be defined to execute the T2 event, namely the compilation of the Global Address List and submission of it to the dirsync requestors.

- **Remote dirsync requestors must be created and configured**   The Exchange server acting as a dirsync server must maintain the list of the dirsync requestors with which it will be communicating. This information is configured by the Exchange administrator by creating a remote dirsync requestor object for each MS Mail postoffice. These objects are created in Exchange Administrator by choosing File ➤ New Other ➤ Remote Dirsync Requestor. One of the most important properties of this type of object is the list of recipient containers that are to be exported to the remote requestor. This information is entered on the Export Containers property page. Attributes on this page include:

  - **Recipient containers**   The Exchange recipient containers to export to this particular remote requestor. These containers can be located in any site.

- **Trust level**   The trust level used to select objects for synchronization with this remote requestor. All Exchange objects in the designated containers with a trust level less than or equal to this value will be synchronized.

- **Configure the MS Mail postoffices that are dirsync requestors**   The MS Mail administrator must configure the dirsync requestors with information about the dirsync server.

Exchange Server as a Dirsync Requestor

If an Exchange server will be a dirsync requestor, the following procedures must be performed:

- **A dirsync requestor object must created and configured**   In Exchange Administrator, choose File ➤ New Other ➤ Dirsync Requestor to configure the dirsync requestor. (When you create this object, make your hierarchy context the Connections container.) The Dirsync Requestor object includes many of the same attributes as the dirsync server, such as name, server, and schedule. On the Export Containers property page you can designate which recipient containers to send to the dirsync server and which trust levels to use. On the Import Container property page you can designate the recipients container in which to create directory entries received from the dirsync server.

- **Configure the Mail dirsync server**   The postoffice serving as the dirsync server must be configured with information about the Exchange server functioning as a dirsync requestor.

Accessing Free/Busy Information

Procedures must be performed in both the Exchange site and the MS Mail network for free/busy information to be accessible from one system to the other system. On the Exchange site, the following must be operational in order for the Schedule+ Free/Busy Connector to work:

- MS Mail Connector

- Directory synchronization between the Exchange site and MS Mail network

The Schedule+ Free/Busy Connector is installed when the MS Mail Connector is installed. If the MS Mail Connector was not installed at the initial Exchange Server setup, run the Exchange Server Setup program in maintenance mode and choose the Add/Remove option to install the MS Mail Connector.

Lotus cc:Mail Connector

The Exchange Connector for Lotus cc:Mail provides both message exchange and directory synchronization between Exchange and cc:Mail systems. This connector is installed using Exchange Server Setup.

The Connector for Lotus cc:Mail uses two Lotus cc:Mail utilities, IMPORT.EXE and EXPORT.EXE. The connector and these two utilities are described here:

- **Lotus cc:Mail Connector**   Transfers messages and synchronizes directories between Exchange and cc:Mail.

- **IMPORT.EXE**   Imports information, both mail messages and directory information, into the cc:Mail environment.

- **EXPORT.EXE**   Exports information, both mail messages and directory information, from the cc:Mail environment.

Figure 15.18 illustrates an organization using the Connector for Lotus cc:Mail.

FIGURE 15.18

The Connector for Lotus cc:Mail

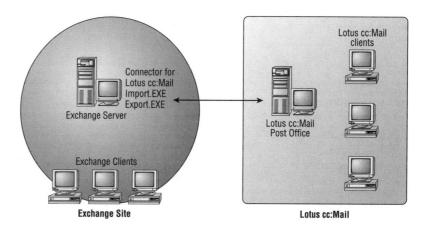

Summary

Exchange Server comes with the tools needed to interoperate, exchange messages, and perform directory synchronization with Microsoft Mail (MS Mail) and Lotus cc:Mail systems.

The MS Mail Connector enables message exchange between an Exchange system and an MS Mail system. This connector creates a temporary storage area (the MS Mail Connector Postoffice) for messages transmitted between Exchange and MS Mail. The MS Mail Connector is implemented as two Windows NT services (components), the MS Mail Connector Interchange and the MS Mail Connector (PC) MTA. The Interchange translates messages from the Exchange format to the MS Mail format, and vice versa. The MS Mail Connector (PC) MTA transfers messages between Exchange and MS Mail systems.

When the MS Mail Connector is installed, the Schedule+ Free/Busy Connector is also installed. The Schedule+ Free/Busy Connector permits the exchange of free/busy information generated by Exchange clients using Schedule 7.5 and MS Mail clients using Schedule+ 1.0.

Environments that contain both Exchange and Lotus cc:Mail can use the Connector for Lotus cc:Mail to enable both message exchange and directory synchronization between the two systems.

Review Questions

1. The MS Mail Connector requires Exchange users to have two mailboxes.

   A. True

   B. False

2. Exchange users CANNOT use the MS Mail Connector to access an MS Mail gateway. They must use an Exchange gateway.

   A. True

   B. False

3. Which of the following does NOT relate to restricting Exchange objects from being synchronized with an MS Mail system?

A. Trust level of the object

B. Trust level of the Exchange dirsync server or requestor

C. The recipients container

D. EXPORT.EXE

4. Which of the following are required when using the Schedule+ Free/Busy Connector?

A. Directory synchronization with MS Mail

B. A Windows NT user account named FreeB

C. IMPORT.EXE running on the designated MS Mail postoffice

D. Both A and C

5. When connecting Exchange and MS Mail environments, one Exchange server must be designated the dirsync server.

A. True

B. False

6. The Connector for Lotus cc:Mail is installed using Exchange Server Setup.

A. True

B. False

7. Schedule+ free/busy information exchanged between Exchange and MS Mail users is stored in the following:

A. A specially designated public folder

B. A specially designated mailbox

C. A specially designated DL

D. The Exchange Directory

8. The MS Mail directory synchronization parameter used by a dirsync server to recompile the Global Address List is:

A. T1

B. T2

C. Newsfeed push

D. T3

9. Directory synchronization between Exchange and MS Mail requires NO configuration on the MS Mail dirsync server.

A. True

B. False

10. If an Exchange object has a higher trust level than the Exchange dirsync requestor is configured for, that object will not be synchronized with the MS Mail dirsync server.

A. True

B. False

CHAPTER

16

Migrating to Exchange

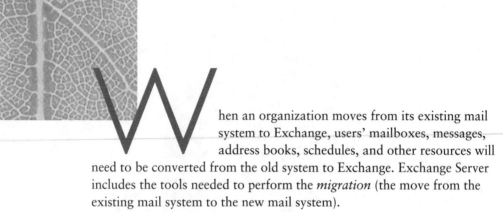

When an organization moves from its existing mail system to Exchange, users' mailboxes, messages, address books, schedules, and other resources will need to be converted from the old system to Exchange. Exchange Server includes the tools needed to perform the *migration* (the move from the existing mail system to the new mail system).

This chapter will discuss the following topics:

- Migration strategies

- Migration tools

- Special migration issues

- Troubleshooting a migration

Migration Strategies

Although there are many different strategies that can be used to perform a migration, we will cover the primary two:

- Single-phase migration

- Multiphase migration

Single-Phase Migration

A single-phase migration moves all the user accounts and data to Exchange at once (see Figure 16.1). This strategy is the most appropriate under the following conditions:

- User accounts and mailboxes are the primary items to be migrated. Not much, if any, data needs to be migrated.

- All the necessary hardware and software is in place to accommodate the additions, including the necessary Exchange client software.

- The necessary personnel is available to complete the entire migration.

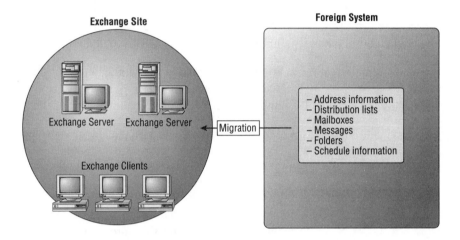

FIGURE 16.1

Single-phase migration

Multiphase Migration

A multiphase migration moves groups of user accounts and data to Exchange in different stages, over a period of time. This strategy is the most appropriate under the following conditions:

- Not all groups or departments can migrate at the same time.

- All the hardware or software requirements for the migration are not in place.

- There is not enough personnel to implement a single-phase migration within the acceptable downtime constraints.

Migration Tools

Three main tools are used to perform a migration:

- **Source extractors**   These programs can copy information from an existing mail system and place it in a format that can be migrated to Exchange at a later time.

- **Migration Wizard**   The Migration Wizard imports information into an Exchange environment. (It includes source extractors for Microsoft Mail and Lotus cc:Mail.)

- **Directory Import and Export**   These two commands can be accessed in Exchange Administrator to make bulk changes to Exchange recipients.

Source Extractors

A source extractor program can copy information out of an existing non-Exchange system and place that information in a format that can be imported into Exchange. The type of information that can be extracted from another mail system includes:

- Address information

- Distribution lists

- Mailboxes

- Messages

- Folders

- Schedule information

Exchange Server comes with source extractors for the following mail systems:

- Microsoft Mail for PC Networks, v3.*x*

- Microsoft Mail for AppleTalk Networks, v3.*x*

- Lotus cc:Mail (database version 6)

- DEC All-In-One, versions 2.3 and later

- IBM PROFS and OfficeVision

- Verimation MEMO MVS, version 3.2.1 and later

- Novell GroupWise

- Collabra Share

You will need to have administrator privileges on the foreign mail system that you will be extracting information from.

You can also create you own source extractor program. The Exchange SDK contains information on this process.

Extracted information is placed in a specific format in specific files. The Migration Wizard uses these files to import the information into the Exchange environment. The following three types of files are created by source extractors:

- **Primary files (*.PRI)**   These files contain the names of mailboxes or custom recipients, personal address book entries, and the message headers of messages being extracted.

- **Secondary files (*.SEC)**   These files contain the message bodies (content), message attachments, and scheduling data.

- **Packing list file (*.PKL)**   This file contains the filenames and other information pertaining to the information in the primary and secondary files.

Because the Migration Wizard uses all three file types, they are collectively referred to as the migration files.

Migration Wizard

The Migration Wizard can import information (such as addresses, mailboxes, messages, folders, and schedules) into an Exchange environment. It can also create Window NT accounts for the users being migrated.

The Migration Wizard is executed from the Microsoft Exchange program group. It can import information from five sources:

- Source extraction files

- Microsoft Mail postoffices

- Lotus cc:Mail post offices (database version 6)

- Novell GroupWise post offices

- Collabra Share forums

The rest of this chapter discusses using the Migration Wizard to migrate a Microsoft Mail (MS Mail) system.

One of your first options will be whether to perform a one-step migration or a two-step migration. The one-step migration extracts information from an MS Mail postoffice and imports it into Exchange. Extraction and importation are performed in one step (at least from the standpoint of the administrator). In the first step of a two-step migration, the Migration Wizard extracts user information from the MS Mail postoffice. This information is placed in a User List file. The administrator can modify the information in this file before the second step of the migration is executed. For example, the user names to be migrated can be modified to conform to the Exchange system's naming standard. In the second step of a two-step migration, the Migration Wizard imports the MS Mail data, using the User List file collected in the first step (which may have been modified by the administrator).

When you begin importing, the Migration Wizard will present a series of options. These options are listed and explained here:

- **Selecting mailboxes to import**   An administrator can select the mailboxes to be imported during the migration. It is not necessary to migrate all the mailboxes of an existing system.

- **Creating mailboxes**   An administrator can create new Exchange mailboxes for each foreign mailbox being migrated or use existing Exchange mailboxes. The default is to create a new mailbox. Some of the additional options pertaining to new mailbox creation are:

  - **Recipient container**   The administrator can choose the recipient container in which to create the new mailboxes.

  - **Templates**   The administrator can choose a mailbox template to use as the pattern for the new mailboxes. This allows an administrator to preconfigure each new mailbox with specific properties, like company name, mailbox storage restrictions, or other properties.

  - **Passwords**   When the Migration Wizard is used to create Windows NT accounts, it can generate random passwords or use the alias name of the corresponding mailbox as the password.

- **Messages and folders** Messages and folders can be migrated. All messages or only messages within a specified date range can be migrated.

- **Shared folders** All shared folders can be migrated to the public folder container of the Exchange site.

- **Personal Address Books (PABs)** The entries in users' Personal Address Books can be imported to Exchange mailboxes.

- **Calendar files** Users' calendar files in the CAL directory on the postoffice can be imported to Exchange mailboxes.

Directory Import and Export

Once recipient objects have been migrated to Exchange, they can still be modified. Obviously, each recipient object can be individually modified by changing its properties. But if a large number of mailboxes need to be changed, changing them individually may be too labor intensive. A better way is to use the Directory Import and Export commands in Exchange Administrator (Tools menu). Directory Export can be used to copy the properties of a large number of Exchange recipients to a text file. This file can be imported into a word processor or spreadsheet program in order to edit its content. For example, a search-and-replace tool can be used to change one particular property of all mailboxes. Directory Import can then be used to import this file back into the Exchange Directory. These two utilities permit an administrator to perform bulk administration.

Special Migration Issues

Any undertaking as potentially complicated as a migration can involve special situations. Three special situations you may encounter are:

- Maintaining external addresses

- Migrating distribution lists

- Replying to migrated mail

Maintaining External Addresses

Migrated users may need to retain their old e-mail addresses. Those addresses can be easily associated with the migrated users' new Exchange mailboxes.

As you learned in Chapter 5, Exchange messages are addressed using names (the display name from the user's perspective, the DN from the system's perspective). However, an Exchange recipient may need to receive mail from a non-Exchange system; therefore, various e-mail addresses are automatically generated for each Exchange recipient. These addresses are also referred to as *proxy addresses*. Proxy addresses for MS Mail, Lotus cc:Mail, SMTP, and X.400 are created automatically for Exchange recipients.

If a migrated user needs to retain his or her old e-mail address, a current proxy address can be modified or a new one created. This can be done through the E-mail Addresses property page of an Exchange recipient. A recipient can even have two different addresses for the same address type. For example, suppose Bob Smith's new SMTP address is `BobS@Chicago.Widget.COM` and his previous SMTP address (before the migration) was `bobsmith@widget.com`. Other SMTP users will probably use his old address, and Bob will not receive his messages. The administrator can easily create a secondary SMTP address of `bobsmith@widget.com` so Bob will get all his mail.

Migrating Distribution Lists

During a multiphase migration, both mail systems will be operational and existing resources will be gradually migrated. This can create various problems. A DL can be migrated to Exchange and remain operational on the existing system. If different changes are made to the two copies of that DL, problems can arise. For example, Exchange recipients might be added to a DL after it has migrated to Exchange. Those recipients might not be added to the corresponding DL on the old system. At a later stage of the migration process, the older copy of that DL (still in use on the foreign system) might be migrated again and overwrite the existing one in the Exchange system. There are five basic methods for managing this situation:

- **Do not migrate the DL until the last phase**   You could decide not to migrate a particular DL until the last stage of a multiphase migration. But since mailboxes will be migrating over to Exchange during the different phases, constant modifications could be required for that DL.

- **Keep duplicate DLs on both systems**   You could have the same DL on both systems. This method would require coordinated changes between both copies of the DL.

- **Convert the DL to a public folder**   An MS Mail DL could be converted to an Exchange public folder. Users would then go to the public folder to view mail sent to the former DL.

- **Maintain the DL only on the Exchange system**   Because there would be only one copy of the DL, there is no problem with coordinating changes. But this method creates more traffic between the two systems. Whenever an existing user sends a message to the DL, the message is sent to the DL recipient in the Exchange system. An MTA then sends messages to the members of that DL, which could include recipients back in the existing system. (Remember, this is a multiphase migration. Both systems will be concurrent for a time.) In this situation, messages could be sent back to the network they originated in, thereby creating additional traffic.

- **Disable the DL on the existing system**   You could notify existing users that a particular DL is not going to be operational until after migration.

Synchronizing DLs in multiphase migration can be difficult. Be sure to plan for contingencies.

Replying to Migrated Messages

When a user replies to a message, the address book provider tries to resolve the address by referencing the Global Address List (GAL) or the user's Personal Address Book.

But when a user whose mailbox and messages have migrated, replies to a migrated message, a special situation can arise. If the sender of the original message (i.e., the message being replied to) has not had his or her mailbox migrated or has migrated with a different name, the user who is replying will have to select the custom recipient, the new mailbox, or in some cases provide a one-off address to the sender.

It is most convenient if custom recipient objects are defined on the Exchange system for recipients who have not had their mailboxes migrated yet. The directory synchronization agent (DXA) can be used to automate custom recipient creation (see Chapter 15).

Troubleshooting a Migration

A migration, like any operation, can run into problems. The Windows NT Event Log, and the Migration Wizard error summary can be used to troubleshoot.

If problems occur during a migration, some of the probable causes are:

- The account used to perform the migration does not have administrator privileges in the existing system.

- The account used to perform the migration does not have administrator privileges on the Exchange server.

- The .PKL, .PRI, or .SEC files were edited improperly.

- The .PKL or .PRI files are missing.

- The .PKL or .PRI files are renamed.

- Network problems occurred during the migration.

- The Private Information Store ran out of space during the migration.

After using the Windows NT Event Log or the Migration Wizard error log to identify the cause of the problem, the administrator can resolve the problem by assigning the necessary permissions, editing the appropriate files, or making more disk space available.

Summary

A migration allows an existing non-Exchange mail system to be moved to an Exchange environment. Resources on the existing system (such as addresses, mailboxes, messages, folders, and schedule information) can all be imported into Exchange.

Special programs, called source extractors, prepare the resources on the existing system for inclusion in Exchange. Source extractors exist for many systems including: MS Mail, Lotus cc:Mail, and Novell GroupWise.

The Migration Wizard program imports the resources of an existing system into Exchange. The Migration Wizard can take information collected by a source extractor, or it can extract and import directly from an MS Mail, Lotus cc:Mail, Novell GroupWise, or Collabra Share system.

Review Questions

1. Which of the following cannot be migrated into Exchange?

   A. Personal Address Book

   B. Schedule information

   C. Messages

   D. Mail gateways

2. Migrations must be performed in one step.

   A. True

   B. False

3. Migrations must include every mailbox on the existing system.

   A. True

   B. False

4. Passwords can be generated for users whose resources are being migrated.

   A. True

   B. False

5. Which property of an Exchange recipient can be used to allow a user to retain his or her pre-migration foreign addresses?

   A. E-mail addresses (also called proxy addresses)

   B. Protocol property

   C. Custom attribute property

   D. Advanced properties

6. Which of the following can be used to modify a large number of Exchange recipients in a bulk manner?

   A. Performance Monitor

   B. User Manager for Domains

   C. Directory Import and Export

   D. Event Viewer

CHAPTER

17

Planning an Exchange Environment

areful planning leads to efficient and effective installation, configuration, and use of an Exchange system. Although Exchange is a highly powerful messaging tool, lack of planning can prevent its full potential from being unleashed. Someone once said that an ox cart is just as useful as a rocket, if you don't know where you are going.

This chapter is not a comprehensive "how-to" on Exchange planning. However, it will help prepare you for the Exchange exam by introducing you to planning issues. It will also help you plan real-world systems. We will discuss planning sites, servers, site connections, connections to non-Exchange systems, and migrations.

Planning the Exchange Topology

The first (and possibly most important) goal when planning your Exchange environment is to design the basic topology of your Exchange organization.

Planning the Exchange topology does not necessarily entail planning the specific properties of objects. Topology planning is mainly concerned with what objects (sites, number of servers, number and type of connectors, etc.) are needed, not how they will be configured. This planning stage focuses on the major organizational units of the Exchange organization. Once it has been determined what and where something is needed (e.g., a public folder for sales leads is needed on Server 1), the specific properties of that object can be planned later. The "big strokes" must be made before the "small strokes."

Three important questions to be addressed are:

- How many sites are needed?

- If you need more than one site, how will you connect them?

- Do you need to connect to non-Exchange systems?

But before answering these, you will need to collect some preliminary information.

What Preliminary Information Must Be Collected?

You need to collect a lot of information before you can begin to make planning decisions. You need information about your network, user needs, Windows NT servers, and non-Exchange mail systems.

Network Topology of Your Organization

A network topology is defined by the number, location, type, available bandwidth, and transport protocols of an organization's networks. Here is a list of some of the characteristics of a network topology:

- **Number of networks**   Networks are usually considered to be separated by a bridge or *router*. Each side of a bridge or router constitutes a network. Sometimes a specific physical network is also called a *network segment*.

- **Type and speed of network**   Ethernet/10 Mbps and Token Ring/4 and 16 Mbps are the most common. ARCnet/2.5 Mbps and ATM/155 Mbps are sometimes used.

- **Available bandwidth**   Use network traffic monitoring utilities in Microsoft Systems Management Server (SMS) or another packet sniffer program to determine the available bandwidth in a network. (A sniffer program is used to monitor activity on a network.)

- **Transport protocols**   For example, TCP/IP, NWLink, NetBEUI, etc.

Windows NT Domain Topology

A Windows NT domain is a group of computers that share the same user account database and security policies. You will need to have quite a bit of information about the domains, including the configuration of any trust relationships between domains, to properly plan your Exchange system.

User Needs

Many factors determine what Exchange resources will be available to users, and where those resources will be placed. You will need a lot of information about the users to efficiently and effectively make these decisions. Some of this information will already be collected in the network inventory. Some information may come from the current messaging system. Other information will need to come from estimates made by the users themselves or from managerial edicts. Here is a list of some of the major pieces of user information you will need to have:

- The network location of each user's computer, also referred to as the *network segment*. (This will be used to estimate performance.)

- The hardware resources of each computer. (Helps determine which Exchange client applications can be used and which computers need to be upgraded.)

- The operating system running on each computer. (Helps determine which Exchange client applications can be used and which computers need to be upgraded.)

- Whether or not each user has a Windows NT domain account. (A factor in determining site location.)

- The messaging services required (for both client and server configurations). Examples include:

  - Exchange Server

  - Microsoft Mail

  - Internet mail

  - Microsoft Fax

- The messaging configuration required (for both client and server configurations). Examples include:

  - Remote access

  - Read message options

  - Send message options

  - New message notification method

  - Advanced security

- The number of messages that will go through the system. (This is a factor in estimating system load.) Microsoft has defined three basic, message volume user profiles (see Table 17.1).

- The message storage requirements. (This will determine the server storage requirements and the number of servers needed.) Users' folders can be stored in either the Private Information Store (which is always located on an Exchange server) or in a personal folder store (which can be located on a user's local computer).

- Public folder planning. The following are some of the important issues involved in public folder planning:

  - Which public folders will be needed initially?

  - What is the estimated size of each public folder? This will help determine storage requirements.

  - Which users will need access to which public folders? This will help you decide on which servers to place specific public folders. For example, if a large number of users located on a single network need access to a particular public folder, you should create the public folder on a server on that network.

  - Based on storage requirements and an analysis of user access, which public folders will be created on which servers?

  - Will public folders need to be replicated across servers? If yes, which servers? Reasons for having multiple replicas of a public folder include load balancing, quicker user access across site boundaries, and fault tolerance.

  - If replication will be used, what replication schedule will be used?

  - Which users will be given permission to create top-level public folders?

  - Will there be individual configurations on specific public folders? Configuration options include user permissions, views, rules, forms, and size restrictions.

- The electronic forms that will be needed.

- The type of remote connections that will be needed to access mailboxes and public folders. You will need to know the number of users who will be remotely accessing Exchange resources, what type of connections they will be using, approximately when they will make those connections, and approximately how long they will need to be connected.

	Parameter	Light User	Medium User	Heavy User
T A B L E 17.1 Message volume user profiles	Maximum inbox size (in messages)	20	125	250
	Old mail processing (per day)	5x	15x	20x
	Total sends per day (average)	7	20	39
	Total received per day (average)	20	56	119

Current Windows NT Servers

You need to have information about the current Windows NT servers, such as their hardware configurations, disk space, and RAM. Once you have determined the requirements for the number and configurations of servers, you can evaluate the current servers to see if you can use any of them or if you will need to install new servers.

Non-Exchange Mail Systems

You need to know if there are any non-Exchange mail systems (Microsoft Mail, Lotus cc:Mail, etc.) in an organization, and if they are to coexist with Exchange or be migrated to Exchange.

How Many Sites Are Needed?

Many small organizations will use a single Exchange site. Large and geographically dispersed organizations may require several sites. However, there are large, geographically dispersed organizations that use a single site. In this section, we will discuss requirements and other factors that help determine a site design.

Using all of the necessary factors, you can determine the number and location of the Exchange sites. If multiple sites will be used, you will also need to plan your intersite connections.

RPC Communication

A site's underlying network must permit RPC communication between clients and servers, and between all the servers in a site. To support RPC, a network must have permanent high-speed connections. The definition of high speed is somewhat arbitrary. Most designers do not recommend a bandwidth less than 128Kbps. Less than that would support only light traffic and would perform poorly. The recommended network speeds for a site are LAN speeds (such as ARCnet at 2.5Mbps, Token Ring at 4Mbps or 16Mbps, or Ethernet at 10Mbps). WAN connections over a T1 line at 1.5Mbps could also support a site, depending on load and other factors. (A T1 line is a leased network connection that provides fairly high bandwidth.)

An organization with six Ethernet networks connected by high-speed routers can support a single site. If this group of six networks also has a temporary low-bandwidth connection of 56Kbps to an additional remote network, two sites are required because the 56Kbps connection will not support RPC communication.

Factors other than RPC communication, like desired messaging performance, can dictate multiple sites. These factors will be discussed shortly.

Transport Protocols

Exchange supports TCP/IP, IPX/SPX, NetBEUI, and Banyan Vines. If a particular network does not support one of the supported Exchange transport protocols, it can not be part of a site.

Windows NT Domains

All of the Exchange servers in a site must use the same site service account for intrasite component communication. A single Exchange site can include more than one Windows NT domain, but all of the domains must be related by trust relationships. The Windows NT domains and the physical networks that make up a site determine the *site boundaries*.

Performance Requirements

You can estimate the performance difference for a single versus a multiple site topology by projecting estimated system loads of both topologies. Even if a network topology can support a single site, the estimated performance level might not meet the requirements.

Connecting Sites

The primary factor when choosing a site connector is the type of network infrastructure between the sites. If that infrastructure can support high-speed connections, the Site Connector is the obvious choice. Another message system can be used as a bridge between sites when there is no high-speed connection. SMTP and X.400 message systems can connect sites when the Internet Mail Service and X.400 Connector are used.

More than one connector can be used between sites in order to increase fault tolerance or balance loads. Each connector will have a cost associated with it so that the MTA's cost-based routing can function.

Connecting to Non-Exchange Systems

If an Exchange implementation will contain connections to non-Exchange systems, the sites that will make those connections can be designed at this stage. This will help determine site requirements, such as how many Exchange servers will be needed in a site, and their configuration.

Organizations should use standardized naming conventions. For example, mailbox names could be "first name last name" or "last name, first name." A general naming convention can be based on geography, company structure, building or floor numbers, etc. A good naming convention makes it easy to identify and add sites, servers, connectors, mailboxes, etc.

During the planning stage, you can also determine many fault tolerance and maintenance procedures. For example, backup routines, server and link monitors, and diagnostic logging can all be standardized.

Figure 17.1 illustrates some of the decisions that are made after the Exchange topology has been determined.

Planning Sites

After the number of sites and their locations have been determined, you can plan site-level messaging parameters that will be inherited by all of the servers in each site. Some of the site-wide parameters that you need to consider are listed in Table 17. 2.

FIGURE 17.1

Decisions made after
determining the Exchange
topology

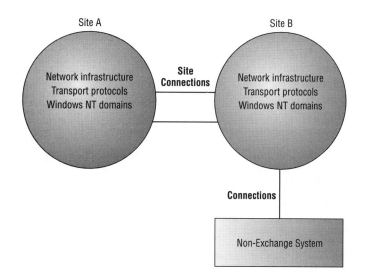

TABLE 17.2 Planning site-level configurations	**Site-Level Object**	**Parameters**
	DS site configuration	■ The Tombstone lifetime (length of time information on deleted directory objects is preserved to notify other servers). The default is 30 days. ■ The Garbage collection interval (interval between the times expired tombstones are deleted). The default is 12 hours. ■ The Offline address book configuration. ■ Custom attributes.
	IS site configuration	■ If message tracking is enabled or disabled for the IS. The default is disabled. ■ Top-level folder creation permissions. ■ Storage warnings schedule. ■ Public folder affinities.
	MTA site configuration	■ If message tracking is enabled or disabled for the MTA. The default is disabled. ■ Messaging defaults (including RTS values, connection retry values, association parameters, and transfer timeouts).

TABLE 17.2 (cont.) Planning site-level configurations	**Site-Level Object**	**Parameters**
	Site addressing	■ E-mail addresses. ■ Routing calculation schedule.
	Encryption	■ Advanced security use. ■ Preferred encryption algorithm. ■ Key Management Server administration.
	Monitors	■ Server Monitors. ■ Link Monitors.
	Protocols	■ Which protocols will be enabled. ■ How protocols will be configured.

Connections and directory replication will be covered in the "Planning Site Connections" section.

Figure 17.2 provides an illustration of the main topics in site planning.

FIGURE 17.2

Site planning main topics

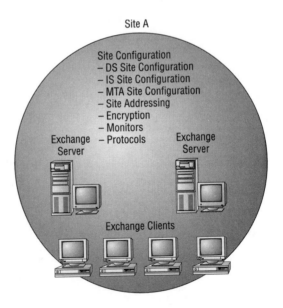

Planning Servers

You need to consider many important issues when you plan servers, including:

- Number and location of servers

- Server-level configurations

- Recipient configurations

- Exchange Server installation and configuration

- Exchange client installation and configuration

Number and Locations of Servers

The number of Exchange servers in a site will depend on factors such as the number and locations of mailboxes, and performance and storage requirements. We will discuss each of these factors in the following text.

Number and Locations of Mailboxes

Determining the number of mailboxes and locating them on specific servers involves many factors. Some of these factors are:

- **Local delivery is a priority**   If the users who will frequently send information to each other are grouped together on the same server, message delivery will remain local to the server.

- **Local network traffic is a priority**   If all the users of a particular network segment are located on servers on that network segment, message transmission will be improved because messages will not have to travel over multiple network segments. (Be careful not to overemphasize this requirement and cause the physical network to be saturated.)

- **Fault tolerance increased through multiple points of failure**   If recipients are spread out between multiple servers, there will not be a single point of failure. (Don't put all your eggs in one basket.)

- **Fault tolerance increased by protecting a single point**   By placing your most important recipients on a single server, that server can utilize high-end fault tolerant features to protect those resources. (Put all your eggs in one basket, but guard that basket!)

Performance and Storage Requirements

In addition to the minimum hardware requirements for an Exchange Server installation (see Chapter 4), additional resources will probably be needed to accommodate the desired performance level, and mailbox and public folder storage needs.

Some of the factors that relate to server performance are:

1. Number of disks

2. Disk speed

3. Amount of memory

4. Processor speed and number of processors

5. Performance of network cards

Storage requirements can become unreasonable (users will try to save everything forever). The following policies can help control this problem:

- Set mailbox storage limits

- Set public folder storage limits

- Set age limits for items in public folders

- Set maximum message sizes

Server-Level Configurations

You need to examine many objects and properties when you plan server-level configurations. Table 17.3 lists some of the things you need to consider.

TABLE 17.3 Planning server-level configurations	**Server-Level Object**	**Parameters**
	Private Information Store	■ Storage limits. ■ The server used to store public folders.
	Public Information Store	■ Storage limits that cause a warning message to be sent to mailbox owners. ■ Storage limits that prevent mailbox owners from sending mail. ■ The server used to store public folders.

	Server-Level Object	Parameters
T A B L E 17.3 *(cont.)* Planning server-level configurations	Message Transfer Agent	■ Message size limits. ■ Distribution list expansion. ■ Conversion of incoming messages to MS Exchange content.
	System Attendant	■ Message tracking log file maintenance.

Recipient Configurations

When you planned the site servers, you decided which servers would house which recipients. Now we will discuss the configuration of the recipients.

The planning phase is a good time to decide which templates to use to create mailboxes, distribution lists, and custom recipients. Templates will make it easier to create and standardize these recipients later in the implementation phase. Some of the properties that can be specified in a template are listed in the following sections. You can also begin to plan the configurations of public folders.

Mailbox

The following are some of the critical properties of a mailbox. These should be carefully considered any time a new mailbox is created.

- Home server

- Hide from address book

- Message size limits

- Information store storage limits

- Distribution list membership

- Delivery restrictions

- Delivery options

- Advanced security

- Protocols

Distribution Lists

The following are some of the critical properties of a distribution list. These should be carefully considered any time a new DL is created.

- Members

- Delivery restrictions

- Message size limits

- Hide from address book

- Hide membership from address book

Custom Recipients

The properties of a custom recipient are basically the same as a mailbox, with the addition of the target (non-Exchange) e-mail address. Planning a custom recipient template entails determining the common properties for a group of foreign users. The target address of each custom recipient will be unique, so this field will not be part of the template.

Public Folders

When you designed the Exchange topology, you determined general information about groupware applications. At this planning stage, you need to design the intrasite. Some of the properties you need to determine are:

- Intrasite replica locations

- Replication schedules

- Age limits

- Storage limits

Whether or not particular public folders will be replicated to other sites can be determined now or when you design the intersite configurations. We will do it later.

Exchange Server Installation and Configuration

Now that you have determined the number, network location, and configuration of the Exchange servers, you need to purchase the necessary copies and licenses for the Exchange Server product and schedule the installation of each server.

Exchange Server Maintenance

The Private Information Store and the Public Information Store are two important areas of an Exchange environment that need to be carefully maintained. Storage being used and public folder replication must be monitored to ensure an efficient and effective Exchange environment.

The Private Information Store permits an administrator to examine the storage levels of individual mailboxes. The Public Information Store permits the examination of individual public folder storage levels, folder replication status, and server replication status.

Server Backup Plan

Consider the following when creating an Exchange server backup:

- How frequently will backups be performed?

- What type of backup will be performed? Options include full, incremental, and differential.

- What time of day should backups be performed? A backup performed over the network can adversely affect network performance and necessitate performing the backup during off-hours.

- What device, or devices, will be used for backups?

- How will offsite storage of backup media be handled?

Exchange Client Installation and Configuration

Earlier you collected an inventory of the user operating systems and computer hardware profiles. Now you can use that information to determine which Exchange client applications will be installed on which client computers.

You also collected messaging service requirements and common configuration requirements. Use that information to create default settings for the client setup program. The EXCHNG.STF and DEFAULT.PRF files holding the default settings are created by the Setup Editor program, and placed in a shared area. Users can run the client setup program from that share point and utilize the default settings.

Planning Site Connections

You have already determined the number of sites, their locations, and which connectors to use between the sites. Now you need to determine the properties of those connectors, the properties of the Directory Replication connectors, and the configuration of public folder replication to other sites. These topics are covered in the following sections.

Connector Properties

Some of the common connector properties that need to be planned include:

- Address space

- Connector costs

- Remote sites with which to connect

- Remote servers with which to connect

If you will be using the Site Connector, you need to plan the following properties:

- Messaging bridgehead server

- Target servers

- Target server costs

If you will be using the X.400 Connector or the Dynamic RAS Connector, you need to plan these properties:

- Connection schedules

- Delivery restrictions

If you will be using the Internet Mail Service, the following decisions need to be made:

- Which Exchange server will run the IMS?

- What type of connection will be used to connect to the Internet or other SMTP hosts?

- How will mail be sent? Your options include forwarding all messages to a single SMTP host or using DNS to resolve addresses and send messages to the recipients' hosts.

- What will be the site address used to generate SMTP e-mail addresses for Exchange users?

- Which recipient will receive IMS notifications?

Directory Replication Connector

Once you have designed your messaging connectors, your Directory Replication connectors can be planned. You need to determine the identity of the directory replication bridgehead servers (both local and remote), which sites to connect, and the replication schedule.

Public Folder Replication between Sites

If you decided that your Exchange topology will include public folder replicas in other sites, you must make plans for replication. Some of the properties that you need to plan to perform replication are the servers that will contain a replica, the schedule for folder replication, and the age limits of replicas.

Planning Connections to Non-Exchange Systems

In this section, we will plan a connection to a Microsoft Mail system. The two primary areas we will discuss are the Microsoft Mail Connector and the Directory Synchronization component.

Microsoft Mail Connector

To provide interoperability between an Exchange system and a Microsoft Mail system, the Microsoft Mail Connector is utilized. You must determine the following properties on this connector:

- Address space
- Interchange properties

- Local postoffice

- Connections

- Connector MTAs

Directory Synchronization Component

Your major decision for directory synchronization is determining which Exchange server will be involved in this process, and what role that server will play: Dirsync Server or Requestor.

If you decide to make your Exchange server a Dirsync Server, the names of the remote dirsync requestors must be collected, and a schedule for synchronization can be defined. If you decide to make the Exchange server a Dirsync Requestor, the name of the remote dirsync server must be known.

Directory synchronization must be coordinated with the administrator of the Microsoft Mail system.

Schedule+ Free/Busy Connector

If Exchange users of Schedule+ 7.5 and Outlook want to share schedule and calendar information with MS Mail users of Schedule+ 1.0, the following components need to be included in the Exchange design plan:

- MS Mail Connector

- Directory synchronization between Exchange and MS Mail

- Schedule+ Free/Busy Connector

Although the previous scenario permits interoperability between the Exchange applications and MS Mail applications, some advanced features of Outlook are not available to Schedule+ 1.0 and 7.5 users. For example, Outlook nontabular views of calendar information are not available in Schedule+ 1.0 or 7.5. Some of the alternatives that can be used in this situation are:

- Manage a mixed environment. Because these applications can exchange information, a mixed environment can be used. Users simply need to understand that certain features of Outlook will not work for Schedule+ users.

- Configure Outlook to use the Schedule+ option for group scheduling.

- Migrate all clients to Outlook. Make sure users do not delete their Schedule+ files (.SCD and .CAL) because Outlook has an Import/Export Wizard that can import Schedule+ data.

Planning Long-Term Administration

You need to plan for more than just the installation and configuration of the Exchange environment. You also need to plan for the long-term care of the system. Some of the issues that you will need to address include:

- How many administrators will be needed? This will depend on the number of servers, sites, connectors, and recipients.

- Will remote administration be needed? If so, which sites and which remote computers will need to be configured? The relevant sites will need a RAS server, and the relevant remote computers will need the RAS client software installed and configured, as well as a local copy of the Exchange Administrator program. User Manager for Domains and Server Manager are two additional programs that can also be installed on the remote computers if they are running Windows NT Workstation.

- Will there be specific administrators for particular Exchange functions or objects? (For example, in a large environment there might be an administrator for recipients and another administrator for connections to other sites and foreign systems.)

- Who will be the Exchange administrators? If they are not already trained, arrangements will need to made to train them.

Planning a Disaster Recovery Strategy

Planning a disaster recovery strategy can involve a large number of considerations. Some of the major ones are listed here:

- What is your organization's definition of a disaster? A mere inconvenience (such as a connector being offline) at one organization can be a major catastrophe at another organization. An organization can define different degrees of disasters with different levels of response.

- What is your organization's definition of acceptable downtime for a particular disaster?

- What is the escalation process and who is to be notified and mobilized in the event of a disaster? How will they be notified (telephone, pager, e-mail, etc.)?

- What are the recovery steps for the defined disasters? These procedures should be written down and tested.

- Is there an inventory of the necessary resources for a recovery process? Resources include hardware (e.g., hard drive) and software (the Exchange Server CD).

Planning Migrations

Many organizations have existing messaging systems that are to be replaced by Exchange. Those existing systems already contain message data and address information that may need to be moved to the Exchange system. You need to determine if that is possible, and if so, how to perform the migration.

The following are some of the main steps for planning a migration:

1. Create a map and inventory of the current messaging systems. You need to know:

   - What systems are connected (so you will know what migrations are possible).

   - What resources are located in each system (so you will know what resources need to be migrated).

   - Which users are using which messaging client applications (so you will know which users need upgrades to their applications and which may need additional hardware).

2. A period of coexistence of the old messaging system and Exchange may be the best way to ease the pain of a migration. This period can be used to perform a phased migration where subsets of the users are migrated during each phase.

3. Design and plan user education. Users must be prepared for the migration and life with the new system.

4. Design and plan client software installation and upgrades.

5. Determine mailbox naming conventions. Decide what naming convention to use for the mailboxes being migrated.

6. Decide what resources will be migrated, such as mailboxes, distribution lists, personal address books, and schedule information.

7. Decide on the migration method, the single-phase or multiphase method.

8. Plan for contingencies. You need to have a fall-back plan if things do not go as planned.

Summary

The planning process is critical to implementing a successful, optimized Exchange organization topology. To plan properly, you will need to determine the number and location of Windows NT domains, and whether the organization will be connected to any non-Exchange systems.

You need to plan intrasite configurations (DS, IS, and MTA) and individual server configurations.

If multiple connected sites will be part of the Exchange organization, you will need to plan the number, types, and properties of the connectors.

Connecting an Exchange system to a non-Exchange system involves coordinated planning by personnel from both systems. When connecting to a Microsoft Mail system, for example, you will need to consider the properties of both the Microsoft Mail Connector and the Directory Synchronization component.

Planning is important when an existing non-Exchange system migrates its message data and address information to Exchange. Issues include what resources will be migrated and what type of migration method to be used. You also need to have a contingency plan in case the migration does not work.

Review Questions

1. The network infrastructure is very important factor in planning sites and site boundaries.

   A. True

   B. False

2. The hardware requirements of an Exchange server are affected by which of the following:

   A. Number of mailboxes

   B. Public folder storage

   C. Message traffic

   D. All of the above

3. Grouping common recipient configurations is NOT part of Exchange planning.

   A. True

   B. False

4. Advanced security planning pertains to what object or objects?

   A. Mailboxes

   B. Connectors

   C. Sites

   D. Both A and C

5. Which of the following properties should be considered when planning a connector?

   A. Storage limits

   B. Scheduled connections

C. Tombstones

D. Both B and C

6. Which of the following is an important planning issue when interoperating with a non-Exchange system?

A. POP3 configuration

B. Mailbox cleanup

C. Home server of the administrator

D. Directory synchronization

7. Which of the following is NOT considered when planning a migration?

A. Assigning foreign users administrative rights

B. What resources will be migrated

C. Choosing a migration method (single-phase or multiphase)

D. Installing or upgrading client software

APPENDIX

A

Review Answers

Chapter 1

1. The type of utility that would allow you to replace a foreign message system with Exchange is:

    A. Administrative tool

    B. Security utility

    C. X.500

    D. Migration tool

    Answer: D

2. This type of mail system has a passive server:

    A. Shared-file mail system

    B. Client/server mail system

    C. Host-based mail system

    D. Exchange Server

    Answer: A

3. Which of the following is NOT a feature of a client/server messaging system:

    A. Distributed processing

    B. Tight security

    C. Passive client application

    D. Reduced network traffic

    Answer: C

4. Microsoft Outlook is a desktop information manager application that runs on the following operating system:

    A. Windows 3.*x*

    B. Windows for Workgroups

C. Windows NT

D. 32-bit UNIX

Answer: C

5. The following types of components can be used to connect Exchange to a foreign messaging system:

A. Gateway

B. Connector

C. Directory Synchronization

D. Key Management

Answer: A, B

6. The universal inbox is part of this software:

A. Exchange Client

B. SMTP clients

C. POP3 clients

D. LDAP clients

Answer: A

7. The following is an e-mail protocol:

A. LDAP

B. PNP

C. PPP

D. POP3

Answer: D

8. Which of the following could NOT be used as an Exchange e-mail client?

   A. Word processing program

   B. Web browser

   C. Internet e-mail program

   D. Microsoft Outlook

   Answer: A

9. Which Exchange Client feature enables e-mail content to include multiple format types, such as fonts, sizes, and colors?

   A. WordPerfect

   B. This software cannot do this

   C. Richman message content

   D. Rich-text message content

   Answer: D

10. This Microsoft technology enables the Exchange Client to create compound documents using drag-and-drop:

    A. OLE

    B. OOP

    C. DLL

    D. SNADS

    Answer: A

11. Recalling a sent, but unopened, message is a feature of what program or programs?

    A. Outlook

    B. Exchange Client

C. Public folders

D. Forms

Answer: A

12. Which of the following relate to the performance of Exchange?

A. Load Simulator

B. 32-bit program

C. Multithreaded

D. Auditing

Answer: A, B, C

13. Since Exchange is scalable, it cannot be used in small to medium environments.

A. True

B. False

Answer: B

14. Exchange could use the Internet as part of its WAN design.

A. True

B. False

Answer: A

15. The following feature enables a Exchange client to create rules for processing incoming mail:

A. Search tool

B. Customized views

C. Universal inbox

D. AutoAssistants

Answer: D

16. What is the name of the mechanism when two Exchange components on the same machine pass instructions and data?

   A. Remote procedure call

   B. Remote instruction call

   C. Local instruction call

   D. Local procedure call

   Answer: D

17. What is the name of the mechanism when a client-read instruction is sent to an Exchange server for execution?

   A. Local procedure call

   B. Local instruction call

   C. Remote instruction call

   D. Remote procedure call

   Answer: D

Chapter 2

1. The following is NOT a core component of Exchange:

   A. Internet Mail Service

   B. System Attendant

   C. Message Transfer Agent

   D. Information Store

   Answer: A

2. The Information Store is made up of these two databases:

   A. SQL and ODBC

   B. Message tracking log

C. Private and public information store

D. MTA and SA databases

Answer: C

3. This component generates new e-mail addresses:

A. Directory Service

B. System Attendant

C. Global Address List

D. Client components

Answer: B

4. This component is involved in advanced security:

A. Directory Service

B. Information Store

C. Key Management

D. Message Transfer Agent

Answer: C

5. This component builds routing tables:

A. System Attendant

B. Key Management

C. Information Store

D. Internet Mail Service

Answer: A

6. This component notifies clients of new mail:

   A. Directory Service

   B. Microsoft Mail Connector

   C. Information Store

   D. System Attendant

Answer: C

7. The Internet Mail Service relates to which protocol?

   A. X.400

   B. RPC

   C. OSF

   D. SMTP

Answer: D

8. Which of the following is NOT an example of a foreign system?

   A. An Exchange server in a different site

   B. IBM SNADS

   C. SMTP system

   D. Microsoft Mail system

Answer: A

9. This component calculates the route a message could take to its destination:

   A. System Attendant

   B. Message Transfer Agent

C. Information Store

D. Internet Mail Service

Answer: B

10. This standard is used as the pattern of the Exchange Directory:

A. X.400

B. SMTP

C. LDAP

D. X.500

Answer: D

11. The following object creates a transparent messaging environment for Exchange users:

A. Site

B. System Attendant

C. Protocols

D. INS

Answer: A

12. The Global Address List is contained in this object:

A. Site

B. Server

C. Enterprise

D. Organization

Answer: D

13. Users must know the name of the server on which a public folder is homed in order to access the public folder.

   A. True

   B. False

Answer: B

14. This component enables World Wide Web users to access Exchange resources:

   A. Active Server Components

   B. SNMP

   C. X.400

   D. X.500

Answer: A

15. The Message Transfer Agent is based on this standard:

   A. SNMP

   B. SMTP

   C. X.500

   D. X.400

Answer: D

Chapter 3

1. The IS communicates with this component to perform a remote delivery:

   A. SA

   B. IS on other server

   C. Key Manager

   D. MTA

Answer: D

2. This component is referenced by other components when resolving an address:

  A. DS

  B. IS

  C. MTA

  D. SA

  Answer: A

3. Intrasite Directory replication uses the MTA to route directory information.

  A. True

  B. False

  Answer: B

4. The IS notifies clients of new messages.

  A. True

  B. False

  Answer: A

5. This component assists in the implementation of advanced security:

  A. IS

  B. SA

  C. MTA

  D. DXA

  Answer: B

6. The Active Server Components run on this system:

A. Microsoft Exchange server

B. Web client

C. Internet router

D. Microsoft IIS server

Answer: D

7. The INS communicates with this component for the storing of USENET content:

A. Microsoft IIS server

B. DS

C. SA

D. IS

Answer: D

8. Connectors, such as the Connector for Lotus cc:Mail, CANNOT place foreign messages in the IS.

A. True

B. False

Answer: B

9. When routing a message, the MTA may communicate with this component for the physical transfer of the message:

A. Connector or gateway

B. MTA on another server

C. Key Manager

D. SA

Answer: B

10. The DS uses this information when performing a directory replication:

   A. Site number

   B. Update Sequence Number (USN)

   C. Server DS number

   D. Combination site and server number

Answer: B

11. The Link Monitor utility uses this component to send test messages:

   A. LDAP

   B. INS

   C. Key Security

   D. SA

Answer: D

12. To expand a distribution list, the MTA references this component:

   A. IS

   B. DS

   C. Key security

   D. SA

Answer: B

13. When addressing messages for delivery within an Exchange organization, this address format is used:

   A. Distinguished Name

   B. MS Mail name

   C. Exchange lengthwise address

   D. cc:Mail name

Answer: A

Chapter 3

1. The minimum amount of RAM needed by Microsoft Exchange Server is:

   A. 24

   B. 48

   C. 64

   D. 128

   Answer: A

2. When the installation option "Typical" is chosen, the Microsoft Exchange Server Administrator program is not installed.

   A. True

   B. False

   Answer: B

3. One of the reasons to install an additional Exchange server in a site is to locate the public or private information stores on another machine.

   A. True

   B. False

   Answer: A

4. The site services account must be configured:

   A. As a regular user account

   B. As a member of the Mail group

   C. After the Exchange installation

   D. As a member of the Domain Administrators global group

   Answer: A

5. A Client Access License (CAL) is not required for the Windows 95 Inbox.

   A. True

   B. False

   Answer: B

6. Which file would be useful in a troubleshooting situation?

   A. Exchange Server Setup.LOG

   B. ERROR.LOG

   C. SETUP.EXE

   D. VIEWLOG

   Answer: A

7. The default location of the Exchange directory is:

   A. \EXCHANGE

   B. \MICROSOFT\EXCHANGE

   C. \EXCHSRVR

   D. \\EXCHANGE

   Answer: C

8. The Microsoft Exchange Server Administrator program can be run on a Windows NT workstation.

   A. True

   B. False

   Answer: A

9. The Internet Mail Service requires this protocol to be running on the Exchange Server:

   A. NWLink

   B. Ethernet

   C. TCP/IP

   D. SNA

   Answer: C

10. This Windows NT-based program analyzes your Exchange Server machine and makes recommendations for better performance:

    A. Administrator program

    B. SETUP.HLP

    C. ANALYZER

    D. Performance Optimizer

    Answer: D

11. If there is a problem with the Exchange Server boot process, one action would be to view:

    A. The Event Log

    B. My Computer

    C. Microsoft Explorer

    D. Administrator Tools/User Manager for Domains

    Answer: A

12. The following is one of the configuration requirements for the operating system that Microsoft Exchange Server uses:

    A. Pagefile size equal to 50 plus the amount of RAM

    B. NETBEUI

C. NWLink

D. Ethernet

Answer: A

13. Two sites, siteA and siteB, were both using version 4.0 of Exchange Server. The two sites also had directory replication configured between them. But after upgrading some of the servers in siteA to version 5.0, directory replication between the two sites stops working. Which of the following is a solution?

   A. Uninstall version 5.0, and reinstall version 4.0.

   B. Directory replication between sites cannot work until all servers have the same version.

   C. Internet Mail Service must be used for directory replication.

   D. Upgrade all directory bridgehead servers to version 5.0.

   Answer: D

14. When adding a Microsoft Exchange Server to an existing site, which two pieces of information do you need to know?

   A. The name of an existing Exchange Server in that site, and the password for the site service account in that site.

   B. Organization name, and site name

   C. Site name, and administrator's user account

   D. Organization name, and administrator's user account

   Answer: A

Chapter 5

1. The Microsoft Exchange Administrator program is the only method for creating Exchange mailboxes.

   A. True

   B. False

   Answer: B

2. The following is an example of a mailbox attribute:

A. Operating system

B. Groups

C. Server operating system

D. Home server

Answer: D

3. Permissions to a mailbox are assigned through:

A. Roles

B. UNIX permissions

C. Custom recipients

D. DLs

Answer: A

4. The following permits easy mass mailing:

A. A mailbox with multiple owners

B. Distribution list

C. A mailbox with multiple users

D. A mailbox set to forward messages

Answer: B

5. A foreign mail user would be this type of Exchange recipient:

A. Mailbox

B. A member of the Custom distribution list

C. Custom recipient

D. A mailbox with a foreign owner

Answer: C

6. An expansion server is the server that sends e-mail messages to their destinations.

   A. True

   B. False

   Answer: B

7. Public folders are created in the Microsoft Exchange Administrator program.

   A. True

   B. False

   Answer: B

8. Which of the following does NOT relate to a feature of a public folder?

   A. Views

   B. Rules

   C. Permissions

   D. Expansion Server

   Answer: D

9. Copies of the same public folder located on several Exchange servers are called:

   A. Clones

   B. Clone folders

   C. Folder images

   D. Replicas

   Answer: D

10. A mailbox can be created that uses the settings of an existing mailbox.

A. True

B. False

Answer: A

11. This menu option relates to selectively deleting messages in a mailbox:

A. Clean Mailbox

B. Purge Mailbox

C. Delete Mailbox

D. Remove Mailbox

Answer: A

12. This feature of a mailbox allows it to store and send messages containing formatting such as underlining, bolding, and fonts:

A. Font format

B. Word format

C. Rich-text format

D. Data compression

Answer: C

13. Microsoft NT User Manager for Domains can be used to create Exchange mailboxes.

A. True

B. False

Answer: A

14. This type of program assists in the creating of mailboxes for NetWare
users:

A. Extract tool

B. NetWare synchtool

C. Microsoft-NetWare synchronization tool

D. Cannot be done

Answer: A

15. The default permission for the primary NT account of a mailbox is:

A. Admin. role

B. Send as

C. Permissions Admin.

D. User

Answer: D

Chapter 6

1. Which of the following is NOT a MAPI-based application?

A. Internet mail with POP3

B. Microsoft Schedule+

C. Microsoft Exchange Client

D. Microsoft Outlook

Answer: A

2. A Web browser cannot be used to access an Exchange mailbox.

A. True

B. False

Answer: B

3. The term used to describe the collection of MAPI configuration settings is:

A. MAPI subsystem

B. Service provider

C. API

D. Profile

Answer: D

4. A PST file is also known as what type of message storage?

A. Personal folder

B. Private folder

C. Offline folder

D. Macintosh folder

Answer: A

5. An inbox assistant is a:

A. Secretary

B. Temporary employee

C. Permissions set on a mailbox

D. A software agent that can apply rules to a mailbox

Answer: D

6. The MAPI-based clients that access an Exchange server require a client access license.

A. True

B. False

Answer: A

7. Which of the following is NOT true for the Microsoft Exchange Client?

A. Has remote mail features

B. Has a delegate access feature

C. Only runs on Windows 95.

D. Can work with electronic forms

Answer: C

8. There is NO Exchange Client version for MS-DOS or Apple Macintosh.

A. True

B. False

Answer: B

9. Which of the following is true for Microsoft Schedule+?

A. Has an alarm feature

B. Is shipped with Microsoft Office 97

C. Will not work with Apple Macintosh

D. Will only run on 32-bit platforms

Answer: A

10. Which of the following features enables Microsoft Outlook to place notices on messages to help prioritize them?

A. Message recall

B. AutoNameCheck

C. Voting

D. Message flags

Answer: D

11. Microsoft Outlook enables schedules, contact lists, and task lists to be published to a public folder.

A. True

B. False

Answer: A

12. Which of the following are two navigational aids in Microsoft Outlook?

A. Outlook Bar

B. Tabbed Windows

C. AutoDate

D. Message recall

Answer: A, B

13. The following relate to the integration of Microsoft Outlook with Microsoft Office 97:

A. Office 97 interface

B. Use of Office 97 attachments

C. Use of Office 97 objects in Outlook forms

D. All of the above

Answer: D

14. The Microsoft Exchange Client for MS-DOS does NOT support a shared installation.

A. True

B. False

Answer: B

15. The Microsoft Exchange Client for Macintosh does NOT support a shared installation.

A. True

B. False

Answer: A

16. The following line would be used to set up a shared installation point for Windows-based clients:

A. SETUP /A

B. INSTALL /N

C. INSTALL /A

D. SETUP /A /N

Answer: A

17. Microsoft Schedule+ enables the grouping of tasks into a:

A. Task commune

B. Task group

C. Project

D. Task community

Answer: C

18. Which of the following does NOT relate to a scripted installation?

A. Setup Editor

B. Client installation point

C. PROFILE.PROF

D. DEFAULT.PRF

Answer: C

19. If you wanted all new client installations to be configured to use IPX and not use of TCP/IP, you would perform which action?

    A. Use Setup Editor to remove TCP/IP from the RPC binding order

    B. Do nothing, that is already the default

    C. This can not be done

    D. Run SETUP.EXE /A

    Answer: A

Chapter 7

1. Which of the following is NOT a default information service in a messaging profile?

    A. Microsoft Fax

    B. Microsoft Mail

    C. Microsoft Exchange

    D. Both A and B

    Answer: A

2. Remote mail supports Dial-Up Networking in Windows 95 clients.

    A. True

    B. False

    Answer: A

3. A Personal Address Book is configured in a profile as an information service.

    A. True

    B. False

    Answer: A

4. Delegate access is a feature of Microsoft Outlook only.

    A. True

    B. False

Answer: B

5. From which programs can the Send On Behalf Of permission be assigned?

    A. Microsoft Exchange Client

    B. Microsoft Outlook

    C. Microsoft Exchange Administrator program

    D. All of the above

Answer: D

6. Which of the following information files does SETUP look for when building a messaging profile?

    A. DEFAULT.PRF

    B. PROFILE.DAT

    C. PROFILE.PRF

    D. DEFAULT.DAT

Answer: A

7. What file contains the profile for an MS-DOS client?

    A. PROFILE.DOS

    B. PROF-MS.DOS

    C. EXCHANGE.PRO

    D. DOS.PRO

Answer: C

8. Which of the following is NOT a feature of remote mail?

    A. PCMCIA cards

    B. Downloading only new messages

    C. Offline folders

    D. Working offline

    Answer: A

9. Which of the following relates to remote mail?

    A. Offline address book

    B. Scheduled connections

    C. ShivaRemote

    D. All of the above

    Answer: D

10. Which of the following file types can be imported by the Exchange Client?

    A. MMX

    B. GIF

    C. MMF

    D. Both B and C

    Answer: C

11. A Microsoft MAPI application can use only ONE information service.

    A. True

    B. False

    Answer: B

12. The profile currently in use can be edited from within Exchange MAPI clients.

  A. True

  B. False

Answer: A

13. A user can designate their mailbox in the Private Information Store as the storage location of their messages.

  A. True

  B. False

Answer: A

14. Exchange clients have which of the following as notification options for new mail?

  A. Play a sound

  B. Blinking screen

  C. Briefly change the pointer

  D. Both A and C

Answer: D

15. Which of the following programs can be used to edit a messaging profile?

  A. WordPad

  B. PaintBrush

  C. Server Monitor

  D. The Mail and Fax applet in the Control Panel

Answer: D

16. Which of the following is required for a folder to be designated for offline use?

    A. It must have a size limitation

    B. It must have a password

    C. It must not have a size limitation

    D. It must be designated as a Favorite folder

    Answer: D

Chapter 8

1. A form that is used to directly input information into a public folder is called:

    A. A Send form

    B. An Input form

    C. A Folder form

    D. A Post form

    Answer: D

2. The Exchange Client can send and receive Outlook forms.

    A. True

    B. False

    Answer: B

3. Outlook forms are not compiled.

    A. True

    B. False

    Answer: A

4. The following procedure makes forms available for use:

  A. Installing or publishing forms

  B. Customizing in Visual Basic

  C. Saving in the FRM format

  D. Saving to the Access database

Answer: A

5. EFD forms are compiled into an executable format.

  A. True

  B. False

Answer: A

6. A Microsoft Office 97 object could be used in an Outlook form.

  A. True

  B. False

Answer: A

7. If a form needed wide availability, it would be installed in this location:

  A. Personal folder

  B. Organization forms library

  C. Administrator's mailbox

  D. A public mailbox

Answer: B

8. Outlook can send and receive forms created in EFD.

  A. True

  B. False

Answer: A

9. Which of the following is NOT a design feature of Outlook Forms Designer?

A. AutoLayout

B. Alignment

C. Visual Basic scripting

D. Lotus Notes formatting

Answer: D

10. EFD saves form information in this database format:

A. Microsoft Access

B. SQL

C. Paradox

D. DB2

Answer: A

Chapter 9

1. Public folders can be assigned the user rights used in Windows NT.

A. True

B. False

Answer: B

2. By default, no users can create folders at the top-level of the public folder hierarchy.

A. True

B. False

Answer: B

3. Which of the following relate to assigning rules to a public folder?

   A. Conditions

   B. Actions

   C. Folder Assistant

   D. All of the above

   Answer: D

4. Public folder permissions are grouped into predefined:

   A. Hives

   B. Clone sets

   C. Roles

   D. Sets

   Answer: C

5. There can be only one user with the Owner role on a public folder.

   A. True

   B. False

   Answer: B

6. Which of the following cannot be done?

   A. Hide a public folder from the hierarchy

   B. Hide the contents of a public folder

   C. Hide a top-level public folder

   D. Hide a public folder from the GAL

   Answer: C

7. If the recipient who is the owner of a public folder is deleted, what can be done in order to allow the administrator to grant permissions to other recipients?

A. Delete the public folder, and recreate it

B. Designate the recipient used by the administrator as the owner

C. Give the administrator account the "right to logon as a service"

D. Restore a backup tape that was made before the previous recipient was deleted

Answer: B

8. What must you do to hide a subfolder from a particular recipient?

A. Revoke the Read Items permission from that recipient at the parent folder

B. Revoke the Read Items permission from that recipient at that subfolder

C. Hide the root folder above that subfolder

D. A subfolder cannot be hidden, only its contents

Answer: A

9. By default, all public folders can be seen in the GAL.

A. True

B. False

Answer: B

10. By default, all public folders are visible in the public folder hierarchy.

A. True

B. False

Answer: A

Chapter 10

1. There can be only one KM administrator.

A. True

B. False

Answer: B

2. Client software must be configured before a user's mailbox can be configured.

A. True

B. False

Answer: B

3. The KM database is made up of the directories and files under which directory?

A. DATA

B. KM\DATA

C. DATA\KM

D. SECURITY\MGRENT

Answer: D

4. Which program can create security tokens in a batch manner?

A. SIMPORT.EXE

B. BATCH.BAT

C. BATCH.EXE

D. SECADMIN.DLL

Answer: A

5. What program is used to revoke a user's keys and certificates?

   A. Exchange Administrator

   B. SIMPORT.EXE

   C. KM database

   D. REVOKE.EXE

Answer: A

6. The MS-DOS-based Exchange client, although slow, can perform signing and sealing operations.

   A. True

   B. False

Answer: B

7. CAST-64 cannot be used in the United States.

   A. True

   B. False

Answer: B

8. What core Exchange component is involved in the initialization of advanced security for a client?

   A. MTA

   B. IMS

   C. POP3

   D. System Attendant

Answer: D

9. What is the extension of the client-side file that stores a user's security information?

A. .EPF

B. .EFP

C. .KMS

D. .KM

Answer: A

10. Which extension enables the Exchange Administrator program to interface with the Key Manager service?

A. SECADMIN.DLL

B. KM.DLL

C. ADMIN.SEC

D. KMSEC.DLL

Answer: A

11. Which of the following must an administrator do to enable advanced security for a user?

A. Enabled advanced security on the Security property page of that user's mailbox

B. Have the user first install and configure advanced security on their computer, then have the user inform the administrator of their configuration

C. Inform the user of their security token which will be used to configure their client software

D. Both A and C

Answer: D

12. What must an administrator do to change the preferred encryption algorithm of a site?

A. Reinstall the Microsoft Exchange Key Manager service

B. Change the preferred encryption algorithm on the Encryption object

C. Recover the security keys for all security-enabled mailboxes

D. Both B and C

Answer: D

Chapter 11

1. The POP3 protocol can be used to both retrieve and send messages.

A. True

B. False

Answer: B

2. The following can be accessed through the POP3 protocol:

A. Public folders

B. Inbox

C. Public folders and Inbox

D. Calendars

Answer: B

3. Web access to an Exchange server requires a Microsoft Internet Information Server (IIS).

A. True

B. False

Answer: A

4. The following is one of the roles of the Active Server:

A. Creates Windows NT accounts

B. Holds public folders accessed by Web users

C. Translates Visual Basic code into C++

D. Translates Exchange content to HTML

Answer: D

5. An Exchange server can publish data to the USENET using NNTP, but cannot receive it.

A. True

B. False

Answer: B

6. The POP3 protocol is configured on an Exchange server using this object:

A. Information Store

B. Global Address List

C. POP3

D. Site addressing

Answer: C

7. After an Exchange server has upgraded from 4.0 to 5.0, what could be the reason POP3 clients can no longer access the server?

A. The site service account does not have the "Act as part of the operating system" right.

B. The POP3 Service needs to be stopped and restarted.

C. The IS needs to be upgraded.

D. POP3 does not work with Exchange Server 5.0.

Answer: A

8. If you wanted to prevent anonymous users using LDAP from seeing a particular Exchange attribute, like telephone numbers, where in the Exchange hierarchy would you have to go to prevent this?

A. Information Store Site Configuration

B. Encryption object

C. Directory Replication object

D. DS Site Configuration

Answer: D

9. If you wanted to reject certain IP addresses of Web clients from accessing your Exchange server, what program would you use?

A. Microsoft Exchange Administrator

B. Network applet in Control Panel

C. Internet Service Manager

D. Link Monitor

Answer: C

10. Which of the following is a reason why POP3 clients could not see e-mail messages in subfolders of their Inbox?

A. POP3 can only access messages in the Inbox, not subfolders of the Inbox.

B. LDAP is not enabled at the mailbox object.

C. NNTP is not enabled at the mailbox object.

D. The IIS computer is down.

Answer: A

11. Which of the following would have to be configured for an anonymous Web client to be able to read a public folder?

    A. The Web client would have to log on using a Windows NT account.

    B. The public folder would have to be listed in the Folders Shortcuts.

    C. The folder owner would have to grant the Read permission to the anonymous user type.

    D. Both B and C

    Answer: D

12. For POP3 clients to be able to send Internet mail from their mailbox, what other component must be operation on the Exchange server?

    A. LDAP

    B. NNTP

    C. Active Server Components

    D. Internet Mail Service (IMS)

    Answer: D

Chapter 12

1. Configuring circular logging for transaction log files increases fault tolerance.

    A. True

    B. False

    Answer: B

2. Which of the following is NOT true for a differential backup of a database?

   A. Backs up new data since the last full backup

   B. Backs up modified data since the last full backup

   C. Takes progressively longer each day

   D. Takes less time than the incremental strategy

   Answer: D

3. Control Panel/Services should NOT be used to start or stop an Exchange service.

   A. True

   B. False

   Answer: B

4. The diagnostic logging performed by Exchange services is written to this location:

   A. Windows NT Event Log

   B. \BIN

   C. \exchsrvr\bin

   D. \logging

   Answer: A

5. Which of the following relates to information about a deleted Directory object?

   A. RTS values

   B. Retry timeouts

   C. Bounce

   D. Tombstone

   Answer: D

6. Some site-level configuration properties can be overridden at a server object.

   A. True

   B. False

   Answer: A

7. Which of the following is required for single-seat administration of multiple Exchange sites?

   A. RPC connections between sites

   B. NNTP

   C. POP3

   D. X.400

   Answer: A

8. Which of the following procedures could help recover significant disk space on an Exchange server?

A. MTACheck

B. Server Monitor

C. Online IS Maintenance

D. Performance Monitor

Answer: C

9. How would you use Exchange Administrator to group Exchange recipients by city?

A. Create an address book view container

B. Autonaming

C. You cannot group recipients

D. Delete the GAL and create Personal Address Books

Answer: A

Chapter 13

1. The IMS permits the scheduling of message transfer over permanent and dial-up connections.

A. True

B. False

Answer: B

2. Which of the following statements is NOT true for the X.400 Connector?

A. Requires a high-speed network connection

B. Can use TCP/IP

C. Can be assigned costs

D. Can connect through a public backbone

Answer: A

3. Which of the following is true for the Site Connector?

A. Sends information between sites in a message format

B. Can schedule connections

C. Permits delivery restrictions

D. Uses RPC

Answer: D

4. Using multiple messaging connectors between two sites can provide:

A. Fault tolerance

B. Load balancing

C. A foundation for multiple directory replication connectors between the two sites

D. Both A and B

Answer: D

5. The IMS uses the Exchange message format with no conversion required.

A. True

B. False

Answer: B

6. When there are multiple connectors between two sites, the primary factor used by the MTA to select a connector is:

   A. Target server costs

   B. Connector cost

   C. Versions of Exchange

   D. Both A and B

   Answer: B

7. The Exchange component that makes routing decisions is:

   A. RAS

   B. SA

   C. IS

   D. MTA

   Answer: D

Chapter 14

1. You can start the IMS by using which of the following?

   A. Internet Explorer

   B. Control Panel/Network

   C. DNS Administrator

   D. Control Panel/Services

   Answer: D

2. The IMS must use a DNS server.

   A. True

   B. False

   Answer: B

3. The MTA is involved in choosing a particular IMS component to deliver a message to a remote SMTP destination.

  A. True

  B. False

Answer: A

4. Which of the following is NOT a role of the IMS?

  A. Automatically generate SMTP addresses for new Exchange recipients

  B. Act as a DNS client

  C. Act as an SMTP server

  D. Act as a mail exchanger (MX)

Answer: A

5. The DNS hierarchical database is sometimes referred to as the domain name space.

  A. True

  B. False

Answer: A

6. The fully qualified domain name (FQDN) SALES.ACME.COM is in what root domain?

  A. COM

  B. SALES

  C. There is no way to tell

  D. ACME

Answer: A

7. The IMS relies on which component to resolve addresses of Exchange recipients on inbound messages?

   A. DNS

   B. SMTP

   C. Resolver program

   D. DS

   Answer: D

8. The IMS component can be configured to use either a DNS server or to send all outbound messages to a designated host called a relay host.

   A. True

   B. False

   Answer: A

9. After a change is made to the IMS configuration, the following should be done:

   A. The IMS should be paused and restarted

   B. The IMS should be reinstalled

   C. The IMS should be stopped and restarted

   D. The DNS server should be rebooted

   Answer: C

10. Which of these connections to an SMTP server or ISP does the IMS support?

    A. Permanent connection using TCP/IP

    B. A dial-up connection using PPP

    C. A dial-up connection using POP3

    D. Both A and B

    Answer: D

11. An Exchange site CANNOT have more than one IMS configured.

    A. True

    B. False

    Answer: B

12. Which of the following must be true for the IMS to use RAS for a dial-up connection?

    A. A SAP agent must be configured

    B. RAS must be installed

    C. An RAS phone book entry must be created for the remote SMTP server or ISP

    D. Both B and C

    Answer: D

13. Which of the following is the default Exchange naming convention for the domain name of a site?

    A. site.organization.com

    B. organization.site.com

    C. com.organization.site

    D. mailbox_name.site.organization

    Answer: A

14. Which process maps domain names to IP addresses?

    A. Address encapsulation

    B. Name resolution

    C. IP wrapping

    D. Address spaces

    Answer: B

15. Soon after the IMS is installed and started, an SMTP address space will be in the GWART.

    A. True

    B. False

    Answer: A

Chapter 15

1. The MS Mail Connector requires Exchange users to have two mailboxes.

    A. True

    B. False

    Answer: B

2. Exchange users CANNOT use the MS Mail Connector to access an MS Mail gateway. They must use an Exchange gateway.

    A. True

    B. False

    Answer: B

3. Which of the following does NOT relate to restricting Exchange objects from being synchronized with an MS Mail system?

    A. Trust level of the object

    B. Trust level of the Exchange dirsync server or requestor

    C. The recipients container

    D. EXPORT.EXE

    Answer: D

4. Which of the following are required when using the Schedule+ Free/Busy Connector?

   A. Directory synchronization with MS Mail

   B. A Windows NT user account named FreeB

   C. IMPORT.EXE running on the designated MS Mail postoffice

   D. Both A and C

   Answer: A

5. When connecting Exchange and MS Mail environments, one Exchange server must be designated the dirsync server.

   A. True

   B. False

   Answer: B

6. The Connector for Lotus cc:Mail is installed using Exchange Server Setup.

   A. True

   B. False

   Answer: A

7. Schedule+ free/busy information exchanged between Exchange and MS Mail users is stored in the following:

   A. A specially designated public folder

   B. A specially designated mailbox

   C. A specially designated DL

   D. The Exchange Directory

   Answer: A

8. The MS Mail directory synchronization parameter used by a dirsync server to recompile the Global Address List is:

   A. T1

   B. T2

   C. Newsfeed push

   D. T3

   Answer: B

9. Directory synchronization between Exchange and MS Mail requires NO configuration on the MS Mail dirsync server.

   A. True

   B. False

   Answer: B

10. If an Exchange object has a higher trust level than the Exchange dirsync requestor is configured for, that object will not be synchronized with the MS Mail dirsync server.

   A. True

   B. False

   Answer: A

Chapter 16

1. Which of the following cannot be migrated into Exchange?

   A. Personal Address Book

   B. Schedule information

C. Messages

D. Mail gateways

Answer: D

2. Migrations must be performed in one step.

A. True

B. False

Answer: B

3. Migrations must include every mailbox on the existing system.

A. True

B. False

Answer: B

4. Passwords can be generated for users being migrated.

A. True

B. False

Answer: A

5. Which property of an Exchange recipient can be used to allow a user to retain his or her pre-migration foreign addresses?

A. E-mail addresses (also called proxy addresses)

B. Protocol property

C. Custom attribute property

D. Advanced properties

Answer: A

6. Which of the following can be used to modify a large number of Exchange recipients in a bulk manner?

   A. Performance Monitor

   B. User Manager for Domains

   C. Directory Import and Export

   D. Event Viewer

   Answer: C

Chapter 17

1. The network infrastructure is very important factor in planning sites and site boundaries.

   A. True

   B. False

   Answer: A

2. The hardware requirements of an Exchange server are affected by which of the following:

   A. Number of mailboxes

   B. Public folder storage

   C. Message traffic

   D. All of the above

   Answer: D

3. Grouping common recipient configurations is NOT part of Exchange planning.

   A. True

   B. False

   Answer: B

4. Advanced security planning pertains to what object or objects?

   A. Mailboxes

   B. Connectors

   C. Sites

   D. Both A and C

Answer: D

5. Which of the following properties should be considered when planning a connector?

   A. Storage limits

   B. Scheduled connections

   C. Tombstones

   D. Both B and C

Answer: B

6. Which of the following is an important planning issue when interoperating with a non-Exchange system?

   A. POP3 configuration

   B. Mailbox cleanup

   C. Home server of the administrator

   D. Directory synchronization

Answer: D

7. Which of the following is NOT considered when planning a migration?

   A. Assigning foreign users administrative rights

   B. What resources will be migrated

   C. Choosing a migration method (single-phase or multiphase)

   D. Installing or upgrading client software

Answer: A

APPENDIX

B

Glossary

ActiveX   The set of Microsoft protocols that specifies how software components can communicate with each other through the use of objects.

Address Encapsulation   Placing a sender's native Exchange address in the form of a valid SMTP address. The encapsulated address is placed in the FROM field of the message.

Address Space   The set of remote addresses that can be reached through a particular connector. Each connector must have at least one entry in its address space.

Application Programming Interface (API)   A collection of programming commands (frequently called interfaces) that can invoke the functions of a program. Other programs can use a program's API to request services or communicate with that program. For example, Windows 95 contains an API referred to as the win32 API. For an application to request a service from Windows 95, it must issue that request using a win32 API.

Architecture   The description of the components of a product or system, what they are, what they do, and how they relate to each other.

Attribute   A characteristic of an object. Attributes of a mailbox include display name, primary Windows NT account, and storage limits. The terms *attribute* and *property* are synonymous.

AutoAssistants   A feature of a mailbox or public folder that can automatically carry out actions based on rules the user defines.

Back-End Program   A server application that provides services to front-end programs (client applications). Exchange Server is an example of a back-end program.

Bulk Encryption Key   The random secret key generated by a client's security DLL used to seal messages.

Caching   Temporarily storing data in random access memory (RAM) where it can be accessed much faster than it could be from the disk.

Certification Authority (CA)   The central authority that distributes, publishes, and validates security keys. Exchange Server can be configured to perform this role. See also public key and private key.

Checkpoint File   The file (EDB.CHK) that contains the point in a transaction log which is the boundary between data that has been committed and data that has not yet been committed to an Exchange database.

Ciphertext   Encrypted data.

Circular Logging   The process of writing new information in transaction log files over information that has already been committed. Instead of repeatedly creating new transaction logs, the Exchange database engine "circles back" and reuses log files that have been fully committed to the database. Circular logging keeps down the number of transaction logs on the disk. These logs can not be used to re-create a database because the logs do not have a complete set of data. The logs contain only the most recent data not yet committed to a database. Circular logging is the default setting of the Exchange Directory and Information Store databases.

Cleartext   Unencrypted data. Synonymous with plaintext.

Client Access License (CAL)   The license, purchased from Microsoft, that legally permits a client to access an Exchange server.

Connectors   Software that manages the transport of data between Exchange sites (e.g., the Site Connector) or between Exchange and a foreign message system (e.g., the X.400 Connector, Microsoft Mail Connector, and the Internet Mail Service). See also gateways.

Connector Cost   A numeric value assigned to a connector. The MTA uses connector cost as a criterion when it chooses between multiple connectors that support the same address space.

Container Object   An object in the Exchange hierarchy that contains and groups together other objects. The organization object is a container object that contains the Folders, Global Address List, and Site objects.

Context Level   Refers to a level in the Exchange hierarchy that does not inherit permissions from other portions of the hierarchy. The three context levels are organization, site, and configuration. Administrative permissions must be assigned to users or groups individually at each of the three levels.

Cryptology   The study and implementation of hiding and revealing information.

Custom Recipient   An Exchange recipient object that represents a foreign message recipient. Custom recipients allow Exchange clients to address messages to foreign mail users.

Datagram   A packet that contains both data to be sent and information related to the transmission of the data, such as the network address of the packet's destination.

Decryption   Translating encrypted data back to plaintext.

Denial-of-Service Attack   A system shutdown cased by too many requests or too much data. Occurs when a computer system receives so many service requests or so much data that it becomes overwhelmed and effectively shuts down.

Desktop Information Manager   An application that can be used to manage many aspects of a user's activities, such as reading and sending e-mail, accessing calendar and scheduling information, and task management.

Digital Signature   A personal and unique number included with a message that proves the sender's identity.

Directory Replication Bridgehead Server   The Exchange server designated as the server that will send site directory information to another site. Only one server in a site can be assigned to replicate information with each remote site. There can be more than one directory replication bridgehead server in a site, but each must connect with a unique remote site. One server can, however, perform directory replication with multiple remote sites.

Directory Synchronization Protocol   The MS Mail protocol used to synchronize directory information between MS Mail postoffices. One server is designated as the dirsync server and the other servers are designated as dirsync requestors. The dirsync server maintains the master copy of a network's directory. The dirsync requestors send any new directory information to the dirsync server, and request a copy of the master directory.

Dirsync Requestor   A type of MS Mail postoffice that sends its new directory information to the designated dirsync server, and requests a copy of the master directory from the dirsync server. See also Directory Synchronization Protocol, T1, and T3.

Dirsync Server   A type of MS Mail postoffice that maintains the master copy of a network's MS Mail directory information. It also responds to requests by sending a copy of the master directory to dirsync requestors. See also Directory Synchronization Protocol and T2.

Discussion Thread   A collection of postings to a public folder related to a single subject.

Distinguished Name (DN)   An X.500-style address that denotes an object's location in the Exchange directory hierarchy. An example DN is: /o=widget/ou=chicago/cn=education/cn=jayw.

Encryption   Scrambling data to make it unreadable. The intended recipient will decrypt the data into plaintext in order to read it.

Expanding a Distribution List   The process of determining the individual addresses contained within a distribution list. This process is performed by the MTA.

Extraction   The process of copying foreign message resources, such as mailboxes, messages, etc. and putting them in a format that can be imported into Exchange. See also source extractors.

Filtering   The ability to display only messages that meet various criteria, such as sender, subject, date, priority, and others.

Folder-Based Application   An application built within a public folder by customizing properties of the folder, such as permissions, views, rules, and the folder forms library to store and present data to users.

Foreign System   A non-Exchange message system.

Frame   The unit of information sent by a Data Link protocol, such as Ethernet or Token Ring.

Front-End Program   A client application, usually running on a user's workstation, that communicates with the back-end program, usually running on a server computer. Outlook is an example of a front-end program for Exchange Server, the back-end program. See also back-end program.

Fully Qualified Domain Name (FQDN)   The full DNS path of an Internet host. An example is `sales.dept4.widget.com`.

Function Call   An instruction in a program that calls (invokes) a function. For example, MAPIReadMail is a MAPI function call.

Gateways   Third-party software that permits Exchange to interoperate with a foreign message system. See also connectors.

Gateway Access Component   The MS Mail software that permits a post-office to send foreign addressed messages to a gateway postoffice for delivery.

Gateway Address Routing Table (GWART)   The routing table that contains all the address space entries for all the connectors in a site.

Gateway Postoffice   The MS Mail postoffice configured to receive messages to be delivered through a gateway.

Groupware   Any application that allows *groups* of people to store and share information.

GWART   See Gateway Address Routing Table.

Hierarchy   The grouping and arrangement of items by rank, order, class, etc.

Home Server   The Exchange server on which an object physically resides.

HTML   See Hypertext Markup Language.

HTTP   See Hypertext Transfer Protocol.

Hypertext Markup Language (HTML)   The script language used to create WWW content. HTML can create hyperlinks between objects on the WWW.

Hypertext Transfer Protocol (HTTP)   The Internet protocol used to transfer information on the World Wide Web (WWW).

Importing   The process of copying foreign message resources, such as mail-boxes, messages, etc., into Exchange.

Inbox   The storage folder that receives new incoming messages.

Information Service   A group of service providers for a specific product or environment. The information service for Exchange Server includes service providers for an address book, message store, and message transport.

Internal Network Number   The network address of a Novell NetWare network.

Interpersonal Messaging (IPM)   The X.400 standard for the format of an e-mail message.

Interoperability   The ability of different systems to work together (for example, the ability of two different messaging systems to exchange messages).

Intersite   Transfer of information across site boundaries.

Intrasite   Transfer of information within one site.

Key   A randomly generated number used to implement advanced security, such as encryption or digital signatures. See also key pair, public key, and private key.

Key Pair   A key that is divided into two mathematically related halves. One half (the public key) is made public. The other half (the private key) is known only by one user.

Leaf Object   An object that does not contain any other objects. A mailbox object is an example of a leaf object.

Lightweight Directory Access Protocol (LDAP)   An Internet protocol used for client access to an X.500-based directory.

Local Delivery   The delivery of a message to a recipient object that resides on the same server as the sender.

Local Procedure Call (LPC)   When a program issues an instruction that is executed on the same computer as the program executing the instruction. See also Remote Procedure Call.

Location Transparency   Being able to access resources without knowledge of their physical location.

Lockbox   An encrypted secret key that is sent with a message.

Mailbox   The generic term referring to a container that holds messages, such as incoming and outgoing messages.

Mail Exchanger (MX)   The designation of an SMTP mail server in a DNS database.

Messaging Application Programming Interface (MAPI)   An object-oriented programming interface for messaging services, developed by Microsoft.

Messaging Bridgehead Server   An Exchange server designated to deliver messages to another site.

Middleware   Software that serves to connect client software to server software.

Migration   Moving resources, such as mailboxes, messages, etc. from one messaging system to another. See also extraction, importing, and Migration Wizard.

Migration Wizard   An Exchange program that extracts data from a foreign message system and imports it into Exchange.

Mismatch   The situation when an Exchange server determines through the Knowledge Consistency Checker (KCC) that it does not have all the Exchange servers in the site in its Replication List.

Multimaster Model   A model where every server in a site has a copy of the site directory.

MX   See Mail Exchanger.

Name Resolution   The DNS process of mapping a domain name to its IP address.

Network News Transfer Protocol (NNTP)   An Internet protocol used to transfer USENET information between clients (newsreaders) and newsgroup servers.

NNTP   See Network News Transfer Protocol.

Newsfeed   The newsgroup data that is sent from one newsgroup server to other newsgroup servers.

Objects   The representation, or abstraction, of an entity. For example, each Exchange server is represented as an object in the Exchange Administrator program. As an object, it contains properties, also called attributes, that can be configured. For example, an Exchange server object can have properties that give certain administrators permission to configure that server.

Object Linking and Embedding (OLE)   The Microsoft protocol that specifies how programs can share objects and therefore create compound documents.

One-Off Address   An e-mail address that does not exist in the Exchange GAL, but is specified as a message recipient by a user. One-off addresses are often used to send messages to Internet addresses that do not have corresponding custom recipients in the GAL.

Originator/Recipient Address (O/R Address)   An X.400 address scheme that uses a hierarchical method to denote where on an X.400 network a recipient resides. An example is: c=us;a= ;p=widgetnet;o=widget;s=wilson;g=jay;.

Plaintext   Unencrypted data. Synonymous with cleartext.

Point-to-Point Protocol (PPP)   An Internet protocol used for direct communication between two nodes. Commonly used by Internet users and their Internet Service Provider on the serial line point-to-point connection over a modem.

Polling   A process that queries a server-based mailbox for new mail.

POP3   See Post Office Protocol 3.

Port Number   A numeric identifier assigned to an application. Transport protocols like TCP use the port number to identify to which application to deliver a packet.

Post Form   A form used to send information directly to a folder without using messaging routing.

Post Office Protocol 3 (POP3)   An Internet protocol used for client retrieval of mail from a server-based mailbox.

Postoffice   An MS Mail server that stores messages.

Private Folder   A server-based folder that is part of a user's mailbox. Private folders are stored on an Exchange server in the private information store. The Inbox and Outbox are examples of private folders.

Private Key   The half of a key pair that is known only by one user and is used to decrypt data and to digitally sign messages.

Property   A characteristic of an object. Properties of a mailbox include display name, primary Windows NT account, and storage limits. The terms property and attribute are synonymous.

Public Key   The half of a key pair that is published for anyone to read and is used when encrypting data and verifying digital signatures.

Push   A procedure where information is sent (i.e., pushed) to users. Users do not need to find and retrieve (i.e., pull) the information. Exchange Server pushes incoming messages to MAPI-based Exchange clients.

Push Feed   A procedure where a newsgroup server sends information to another newsgroup server without requiring the receiving server to request it. The opposite of a pull feed.

Pull   A procedure where a user finds and retrieves information, such as when browsing a public folder. Users accessing a public folder containing a company's employee handbook is a type of pull communication.

Pull Feed   A procedure where a newsgroup server requests newsfeed information from another newsgroup server. The opposite of a push feed.

Public Folder   A folder used to store data for a group of users. Some of the features of a public folder are permissions, views, and rules.

Recipient   An Exchange object that can receive a message. Recipients objects include mailboxes, distribution lists, public folders, and custom recipients.

Replica   A copy of a public folder located on an Exchange server.

Remote Delivery   The delivery of a message to a recipient that does not reside on the same server as the sender.

Remote Procedure Call (RPC)   A set of protocols for issuing instructions that can be sent over a network for execution. A client computer makes a request to a server computer and the results are sent to the client computer. The computer issuing the request and the computer performing the request are remotely separated over a network. Remote procedure calls are a key ingredient in distributed processing and client/server computing. See also Local Procedure Call.

Replication Latency   The delay period (the latency) that occurs after a change to the directory before the DS begins the directory replication process. Latency allows multiple directory changes to be sent during directory replication. The default replication latency period is 300 seconds.

Resolver Program   Client software that queries a DNS database to map a domain name to its IP address.

Resolving an Address   The process of determining where (on which physical server) an object with a particular address resides.

Role   A group of permissions that define what activities a user or group can perform with regards to an object.

Scalable   The ability of a system to grow to handle greater traffic, volume, usage, etc.

Schema   The set of rules defining a directory's hierarchy, objects, attributes, etc.

Sealing   The process of encrypting data.

Secret Key   A security key that can be used to encrypt data and that is only known by a sender and the recipients the sender informs.

Send Form   A stand-alone form that is sent from one user to another user.

Service Provider   A MAPI program that provides messaging-oriented services to a client. There are three main types of service providers: address book, message store, and message transport.

Shadow Postoffice   A postoffice without mailboxes. The Exchange MS Mail Connector Postoffice is referred to as a shadow postoffice because it does not contain user mailboxes and only temporarily stores incoming and outgoing MS Mail messages.

Signing   The process of placing a digital signature on a message.

Simple Mail Transfer Protocol (SMTP)   The Internet protocol used to transfer mail messages.

Single-Instance Storage   Storing only one copy. A message that is sent to multiple recipients homed on the same server has only one copy (i.e., instance) stored on that server. Each recipient is given a pointer to that copy of the message.

Site   A logical grouping of Exchange servers that are connected by a full mesh (every server is directly connected to every other server) and communicate using high-bandwidth RPC. All servers in a site can authenticate one another either because they are homed in the same Windows NT domain or because of trust relationships configured between separate Windows NT domains.

Site Services Account   The Windows NT user account that Exchange Server components within a site use to communicate with each other.

Source Extractors   Software programs that can copy messaging resources, such as mailboxes and messages, from a foreign mail system and put the information in a format that can be imported into Exchange.

Store-and-Forward   A delivery method that does not require the sender and recipient to have simultaneous interaction. Instead, when a message is sent, it is transferred to the next appropriate location in the network, which temporarily stores it, makes a routing decision, and forwards the message to the next appropriate network location. This process occurs until the message is ultimately delivered to the intended recipient, or an error condition causes the message to be returned to the sender.

Subsystem   A software component that, when loaded, extends the operating system by providing additional services. The MAPI program, MAPI32.DLL, is an example of a subsystem. MAPI32.DLL loads on top of the Windows 95 or Windows NT operating system and provides messaging services.

Target Server   An Exchange server in a remote site that is designated to receive messages from the local site.

Token   The packet of security information a certification authority sends to a client during advanced security setup. Information in the packet includes the client's public key and its expiration. A token is synonymous with a certificate.

Tombstone   Information created by the DS about a deleted directory object. The tombstone is replicated to other Exchange servers in a site to inform them of the deletion.

Tombstone Lifetime   The length of time a tombstone is kept before it is deleted.

T1   The interval used by dirsync requestors to send their postoffice address list to the designated dirsync server.

T2   The interval used by the dirsync server to compile a new Global Address List and to send that list to the dirsync requestors.

T3   The interval used by the dirsync requestors to rebuild their postoffice address list.

Universal Inbox   One inbox folder that receives incoming items from all outside sources and of all types, such as e-mail, voice mail, faxes, pages, etc.

Update Sequence Number (USN)   A tracking device used during directory replication to ensure that all new changes to a directory are replicated throughout the site.

User Profile   A collection of information for MAPI client configuration that specifies the services a user wants to use and how MAPI client applications are to look and behave.

Web   The World Wide Web.

Workflow Application   An application that can route electronic forms to users based on various criteria.

World Wide Web (WWW)   The collection of computers on the Internet using protocols such as HTML and HTTP.

WWW   See World Wide Web.

X.400   An International Telecommunications Union (ITU) standard for message exchange.

X.500   An International Telecommunications Union (ITU) standard for directory services.

Index

Note to the Reader: First level entries are in **bold**. Page numbers in **bold** indicate the principal discussion of a topic or the definition of a term. Page numbers in *italic* indicate illustrations.

S

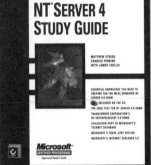